Professional Masters

Torts

Macmillan Professional Masters

Law titles   Law Series Editor: Marise Cremona

Basic English Law   W. T. Major
Company Law   Janet Dine
Conveyancing   Priscilla Sarton
Constitutional and Administrative Law   John Alder
Contract Law   Ewan McKendrick
Criminal Law   Marise Cremona
Employment Law   Debbie Lockton
European Community Law   Josephine Shaw
Family Law   Kate Standley
Land Law   Kate Green
Landlord and Tenant Law   Margaret Wilkie and Godfrey Cole
Law of Trusts   Patrick McLoughlin and Catherine Rendell
Legal Method and Thinking   Ian McLeod
Tort   Alastair Mullis and Ken Oliphant

Business titles

Communication   Nicki Stanton
Company Accounts   Roger Oldcorn
Cost and Management Accounting   Roger Hussey
Data Processing   John Bingham
Employee Relations   Chris Brewster
Financial Management   Geoffrey Knott
Management   Roger Oldcorn
Marketing   Robert G. I. Maxwell
Marketing for the Non-profit Sector   Tim Hannagan
Office Administration   E. C. Eyre
Operations Management   Howard Barnett
Personnel Management   Margaret Attwood
Study Skills   Kate Williams
Supervision   Mike Savedra and John Hawthorn
Systems Analysis   John Bingham and Garth Davies

Torts

Alastair Mullis
*Lecturer in Law at King's College
University of London*

and

Ken Oliphant
*Lecturer in Law at King's College
University of London*

Law series editor: Marise Cremona
*Senior Fellow, Centre for Commercial Law Studies
Queen Mary and Westfield College, University of London*

M
MACMILLAN

First published 1993 by
THE MACMILLAN PRESS LTD
Houndmills, Basingstoke, Hampshire RG21 2XS
and London
Companies and representatives
throughout the world

ISBN 0-333-56418-9

A catalogue record for this book is available
from the British Library.

Copy-edited and typeset by Povey–Edmondson
Okehampton and Rochdale, England

Printed in Hong Kong

10 9 8 7 6 5 4 3 2
02 01 00 99 98 97 96 95 94

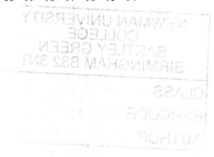

Contents

Preface

Torts make headline news. From mass disasters like Hillsborough and King's Cross to scandal-mongering in the popular press, torts are seldom far from the front pages. Yet, despite its human interest, the law of torts is notoriously difficult for students

We aim in this book to provide an accessible introduction to the law of torts. We cover the basic principles of the law and examine them in context of those torts which most commonly feature in degree courses. In doing so, we direct the reader towards the complexities of the subject and its relationship with society.

Our thanks are due to several colleagues and students who gave us help and encouragement in the venture. Ian Kennedy, Mark Lunney, Robin Morse, Kristina Stern and Paul Sutherland read and made helpful comments on various chapters. Andrew Grubb read virtually the entire book and we are particularly indebted to him. We are also indebted to our external reader for his constructive and thorough criticisms. Others to whom we are grateful include Janet Dine, Marise Cremona, Keith Povey and (for his immense patience and unfailing good humour) John Winckler. Alastair Mullis's special thanks are due to Camilla and Lara for their love and support.

In accordance with the developing modern practice, 'he' and 'she' are used in alternating parts of the book.

We have endeavoured to state the law on the materials available to us on 1 December 1992.

ALASTAIR MULLIS
KEN OLIPHANT

Table of Cases

Table of Statutes

1 Introduction

1.1 What is a Tort?

'Tort' is the French word for wrong. (Other terms derived from this root are the adjective 'tortious', the adverb 'tortiously' and 'tortfeasor', the name for one who commits a tort.) Yet, just as all dogs are animals but not all animals are dogs, so all torts are wrongs but not all wrongs are torts. To make sense of this conundrum, we must distinguish (a) civil wrongs from criminal wrongs; (b) equitable civil wrongs from common law civil wrongs; and (c) the different varieties of common law civil wrongs, some of them known as 'torts', some going under different names.

Criminal and Civil Wrongs

If I punch you in the face, that is both a crime and a civil wrong (both the crime and the tort of battery). The one event gives rise to two legal responses. First, I may be prosecuted by the state for committing the criminal offence and, if found guilty by the court, made to pay a fine to the state, or sent to prison or punished in some other way. Secondly, I may be sued by you in the civil courts (the County Courts or the High Court) and, if found liable, ordered to pay you a sum of money (damages) or to change my behaviour in the future (by an injunction). Unlike criminal proceedings, civil actions are brought by individuals, not the state. Furthermore, it is those individuals, again not the state, who stand to benefit directly from a court judgment against the defendant. Because of this, and because the defendant who is held liable is not exposed to the stigma of a criminal conviction, civil actions are possible in many circumstances in which no criminal liability arises. It should be noted, however, that not all crimes are also torts: this is true especially of so-called victimless crimes (e.g., possession of drugs) which have no effect upon other people.

Some would press the distinction between criminal and civil law further and say that the criminal law is designed to punish the defendant while the civil law aims only to vindicate the plaintiff's rights, but we should not pursue doctrinal purity at the expense of practical convenience. Medieval English law certainly knew no such purity. Criminal proceedings were originally instituted by individuals, for the law enforcement arm of the state did not develop until much later. Furthermore, many proceedings we would now recognise as civil were at least semi-criminal in character: the unsuccessful defendant would be punished as well as being obliged to pay damages, while the defendant who failed to appear in court would not only lose her case but would also be liable to arrest and imprisonment (see Maitland, 1936, pp. 39–40). In view of these beginnings, and of the pragmatic nature of English lawyers throughout history, it is no surprise that the modern criminal and civil law borrow elements from each other. Thus a criminal court may order the guilty party to pay compensation to the victim under section 35 of the Powers of Criminal Courts Act 1973 as well as passing a criminal sentence. Conversely, the damages awarded by a civil court may include a punitive element designed not to vindicate the plaintiff's rights but to punish the defendant for her wrongdoing (see 23.2)

Equitable and Common Law Wrongs

Within the category of civil wrongs, history obliges us to make a fundamental distinction between wrongs at common law and wrongs in equity (see Baker, 1990, Chapter 6). Before 1875, two distinct court systems existed side by side. The first to evolve had been the common law courts of the King's Bench and Common Pleas. The law applied in these courts was embodied in the 'forms of action', the verbal formulas written on the 'writs' purchased from the Chancellor's office (the Chancery), which authorised citizens to commence an action. In order to mount successful proceedings, medieval litigants had to ensure that the form of words written on the writ matched the substance of their complaint. In the case of the writ of trespass to the person, for example, this required them to establish that, in the florid language of the writ, they had been beaten, wounded and maltreated by force and arms, against the King's peace. With the passage of time, the forms of action became more or less set in stone. Such rigidity in the law led to injustice as litigants were denied the remedy they deserved simply because none of the existing forms of action covered their case.

It was to remedy this injustice that the equitable jurisdiction was developed. (The common law's response to the same problem was to recognise the flexible 'action on the case'; even this did not go far enough and the writ system was finally abolished in the Judicature Act 1873.) Some of the victims of such injustice took to petitioning the King for help, and in time these petitions came to be passed on to the Chancellor who proved willing in some cases to grant relief when the common law provided no remedy. The grant of this relief was at first purely discretionary, but after a while a body of established rules and principles evolved. A primary concern of these rules was to lay down the circumstances under which property, whose official 'legal' title was held by one person, should be held on trust for another. They thus laid the foundation for our modern law of trusts. For present purposes, the rules are significant for their recognition of the equitable wrong of breach of fiduciary duty. Examples of breach of fiduciary duty might include an employee 'stealing' a trade secret from her employee in the hope of selling it to a rival, or a company director accepting a bribe to ensure that the company enters into contracts with a particular supplier. The remedies that equity gave in respect of these wrongs differed from the normal common law remedy of damages: the employee might be subjected to an injunction forbidding her to pass on the trade secret to anyone else, while the company director might be required to 'account for' (hand over) the value of the bribe she received.

This equitable jurisdiction, and these equitable remedies, grew up outside the common law courts; however, the Judicature Act 1875 'fused' the two separate systems so that, from that time on, both common law and equitable principles were applied by the same courts. Nonetheless, and despite the views of many judges who – like Lord Diplock in *United Scientific Holdings Ltd v. Burnley Borough Council* [1978] AC 904 – believe that 'the waters of the confluent streams of law and equity have surely mingled now', most commentators continue to regard breach of fiduciary duty as entirely distinct from the civil wrongs at common law (cf. North, 1972). The result is not only that the subjects are treated in different textbooks (breach of fiduciary duty being consigned to books on equity and trusts), but also that certain equitable remedies, particularly the account of profits made by a wrongdoer, are generally held not to be available in respect of common law wrongs.

Torts and Other Common Law Wrongs

Common law wrongs themselves come in different varieties, breach of contract, tort and unjust enrichment being the most familiar. This sub-division of the common law wrongs was unknown to the medieval law and only took shape closer in time to the modern era when lawyers looked to impose some order on the many disparate forms of action that history had bequeathed them (see Baker, 1990, pp. 454–5). Their first move was to seize upon a body of law dealing with undertakings or promises and, sharply differentiating breach of promise from other forms of wrong, to develop a set of rules that we recognise today as our law of contract. A comparable, and ongoing, endeavour has been the attempt to formulate a law of unjust enrichment by drawing together certain examples of both common law and equitable wrongs (see Birks, 1985, Chapter X). The common element of such cases is that the defendant has acquired a benefit which the law requires her to surrender to the plaintiff. The law of tort is what is left behind after cases of breach of contract and unjust enrichment have been withdrawn from the list of common law wrongs and may be accurately described as 'our residual category of civil liability' (Gilmore, 1974, p. 87).

1.2 The classification of torts

The status of the law of tort as our residual category of civil liability means that it consists of a 'rag-bag' of disparate types of case which very often have little connection with one another. This fact makes efforts to elaborate general principles of the law of tort, in order to match the general principles of the law of contract which have been developed over the years, fraught with difficulty. The considerations raised by a road traffic accident are very different from those raised by a smear campaign of a public figure conducted in the popular press, which in turn are very different from those raised by industrial action taken by disgruntled employees. All these incidents might lead to liability in the law of tort, but it would be impossible to apply the same principles in relation to each. So when we turn to modern works on the law of tort, we find chapters dealing with principles said to be common to all torts intermixed with discussions of the divergent rules applicable to different kinds of case. These rules are generally listed under the name of a particular tort, but they may come under a heading under which a number of different torts are grouped together. These groupings may be justified on the grounds that the torts are all relevant in a particular context (e.g. 'Liability for Land and Structures'), that they all serve to protect a particular interest (e.g. 'Interests in Reputation'), that they can all be traced back to one medieval form of action (e.g. 'Trespass'), or that they share a common mental element (e.g. 'Intentional Wrongs').

The different torts that we can identify today often overlap with one another. They are a mixture of 'hand-me-downs' from the age of the forms of action, abolished in 1875, whose names recall the names of the original writs (e.g. trespass), and later creations, both judicial and legislative. These later judicial creations were attempts to draw together different instances of liability recognised under the old forms of action. The most notable of these is the tort of negligence, which united a variety of instances of liability for damage caused by negligence and was recognised as a fully-fledged tort in its own right in 1932 (see section below). Since that time it has done the work of a number of the older torts and has become the favoured head of claim of many plaintiffs, being the purest expression recognised by the law of the moral notion that wrongdoers should pay for their wrongs.

1.3   The Organisation of this Book

This book conforms to type in giving separate treatment to the general principles of tortious liability (Part V) and to the various discrete torts (Parts I–IV). In dealing with the latter, we start with the tort of negligence (Part I) which merits this prime position by virtue of its present practical importance and its tendency with the passage of time to subsume the other torts under its mantle. When we come to dealing with the remaining torts, we make no pretence of completeness: this is a student book and the torts covered in depth are those that typically feature in tort courses in university. We have omitted detailed coverage of areas of the law that are generally found in the syllabuses of other subjects (thus conversion has been left to the commercial lawyers and intimidation, conspiracy, etc., to teachers of labour law). Despite these exclusions, we have been left with a wide-ranging though ramshackle body of law, as befits tort law's status as the great dustbin of civil liability.

To impose some order on this expanse of materials, we have looked at the various torts in terms of the interests they may be said primarily to protect, dealing in turn with interests in the person and personal property (Part II), interests in land (Part III) and interests in reputation and privacy (Part IV). We preface our discussion of the torts selected under each heading with a few words on the extent to which negligence provides protection in each area, and on the continuing importance of the other torts in furnishing additional relief. One major interest has been omitted: that in financial well-being. As financial well-being is largely dependent on one's ability to exploit one's labour, goods and land, it is protected by those torts which provide relief in respect of physical interference with the person and personal property (Part II) and with land (Part III). Other torts provide relief even where there has been no physical interference with these interests, as where *I pass off* my goods as yours so that I can sell at a better price or where *I conspire* with militant workers to picket your factory and cause you to cease trading by *intimidating* you with threats of personal violence. The torts of passing off, conspiracy, intimidation and others are omitted for the reason given above, namely that they are best left to be considered in depth in other books.

Summary

1.1 A tort is a civil, as opposed to criminal, wrong. The category of civil wrongs contains breaches of contract and equitable wrongs as well as torts.
1.2 Different torts deal with different types of wrongful conduct and developed, often haphazardly, over the course of time. This makes it difficult, if not impossible, to identify general principles about the law of tort.
1.3 In this book, we look at (a) the tort of negligence, the most important tort in both theory and practice; (b) a selection of other torts arranged according to the interest they primarily protect; and (c) such general principles as do exist.

Part I

The Tort of Negligence

2 Negligence: Introduction

2.1 Origins

It all began in August 1928. The scene was Minchella's cafe in Paisley, near Glasgow. A certain Mrs Donoghue had gone in for a drink. This is her story: a friend bought her a bottle of ginger beer; she began to drink it; then, as her friend topped up her tumbler, she watched in horror as the decomposed remnants of a snail floated out with the ginger beer; she suffered shock and an upset stomach. Now Mrs Donoghue's injuries may seem of less than earth-shattering importance to us today but it is to these unlikely beginnings that the modern law of negligence owes its existence. Mrs Donoghue, unable to sue Minchella in the law of contract because she had not bought the bottle herself (there was no 'privity of contract'), brought an action in tort against the manufacturer, Stevenson. She alleged that he had been negligent in producing the drink. In response, Stevenson denied that those injured by a negligently manufactured product had any right to recover damages outside certain exceptional categories (e.g. inherently or patently dangerous products like firearms). The case reached the House of Lords which found in favour of Mrs Donoghue. It was not a unanimous decision: two powerful dissents were registered. Neither was the decision of the majority clear and unambiguous in every respect: was it to be a rule confined to defective products or was it to have wider effect? Today, however, its status is unquestioned and its effect plain for all to see, for *Donoghue* v. *Stevenson* [1932] AC 562 is the case that changed the face of the law of negligence.

Up to that time, liability for negligent conduct had been recognised only in certain carefully defined circumstances, for example where innkeepers were careless in looking after property in guests' rooms or where fire damage resulted from negligence. The courts allowed actions for damages in these cases because – they said – the special circumstances gave rise to a 'duty of care'. The significance of *Donoghue* v. *Stevenson*, and of Lord Atkin's speech in particular, was that it sought to unify these disparate duties of care in a single general theory. Lord Atkin noted that the courts had previously been 'engaged upon an elaborate classification of duties' as they existed in various fact situations, and urged them to recognise that 'the duty which is common to all the cases where liability is established must logically be based upon some element common to the cases where it is found to exist'. He continued:

'[I]n English law there must be and is some general conception of relations giving rise to a duty of care, of which the particular cases found in the books are but instances. The liability for negligence . . . is no doubt based upon a general public sentiment of moral wrongdoing for which the offender must pay. But acts or omissions which any moral code would censure cannot in a practical world be treated so as to give a right to every person injured by them to demand relief. In this way rules of law arise which limit the range of complainants and the extent of their remedy. The rule that you are to love your neighbour becomes in law: You must not injure your neighbour, and the lawyer's question: Who is my neighbour? receives a restricted reply. You must take reasonable care to avoid acts or omissions which you can reasonably foresee would be likely to injure your neighbour. Who then, in law, is my neighbour? The answer seems to be persons who are so closely and directly affected by my act that I ought reasonably to have them in contemplation as being so affected when I am directing my mind to the acts or omissions which are called in question.'

2.2   The Elements of the Tort of Negligence

Negligence is a common word, used to refer to a species of fault, and it is often treated as synonymous with 'carelessness'. But since *Donoghue* v. *Stevenson* it has also become the name of a self-contained tort with its own internal framework of rules. The elements of liability in the tort of negligence can be outlined as follows:

(a)   the defendant must owe the plaintiff a *duty of care*;
(b)   the defendant must be in *breach* of that duty (i.e. she must be careless or negligent);
(c)   this must *cause* the plaintiff loss;
(d)   that loss must not be too *remote* (i.e. it must be foreseeable);
(e)   the defendant must not be able to raise any *defence* to the plaintiff's claim.

This list makes it plain that one will not be held liable in the tort of negligence for every harmful result of her carelessness. Although Lord Atkin appealed – in his 'neighbour principle' – to our moral intuitions which suggest that there should be general recognition of tortious liability for harm caused by negligence, he himself stressed the need for 'rules of law . . . which limit the range of complainants and the extent of their remedy'. This task is done by means of the concepts of the duty of care, causation and remoteness of damage, and of the law relating to defences. Because they have this function, those concepts and the various defences can be thought of as limitation mechanisms or control devices in the tort of negligence, keeping liability for negligence within acceptable bounds.

2.3   The Abstract Nature of the Tort of Negligence

The above discussion will have given the reader an inkling that the tort of negligence makes use of a good deal of abstract conceptual language.

Indeed, it uses rather too much – at least, so far as many students are concerned – and negligence is often contrasted unfavourably in this respect with subjects such as contract and property law which contain a wealth of concrete rules, giving students something to get their teeth into. In part, this contrast is an illusion. There are in fact detailed rules prescribing when liability for negligence arises and when it does not, though these rules are often obscured by the excessively theoretical language of which the law reports are full. In part, however, the charge has some substance. The tort of negligence remains in its adolescence and has not yet reached full maturity. In many areas, the question whether liability arises has yet to be determined. Courts encountering unprecedented claims will grapple with a number of grand-sounding concepts, but they will rarely provide a clear answer to whether a claim should be allowed or not. All too frequently, the concepts will prove to have no settled meaning or to consist merely of vague appeals to what is reasonable in the circumstances.

The open-textured nature of central concepts such as the duty of care, causation and remoteness has led to a certain degree of scepticism about the way judges decide cases in the tort of negligence. Some feel that conceptual language is used inconsistently and instrumentally, in order to give an aura of legal respectability to decisions reached on non-legal (policy) grounds. The following, typically bold expression of this view comes from a judgment of that leading judicial sceptic, Lord Denning:

'The truth is that all these three, duty, remoteness and causation, are all devices by which the courts limit the range of liability for negligence . . . As I said recently . . . "it is not every consequence of a wrongful act which is the subject of compensation." The law has to draw a line somewhere. Sometimes it is done by limiting the range of persons to whom a duty is owed. Sometimes it is done by saying that there is a break in the chain of causation. At other times it is done by saying that the consequence is too remote to be a head of damage. All these devices are useful in their way. But ultimately it is a question of policy for the judges to decide.' (*Lamb* v. *Camden LBC* [1981] QB 625)

Lord Denning perhaps puts his case too strongly, for it would be wrong to suggest that judges feel free to disregard rules laid down in previous cases and to impose whatever solution they feel is warranted in terms of public policy. Nevertheless, his words stand as a useful indication of the imprecision that surrounds the use of the key concepts in the tort of neligence and of the scope that this imprecision allows for judges to give effect to policy choices.

2.4   The Role of Policy in the Tort of Negligence

As the above discussion makes plain, matters of social and economic policy are of paramount importance in considering the tort of negligence.

In this context, 'policy' is contrasted with 'principle', the latter referring to rules which can be derived from judicial decisions and other legal sources. In the tort of negligence, the relevance of policy matters is not limited to the evaluation of the existing law and of proposals for reform: policy actually dictates what rules the courts will apply when they encounter novel fact situations. In the course of time, certain concerns have been raised time and time again by the courts and, by identifying those concerns, we equip ourselves to predict how the law will develop in those 'grey areas' beloved of examiners.

The extent to which policy choices are aired openly in judicial decisions varies from one judge to another. Understandably, many judges have been keen to play down their political role by emphasising that their task is merely to apply principles developed over the course of time, in case after case. They recognise that they have no special training or democratic mandate to determine issues of social or economic policy and that a trial involving only two parties may deny a hearing to many with a legitimate interest in its outcome. The best-known elaboration of this position is found in Lord Scarman's speech in *McLoughlin* v. *O'Brian* [1983] AC 410:

> 'By concentrating on principle the judges can keep the common law alive, flexible and consistent, and can keep the legal system clear of policy problems which neither they, nor the forensic process which it is their duty to operate, are equipped to resolve. If principle leads to results which are thought to be socially unacceptable, Parliament can legislate to draw a line or map out a new path.'

Lord Scarman provides a useful barometer reading of current judicial hostility to overt law-making. He has, however, been criticised for trusting too much in Parliament's willingness to intervene where the common law produces injustice, and his speech attracted a sharp rebuke from Lord Edmund-Davies in the very same case. The latter asserted that public policy issues are 'justiciable', and we agree. In fact, we would go further and suggest that the shape of the modern law of negligence cannot be understood – or justified – without some appreciation of the policies that have influenced its development. Accordingly, in the paragraphs that follow we give an introductory explanation of the policy factors that seem to us to have exerted the most crucial influence on the law in this area.

2.5   Selected Policy Considerations in the Tort of Negligence

Compensation

The provision of compensation is so central to the tort of negligence that it is often regarded as the *objective* of the tort, rather than just as one of its policies. It is, however, helpful to view it as one of many policies pursued in the tort of negligence, for this emphasises that in some circumstances it may be outweighed by other, competing, policy considerations.

It is important to be clear what we mean when we talk of compensation. 'Compensation' is the goal both of the tort of negligence and of the social security system, but the meaning of the term varies according to the context. In the former, it is part of a regime of corrective justice; in the latter, part of a regime of distributive justice. This is reflected in two ways. First, the payment of compensation in negligence depends on a finding that the plaintiff's loss was caused by fault. In the context of social security, fault is generally irrelevant. Thus we can say that, whereas tort damages are awarded as a matter of individual responsibility, social security benefits are paid as a matter of social responsibility. Secondly, the amount of compensation paid differs according to the context. Damages are designed to compensate for *loss*: the sum awarded is that needed to restore the plaintiff, as nearly as possible, to the position she would have been in but for the defendant's negligence. Social security benefits, in contrast, aim to compensate for *needs*, and benefits are generally limited to the amount necessary to sustain the recipient at an acceptable standard of living.

This is not to say that there has been no cross-fertilisation between the notions of compensation adopted in negligence and social security respectively. Entitlement to social security payments may depend on proof that the claimant's injuries were caused by someone else's fault. This is the case under the Criminal Injuries Compensation Scheme which provides for the payment of compensation in respect of personal injury attributable to a criminal offence, the arrest of a suspect or the prevention of crime (see Criminal Justice Act 1988, ss. 109–115). Awards are assessed in the same way as common law damages, to reflect the claimant's loss rather than her needs. Other social security benefits reflect loss rather than need to some extent: thus, the amount of statutory sick pay awarded to employees who are off work through sickness depends on average weekly earnings before the sickness started. Concerns of social responsibility which underpin the compensation objectives of the social security system have also had an influence on the development of the law of tort, both in the tort of negligence and elsewhere. Certain tort doctrines (the vicarious liability of employers for the torts of their employees, see Ch. 22; liability for the breach of strict statutory duties imposed in the workplace, see Ch. 16) serve to direct losses away from individuals towards defendants whose 'deep pockets' can easily bear the cost, irrespective of whether they were personally at fault. The influence of such considerations is evident within the tort of negligence itself, notably in the observed tendency of the courts to characterise blameless and inevitable slips as negligence in contexts in which liability insurance is widespread (see 9.3).

The courts have on occasion expressly adverted to the contrast between the two conceptions of compensation. An example is *Hodgson* v. *Trapp* [1989] AC 807, in which the issue was whether the social security attendance and mobility allowances paid to the plaintiff after a road accident should be deducted from damages awarded to her. The House of Lords overturned Court of Appeal authorities to hold that they should, Lord Bridge stating that to do otherwise would 'only add to the enormous disparity . . . between the position of those who are able to establish a third party's fault as the cause of their injury and the position of those who are not'.

Deterrence

In recent times, many have come to view compensation under the social security system as superior to that awarded as damages in the tort of negligence. This has prompted others, seeking some justification for the continued existence of the tortious remedy, to identify deterrence as its primary objective. They argue that negligence has a major role to play in the prevention of accidents as the threat of liability both (a) encourages people to take care in what they do and (b) scares them away from activities that are fraught with unnecessary danger. These two aspects of 'deterrence theory' can be illustrated as follows. (a) If a manufacturer of fizzy drinks thinks that the installation of an Acme Patent Snailguard on her bottling line will reduce the risk of consumers suffering food poisoning, and hence of her paying out awards of damages, she will have an incentive to go ahead and have one fitted. (b) If a fizzy drinks manufacturer discovers that she cannot produce her product without an unacceptable risk of food poisoning, the liabilities she incurs will force her to raise her prices to an extent where she may no longer be able to compete in the market. Of course, the threat of liability is not the only incentive our fizzy drinks manufacturer may have to ensure her products are safe: she may also be motivated by the need to maintain her reputation for quality or even, strange as it may seem to lawyers, by compassionate concern for the well-being of others. Nevertheless, there is reason to believe that the tort of negligence has a powerful deterrent effect on potential tortfeasors, especially in the commercial context.

Deterrence theory is now particularly associated with the economic analysis of law. Proponents of such analysis view the law as a series of incentives designed to promote a state of economic efficiency in which the wealth of society is maximised (see Atiyah, 1987, Ch. 24). Looking at the law exclusively in these terms is regarded by many as morally disreputable for it pays no heed to individual rights which should not be sacrificed in the public interest (see Dworkin, 1986, Ch. 8). In any case, attempts to evaluate the law of negligence in terms of economic efficiency tend to rely on too many unproven assumptions for them to be of significant practical value. Sometimes, however, economic analysis can throw interesting light on court decisions and judicial reasoning and, for this reason, occasional references to the economic analysis literature will be made in the course of this book.

'Floodgates'

The so-called floodgates argument has often been deployed as a justifica-tion for the refusal to recognise alleged liabilities in negligence. However, despite the frequent judicial recourse to the argument, there is consider-able confusion as to what it stands for and what weight should be attached to it (see 3.2). The argument takes many different forms (see Bell, 1983, Ch. 3) and it is not always clear in which sense a court means to use it. Sometimes it focuses attention on the administration of the courts and points to the risk that the courts, were they to allow a particular type of claim, might be swamped with more claims than they could handle. This form of the argument seems rather weak, for the more people that suffer a particular wrong, the more the courts should be concerned to redress it. Another variation of the floodgates argument commands greater respect. This focuses on the defendant and asks whether it is fair to expose her to liability. A court may find that it is not where the extent of the liability would be too great ('excessively burdensome') or too indeterminate: as the American judge Cardozo CJ remarked, and as many English judges have repeated, the courts should be wary of imposing 'liability in an indeterminate amount for an indeterminate time to an indeterminate class' (*Ultramares Corporation* v. *Touche* 174 NE 441 (1931)).

The floodgates argument is becoming increasingly linked with fears about the ability of the liability insurance industry to cope with the demands placed on it (liability insurance being the practice of insuring against future liabilities). If these fears were well-grounded this would be a serious matter, for the ability of the tort of negligence to furnish the victims of accidents with compensation depends on the efficient operation of the liability insurance market. Without such insurance, many judg-ments obtained as the result of litigation would remain unsatisfied and the process of compensation through the tort of negligence would grind to a halt. This fact explains why Parliament requires those engaged in certain activities to take out liability insurance: the most common types of accident generating claims in negligence are accidents on the roads and at work, and in both these areas liability insurance (on the part of vehicle owners and employers) is compulsory. The development of the tort of negligence since *Donoghue* v. *Stevenson* has provided liability insurers with business opportunities. It now appears, however, that the courts fear that any further expansion of negligence liability into certain areas might cause the liability insurance system to break down, opening up, in the words of Lord Oliver, 'a limitless vista of uninsurable risk' (*Caparo Industries* v. *Dickman* [1990] 2 AC 605).

Two aspects of the expansion in negligence liability, corresponding with the 'excessive burden' and 'indeterminacy' branches of the floodgates argument respectively, have been problematic for the insurance industry. First, insurers now face vastly increased potential liabilities. Not only does this make them wary of undertaking new business (see Alexander, 1972) but it also threatens their continued existence, for their liabilities under policies they have already issued may considerably exceed their estimates (which may not have taken account of recent developments in the law). Secondly, the liabilities that insurers face have become increasingly indeterminate in size. This is attributable above all to recent judicial willingness to allow claims by so-called 'secondary victims' of accidents whose injury – typically psychiatric illness or financial loss – flows from the injury suffered by others (the 'primary victims'). Stapleton (1991) illustrates the indeterminate nature of the losses suffered by secondary victims by considering the effects of an accident which blocks the Dartford Tunnel. No one could predict in advance how many vehicles would be held up (would the blockage occur in rush hour or at midnight?), or how the delay would affect each of the drivers (would it cause their business to lose profits, and if so, would their business clients and suppliers also lose out?). The total loss flowing from the accident would be indeterminate.

Such indeterminacy makes life very difficult for insurers as the key to success in the insurance industry is the ability to forecast the extent and likelihood of various contingencies as accurately as possible. The more accurately this can be done, the lower the insurer can set her premiums. Insurers facing losses of an indeterminate nature would be hard-pressed to set their premiums accurately and would have to play on the safe side by setting high premiums. As premiums rose, clients would find themselves unable to afford to take out insurance at all. Ultimately, insurers might see their client base unravel and be obliged to withdraw from areas of the liability insurance market altogether. It has been argued that the only way to reverse this trend is to limit the scope of liability in negligence and encourage potential victims to take out first-party insurance which presents fewer problems (see Priest, 1987). Against this it can be said that it is wrong to deprive the plaintiff in one case of an action because of fears about the ability to pay off defendants in other cases. Furthermore, a regressive step of the sort advocated would remove the threat of tort liability as a deterrent to potential wrongdoers.

The Danger of Overkill

Just as the floodgates arguments warns of the risk of pursuing a policy of *compensation* too single-mindedly, the overkill argument points out the deleterious consequences that arise if the *deterrent* effect of negligence liability is too great. In 'the overkill scenario', those threatened with liability respond by taking unnecessary safety precautions, or by giving up a socially beneficial activity altogether. Ideally, the law would give potential tortfeasors incentives to take some precautions but not so many that their freedom to pursue their activities is unduly restricted: we all want people to drive safely but we would not go so far as to recommend that all cars be preceded by a pedestrian waving a red warning flag. This crucial point was at the heart of a pioneering study by Calabresi

(1970) in which he argued that the concern of negligence law should be to minimise 'the costs of accidents' across society as a whole rather than their frequency.

In fact, the danger of overkill can be exaggerated. Liability in negligence will not arise merely because one exposes others to the risk of harm; one is only negligent if it is *unreasonable* to do so. Nevertheless, in some contexts, the danger of overkill has exerted a powerful influence upon judicial decisions. It was considered in some depth by Lord Keith in *Rowling* v. *Takaro Properties Ltd* [1988] AC 473. One situation in which he thought the danger might arise was if local authority inspectors were held liable for failing to spot defects in foundations of inspected buildings. In his view, this might lead them unnecessarily to increase the requisite depth of foundations, thereby imposing a substantial and unwarranted financial burden on members of the community. Yet, although there is sometimes a sound basis for the overkill argument (this is one area in which economic analysis has produced interesting insights into the law: see 5.9), all too often it seems to rely less on hard facts than on speculation and secondhand knowledge of the alleged 'liability crisis' in the USA. The following statement, taken from the judgment of Purchas LJ in *Greater Nottingham Co-operative Society Ltd* v. *Cementation Piling and Foundations Ltd* [1989] QB 71, may be construed as exhibiting this shortcoming:

'That this is a field in which the law has properly applied policy restrictions [on the scope of liability] is justified by a glance at the position reached on the other side of the Atlantic where damages awarded in respect of medical and surgical negligence is, it is believed, affecting the proper execution by surgeons of their professional tasks to the detriment of the patients.'

It is one of the themes of Part I of this book that it is possible to develop a more critical understanding of the policies that shape the law of negligence than can be derived from a mere 'glance' across the Atlantic. Accordingly, the following chapters endeavour to explain and analyse the most important of these policies with the aim of promoting a fuller understanding of the current law.

Summary

2.1 In *Donoghue* v. *Stevenson*, the House of Lords recognised for the first time a general rule of liability for harm caused by negligence. As a result, it became possible to talk of a tort of negligence.

2.2 Notwithstanding this general rule, liability for the consequences of carelessness is limited by the requirements of the duty of care, causation and remoteness, and by the various defences that the defendant might raise.

2.3 The tort of negligence abounds with high-flown conceptual language which tends to obscure the fact that detailed rules have developed in many areas to govern the imposition of liability. In other areas, however, the question of liability has yet to be settled and judges may find policy considerations of more assistance than vague legal concepts in deciding whether liability should arise.

2.4 Policy considerations, though not always expressed, influence judicial views as to the precise contours of the existing law and as to the way the law should be developed as and when novel cases arise.

2.5 Important policies that have influenced the shape of the tort of negligence include compensation, deterrence and the fear of 'opening the floodgates' or of engaging in 'overkill'.

Exercises

2.1 What was the significance of *Donoghue* v. *Stevenson*?

2.2 In addition to showing that the defendant was in fact negligent, what else must the plaintiff in a negligence action establish?

2.3 What is the difference between 'policy' and 'principle'? Should judges be concerned with both?

2.4 What impact has the desire to compensate the needy had on the development of the tort of negligence? Why should the courts ever want to deny the claim to compensation of someone injured by another's negligence?

2.5 What role might the tort of negligence have in accident prevention? Is there a danger of going too far?.

---

3   The Duty of Care Concept

3.1   The Nature of the Duty of Care Concept

Not every instance of carelessness resulting in harm will lead to liability in the tort of negligence. Liability is limited by reference to various 'control devices' (see 2.2) of which the most significant is the duty of care. To be held liable in negligence, the defendant must first be found to owe the plaintiff a duty of care. In most cases encountered in practice – particularly cases of physical injury suffered in accidents at work or on the roads – the existence of a duty of care will be presumed without argument (see *Alcock* v. *Chief Constable of South Yorkshire Police* [1992] 1 AC 310). The only question will be whether the defendant was in fact negligent (in breach of duty). In such cases, the moral imperative expressed by Lord Atkin in his 'neighbour principle' points towards liability on the part of the person at fault.

Other cases are not so simple, however. Certain aspects of a case might prompt the courts to be wary of imposing liability on the blameworthy party. This wariness might be linked to doubts as to whether the loss of which the plaintiff complains should be recoverable (especially in cases of nervous shock or pure economic loss). It might stem from the way in which the plaintiff's loss was caused (especially where it was caused by the defendant's statement or omission). Alternatively, it might be associated with the identity of the plaintiff or the defendant. Where a case has features such as these, the court might respond by saying either that no duty of care will ever be owed where those features are present or that it will be owed only if special requirements are met. Chapters 4–8 identify the various features that cause the courts to adopt a restrictive approach and the rules that determine under what circumstances, if any, liability will arise when these features are present.

3.2   Testing the Existence of a Duty of Care

The role of the duty of care concept, then, is a simple one: that of marking out problem areas and laying down the rules limiting liability in each. But how do we know when a duty of care exists and when it does not? The obvious answer is to look at the case law: there we will find numerous decisions as to whether a duty exists on given facts. There will, however, be cases that are not covered by existing decisions: in these, the courts need to take a somewhat different approach.

A notorious attempt to address the need for such an approach was made by Lord Wilberforce in delivering the opinion of the House of Lords in *Anns* v. *Merton London Borough Council* [1978] 1 AC 728. He laid down a two-stage test of the existence of a duty of care:

> 'First one has to ask whether, as between the alleged wrongdoer and the person who has suffered damage, there is a sufficient relationship of proximity or neighbourhood such that, in the reasonable contemplation of the former, carelessness on his part may be likely to cause damage to the latter, in which case a prima facie duty of care arises. Secondly, if the first question is answered affirmatively, it is necessary to consider whether there are any considerations which ought to negative, or to reduce or limit, the scope of the duty or the class of person to whom it is owed or the damages to which a breach of it may give rise.'

The most natural interpretation of this passage is that it lays down a presumption of liability where the defendant, in the circumstances in which she found herself, *ought to have foreseen* injury to the plaintiff. This will be a question of fact to be determined by the judge in every case. The judge then has to decide whether to decline to allow recovery on grounds of public policy. This interpretation of Lord Wilberforce's words found favour for some time and judges soon began to adopt them enthusiastically as a simple test of liability in negligence. More recently, however, the courts have expressed dissatisfaction with this way of proceeding.

So what was wrong with Lord Wilberforce's 'two-stage' test? Essentially, the problem was that it provided the springboard for a massive expansion of liability in the late 1970s and early 1980s. The first stage of Lord Wilberforce's test presented no hurdle to litigants at all: almost everything in life is foreseeable if you have a vivid enough imagination. This meant that the courts were left to restrict the scope of negligence liability by reference to the policy considerations that come in at the second stage of Lord Wilberforce's test. In fact, judges proved unwilling to let matters of public policy stand in the way of their understandable sympathy for the injured plaintiffs in court before them. As Lord Keith subsequently observed: '[A] too literal application of the well-known observation of Lord Wilberforce in *Anns*... may be productive of a failure to have regard to, and to analyse and weigh, all the relevant considerations in considering whether it is appropriate that a duty of care should be imposed' (*Rowling* v. *Takaro Properties Ltd* [1988] 1 AC 473).

In key cases such as *McLoughlin* v. *O'Brian* [1983] 1 AC 410 and *Junior Books* v. *Veitchi Co Ltd* [1983] 1 AC 520 (see 4.2 and 5.3), judges roundly condemned the policy arguments which were said to justify restrictions on liability. The 'floodgates' argument (see 2.5), in particular, was dismissed in cavalier fashion. The results were twofold. First, the courts recognised duties of care in a wide variety of situations that had not previously come before the courts (e.g. in respect of 'wrongful birth': see 7.3). Secondly and more controversially, judges used the two-stage test as a justification for recognising duties of care whose existence had previously been denied, thereby casting aside restrictions on liability that had been recognised in older cases (particularly in the context of economic loss and omissions).

3.3 The Retreat from *Anns*

Unhappy with the way things were shaping up, the courts have recently sought to reverse many of the developments of the last 20 or so years. This has led to talk of a 'retreat from *Anns*'. The retreat is typified by a certain amount of rhetorical posturing on the part of the courts. The following propositions (not always consistent with one another) can be regarded as recurrent themes: first the two-stage test cannot be used to justify overturning established restrictions on liability for negligence (see *Leigh & Sillivan Ltd* v. *Aliakmon Shipping Co Ltd* [1986] AC 785). Secondly, the first stage of Lord Wilberforce's test does not simply raise questions as to what was *in fact* foreseeable but also questions as to what *the law* regards as foreseeable, foreseeability in this latter (restricted) sense sometimes being called 'proximity' (see *McLoughlin* v. *O'Brian* [1983] 1 AC 410. Thirdly, in certain contexts, the courts might have to lay down conditions of liability other than those given by Lord Wilberforce (e.g. that there should be a 'close and direct' relationship between the parties or that it should be 'just and reasonable' to impose liability: see *Peabody Donation Fund* v. *Parkinson* [1985] AC 210). Finally, the courts should abandon 'the modern approach' of looking for a single general principle underlying the tort of negligence and revert to the 'traditional approach [of identifying] a wide variety of duty situations, all falling within the ambit of the tort of negligence, but sufficiently distinct to require separate definition of the essential ingredients by which the existence of the duty is to be recognised' (*Caparo* v. *Dickman* [1990] 2 AC 605 per Lord Bridge*)*. From this base, the scope of the tort should only be expanded 'incrementally and by analogy with established categories of liability' (*Sutherland Shire Council* v. *Heyman* (1985) 60 ALR 1, per Brennan J).

3.4 Where Now?

What all this amounts to is debatable. Certainly, the courts have arrested the expansion of liability for negligence and re-asserted old limitations on the scope of the duty of care. Decided cases must be carefully analysed so that the scope of existing duties of care can be ascertained. But it can be doubted whether the courts have left us with any guidance as to how novel cases should be addressed. Words and phrases such as 'proximity', 'close and direct' and 'just and reasonable' provide little or no concrete assistance. Lord Bridge admitted as much in *Caparo* v. *Dickman*:

> '[Such concepts] are not susceptible of any such precise definition as would be necessary to give them utility as practical tests but amount in effect to little more than convenient labels to attach to the features of different specific situations which, on a detailed consideration of all the

circumstances, the law recognises pragmatically as giving rise to a duty of care of a given scope.'

This suggests that the first concern of students of the tort of negligence should be to analyse the *results* of decided cases rather than the conceptual *reasoning* employed to reach such results. A second concern should be with the policy considerations to which those decisions give effect, for those considerations at least give us a starting point as we attempt to predict whether existing liabilities will be expanded – incrementally – to cover the facts of cases which come before the courts for the first time.

Summary

3.1 The existence of a duty of care is a prerequisite of liability in the tort of negligence. In cases where the positive acts of a private individual cause physical damage, the existence of such a duty can be assumed. Outside this simple instance of negligence liability, the question whether a duty of care exists may call for detailed consideration of rules of law.

3.2 The question whether a duty of care arises can often be answered by examining the case law. This is not possible where a case raises novel issues. In such cases, the courts for some time applied Lord Wilberforce's two stage test from *Anns* to determine whether a duty of care would arise. This approach has now fallen out of favour as it was felt that it resulted in an undesirable expansion of the scope of liability in negligence.

3.3 The last few years have seen a retreat from *Anns* in which the courts have restricted liability by reference to a number of requirements which were not given sufficient emphasis, if any, in Lord Wilberforce's test. Most significant amongst them is the requirement of 'proximity'. Instead of following Lord Wilberforce in pursuit of a single general principle of liability, the courts now prefer to develop different categories and sub-categories of liability (the 'incremental' approach).

3.4 The result of this change of tack is that the tort of negligence is in a state of flux. Concepts such as proximity have yet to be given any concrete meaning; indeed, they may simply be indefinable. For the time being, the best way to predict how liability in negligence will develop is to pay close attention to the facts of decided cases and to the policy factors that have influenced them.

Exercises

3.1 What purpose does the duty of care concept serve?

3.2 What considerations do you think Lord Keith had in mind when he said that 'a too literal application of the well-known observation of Lord Wilberforce in *Anns. . .* may be productive of a failure to have regard to, and to analyse and weigh, all the relevant considerations in considering whether it is appropriate that a duty of care should be imposed' (*Rowling* v. *Takaro Properties Ltd*)?

3.3 What differences are there between the approach of the courts to the duty of care concept at the beginning of the 1980s and their approach at the beginning of the 1990s.

4 Nervous Shock

4.1 What is Nervous Shock?

The law of tort gives no damages for grief, anxiety and depression independent of physical injury. These are dismissed as normal human emotions which any normal person experiences after a particularly traumatic event. To claim damages in tort, a plaintiff must prove that she is suffering from what Lord Bridge has described as a 'positive psychiatric illness' (*McLoughlin v. O'Brian* [1983] AC 410), but what is commonly known amongst lawyers as 'nervous shock'. Whether the plaintiff's mental condition amounts to such an illness is a matter for the court after hearing expert evidence from psychiatrists. As the medical profession's understanding of psychiatric conditions develops, so the law may admit new varieties of nervous shock. Recently, attention has focused upon Post-Traumatic Stress Disorder (PTSD). Awareness of this condition was heightened by studies of veterans of the Falklands War and that experience was invaluable in the treatment of victims of a number of man-made disasters that have occurred since (the sinking of the ferry *Herald of Free Enterprise* in Zeebrugge harbour and the fire at King's Cross Underground station are prominent examples). The condition first received judicial recognition in the litigation that followed the Hillsborough football stadium tragedy in which 95 fans were crushed to death after the police had negligently let too many fans on to the terraces at the Leppings Lane end of the ground (*Alcock* v. *Chief Constable of South Yorkshire* [1992] 1 AC 310). Many relatives and friends of those caught up in the crush complained of PTSD, the effects of which were described in the following terms by the psychiatrist whose evidence was accepted at the trial:

It follows on a painful event which is outside the range of normal human experience, the Disorder includes preoccupation with the event – that is intrusive memories – with avoidance of reminders of the experience. At the same time there are persistent symptoms of increased arousal – these symptoms not being present before the event. The symptoms may be experienced in the form of sleep difficulty, irritability or outbursts of anger, problems with memory or concentration, startle responses, hypervigilence [*sic*] and over-reaction to any reminder of the event.

4.2   The Approach to be Taken

In asking whether a duty of care arises in cases of nervous shock, the courts have wavered between the two broad types of approach identified by Lord Bridge in *Caparo* (see 3.3). This equivocation was readily apparent in what was, before Hillsborough, the leading case: *McLoughlin v. O'Brian*. Mrs McLoughlin suffered nervous shock after a car crash involving her husband and three children. One child was killed; the others were badly injured. Mrs McLoughlin had been at home at the time the accident happened. She was told the grim news an hour or so afterwards by a friend who drove her to the hospital. There, Mrs McLoughlin saw the surviving members of her family – bruised and battered, covered in mud and oil – and heard their sobs and screams. Subsequently, she suffered the condition of which she complained.

Her claim for damages was unanimously allowed by the House of Lords although the approach of the different members of the House differed markedly. Lord Wilberforce adopted a very traditional approach, focusing narrowly on the facts of previous cases, which is somewhat surprising given the approach he had previously taken in *Anns*. By contrast, the other members of the House preferred simply to ask whether the harm suffered by Mrs McLoughlin was reasonably foreseeable and then (with the exception of Lord Scarman) to enquire whether any argument of policy militated against recovery in the present case. Paradoxically, it was precisely this approach that Lord Wilberforce had seemed to advocate in *Anns*. Let us now examine the two approaches in more detail.

Lord Wilberforce endorsed the method employed in cases which had previously expanded liability for nervous shock. He noted that '[t]hroughout these developments. . . the courts have proceeded in the traditional manner of the common law from case to case, upon a basis of logical necessity,' adding that '[t]o argue from one factual situation to another and to decide by analogy is a natural tendency of the human and legal mind'. In determining whether Mrs McLoughlin's case was analogous to those in which the courts had already allowed recovery, Lord Wilberforce measured her claim against three criteria: 'the class of persons whose claims should be recognised; the proximity of such persons to the accident; and the means by which the shock was caused'.

With regard to the first of these criteria, the law originally adopted the position that no damages could be recovered for nervous shock unless it was accompanied by actual physical injury. From there the law advanced to allow claims to those who reasonably feared immediate personal injuries to themselves and subsequently to those who feared, not for themselves, but for close relatives. Lord Wilberforce explained in *McLoughlin* that this process illustrated how the common law develops incrementally from case to case: 'If a mother. . . could recover on account of fear for herself, how can she be denied recovery on account of fear for her accompanying children?' By the time of *McLoughlin* v. *O'Brian* itself, it was well established that plaintiffs could recover for nervous shock induced by fear for the well-being of their children or spouses: accordingly Mrs McLoughlin had no difficulty surmounting this hurdle.

Lord Wilberforce's second requirement was that the plaintiff should be in close proximity to the accident in time and space. Early cases allowed recovery only where the plaintiff was at the scene of the accident. But this requirement had been relaxed to justify damages awards to those who, though not witnessing the accident itself, came upon its 'immediate aftermath'. This move was approved by Lord Wilberforce in *McLoughlin* who applied the 'aftermath' doctrine to the facts before him. Although Mrs McLoughlin had come across her family not at the scene of the accident but at the hospital, she still fell within the 'aftermath' doctrine. In coming to this conclusion, Lord Wilberforce emphasised that her relatives 'were in the same condition, covered with oil and mud, and distraught with pain'.

The final limitation identified by Lord Wilberforce in *McLoughlin* concerned the means by which the shock was caused. He contrasted cases where an accident, or its immediate aftermath, was witnessed in person with those in which the victim was told of the accident by a third party. Only in the former type of case would liability arise. He reserved his judgment on the question of whether watching live television coverage of an accident, or any other 'equivalent of sight or hearing', would satisfy this requirement.

In contrast to Lord Wilberforce's incremental approach, other judges in *McLoughlin* disavowed the arbitrary and rigid limitations on recovery adopted in previous cases. They preferred to start from the presumption that, if nervous shock was the foreseeable consequence of the defendant's carelessness, then the victim was entitled to damages. The case for this approach was put most powerfully by Lord Bridge: 'we should resist the temptation to try yet once more to freeze the law in a rigid posture which would deny justice to some who. . . ought to succeed'. Illustrating the injustice that might follow from this, Lord Bridge gave an example that seems to go much further than Lord Wilberforce would have allowed. Suppose a mother suffers nervous shock after learning of the death of the rest of her family in a hotel fire and seeing a newspaper photograph of unidentifiable victims trapped on the top floor waving for help from the windows: can she recover for her psychiatric injury? Lord Bridge thought that she could. In his view, it should make no difference whether her condition was brought about 'by her imagination of the agonies of mind and body in which her family died, rather than direct perception of the event': the mother should not be denied damages by the operation of hard and fast legal rules.

Powerful as Lord Bridge's argument is, it is now apparent that it is the Wilberforce approach which prevails. This was made clear by the House of Lords in the Hillsborough litigation, at the end of which all the claims brought before the House were rejected. Their Lordships gave short shrift to the argument that Lord Wilberforce was actually in the minority in

McLoughlin in terms of the approach he adopted. Cases decided since *McLoughlin* which adopted the analysis of Lord Bridge must now be treated with some caution. Nervous shock can no longer be looked at as an unexceptional form of personal injury, raising no more difficulty than a broken arm or leg. For other personal injuries, the plaintiff need generally only show that injury to her of that sort was foreseeable; however, where she complains of nervous shock alone, she must tread a precarious path through a minefield of complicated legal rules. In nervous shock cases, the courts adopt the incremental approach to the establishment of a duty of care and scrutinise the facts of decided cases to identify the precise extent of the liabilities recognised therein. The frontiers of liability may be pushed forward marginally over the course of time – and indeed the Hillsborough plaintiffs sought to convince the House of Lords that it was appropriate to take small steps forward in a number of respects – but the boundary posts must be pushed back slowly, not removed in one fell swoop. Let us now turn to the rules that come from the decided cases and try to see how far the Hillsborough decision has expanded the scope of liability for nervous shock.

4.3   The Class of Plaintiff Able to Recover

Their Lordships in the Hillsborough case (four of whom delivered full speeches) agreed that the law should not be frozen in a rigid posture: new categories of plaintiffs entitled to recover could be added to those recognised in existing cases. However, they felt that a cautious approach was in order and the law was not yet such that anyone who might foreseeably suffer nervous shock as a result of an event could claim. The existing categories should be expanded incrementally rather than cast aside and replaced by an open-ended test of foreseeability.

A useful starting point, adopted by Lord Oliver and Lord Jauncey, is to look at cases in which the plaintiff was personally involved as a participant in the shocking events. In such cases, the plaintiff would benefit from a duty of care almost as of right. Under this heading come cases where the plaintiff was herself threatened by the relevant events (as where a car crash leaves the passenger with no physical scars) and those where the plaintiff gives assistance in the rescue operations (see *Chadwick* v. *British Railways Board* [1967] 1 WLR 912). Also under this heading are cases in which the plaintiff is the unwitting instrument of another's misfortune. This rule would allow recovery by the crane operator who sees the rope carrying the load snap and the load plummet onto people below, and by the train driver who is misdirected at the points and ploughs into workers busy on the tracks (see *Dooley* v. *Cammel Laird & Co* [1951] 1 Lloyd's Rep 271 and *Galt* v. *British Railways Board* (1983) 133 NLJ 870).

The second type of case identified by Lord Oliver is where the plaintiff is not herself involved in the shocking events but merely witnesses them.

In such cases, she must generally be able to point to a sufficient relationship of love and affection with the victim. This condition serves to limit the range of claimants. Precisely how one measures love and affection is an issue on which the judges were silent; however, Lord Keith and Lord Ackner stated that courts are entitled to presume that there is sufficient love and affection in certain relationships, such as those of parent and child, spouses and – going beyond the relationships specified by Lord Wilberforce in *McLoughlin* – fiancées (Lord Keith only). However, the relationship between brothers is not such as to allow the same presumption to be made, and for this reason the claim of one of the Hillsborough plaintiffs was dismissed. In these and other relationships, the plaintiff must specifically prove that a special bond of affection existed between her and the victim. (Is the judiciary ready to hear our courtrooms swell with the sounds of wailing and gnashing of teeth on the part of plaintiffs seeking to establish their love and affection for the deceased?) Conversely, in the case of relationships in which a special bond is to be presumed, it is open to the defendant to seek to rebut the presumption of liability (e.g. by showing that a married couple had fallen out several years ago and were virtual strangers).

Although in the majority of cases the plaintiff will have to prove the existence of a special bond of affection between herself and the victim, the House of Lords was not prepared to rule out the possibility that a mere bystander might recover if the circumstances of a catastrophe occurring close to the bystander were especially horrific. As an example of circumstances under which a mere bystander might recover, Lord Ackner envisaged the case of a passer-by witnessing a petrol tanker careering out of control into a school in session and bursting into flames. He failed to explain, however, why this would be regarded as more horrific than the terrible events at Hillsborough.

4.4 The Type of Event that may give Rise to Liability

Although people do in fact suffer psychiatric illness in a variety of situations, the law limits their right to recover damages to cases where the circumstances causing the illness take a certain form. Two issues require consideration: first, the requirement that the event that induces the shock be *traumatic* in nature; secondly, the possibility that, even within the class of traumatic events, there are some that give rise to liability and some that do not.

The plaintiff's injury must be caused by a traumatic event in the nature of an accident: it is not enough that the injury was caused by a series of events which result in the gradual accumulation of pressures on the nervous system. This as least was the view of Lords Ackner and Oliver in *Alcock*, the former illustrating the sort of case in which he felt there would be no liability by instancing the spouse who has been worn down by caring for a tortiously injured husband or wife, and the parent made distraught by the wayward conduct of a tortiously brain-damaged child. In Lord Ackner's view, an element of *suddenness* was necessary for liability to arise.

Even when this element of suddenness is present, there remains the question as to how far, if at all, the courts will discriminate between different factual situations in determining whether the defendant should be held liable. It is clear that liability may be imposed where the shock is caused by witnessing actual *injury* suffered by another person, and it seems also that there will be liability where shock is suffered as the result of seeing another placed in extreme jeopardy, even if in the event the other escapes unharmed (see Lord Oliver in *Alcock*). It is not clear what the situation is where the defendant is mistaken as to the existence of a threat to the physical safety of another. Similar uncertainty surrounds the case where the accident in question involves not people but property. In *Alcock*, the House of Lords made no reference to the Court of Appeal decision in *Attia* v. *British Gas* [1988] QB 304, which accepted that a duty of care was owed in relation to nervous shock suffered by Mrs Attia when she returned home to find her house in flames due to the negligence of British Gas. In view of the Court of Appeal's reliance in that case upon the approach of Lord Bridge in *McLoughlin*, the decision must now be regarded as questionable.

4.5   The Requisite Means of Witnessing the Event

The rule – stated by Lord Wilberforce in *McLoughlin* and reiterated in the Hillsborough decision – is that the plaintiff must either actually perceive the shocking event by sight or hearing or come upon its immediate aftermath. Merely being told about it is not enough. In the Hillsborough case, the House of Lords was faced for the first time with the question, which Lord Wilberforce had been content to leave open in *McLoughlin*, of whether viewing shocking events on television might be regarded as equivalent to actually seeing or hearing them. On the facts, the House concluded that those plaintiffs who had only viewed the disaster on television or listened on the radio, or who had merely been told about it, were barred from recovering for that reason. Their Lordships urged that the interpolation of television coverage between event and observer robbed the scenes of their sudden impact upon the senses. All their Lordships, however, confined their decision to the facts in front of them, and Lord Ackner was prepared to accept that there might be occasions on which television pictures would have at least as great an impact on observers as actual presence at the scene. An example of such a case would, he said, be where parents viewed live television pictures of a special event of children travelling in a hot-air balloon, in which the balloon suddenly burst into flames and plummeted to the ground. Perhaps the crucial distinguishing factor in this case is that the parents knew that their children would be injured whereas in the Hillsborough case the television viewers, unable to make out recognisable individuals in the crowd, merely feared that their friends and relatives would be caught up in the crush. It is not clear whether this rule applies to those who rely not merely upon their witnessing the event but upon the fact that they were personally involved as a *participant* in the event (e.g., the mining engineer who supervises on closed-circuit television a rescue operation of those trapped when the roof of a mine collapsed on workers).

The plaintiff need not suffer nervous shock as a result of experiencing the traumatic event unfold: it is sufficient that she comes upon its 'immediate aftermath'. The issue of what counts as the immediate aftermath of such an event remains problematic despite attempts to clarify it in the leading cases. In *McLoughlin*, Lord Wilberforce had been content to treat Mrs McLoughlin as coming on the immediate aftermath even though she did not go to the scene of the crash but only went to the hospital. He stressed, however, that the scenes at the hospital were particularly horrific. In the Hillsborough decision, there was general agreement that the immediate aftermath did not extend to cover those who had attended at temporary mortuaries some nine hours or more after the disaster in order to identify bodies. Lord Jauncey's reasons for taking this view were that too much time had lapsed and that the visits were made for the wrong purpose: they were made not for the purpose of rescuing or giving comfort to the victim but purely for the purposes of identification. Lord Jauncey warned, however, against attempting to draw up any exhaustive catalogue of examples that would fall within the immediate aftermath, and his words should not be treated as precluding claims by those who do not come upon the aftermath in order to make a rescue or give comfort. Thus the woman who returns home to find the charred body of her husband, electrocuted by a defectively wired product, should be able to argue she had come upon the immediate aftermath of the accident.

4.6 The Class of Defendant Potentially Liable

It seems odd to suggest that nervous shock claims require special rules as to the class of those who can be held liable. However, the House of Lords in the Hillsborough case was content to accept that this was so. For no very obvious reason, Lord Oliver suggested that a defendant who imperils or injures herself would be unlikely to be held liable to those who suffer shock as a result (cf. 7.2). This would mean that there would be no liability on the part of the son who, watched by his mother, negligently walks in front of an oncoming motor car or (more gruesomely) on the part of the negligent window-cleaner who loses her grip and falls from a height, impaling herself on spiked railings. Remarkably, Lord Oliver was prepared to countenance this result in spite of his recognition that the rule might produce injustice where a third party shared responsibility for the shocking event with the person imperilled or injured. In such a case, the third party would have to compensate the plaintiff in full, even if her fault was trivial, while the person imperilled would pay nothing even if the incident had arisen primarily as a result of her negligence. Another type of defendant against whom an action would be problematic is the *communicant* of shocking news. Two types of case can be imagined. The first is where the communicant passes on erroneous information about the fate of a close relative. In Australia, it has been held that the communicant owes a duty of care to the relative and liability was imposed on one who told the plaintiff falsely that her husband had been admitted to an asylum (*Barnes* v. *Commonwealth* (1937) SR (NSW) 511). The second case is where the communicant tells no lies but pays no regard for the sensibilities of the plaintiff by giving all the gory details of her loved one's fate. Suppose the live television broadcasts coming from the Hillsborough stadium had included – in breach of the broadcasters' code of practice – close-up pictures of individuals being crushed to death: could relatives claim that the television company was at fault in showing the pictures and liable for PTSD suffered as a consequence of seeing them?

4.7   Policy Considerations

The floodgates argument has exerted a crucial influence on the development of the law relating to nervous shock. However, in *McLoughlin*, there was general agreement that the fears aroused by this argument had been exaggerated. The majority of the House of Lords was not persuaded that this consideration required them to lay down, in advance, rules restricting liability for nervous shock. Lord Wilberforce, on the other hand, did feel the need to set down legal limitations on the extent of admissible claims. This need, he thought, arose 'just because "shock" in its nature is capable of affecting so wide a range of people'. These sentiments were echoed by the House of Lords in the Hillsborough case and used as a justification for the restrictive approach adopted there.

One might question whether such a restrictive approach is in fact called for. Psychiatric illness is relatively uncommon as compared to physical injury and it is, in any case, less likely to be caused by another's culpable conduct. Furthermore, even the largest awards of damages for nervous shock are but a tiny fraction of many awards for physical injury. While we must accept that large numbers of people might suffer nervous shock as the result of one event, we should also note that the same is true of physical injury: some 500 people were killed or injured at Hillsborough. In view of these considerations, we might doubt whether treating nervous shock as an unexceptional category of personal injury calling for no special rules would result in a flood of claims, excessively burdening defendants, insurers and the courts.

Summary

4.1 The plaintiff in a nervous shock case must prove that she is suffering from a positive psychiatric illness, and not merely grief, anxiety or depression.

4.2 The Hillsborough case makes it clear that courts should take the incremental approach associated with Lord Wilberforce in *McLoughlin* to the duty of care in nervous shock cases, rather than regarding the foreseeability of nervous shock as the sole test of liability (the approach associated with Lord Bridge in *McLoughlin*).

4.3 As a general rule, only participants in the traumatic events and close relatives (parents, children and spouses, but not siblings) who witnessed those events, can recover for nervous shock. However, if the traumatic event is particularly horrific, a mere bystander might be able to recover.

4.4 The plaintiff's injury must have been caused by a traumatic event rather than by continual stress. The trauma must derive from concern about the fate of people; concern about the fate of property is probably not enough.

4.5 The plaintiff must generally perceive the traumatic event by means of her own senses rather than through the medium of television. It is sufficient that the plaintiff come upon the immediate aftermath of the event.

4.6 Doubts exist as to whether a defendant can be held liable in respect of an act of folly which endangers herself and thereby causes shock to the plaintiff. Similar doubts arise where the defendant does not cause the occurrence of the traumatic event but negligently communicates information about it to the plaintiff.

4.7 The floodgates argument has caused the courts to adopt a restrictive approach to recovery in respect of nervous shock, though it can be argued that its weight has been exaggerated.

Exercises

4.1 Is nervous shock to be treated as an unexceptional type of personal injury in respect of which the sole criterion of liability is foreseeability or is it a type of injury that requires the scope of the duty of care to be limited? If the latter, what is it about nervous shock that calls for a restrictive approach?

4.2 Explain the distinction made by Lord Oliver in *Alcock* between participants in a traumatic event and mere witnesses to it.

4.3 In what circumstances might brothers and sisters of a deceased claim damages for nervous shock after witnessing her death? What evidence about their relationship with the deceased would they have to produce in court?

4.4 Must the plaintiff in a nervous shock action always actually see the traumatic event in person? What if the plaintiff is blind?

4.5 Two years ago a fatal train crash occurred at Thames Junction. The 7.20 a.m. from Fleet was directed down the wrong tracks through the negligence of a railway employee and ploughed into a group of workers laying new track. Three of the workers were killed; two were seriously injured. Only G escaped being caught in the impact, though she had felt sure that she was doomed. None of the passengers in the train, driven by H, was hurt. J, the station supervisor and the twin sister of one of those killed, had watched the accident as it happened on closed circuit television; she proceeded bravely to co-ordinate the rescue attempts from her office with the aid of the television cameras. It took several hours to recover the bodies of the dead and wounded from the wreck. As they were laid by the side of the track, relatives were allowed to approach. K saw her daughter wracked with pain and attempted to give her comfort; L saw the lifeless body of her son and kissed him farewell. Railway staff refrained from telling K that her daughter, having been designated look-out, was partly responsible for the injuries suffered. The whole proceedings, from the moment of the crash on, were observed by M, a 5 year old child. G, H, J, K, L and M all suffered PTSD as a consequence of their experiences. N, the lover of one of those injured in the crash, nursed her loved one slowly back to health but herself suffered a nervous breakdown as a result of the strain which this caused. Advise the parties as to their rights and liabilities in tort.

5 Economic Loss and Negligent Misstatement

5.1 What is 'Pure Economic Loss'?

The tort of negligence provides compensation for all sorts of loss that are financial in nature. If you were to be run over by a negligent car driver, your damages would represent not only your physical injuries (your pain and suffering, etc) but also the financial consequences of those injuries ('consequential economic loss'). Thus you would be able to recover in respect of any medical costs incurred and any wages lost. However, when the courts are faced with loss that is *purely* economic in nature – that is, which does not stem from any physical damage to the plaintiff or her property – their approach is very different. Pure economic loss is, by and large, irrecoverable.

The distinction between recoverable and irrecoverable economic loss can be demonstrated by the case of *Spartan Steel and Alloys Ltd* v. *Martin & Co Ltd* [1973] QB 27. Martin were building contractors carrying out road works near Spartan Steel's metal-processing plant. Their men were careless in digging up the road and damaged the electricity cable running to the plant. The power was cut off for several hours. Spartan Steel sued Martin for their lost profits. The Court of Appeal allowed the claim only in part. The majority of the court made the following distinction. The profits lost on the metal that was being processed at the time the electricity was cut off were recoverable. This metal was actually damaged by the power cut and so these profits could be regarded as consequential economic loss stemming from physical damage to the plaintiff's property. The rest of Spartan Steel's loss, however, was purely economic. This loss arose from the fact that Spartan Steel was not able to process other lots of metal in the time the power was off: it did not stem from damage to any of these lots. Admittedly, the electricity cable had been damaged, but the cable belonged to the electricity board, not to Spartan Steel: to recover financial loss you have to establish that it was caused by physical damage to your own person or property.

5.2 Defective Product Economic Loss

We must now elaborate our definition of pure economic loss to take into account the question of defective products (see Stapleton, 1991, pp. 267–77). The courts insist that the manufacturer of a defective product will only be liable in respect of damage that the product causes to another's

person or property. If a product is simply no good, or merely physically
deteriorates, even if it blows up and destroys itself, any financial loss that
flows from this is pure economic loss. So, while Mrs Donoghue's claim for
compensation for being ill after drinking her fabled bottle of ginger beer
would today be unanswerable, she would not be entitled to recover the
cost of a replacement bottle of ginger beer.

This rule was applied in what has become known as the 'lobster case'
(*Muirhead* v. *International Tank Specialities Ltd* [1986] QB 507). Mr
Muirhead was a wholesale fish merchant who thought he had spotted a
way of making a killing out of lobsters. However, his plan was to work
out rather too literally for his liking. The essence of his scheme was that he
would buy lobsters in the summer, when they were cheap, and sell them at
Christmas, by which time the price would have soared. To do this, he
required storage facilities, which he bought from ITS. These consisted of a
large tank and a number of pumps designed to stop the water going stale.
Sadly for Mr Muirhead, the pumps – made in France – were not suitable
for use on the electricity mains in the United Kingdom. A few days after
he had installed the storage tank and the lobsters in it, the pumps cut out
and the entire stock of lobsters died. Unable to recover damages from
ITS, which had gone into liquidation, Mr Muirhead sought compensation
from the French manufacturers of the pumps, who were found to have
been negligent. The Court of Appeal allowed him to recover all the loss he
claimed which flowed from the death of the lobsters, but declined to
award damages to represent the money he had spent on the purchase of
the pumps and on attempts to repair them. These latter heads of loss were
purely economic as they were sustained simply because the pumps did not
work.

The notion of a defective product applies to buildings as well as to
goods. This was recently confirmed by the House of Lords in *Murphy* v.
Brentwood DC [1991] AC 398 (see Fleming, 1990; the decision overruled
Anns v. *Merton LBC* [1978] AC 728: see 5.4). In Murphy, as in *Anns*,
defective foundations were the cause of subsidence and of cracks that
appeared in the walls of the plaintiff's house. The House of Lords held
that the money Mr Murphy lost on the subsequent sale of his house was
purely economic as it was caused by the deterioration of a defective
product, not by any damage caused to his other property. The plight of
those in Mr Murphy's situation is compounded by the fact that the law of
contract also operates harshly in this area. Had Mr Murphy sued the
previous owner on the contract of sale, he would have been met by the
response that the law implies no warranty as to safety or fitness for
habitation into contracts for the sale of real property (contrast the implied
warranty of merchantable quality under the Sale of Goods Act 1979,
s.14(2)). The purchase is at the buyer's risk: *caveat emptor* (let the buyer
beware).

To mitigate the harshness of the common law rules, Parliament has
allowed homeowners a statutory right to compensation in certain
circumstances. By section 1 of the Defective Premises Act 1972, archi-

tects, builders and others involved in the construction of dwellings may be held liable to owners of those dwellings if they fail to carry out their work in a workmanlike or professional manner and this failure results in the building being unfit for habitation. The Act only applies to 'dwellings': commercial properties are excluded. Also excluded are houses erected under schemes approved by the Secretary of State (see Hepple and Matthews, 1991, p. 483).

One large area of doubt remains in the area of defective product economic loss. This centres upon the 'complex structures' argument first advanced by Lord Bridge in *D & F Estates* v. *Church Commissioners* [1989] AC 177 and developed by Lord Bridge and other members of the House of Lords in *Murphy* v. *Brentwood DC*. The argument suggests a qualification to the general rule preventing recovery in respect of damage which a product sustains to itself because of a defect: certain products might be analysed as 'complex structures' so that the owner would be able to sue in respect of damage to one part of the product caused by a defect in another part. Such damage would not be considered pure economic loss and would be recoverable under normal *Donoghue* v. *Stevenson* principles. Doubts exist as to the circumstances in which the complex structures analysis might operate. Lord Bridge in *Murphy* said that it would apply if a defective central heating boiler in a house were to cause a fire damaging the house; the owner might then be able to obtain damages from the boiler manufacturer. However, the House of Lords in *Murphy* was adamant that the complex structures argument had no place in the case before it: it could not be said that the cracks in the walls of Mr Murphy's house were damage to a part of the building separate from the defective foundations which were the root of the problem. Whether the complex structures argument will find favour with the courts, and (if so) how it will be applied, is as yet uncertain (see Fleming, 1989b; Grubb and Mullis, 1991).

5.3 Attempts to Circumvent the Rule

The law relating to the recovery of pure economic loss has been considerably simpified by the decisions of the House of Lords in *D & F Estates* and *Murphy*. It is now safe to say that, as a general rule, such loss cannot be recovered in the tort of negligence. Yet the matter was not always so clear. As the expansion of the tort of negligence continued apace up to the early 1980s, the restrictive rule that pure economic loss could not be recovered came under increasing pressure. This pressure produced attempts either to admit exceptions to the rule or even to abandon the rule altogether. Although most of these attempts were subsequently disavowed by the courts, one or two loose ends remain to be tidied up.

The first major landmark in this process was the decision in *Hedley Byrne & Co* v. *Heller & Partners* [1964] AC 465. In that case, the House of Lords accepted in principle that pure economic loss caused by reliance upon a negligent misrepresentation could be recovered. The case spawned a line of authority that is regarded as analytically distinct from the rest of the law derived from *Donoghue* v. *Stevenson*. It has generally been seen as an exception to the general rule that pure economic loss is not recoverable rather than as a denial of that rule. The case and its progeny are examined in detail in the section on negligent misrepresentation (5.5).

Subsequent cases, however, took a more radical approach and claimed to be founded on normal *Donoghue* v. *Stevenson* principles, rather than on the narrower rule in *Hedley Byrne*. In *Ross* v. *Caunters* [1980] Ch. 297, the intended beneficiary under a will had been deprived of his inheritance by the incompetence of the solicitor drawing up the will. Sir Robert Megarry V-C held the solicitor liable and awarded damages to the intended beneficiary. The liability, he said, resulted from a direct application of Lord Wilberforce's two-stage test in *Anns*, itself an attempt to encapsulate the basis of *Donoghue* v. *Stevenson* in a single general principle. At the first stage, the Vice-Chancellor found that the plaintiff's loss was readily foreseeable, while he thought that there were no policy considerations at the second stage sufficient to negate any duty of care. For this reason, there was no need to apply the stricter test of liability derived from *Hedley Byrne*. In any case, the Vice-Chancellor had doubts whether the rule in *Hedley Byrne* could apply where the cause of the plaintiff's loss was not her reliance upon the defendant but the reliance upon the defendant of a third party, namely the testator (see also *Ministry of Housing and Local Government* v. *Sharp* [1970] 2 QB 223).

Lord Wilberforce's approach to the duty of care was also adopted by Lord Roskill, delivering the leading speech of the House of Lords in the problematic case of *Junior Books Ltd* v. *Veitchi Co Ltd* [1983] AC 520. By a majority, the House of Lords held Veitchi liable in respect of defective product economic loss representing the cost of replacing a floor which they had negligently laid in a factory owned by Junior Books. No contractual claim was possible because Veitchi had been engaged by a firm of builders employed by Junior Books, and not by Junior Books itself. Emphasising that Junior Books had directed the builders to engage Veitchi and had relied on Veitchi's expertise, Lord Roskill found there was sufficient proximity to satisfy the first stage of Lord Wilberforce's test. Furthermore, at the second stage of the test, there were no reasons to restrict the duty of care, the fears aroused by the 'floodgates' argument being unfounded.

The precise *ratio* of *Junior Books* remains unclear. What is clear, however, is that the case was founded on the two-stage test in *Anns* and was thus sited in the mainstream of *Donoghue* v. *Stevenson* liability. Unlike *Hedley Byrne*, which could be regarded as a narrowly confined exception to the general rule, *Junior Books* threatened to allow recovery for pure economic loss across the board. Courts in subsequent cases, unhappy with this prospect, began to cast doubt on the majority speeches in *Junior Books* and expressed a preference for the dissenting reasoning of Lord Brandon. Every time a plaintiff sought to rely upon *Junior Books,* the court was able to distinguish that case on the facts (see *Muirhead* v. *International Tank Specialities Ltd* [1986] QB 507; *Simaan General Contracting Co* v. *Pilkington Glass Ltd (No 2)* [1988] QB 758; *Greater Nottingham Co-operative Society Ltd* v. *Cementation Piling and Foundations Ltd* [1989] QB 71). Consigning the case to what may be early oblivion, Lord Bridge described it (in *D & F Estates*) as depending upon a 'unique' relationship between the parties and asserted that 'the decision cannot be regarded as laying down any principle of general application in the law of tort'. (Note, however, the suggestion that *Junior Books* was merely an application of the rule in *Hedley Byrne*: see 5.5.)

5.4 Preventative Damages

Another, more limited, attempt to allow recovery for pure economic loss was equally ill-fated. In *Anns* itself, the House of Lords had allowed a building-owner to recover compensation for the cost of repairs required to avert imminent danger to the health and safety of occupants arising from the weakness of the building's foundations. Such 'preventative damages' are properly regarded as compensating for pure economic loss because the loss sustained was not consequential upon damage to property other than the defective building itself. As was the case with *Junior Books*, certain aspects of the decision in *Anns* were obscure (e.g. did the House of Lords realise it was dealing with pure economic loss at all?). The case also posed further difficulties in that it recognised liability on the part of a local authority for failing to inspect the foundations and thus raised issues of omissions liability and the liability of public bodies in addition to the issue of pure economic loss. However, *Anns* seemed to express a sound principle: that it makes sense to spend money to prevent a house collapsing and causing injury rather than waiting until disaster strikes.

However, seeing how the two-stage test had been at the root of the expansion attempted in *Junior Books*, judges began to cast doubt on Lord Wilberforce's well-known *obiter dicta*. The actual decision in *Anns* suffered by its association with the Wilberforce approach and was tarred with the same brush. In *D & F Estates Ltd* v. *Church Commissioners* [1989] AC 177, the House of Lords effectively undermined the decision by holding that expenditure on accident prevention – recovered in *Anns* from the local authority – could not be recovered from the builder who had actually done the defective construction work. In their Lordships view, the presence of an imminent danger to the health and safety of occupants did not justify a departure from the general rule that defective product economic loss is not recoverable. After this, it was inevitable that *Anns* would have to be overruled, for there was no earthly reason why a local authority should have to pay damages in respect of shoddy work carried out by builders when the builders themselves were immune from liability. Surely enough, a seven-judge panel of the House of Lords, sitting in *Murphy* v. *Brentwood DC* [1991] AC 398, exercised its power to depart from its previous decisions (see Fleming, 1990). It was only the eighth time in the 25 years of its existence that the power had been used.

The speeches delivered in *Murphy* address the argument that it would be absurd to insist that owners wait until their buildings fall down and cause injury to person or property before claiming damages. The response of the House of Lords was that an owner who knew the full extent of dangerous defects in her building would be regarded as the author of her own misfortune if she continued in occupation and suffered injury when the building collapsed. This seems a harsh rule: the defence of voluntary assumption of risk that seems to underlie this analysis only operates against those who fail to take a reasonable opportunity to avoid injury (see 12.3), and one can hardly demand that a home owner abandon her property as unfit for habitation. This, though, is effectively what the House of Lords said she should do. But what if the defective premises threaten to injure those in neighbouring houses or on the street? In such circumstances, Lord Bridge was prepared to contemplate an exception to the general rule and allow the owner to recover the cost of demolition or repair to remove the danger to third parties. (Lord Oliver, however, was sceptical.) This leaves the law in a puzzling state for it entails the conclusion that, while a property owner is expected to abandon her property to save herself from harm, she is not expected to bear the costs of demolition or repair work to protect others from it.

5.5   Negligent Misrepresentation

The one secure basis for the recovery of pure economic loss under the present law is under the principle of *Hedley Byrne & Co* v. *Heller & Partners* [1964] AC 465, which deals with loss suffered in reliance upon a negligent misrepresentation. The fact the loss was caused by something said rather than by something done raises policy questions of its own. Also, it should be noted that negligent misrepresentation can cause physical damage as well as pure economic loss. In light of these considerations, we will begin with a few words on negligent misrepresentation in general before turning to the more particular issue of negligent misrepresentation leading to pure economic loss.

'Words are more volatile than deeds. They travel fast and far afield. They are used without being expended.' These cautionary words, uttered by Lord Pearson in *Hedley Byrne*, suggest that the courts might be justified in taking a more restrictive approach to liability for negligent words than for negligent acts. Whereas the destructive potential of acts is generally exhausted after one event, words might be relied on by many different people, in many different places, on many different occasions. Each time the results might be disastrous. However, these fears have had little effect on the development of the law. Where negligent words cause physical harm, courts have shown little inclination to restrict liability, and it seems that the plaintiff need only prove that such harm was foreseeable in order to succeed. This was the view expressed by Lord Oliver in *Caparo* v. *Dickman* [1990] 2 AC 605. He indicated his approval of the finding in *Clayton* v. *Woodman* [1962] 2 QB 533 that an architect who negligently instructs a brick layer to remove the keystone of an archway might be held liable to someone injured when the archway collapses. It would be the same, said Lord Oliver, where physical injury results from the mislabelling of a dangerous medicine or from negligent medical advice about the treatment of an illness.

When it comes to negligent misrepresentation causing pure economic loss, however, foreseeability of the loss is not enough to establish liability. The plaintiff must satisfy certain additional requirements in order to obtain judgment. The nature of these requirements can only be gleaned by a close examination of the case law, beginning with the leading case, *Hedley Byrne* v. *Heller* (see Stevens, 1964). Hedley Byrne was a firm employed to conduct an advertising campaign for one of its customers, Easipower Ltd. In the course of this engagement, Hedley Byrne became personally liable under a number of contracts for advertising time and space. As a precautionary measure, the firm had its bank check Easipower's credit-worthiness by writing to Heller & Partners, the bankers with whom Easipower had an account. Heller & Partners replied, in a letter marked 'without responsibility', that Easipower was in a sound business position. This turned out to be wrong and Hedley Byrne lost several thousands of pounds under the contracts when Easipower went into liquidation. Hedley Byrne sued Easipower's bankers to try to recover this money. Its claim was rejected by the House of Lords on the grounds that Heller & Partners had successfully excluded any liability to Hedley Byrne by making it clear that they supplied the information requested 'without responsibility' (see 12.2). The House of Lords did, however, accept that the bankers would have been liable for Hedley Byrne's pure economic loss had they not made this disclaimer of responsibility. This was a major breakthrough. Although the courts had previously recognised the right to compensation for pure economic loss in the tort of deceit, negligence is not sufficient to make out liability in deceit (*Derry* v. *Peek* (1889) 14 App Cas 337), and the Court of Appeal (Denning LJ dissenting) had ruled in *Candler* v. *Crane, Christmas & Co* [1959] 2 QB 164 that no liability would arise in the tort of negligence. The latter decision was overturned by *Hedley Byrne* and the dissent of Denning LJ approved.

As we have noted (5.3), the House of Lords made it plain that liability under *Hedley Byrne* was distinct from, and more restricted than, that under *Donoghue* v. *Stevenson*. The judges in the case emphasised this by pointing to various requirements, over and above those required generally in the law of negligence, that had to be satisfied for liability to arise under *Hedley Byrne*. Different requirements appealed to different judges: it was said that the crucial question was (a) whether there was a 'special relationship' between the parties such that the defendant knew or ought to have known that the plaintiff might reasonably rely upon the defendant's representation (Lord Reid); (b) whether there was a 'voluntary assumption or undertaking of responsibility' by the defendant towards the plaintiff (Lord Morris and Lord Devlin); and (c) whether the relationship between the parties was 'akin to contract' (Lord Devlin). Each of the analyses may now be regarded as flawed, as explained below.

(a) The requirement of a 'special relationship' as defined by Lord Reid must now be regarded as too lenient because it approximates to the discredited view that the foreseeability of loss by the person to whom the defendant communicates the information is sufficient to justify the imposition of liability. This criticism is aimed particularly at Lord Reid's focus upon what the defendant *ought to have known*, which is just another way of asking what was foreseeable. It may be possible to salvage something of the 'special relationship' test if a restrictive meaning is given to the concept of 'reasonable reliance' which is one aspect of the test. But reliance is a problematic concept: there is a sense in which all negligence cases involve reliance, 'as every motorist relies upon every other motorist in the vicinity to drive carefully' (*Muirhead* v. *International Tank Specialities Ltd* [1986] QB 507, per Robert Goff LJ). In order to makes sense of the reliance requirement, we must regard it as referring either to reliance upon a voluntary assumption of responsibility (see below) or to reliance upon a specific statement. The latter interpretation is both too narrow and too wide at the same time. It is too narrow because reliance is used in cases involving negligent acts as well as negligent words: *Junior Books*, for example, has been said to involve the same sort of reliance as *Hedley Byrne* (*Murphy* v. *Brentwood DC* [1991] AC 398). It is too wide because it is not every case in which the plaintiff foreseeably relies upon the defendant's statement that she will be able to recover (see *Caparo Industries* v. *Dickman* [1990] 2 AC 605: 5.7) In the final analysis, it seems probable that Lord Reid did not mean to attach any great significance to the concept of reliance but merely used it because it reflects the manner in which misrepresentations most usually cause loss (viz. by the plaintiff's detrimental reliance on them).

(b) The view that *Hedley Byrne* liability depends on the existence of such a voluntary assumption of responsibility is now discredited. In *Smith* v. *Eric S Bush* [1990] AC 831, Lord Griffiths said 'I do not think that voluntary assumption of responsibility is a helpful or realistic test for liability.' His particular criticism of the test was that it suggested – falsely – that the defendant had freely agreed to accept the risk of liability; he had little doubt that, had the defendant been asked if this were the case, she would have replied: 'Certainly not.' In truth, *Hedley Byrne* liability is not accepted by the defendant but imposed by law.

(c) The notion of equivalency to contract provides little more guidance. First, it is used inconsistently. In *Smith* v. *Eric S Bush*, surveyors valued a house at the request of a lending institution which passed the information on to its customer; the customer purchased the property in reliance upon the valuation which had overstated the property's value. Lord Templeman considered that the relationship between the purchaser and the surveyor was akin to contract because the latter was paid out of the fee imposed by the lending institution on the former. This, as Lord Jauncey pointed out in the same case, is not the sense in which Lord Devlin used the phrase 'akin to contract' in *Hedley Byrne*: in *Hedley Byrne*, the parties were dealing directly (in 'privity') with one another albeit that the defendants received no consideration for their efforts, whereas in *Smith* v. *Eric S Bush* the defendants did receive payment but there was no privity of contract with the plaintiff. A second, more general, criticism of the notion of equivalency to contract is that it threatens to subvert basic principles of the law of contract: if the courts can impose liability in tort wherever lack of privity or consideration precludes liability in contract, those requirements of the law of contract become utterly redundant.

The true basis of *Hedley Byrne* liability remains obscure and we make no attempt here to encapsulate it in a simple formula. This is in keeping with the modern preference for the traditional approach to the duty of care of seeking analogies with decided cases rather than trying to identify a single general principle underlying those cases. Indeed, in *Caparo*, Lord Oliver warned that even within the category of negligent misrepresentation cases 'circumstances may vary infinitely and, in a swiftly developing field of law, there can be no necessary assumption that those features which have served in one case to create the relationship between plaintiff and defendant on which liability depends will necessarily be determinative of liability in the different circumstances of another case'. In view of the lack of principles in this field, we consider the most fruitful approach is, first of all, to identify those who are potentially liable under *Hedley Byrne* and then to turn our attention to the precise circumstances in which each of these potential defendants may be held liable.

5.6 *Hedley Byrne*: The Range of Possible Defendants

The most significant analysis of the range of those who may face *Hedley Byrne* liability is found in the decision of the Privy Council in *Mutual Life and Citizens Assurance Co* v. *Evatt* [1971] AC 793. The opinion of the majority was that liability should be restricted to those who give advice in a professional capacity: architects, surveyors, accountants and the like. Applying that rule, the Privy Council held that the plaintiff was not entitled to damages from his insurance company who had carelessly given him false information about the financial stability of an associated company in which he invested: the defendant was not in the business of giving advice about investments. A dissenting opinion was offered by Lords Reid and Morris. In their view, it was sufficient that considered advice was sought from a businessman in the course of his business, which was clearly the case on the facts before them. This broader conception of *Hedley Byrne* liability has been preferred in the English courts to the narrow view of the majority. It was applied by the Court of Appeal in *Esso Petroleum Co Ltd* v. *Mardon* [1976] QB 801 in which Esso was held liable under the *Hedley Byrne* doctrine, as well as under contract, to the owner of a petrol-filling station whom it had negligently advised about the likely profitability of his investment in the station.

5.7   *Hedley Byrne*: The Circumstances in which each Defendant may be held Liable

Although it may be well established that a particular person comes within the scope of the *Hedley Byrne* doctrine, it does not follow that she will be liable on every occasion that her negligent words cause loss. Most notably, it is doubtful whether one can be held liable for advice given on a purely social occasion. Even when it comes to advice given in a business context, however, the courts have placed limits on the circumstances in which liability will arise. They insist that it is not every person who suffers through reliance on a negligent statement who can recover. Neither is it necessarily the case that someone entitled to damages after relying on a negligent statement in one transaction will be similarly entitled in respect of another transaction. So if you request a banker's reference about the financial health of a company to which you are considering extending credit, it may be that the bank would be held liable to you if the reference was inaccurate and your money lost, but it is doubtful that I would have the same remedy if you passed the reference on to me and I too extended the company credit. Equally, while you might be able to sue in respect of money lost when you extended credit to the company, you would probably not be able to sue if you had decided to take out shares in the company on the strength of the reference as that would be a very different transaction from the one contemplated.

As the above discussion suggests, the courts are able to limit liability by reference to two factors: the class of plaintiffs who can sue and the class of transactions in relation to which they can do so. Yet, while the cases may share a common vocabulary, recent House of Lords decisions make it clear that specific rules will have to be developed to govern the liability of each and every sort of advice-giver. The rules developed in one area need not be relevant in another. A full account of the law would demand a treatment of each type of advice-giver in turn (see Jackson and Powell, 1992); here, for reasons of space, we must focus on just two – surveyors and auditors – whose positions were considered by the House of Lords in *Smith* v. *Eric S Bush* [1990] AC 831 and *Caparo Industries* v. *Dickman* [1990] 2 AC 605 respectively.

The question in *Smith* v. *Eric S Bush* was whether the purchaser of a house, who relies upon a surveyor's valuation of the property in proceeding with the purchase, is able to recover damages from the surveyor if the latter negligently failed to identify defects in the property. Property valuations are designed primarily to reassure lending institutions that the property in question represents adequate security for a home loan. Nevertheless, it has become common practice for house purchasers to treat such valuations as warranting the structural soundness of the property; very few go to the additional expense of commissioning a full structural survey. The House of Lords held, at least so far as modest residential properties are concerned, that the valuer may be held liable to the purchaser and that the Unfair Contract Terms Act 1977 prevents this liability being excluded. It is still to be decided how far the class of plaintiffs who may recover will extend. The position of a valuer who, by negligently *under*valuing a property, causes its *seller* unnecessarily to reduce the asking price has yet to be considered.

In *Caparo Industries* v. *Dickman*, the issue was whether accountants performing their task of auditing company accounts at the end of each business year will be held liable to those who invest in the company in question in reliance upon those accounts and suffer losses as a consequence. The House of Lords made it clear that, as a general rule, they will not. Their Lordships accepted, however, that liability may arise in exceptional circumstances. These circumstances would be present where the auditor was sufficiently aware of the people who might suffer loss by relying on the audited accounts and of the transactions in which they might rely upon them. This suggests that where the audit of the accounts is specially requested, (e.g. by a bank considering whether to grant a business loan) liability will arise. Awkward cases which fall somewhere between such a case and the facts of *Caparo* would include a situation where a company, learning of a prospective take-over bid, prepares a 'defence document' designed to convince shareholders that their shares are worth more than the bid price, and the account information in the document is relied upon by the bidder in raising its offer (see *Morgan Crucible Co* v. *Hill Samuel Bank* [1991] Ch. 259).

5.8 Where Are We Now?

While recent decisions have shown the courts setting their store against the recovery of pure economic loss, it is possible to argue – with varying degrees of conviction – that the authorities support a number of exceptions to the general rule. In order to tie up all the 'loose ends', we set out below a brief review of the current status of the decisions and *dicta* that can be viewed as supporting those exceptions:

1. *Hedley Byrne & Co* v. *Heller & Partners* is the one undeniable head of recovery for pure economic loss. Its authority has never been doubted' and it was recently applied by the House of Lords in *Smith* v. *Eric S Bush*. However, its theoretical basis remains obscure, as do the precise limits of the principle. An interesting possibility is that it might extend to negligent *acts* as well as negligent *words*: in both *D & F Estates* and *Murphy*, it is said that *Junior Books*, an 'acts' case, might be justified as an example of *Hedley Byrne* liability.

2. It is not clear whether *Ross* v. *Caunters* is a case that falls under the *Hedley Byrne* head of liability (see also *Ministry of Housing and Local*

Government v. *Sharp*). It differs from the latter in that there was no reliance by the plaintiff on anything said or done by the defendant. We await further judicial clarification as to whether such reliance is an essential element of *Hedley Byrne* liability and, if it is, whether the decision in *Ross* v. *Caunters* can be sustained on an independent basis.

3. *Junior Books*, once distinguished almost out of existence, may be making a comeback as the case which applies *Hedley Byrne* principles to acts as well as words (see 5.5).

4. The concept of preventative damages was practically buried for good by the House of Lords in *Murphy*, although Lord Bridge thought that there might be some scope for such damages where a building threatened to harm those on the highway or on neighbouring property. He furnished no convincing legal basis for this exception and Lord Oliver expressed reservations on the subject in the same case.

5. The 'complex structures' argument, considered in *D&F Estates* and *Murphy,* may allow recovery for what has hitherto been treated as defective product economic loss. This is not in truth an exception to the bar against the recovery of pure economic loss as the argument characterises the loss in question as physical damage rather than pure economic loss. It has yet to be tested in court.

5.9   Policy Considerations

The law's hostility to the recovery of pure economic loss is often said to be entrenched in precedent, but this begs the question why the courts have reverted to a rigid, compartmentalised view of the law in this area rather than allowing recovery purely on the basis of foreseeability. The reason for this is not to be found in deductive reasoning from decided cases but in fears as to where such recovery might lead. As Lord Oliver pointed out in *Murphy* v. *Brentwood DC*, the law has identified rules restricting liability for pure economic loss 'not by the application of logic but by the perceived necessity as a matter of policy to place some limits, perhaps arbitrary limits, to what would otherwise be an endless, cumulative causative chain bounded only by theoretical foreseeability'.

The policy argument most often employed in the case law is the 'floodgates' argument (see 2.5). Increasingly, this focuses on the (alleged) inability of the insurance industry to provide cover in respect of large and indeterminate liabilities. This concern seems to have been in the minds of the courts as they have declined to impose liability in cases where the range of potential plaintiffs is very wide. In *Spartan Steel*, Lord Denning pointed out that the cutting of the supply of electricity may affect 'a multitude of persons'. In his view, it was better for those whose loss would be large themselves to take out insurance against the interruption in the supply. In *Caparo*, in which the class of potential plaintiffs extended beyond the shareholders in the audited company and included those in the market for the buying and selling of shares, similar considerations seem to have been important, at least to Lord Oliver who expressed his fear that the imposition of liability would open up 'a limitless vista of uninsurable risk'.

The floodgates argument loses its force, however, when it comes to cases in which the range of plaintiffs is limited and the loss each might suffer known. This is true in cases such as *Junior Books* in which a product is tailor-made by the defendant for the plaintiff. In such a case, the fact the product turns out to be defective will generally only cause loss to the plaintiff and that loss will generally be limited to the value of that product to the plaintiff. It is also true in some negligent misrepresentation cases, such as *Smith* v. *Eric S Bush*, in which the information supplied by the defendant is of use only to a limited class of people. A common feature of these cases is that they tend to involve 'voluntary relationships' between the parties, unlike cases such as *Spartan Steel* where the parties are thrown together unexpectedly and 'involuntarily' (see Harris and Veljanovski, 1986).

The fact that the parties are in a voluntary relationship diminishes the importance of the floodgates argument, but it also gives rise to problems of its own. In particular, it raises concerns lest business arrangements between the parties are subverted by the imposition of tort liability (see Stapleton, 1991). In such cases, the courts respond to these concerns by emphasising the primacy of the law of contract over the law of tort. The law of contract, expressing a *laissez-faire* ideology, assumes that entrepreneurs are able to negotiate appropriate contractual guarantees from those they rely upon in their business affairs; if they do not do so, that is presumed to be because they have agreed to take the risk of faulty performance and have received compensation for doing so by means of a reduction in the price paid. In the interests of certainty, the courts will decline to 'un-make' a bad bargain. This provides an explanation for the courts' hostility to the decision in *Junior Books* and their unwillingness to apply it in subsequent cases: the plaintiff had the opportunity to deal directly with the defendant rather than contracting only with the main contractor and the fact that it failed to do so is deemed to be reflected in the price paid for the defendant's services (For evidence – not heard in court – that the plaintiff had already accepted compensation for the risk that the floor might prove defective, see Atiyah, 1989, p. 397).

The assumption that contracting parties are able to look after their own best interests only stands up, however, when we are concerned with members of the business community. Consumers should be treated very differently for they have neither the bargaining power nor the detailed legal knowledge necessary to protect themselves fully. Thus the imposition of liability in favour of the purchaser of a modest family home in *Smith* v. *Eric S Bush* can be justified on the grounds that the primacy of contract should only be asserted in the commercial context.

The protectionist stance adopted by the courts in *Smith* does not, however, extend to cases involving defective products. Even in *Junior Books*, Lord Roskill sought to distinguish the facts of the case in front of him from those of the typical consumer purchase of a product from the supermarket shelf. While the consumer's loss in respect of the purchase of a defective (but not dangerous) bottle of ginger beer may be dismissed as trivial, the same cannot be said of all consumer purchases. In this respect, the decision in *Murphy* v. *Brentwood DC* that no tort liability will arise in relation to the purchase of a defective family home looks particularly harsh, and sits uneasily with the decision in *Smith* v. *Eric S. Bush* (see Stapleton, 1991, pp. 277–83).

In addition to the policy considerations already mentioned, the 'overkill' argument may also point towards a restrictive approach to the recovery of pure economic loss (see Lord Keith in *Murphy*). In this area, overkill arguments of some sophistication have been put forward by economists. The root of these arguments is what Harris and Veljanovski (1986) call the 'asymmetric treatment of losses and gains' in the law of tort. This reflects the fact that the sole concern of tort law is compensation for losses caused by the defendant; tort gives the defendant no credit for the benefits which people (other than the plaintiff) take from her activities. Generally this is not a problem, as the benefit rendered to others will be done under contract and the defendant will receive consideration for her performance of the contract. But it will not always be possible for the defendant to demand payment from all those who benefit from her activities. Where she cannot, she may be prompted to take excessive precautions in order to avoid liability, wasting scarce societal resources. Ultimately, she might even be obliged to give up her activities altogether, even though they can be considered beneficial from the point of view of society as a whole.

The prospect of overkill arising from the asymmetric treatment of the defendant's losses and gains arises most especially in two types of economic loss case. First, there is the case where the plaintiff's loss stems from the interruption of her business activities by the defendant. In such cases, the plaintiff's competitors in the marketplace are likely to gain from her misfortune. As Bishop (1982) points out, for every Spartan Steel that suffers a loss of production, there may be an Athenium Steel ready to to step in and supply the goods required. He argues that, in such circumstances, potential tortfeasors would be too cautious if threatened with liability reflecting all of the plaintiff's losses: in the *Spartan Steel* situation, for example, construction firms digging up the street might have unnecessary surveys done before starting work. Bishop argues that the law can avoid overkill while still giving potential tortfeasors an incentive to take care if it allows the Spartan Steels of this world to recover in respect of any property damage it suffers but not in respect of its purely economic losses.

Secondly, the problem of overkill arises in relation to negligent misrepresentation cases. Information is easily transmissible and it is very difficult to control its dissemination. As a consequence, information-providers may find it impossible to pursue all those who benefit from the information for payment and may respond by becoming overcautious or even giving up their activities altogether (see Bishop, 1980). This may be regarded as a potent fear in a *Caparo*-type situation as company auditors have no means of demanding payment from the investors who derive assistance from audited company accounts. Indeed, there are widespread fears about the exposure of auditors to tort liability, and a government enquiry has warned of the danger of overkill (Likierman, 1989). It suggests that auditors faced with increasing liabilities might carry out more extensive checks on their work which serve no purpose other than to protect the auditor in the event of a claim; that they might reject categories of clients who seem to raise particular risks; and that people might be deterred from entering the accountancy profession to the detriment of the British business community which depends on having a highly-qualified audit service. Other negligent misrepresentation cases do not raise such problems, for it is often the case that the information produced by the defendant is of interest only to a very limited class of people from whom the defendant can demand payment. This is true in cases like *Smith* v. *Eric S Bush*: the information contained in a house valuation report is of interest to a potential purchaser of the property but not to people generally, and it is common practice for the purchaser to pay a fee for the work done (the fee is generally paid to the prospective mortgagee which then in turn pays the valuer). This factor may help to explain the difference in result between *Smith* and *Caparo*, and why the House of Lords in the latter case insisted that, in order for liability to arise, the dependent must have knowledge of the plaintiff's likely reliance upon the information in transaction subsequently entered.

Summary

5.1 Pure economic loss is financial loss not consequent upon damage to the property of the plaintiff.
5.2 Any harm which a defective product causes to itself is pure economic loss: a claim can generally only be made in respect of a defective product if it damages *other* property. Parliament has, however, created a statutory liability in respect of defective dwellings (Defective Premises Act 1972). It may be that some products are to be treated as 'complex structures' so that damage to one part of the product, if caused by a defect in another part, will count as damage to other property.
5.3 Recent decisions of the House of Lords have reversed the trend, of which the high-water mark was *Junior Books* v. *Veitchi*, to allow the recovery of pure economic loss more generally.
5.4 As part of this trend, the House of Lords in *Anns* allowed the recovery of 'preventative damages' representing the cost of repairs to a building which were necessary to avert imminent danger to the health and safety of its occupants. This decision has now been reversed, though there remains the possibility that preventative damages may be recovered where there is imminent danger to the health and safety of users of the highway or of neighbours.
5.5 Negligent misrepresentations may cause physical loss, in which case foreseeability seems to be the sole criterion of liability, or pure economic loss. The

latter type of loss is recoverable under the principle of *Hedley Byrne* v. *Heller*, the theoretical basis of which remains obscure.

5.6   *Hedley Byrne* liability may be imposed upon professional advice givers and, probably, all those giving advice in the course of their business.

5.7   Liability under *Hedley Byrne* may be limited by reference to (a) the class of plaintiffs entitled to rely upon the representation and (b) the class of transactions in which they are entitled to do so. How these limitations are applied in practice varies according to the type of defendant in question.

5.8   While liability for pure economic loss can certainly arise under *Hedley Byrne* principles, it is not clear (a) whether that principle applies to acts as well as words or (b) in what circumstances pure economic loss is recoverable outside these principles. A brief survey of the field is given in the text above.

5.9   The fear of opening the 'floodgates' and of engaging in 'overkill' has prompted the courts to adopt a restrictive approach to the recovery of pure economic loss. Even when these arguments seem to lack force on the facts of a given case, the courts are unwilling to impose liability for pure economic loss for fear of subverting contractual bargains.

Exercises

5.1   Is the loss suffered in the following examples to be counted as pure economic loss?

(a)   A's hotel is damaged by fire. It has to close for repairs. A suffers a loss of profits as a consequence.

(b)   B's hotel has to close for repairs after the plaster on the dining room ceiling collapses, damaging furniture underneath. It takes one week to replace the furniture and two further weeks to have the room replastered. B suffers a loss of profits as a consequence.

(c)   C, a newsagent, is injured in a car crash and has to close the shop for two months while she recuperates. She suffers a loss of profits as a consequence. D, who delivers newspapers for C, suffers a loss of earnings while the shop is closed.

5.2   Lord Wilberforce in *Anns* classified the loss suffered by the plaintiff in that case as 'material, physical damage'. Discuss.

5.3   In *Spartan Steel*, Edmund Davies LJ (dissenting) stated that 'an action lies in negligence for damages in respect of pure economic loss, provided that it was a reasonably foreseeable and direct consequence of failure in a duty of care'. In *Junior Books*, Lord Roskill suggested that Edmund Davies LJ's reasoning might be preferred to that of the majority of the Court of Appeal in *Spartan Steel*. Do you think it would?

5.4   In what circumstances (a) was pure economic loss recoverable in 1983 and (b) is it recoverable now?

5.5   Is the basis of *Hedley Byrne* liability (a) foreseeability, (b) reliance, (c) voluntary assumption of responsibility, (d) equivalency to contract or (e) none of the above?

5.6   Why should the courts adopt a restrictive approach to the recovery of damages for negligently-inflicted pure economic loss? Would the argument in favour of liability be stronger or weaker if the loss were *intentionally*-inflicted?

5.7   P is a keen wine collector who used to seek advice from Q, a wine consultant, who gave her advice without payment as P was a friend. Q negligently advised

P to keep cases of Woolloomooloo White, an Australian wine which she already possessed, far too long. When P opened the first bottle, she found that the wine had turned to vinegar. Her tasting of other bottles confirmed that all of them were spoiled. She was doubly dismayed as she had arranged to sell a couple of cases of the wine at a large profit. Q had also advised P to put in a bid at auction for some very old wine labelled Chateau Mutton. P succeeded in buying the wine for £500 but later discovered that Q had confused the name of the wine at the auction for that of a far superior producer, Chateau Mouton. The wine turns out to be undrinkable. P also had in her cellar two cases of English table wine, Chateau Strand and Chateau Aldwych, which she had received as a gift. These also turn out to be spoiled. This time the cause is a mould which was present in the corks of the bottles. The corks in the bottles of Chateau Strand had been produced for the winery by R Ltd. Those in the bottles of Chateau Aldwych, also produced by R Ltd, had been inserted by Q by way of replacement of the original corks after the bottles had come into P's possession. Advise the parties as to their rights and liabilities in tort.

6 Omissions

6.1 Introduction

In formulating his general statement of principle in *Donoghue* v. *Stevenson*, Lord Atkin took as his starting point the biblical command that you are to love your neighbour, a command that stemmed from the parable of the good Samaritan. Some 40 years or so later, Lord Diplock returned to that parable to illustrate the limits of the 'neighbour' principle, particularly in the context of omissions. According to Lord Diplock, although the priest and the Levite who passed by on the other side of the road might attract moral censure, they would have incurred no civil liability in English law (*Home Office* v. *Dorset Yacht Co* [1970] AC 1004).

The traditional approach of the common law has been to adopt the general rule that there is no liability for omissions or, to put it another way, that there is no duty to act to prevent harm. This approach is premised upon a highly individualist political theory which holds that people should be concerned purely and simply with their own self-advancement and should not be burdened with the chore of taking care of others. This, the theory suggests, is the most effective way of maximising individuals' freedom of action (see Smith and Burns, 1983). In addition to the fear of unduly burdening individuals, another justification for the general rule of no liability for omissions is the pragmatic concern that there may be no reason for holding any particular defendant liable for harm she could have prevented rather than all the others who were just as able to intervene. Why pick on the priest and the Levite when countless others might have passed by on the road to Jericho that fateful afternoon?

With the advance of community values, evident in particular in the institution of the welfare state, a categorical denial of liability for omissions looks out of touch with reality. Conscious of this, judges have begun to admit exceptions to the general rule. The exceptions have arisen where the two responses identified above – 'Don't burden me' and 'Why pick on me?' – are weakest. Thus, for instance, it does not seem unfair to burden an employer with the duty actively to take precautions for the safety of her workforce as she at the same time takes the benefit of their activity. Furthermore, this provides a clear reason for picking on the employer rather than, say, those passing by in the street who see that the working practices are unsafe yet do nothing about it. Yet, despite the growing number of cases of liability for omission, the general rule of no liability remains. In cases which fall outside the exceptions, often labelled cases of 'pure' omissions, people can ignore their moral responsibilities towards others without legal sanction. It is, for instance, quite unthinkable that there should be 'liability in negligence on the part of one who sees another about to walk over a cliff with his head in the air and forbears to shout a warning' (*Yuen Kun Yeu* v. *A-G of Hong Kong* [1988] AC 175, per Lord Keith).

The exceptional cases in which the courts have imposed liability for omission defy easy categorisation. A number of cases suggest that the basis of the liability is an 'assumption of responsibility' on the part of the defendant, but this seems to be no help in deciding whether the court should recognise a duty to act. Rather, it seems merely to be a label attached to those cases in which omissions liability is recognised. All in all, the most fruitful way of gaining some idea of the family resemblqnce between these cases is to look at them under four headings. We shall consider, first, cases in which there is a duty to protect another; secondly, cases in which there is a duty to control the activities of another; thirdly, cases in which there is a duty to exercise control over property; and, last, cases in which the defendant has innocently endangered the plaintiff and for that reason owes her a duty.

6.2 Duty to Protect Others

In stark contrast to the law of tort, the law of contract is all about holding people under a duty to act in particular ways. Accordingly, it is no surprise that the courts are most willing to hold people liable in tort for their negligent omissions in cases where they have agreed to take on responsibility for the welfare of others. The fact that they have freely undertaken this responsibility can be taken to indicate that they regard their conduct as advancing their own interests, and accordingly the 'Don't burden me' objection is weakened. Thus it seems likely that the lifeguard who sits back while a swimmer drowns and the doctor who refuses to treat a sick patient will both be liable if the result of their omission is death or injury. In both cases, it is their job to take steps to prevent this very eventuality. Things would be very different if they were in their free time: it is often said that a doctor has no duty to administer first aid to an accident victim she comes across in the street. However, it is probably not necessary for the defendant to be acting in a professional context: it should be enough, first, that she has represented, expressly or impliedly, that she will be responsible for the welfare of others and, secondly, that those others act in reliance upon the representation. Suppose you take it upon yourself to sit, in swimwear, in the lifeguard's chair at the local pond. Suppose also that you sit there twirling a whistle and shouting out instructions to those swimming in the pond. If a child, left there by her parents who saw that the pond was guarded, were to start floundering, you might well be held to be under a duty to fish her out.

The same principles apply where one person agrees to look after another's property. Where a decorator is left alone in your house and leaves the place unlocked while she goes off to fetch some more wallpaper, she may be liable to you for the value of any goods stolen by thieves while she is gone. This was the decision in *Stansbie* v. *Troman* [1948] 2 KB 48, a case decided by reference to an implied term in the contract between home owner and decorator. There can be little doubt that the same result would be reached by the law of negligence, even in the absence of a contract between plaintiff and defendant. This situation might arise where, say, the services of the decorator had been paid for by a relative as a wedding-gift to a newly-wed couple, or where the property stolen belonged to a guest in the house.

A duty to protect others may arise even in the absence of a voluntary undertaking. The premise of individualistic political theory – that people are best off if left to their own devices – is clearly false when applied to particular groups of people. The most obvious examples are young children: manifestly they are incapable of looking after themselves. Thus, parents and those *in loco parentis* must take steps to ensure that children in their care are reasonably safe: teachers who carelessly let small schoolchildren wander out of the playground on to the road will be held liable if the children are run over. The mentally disabled have an equal claim to special consideration and it is clear that warders at mental hospitals owe a duty to prevent the patients harming themselves. An example is provided by the case of *Kirkham* v. *Chief Constable of Greater Manchester Police* [1990] 2 QB 283. In that case, the Court of Appeal was faced by an unlikely-sounding claim by the widow of a man who had committed suicide whilst remanded in custody. The widow alleged that the police who had arrested her husband, and who knew he had mental problems and associated suicidal tendencies, should have informed the remand authorities of this. If the authorities had known Mr Kirkham was a special risk, they would have put him under close supervision and prevented his suicide attempt. The court agreed that the police had a duty to relay this information and awarded Mrs Kirkham damages for loss of dependency. Cases like this will be rare, because the court will normally find that people like Mr Kirkham were the cause of their own loss. However, such cases may succeed if it is impossible to say that the acts of the plaintiff were the voluntary acts of a responsible agent (for instance, where plaintiff is a young child or is mentally impaired).

6.3   Duties to Control Others

Just as the basic rule is that I have no duty to protect others from harm, so too I generally have no responsibility for the actions of others. Exceptionally, however, I might be required to exert control over the actions of another person. Some cases have imposed liability for harm caused by a third party under the care and control of the defendant. One category of such cases deals with young children. These, as we have seen, cannot be regarded as responsible agents whom we might justifiably leave to their own devices. Thus, in *Carmarthenshire County Council* v. *Lewis* [1955] AC

549, the House of Lords held a local authority liable for its failure to secure a school playground which allowed a small child to wander on to the road, causing a lorry to swerve and crash. The mentally handicapped are probably to be treated in the same way as young children. Those held responsible for the acts of an irresponsible agent will include those with a lasting relationship with her, such as parents and teachers, but it seems unlikely that those with purely transient relationships with the individual will be liable for harm she causes. If you were to be accosted on the street by a woman with a crazed look in her eyes who told you she was about to knife the newspaper vendor, you would probably not be under a duty to warn anyone about her intentions. It might well be different if you were a psychiatrist and the confession had been made in the course of a consultancy in your surgery: then the fact that it was your job to treat your patients, for the benefit of themselves and of others, might justify obliging you to act.

A second category of cases deals with those, like prisoners or the mentally disturbed, who were held in the defendant's lawful custody as a matter of public safety. Prison authorities would be responsible for harm caused by one inmate to her fellows while in custody or even for harm caused to those in the vicinity by escaping inmates. In *Home Office* v. *Dorset Yacht Co*, Borstal officers had, in breach of instructions, left their charges unsupervised while on a training exercise. A number of young offenders made good their escape; in the course of this they damaged a yacht. The House of Lords held the Home Office vicariously liable for this damage. It would, however, have been excessive to have burdened the custodians with responsibility for all the harm subsequently done by the escapees and Lord Diplock, whose speech seems the one most in tune with current judicial attitudes, made it clear that he would impose liability only in respect of harm caused in the course of the escape, at roughly the same time and in the vicinity. Thus it seems that the Home Office would not have been liable if the complaint had been that the escapees had some weeks later robbed a post office in another part of the country. It is important to emphasise that it is not sufficient that the defendant had the ability to control the activities of the third party: she must have been obliged so to do. The police may arrest those suspected of criminal activities but they are not responsible for injuries inflicted by suspects they carelessly fail to arrest. In *Hill* v. *Chief Constable of West Yorkshire* [1989] AC 53, an action was brought against the police by the estate of one of the victims of the so-called 'Yorkshire Ripper', Peter Sutcliffe. The House of Lords held that the police owed no duty of care on the facts of the case, distinguishing the *Dorset Yacht* case on the grounds that Sutcliffe had never been taken into police custody. It seems unlikely that the courts will extend liability far beyond those cases in which a custodial relationship is present. Canadian authorities which have employed the 'control' test to justify holding bar owners liable for road accidents caused by the drunk driving of their customers are unlikely to be followed in English courts.

6.4   **Control of Property**

If you were to allow your property to cause damage to others, it might be just as appropriate to describe your conduct in terms of an omission as in terms of an act. Take the facts of *Haynes* v. *Harwood* [1935] 1 KB 146: the driver of a horse-drawn cart left the horses unattended in the street; the horses were startled and ran away, whereupon a policeman grabbed the horses in an effort to stop them and rescue those in the street from danger; in doing so, he suffered injuries. The default of the driver (the defendant's employee) could be described either as the failure to watch over his horses (an omission), or as the negligent performance of his duties as driver of the horse-drawn cart (an act). In truth, it of no importance which description is chosen: all that matters is that owners of property, and others left in charge of property, are held liable for negligently allowing it to harm others. This indeed was the result reached in *Haynes*, and the court wasted no time considering whether the conduct in question was an act or omission.

Land, however, should perhaps be treated differently from other property. Whereas we can generally choose whether or not we should make use of items of personal property and thereby expose others to risk, land can represent a risk to others even if it is not in use. Rocks may slide off our land on to neighbouring property below, while a fire started by lightning might extend beyond the edge of our property. Should we be required by law to take steps to prevent this? The cases which have considered this issue have straddled the boundaries between the torts of negligence and nuisance, some being based on the former, some on the latter. However, it is difficult to believe that this difference in legal classification could make any difference to the final result (see 18.2).

We should note in the first place that the liability of landowners to those who come on to their land and are injured by the state of the land is governed by statute (see Ch. 14), though it seems probable that the tort of negligence would have developed to impose similar liabilities. When it comes to losses suffered by people not on the defendant's land, but perhaps on neighbouring property or on the public highway, the question of liability is more problematical. It probably makes a difference whether a case involves a danger arising from the action of natural forces on the land or one arising from human agency. Liability is more likely to arise in the former case as the latter elicits the individualistic response that one ought not be held responsible for the actions of others. However, where I have allowed people on to my land and they cause you loss, there is an argument for requiring me to take reasonable steps to make sure they behave while they are there: my choice to let them on to my land suggests I am deriving some benefit from their presence and should therefore take the burden of supervising their activities. Consider the case of a football club that allows known hooligans into its ground for a match, appreciating that there is a risk that they will tear up lumps of concrete for use as missiles as the terracing is in a state of disrepair. If the hooligans were to throw the lumps of concrete at police gathered in the street beside the ground, injuring some of them, it is probable that the club would be held liable for their actions. The club after all derived the benefit of the admission fees paid by the hooligans (see *Cunningham* v. *Reading FC Ltd* (1991) *The Times*, 22nd March).

These considerations of benefit and burden apply primarily where the third parties in question are visitors on the defendant's land. Where those others are trespassers, the case for liability is much weaker. However, liability for the acts of trespassers who spark off a danger on one's land may arise in exceptional circumstances. This was accepted by the House of Lords in *Smith* v. *Littlewoods Organisation Ltd* [1987] AC 241. In that case, a fire was started by vandals on the site of a disused cinema bought by Littlewoods, who wanted to locate a supermarket there. The fire spread to neighbouring properties, causing serious damage, and the owners of those properties sued the supermarket chain. All members of the House of Lords agreed that liability could be imposed for the acts of trespassers on one's land only in exceptional circumstances, and that those circumstances were not present on the facts of the case. However, the approach of the various judges differed significantly.

Lord Goff adopted the traditional approach favoured by Lord Bridge in *Caparo* (see 3.3). First of all, he denied that there was any general duty placed on owners or occupiers of property to take reasonable precautions against the wrongdoing of third parties. Then he explained how to identify the exceptional cases in which liability might arise: 'having rejected the generalised principle, we have to search for special cases in which, upon narrower but still identifiable principles, liability can properly be imposed'. In his view, the case law identified two such principles. In the first place, where a landowner has knowledge, or means of knowledge, that intruders have created the risk of fire on her property, she may be liable for failing to take reasonable steps to prevent any such fire damaging neighbouring property. On the facts before him, he could see no reason why Littlewoods should have known that vandals were creating a fire risk; it was not enough to point to a foreseeable possibility that this might have been the case. The second principle applied where a landowner creates, or allows to be created, an unusual source of danger on her land. Lord Goff illustrated this principle by considering the case of a villager deputed to buy the fireworks for the village Guy Fawkes night display who stores the fireworks in an unlocked garden shed. He suggested that the villager might be liable if mischievous children from the village were to sneak into the shed and, playing with the fireworks, start a fire which burns down the neighbouring house. However, he concluded that an empty cinema was not an unusual danger in the nature of a stock of fireworks.

Whereas Lord Goff made an effort to isolate a number of rules governing the liability of landowners for the acts of third parties, the other members of the House of Lords spoke in much more generalised terms. The common theme of these other speeches was that the outbreak of fire was not sufficiently likely to justify holding Littlewoods liable, particularly in view of the burdensome nature of the precautions necessary to stop the vandals: only a 24-hour guard would have have been likely to prevent the fire. As Markesinis (1989) points out, it is not clear whether these other Law Lords dismissed the claim for damages because Littlewoods owed its neighbours no duty of care or because, although there was a duty of care, Littlewoods' behaviour could not have been regarded as unreasonable. Markesinis claims the latter is the better interpretation of the speeches and suggests that, where the burden of precautions is less, the courts might well hold a landowner liable. More ambitiously, Markesinis claims that the majority opinion heralds 'an unnoticed revolution'. In his view, the case is a significant forward step towards a generalised liability for omissions and 'may mark a new beginning for the law of negligence'. However, it is unlikely that the case will be regarded as authority outside the area of the liability of landowners and the categorical denial of liability for 'pure' omissions seems no less insistent now than ever before.

6.5   Innocently Causing Another's Plight

Suppose you are out driving and, through no fault of your own, you run down a pedestrian who suddenly dashes across your path. Your moral duty is clear: you should stop to check if the pedestrian is all right and, if necessary, call an ambulance. Now, legal duties are often at odds with moral duties, but arguably the two would coincide in the case just considered. The foundation of a legal duty to stop and help your victim would be the common sense notion that you had put her into this mess and it was therefore your job to get her out of it. This would be sufficient to distinguish you from all others coming to the scene of the accident. Under English law, they would be free to follow the example of the priest and the Levite and pass by on the other side of the road. Suppose now that the accident happened just over the crest of a hill and that there was a risk that traffic coming up the hill might have to swerve to avoid the injured pedestrian; in those circumstances, you might have a responsibility not only to the pedestrian but also to the motorists coming up the hill. The law might well impose on you a legal duty to warn the oncoming traffic to slow down to avoid any further carnage. The basis of your obligation would be that you had brought about the state of affairs that placed the other drivers in peril. *Home Office* v. *Dorset Yacht Co* was a case of this sort: taking the young offenders on a training exercise in the vicinity of the yacht club served to increase the risks faced by owners of the yachts even though the decision to do so was unimpeachable. Lord Diplock noted this factor as providing one justification for holding the Home Office liable.

Summary

6.1 The courts have been wary of imposing liability for omissions because they fear unduly burdening individuals and recognise the pragmatic difficulty of determining which of those who could have intervened should be held liable. Nevertheless, liability has been recognised in exceptional cases.

6.2 On occasion, a duty to protect others (and their property) may arise. The duty may be founded upon a specific undertaking upon which the plaintiff relies, or it may be founded upon a pre-existing relationship with the plaintiff when the latter is an infant or otherwise incapable of looking after herself.

6.3 A duty to control others may also sometimes arise. A parent looking after an infant and a nurse in charge of a mental patient might both owe a duty to take care that their charges do not cause harm to others. Where the third party is a responsible adult, liability for her acts is less likely to arise, but it may do so where the third party is a prisoner in the defendant's custody.

6.4 Owners of chattels seem generally to have a duty to take care lest their property injures others. Owners of land may be in a different position, for the obligations of a landowner might be unduly onerous if liability were imposed indiscriminatingly. It seems that liability will readily be imposed in respect of loss caused by natural hazards or visitors on the land, but that loss caused by trespassers will rarely be actionable.

6.5 Liability for a negligent omission to act may arise where the defendant had previously injured or endangered the plaintiff by her innocent act.

Exercises

6.1 Is this an area of the law where the courts have adopted, in the words of Lord Bridge in *Caparo*, the 'modern approach' of looking for a single general principle that can be applied in all cases, or is it one in which they have preferred the 'traditional approach' of developing the law incrementally and by analogy with established heads of liability?

6.2 Will the law, in any circumstances, impose liability for failing to shout a warning at someone who is about to walk over the edge of a cliff?

6.3 What is the significance of the decision of the House of Lords in *Smith* v. *Littlewoods Organisation Ltd*?

6.4 Might liability in negligence arise in the following circumstances?

(a) A fails to brake as she approaches an intersection in her car and crashes into B.

(b) C receives a telephone call to say that her daughter, who ought to have been at school, is standing in the middle of a busy road. C does nothing. D is injured when she swerves to avoid the girl. (Would it make any difference whether the girl was aged 5 or 15?)

(c) E sells F a pistol. Before F leaves the premises, she tells E that she plans to shoot her mother. E does nothing. F is in fact mentally ill and she shoots her mother later that day.

---

7 Problem Plaintiffs

7.1 Foreseeable and Unforeseeable Plaintiffs

It is often said that liability in negligence is limited to those who might foreseeably be affected by the defendant's carelessness. This is justified by saying that the defendant must be in breach of a duty of care owed to the plaintiff rather than to the world at large: what singles the plaintiff out is that she is the foreseeable victim of the defendant's wrong. The rule serves to weed out claims by those whose injuries are regarded as farfetched in much the same way as the *Wagon Mound* rule of remoteness of damage weeds out heads of damage that are unforeseeable consequences of the defendant's negligence (see Chapter 11).

The most famous elaboration of the principle that only the foreseeable plaintiff can recover damages in negligence is that attempted by Cardozo J in the New York Court of Appeals in *Palsgraf* v. *Long Island Rail Road* 248 NY 339 (1928). The case also provides a memorable example of the principle at work. Mrs Palsgraf was injured while standing on a railway platform. Some distance away, commotion had broken out as a man, running to catch a train that was beginning to move out of the station, was pushed on board by railway employees. The man dropped an innocuous-looking paper package. It contained fireworks and exploded on contact with the ground. The shock waves caused heavy metal scales near to Mrs Palsgraf to topple over and strike her, causing her injury. The majority of the court held that the railway employees owed her no duty of care as she was not a foreseeable victim of their negligence; it was not enough that their negligence exposed others to risk. Cardozo J explained:

> 'One who seeks redress at law does not make out a cause of action by showing without more that there has been damage to his person. If the harm was not willful [sic], he must show that the act as to him had possibilities of danger so many and so apparent as to entitle him to be protected against the doing of it though the harm was unintended. The victim does not sue derivatively, or by right of subrogation, to vindicate an interest invaded in the person of another. He sues for a breach of a duty owing to himself.'

In England, the same sort of analysis was soon to appeal to the House of Lords in the case of *Bourhill* v. *Young* [1943] AC 92. The case arose out of a motorcycle accident. The motorcyclist, John Young, who was killed, had been travelling too fast and had collided with a car a short distance away from where Mrs Bourhill was standing. She was eight months pregnant at the time of the accident and she alleged, in a suit against

Young's estate, that hearing the impact and seeing the pool of blood afterwards had caused her to miscarry and to suffer nervous shock. The House of Lords found that Young could not have been expected to foresee that anyone in the position of Mrs Bourhill could be affected. The following words of Lord Wright call to mind the reasoning of Cardozo J:

> 'John Young was certainly negligent in an issue between himself and the owner of the car which he ran into, but it is a different issue whether he was negligent *vis-à-vis* the appellant. She cannot build upon a wrong to someone else. Her interest, which was in her own bodily security, was of a different order from the interest of the owner of the car.'

The requirement of the foreseeable plaintiff has attracted criticism on the grounds that, as between innocent victim and careless injurer, the equities favour the former (see Fleming, 1992, p. 143). It may also be criticised in that the test of foreseeability is easily manipulated and may serve merely to obscure the policy considerations that have caused the courts to develop the law as they have. This is particularly true when we come to the question of losses to so-called 'secondary' victims (see also trespassers: 14.7). Even the most typical of tort cases may involve losses that extend beyond the immediate victim of the tortfeasor. Those who suffer as a result of a car accident may include those injured in rescue attempts, the bystanders who suffer psychiatric illness as a result of witnessing the scenes of carnage, the relatives who have to spend time and money to care for their disabled family members and the taxpayer whose contributions fund the emergency services and the National Health Service (NHS). None of these losses can be regarded as far-fetched. Nevertheless, some types of secondary victims habitually gain compensation in the courts on the grounds that they are foreseeable plaintiffs while others – regarded as unforeseeable – have to go without. This has nothing to do with the probability of loss to the various parties; rather it reflects the law's view of the desert of each and of the consequences of recognising liability. This was seen clearly by Andrews J when, in his dissenting judgment in *Palsgraf*, he derided the manipulation of the foreseeability device in such cases as 'merely an attempt to fit facts to theory'. As a response to such criticisms, courts today are inclined to use the concept of 'proximity' to justify differential treatment of different plaintiffs where previously they may have talked solely in terms of foreseeability.

7.2 Rescuers

One area of the law in which manipulation of the foreseeability test is evident is that concerning injuries suffered in the course of rescue attempts. The courts' sympathy for those who have selflessly exposed themselves to danger for the sake of others, allied to their desire not to deter those who might undertake rescues, has caused them to take a lenient view of the requirements for liability in the tort of negligence. Thus rescuers responding to an emergency situation are inevitably held to be foreseeable victims of the negligence of those who caused the emergency in the first place. As the American judge Cardozo CJ remarked: 'Danger invites rescue. The cry of distress is the summons to relief. The law does not ignore these reactions of the mind in tracing conduct to its consequences. It recognises them as normal. It places their effects within the range of the natural and probable' (*Wagner* v. *International Railway Co* 122 NE 437 (1921)).

A similar leniency is apparent when it comes to consideration of the defences that might be raised against those injured in a rescue attempt: courts are very loath to say that the actions of a rescuer negatived any causal connection between her injury and the defendant's negligence; or indeed that she was contributorily negligent or voluntarily assumed the risk of injury (see Chapter 12). These issues were canvassed in the leading case of *Baker* v. *T.E. Hopkins & Sons Ltd* [1959] 1 WLR 966. Dr Baker had descended into a well containing poisonous fumes in an attempt to rescue two workers who were feared to be in difficulty. The rope by which the doctor was lowered into the well became caught and both he, and the workers, were fatally overcome by the fumes. An action in respect of the doctor's death was brought against the employers of the dead workers. The Court of Appeal came down in favour of the doctor. First, it held that the doctor was owed a duty of care as it was reasonably foreseeable that, if the employees were imperilled, someone would seek to rescue them from their peril. Second, it denied that principles of causation or the law relating to defences barred the doctor's claim. The court emphasised especially that a rescuer will very rarely be found to have been contributorily negligent. Such a finding would only be appropriate where the rescuer was 'so foolhardy as to amount to a wholly unreasonable disregard for his own safety' (per Willmer LJ). For an example of a case where such a finding was made, see *Harrison* v. *British Railways Board* [1981] 3 All ER 675.

The last-named case deals with the issue of whether a rescuer may recover damages from the person imperilled if the latter was negligent in exposing herself to danger. In that case the plaintiff, a train guard, attempted to assist another person who, attempting to board a moving train, found himself in difficulty. The plaintiff was pulled from the train and sued in respect of his personal injuries. Boreham J held that the plaintiff was entitled to recover damages (subject to a reduction for his contributory negligence): there was no reason to deny the existence of a duty of care simply because the defendant was also the person imperilled. Implicit in this conclusion is the premise that the duty owed to the rescuer is an independent duty, not merely one derived from that owed to the person imperilled (see *Videan* v. *British Transport Commission* [1963] 2 QB 650; cf. 4.6).

Another interesting issue is whether one rescuer owes a duty of care to others who attempt to assist the person imperilled. This issue was considered in the Canadian case of *Horsley* v. *Maclaren* (1972) 22 DLR (3d) 545. The case concerned a boating accident: a guest on Maclaren's vessel fell overboard and Maclaren tried to manoeuvre the boat in order to carry out a rescue; this was unsuccessful and another guest, Horsley, dived in to do what he could; both guests died. The Supreme Court of Canada held that, on the facts, Maclaren had not been negligent; if he had been, however, the court would have been prepared to hold him liable to Horsley provided that his rescue attempts had placed the first guest in a 'new situation of peril' (per Ritchie J) distinct from that to which he was originally exposed. While it seems equitable that one rescuer should be liable to another, the 'new situation of peril' requirement imposed by the Supreme Court may be too restrictive. Liability should not be limited only to a case in which the defendant, by increasing the danger to the plaintiff, has made a second rescue attempt more likely; it should also arise in a case where the defendant makes the rescue attempted by the second rescuer more risky than it would otherwise have been.

7.3 The Unborn Child

In the case of children born after suffering congenital disabilities, the only requirement is that injury to the mother was foreseeable; there is no need to establish that the unborn child was a foreseeable victim of the defendant's negligence. This rule is set out in the Congenital Disabilities (Civil Liability) Act 1976 which was implemented because of confusion as to the rights of the unborn child at common law. It is now clear, however, that a claim can be brought at common law in respect of births occurring before the Act (*Burton* v. *Islington HA* [1992] 3 All ER 833); only the statutory claim is possible in respect of births since that time.

The liability under the Act is derivative in that the child's claim is dependent upon the defendant owing a duty of care to the parent; however, there is no need to prove that the parent suffered actionable injury (s.1(3)). The derivative nature of the action is also evident in the rule that the child's claim may be reduced to reflect the parent's share of responsibility for the disability (s.1(7)). Similarly, there is no right to recover where both the parents (or just the father if he is the defendant) knew of the risk of the child's disability before she was conceived (s.1(4)). The child may sue her own father, but she can only recover damages from her mother where the latter's negligence occurred while driving a motor vehicle (s.2). In such a case, the desire to maintain harmonious relations between mother and child is outweighed by the recognition that the mother will carry compulsory insurance against such an eventuality.

The Act only applies to those who suffer congenital disabilities as the result of another's tort. It does not cover 'wrongful life' claims by those whose disability is attributable to natural causes but who allege negligence on the part of a doctor who could have prevented the birth in the light of the likely extent of the child's disability. At common law, such claims were held to be contrary to public policy by the Court of Appeal in *McKay* v. *Essex Area Health Authority* [1982] QB 1166. The court in that case rejected a claim for damages by an infant who was born disabled after her mother contracted German measles during pregnancy, and who claimed that the mother's doctor should have advised her of the baby's condition and thereby given her an opportunity to seek an abortion. The court also held that the 1976 Act excluded the possibility of such claims in respect of any birth subsequent to its coming into effect..

To be distinguished from a 'wrongful life' claim is one in respect of a 'wrongful birth'. In such an action, it is the parents who sue in respect of the financial, psychological and other consequences of giving birth to a child whom they would rather not have had and whose birth should have been avoided by the defendants. In *Emeh* v. *Kensington and Chelsea and Westminster Area Health Authority* [1985] QB 1012, the Court of Appeal accepted that all foreseeable losses of that nature were recoverable. Accordingly, it awarded damages to a woman who became pregnant after a sterilisation operation, performed negligently by the defendant, proved ineffective.

Summary

7.1 A duty of care is owed only to the foreseeable victims of the defendant's negligence. This foreseeability requirement has been manipulated by the courts in order to give effect to policy decisions about the desert of different types of plaintiff. Recently, this has been recognised more openly by regarding the entitlement of each plaintiff as a matter of proximity as well as foreseeability.

7.2 Rescuers are invariably held to be foreseeable plaintiffs and are rarely defeated by claims that they unreasonably exposed themselves to the risk of injury. It seems that a rescuer may even succeed against the person imperilled or a fellow rescuer if either of the latter were negligent.

7.3 Two types of action are currently available in respect of pre-natal negligence. First, there is the action under the Congenital Disabilities Act 1976 brought by a child born disabled as a result of negligence. Secondly, there is the common law action for 'wrongful birth' brought by the parents of a child who would not have been born but for the defendant's negligence. Neither the common law nor under the 1976 Act is it possible for a disabled child to bring a 'wrongful life' action claiming she should not have been born.

Exercises

7.1 'It may well be that there is no such thing as negligence in the abstract. . . In an empty world, negligence would not exist. It does involve a relationship between man and his fellows, but not merely a relationship between man and those whom he might reasonably expect to injure; rather a relationship between him and those whom he does in fact injure' (*Palsgraf* v. *Long Island Rly*, per Andrews J).

Discuss.

7.2 Is the duty of care owed to a rescuer a 'derivative' duty or one owed to her in her own right? What difference does it make?

7.3 In what circumstances will the birth of a child give rise to an action in negligence? In what circumstances will the conception of a child give rise to such an action?

7.4 Should the courts allow an action for 'wrongful life'?

8 Problem Defendants

For reasons of public policy, defendants engaged in certain activities may be immune from negligence liability. The following paragraphs consider the immunities of governmental agencies, the police and the legal profession. This is not a complete list of those with immunities from suit: others have been, or may yet be, added to the list. It has been decided for instance, as the authors are pleased to note, that the examiners of the University of London LLB cannot successfully be sued by candidates who allege that their scripts were marked negligently (*Thorne* v. *University of London* [1966] 2 QB 237).

8.1 Public Bodies

Courts are wary of holding public bodies liable in negligence for a number of reasons. One that we have already encountered is that, in most cases, their purported negligence consists in an omission to act: the failure of a local authority to ensure that builders keep to the approved plans and do not skimp on the foundations; the failure of a government department to check the credentials of a new investment fund which folds, leaving investors penniless; and so on. Another reason is that the function of the body in question may be to service the population at large, in which case the imposition of liability would raise the spectre of the 'floodgates' argument. As a consequence, the courts are only willing to impose liability where the body's function may be said to be to protect particular individuals from the particular damage that results (see *Curran* v. *Northern Ireland Co-ownership Housing Association* [1987] AC 718; *Yuen Kun Yeu* v. *A-G of Hong Kong* [1988] AC 175). However, omissions liability is established in certain cases, and some would argue that the fact that a governmental agency is entrusted with a task, and given funds to perform it, is reason enough to hold it accountable to individuals who suffer through its negligence (see Fleming, 1990). Yet there are other very good reasons for allowing public bodies substantial immunity from suit.

In the first place, the decisions they have to make often require too wide-ranging an investigation for the court-room. For instance, no court is equipped to make the decision whether the Home Office is right to operate an 'open' borstal policy and, as part of it, to take young offenders away from safe confinement in highly secure institutions on training exercises. This decision requires the balancing of considerations that the courts are scarcely able to identify, never mind weigh: How much does it cost to operate an open borstal system as opposed to a closed one? Should the object of the system be to punish young offenders or to rehabilitate them? What additional risks are imposed on the local community by allowing young offenders more freedom of movement? Such is the diversity of the issues which might be relevant that it is inconceivable that the two parties represented in court would raise them all. Matters like these should be decided only after a public enquiry has given all interested parties an opportunity to air their views. This suggests a second reason why courts should stay clear of cases that raise these matters: the decisions made by public bodies are often the product of the democratic process and it would be unconstitutional for the courts to undermine this by challenging those decisions. This consideration is particularly weighty when the public body in question is an elected one (e.g. a local authority). Where this is the case, the body is accountable to its electorate and there is a strong argument for saying the electorate alone should pass judgment on it.

These concerns are all too familiar to public lawyers. As a matter of public law, actions of public bodies are not reviewable by the courts unless *ultra vires* (i.e. in excess of their powers). This seems to present an additional hurdle to the plaintiff in a negligence action: not only must she prove that the public body was negligent, she must also establish that the public body acted in an *ultra vires* fashion (see *Home Office* v. *Dorset Yacht Co Ltd* [1970] AC 1004; Craig, 1989, pp. 448–58). In practice, however, these two questions may merge into one, for negligent actions by a public body may be considered automatically *ultra vires*. As Lord Reid said in the *Dorset Yacht* case, 'there must come a stage where the discretion is exercised so carelessly or unreasonably that there has been no real exercise of the discretion which Parliament has conferred. The person purporting to exercise his discretion has acted in excess of his power.' The question then is whether and in what circumstances the courts are able to brand the conduct of a public body negligent without offending the policies for granting public bodies substantial immunity from suit. The mechanism employed by the courts to answer that question is a distinction, made by Lord Wilberforce in *Anns* v. *Merton London Borough Council* [1978] AC 728, between a public body's formulation of a policy and its operation of that policy. According to Lord Wilberforce, the more 'operational' the matter before the court is, the easier it is for the court to regard the public body as owing a common law duty of care. He considered the distinction was probably a matter of degree, and it seems that matters will be regarded as 'policy' (no duty) or 'operational' (a duty of care may exist) on the basis of whether they are appropriate for judicial scrutiny ('justiciable'). Thus Lord Keith has said:

'[T]his distinction does not provide a touchstone of liability, but rather is expressive of the need to exclude altogether those cases in which the decision under attack is of such a kind that a question whether it has been made negligently is unsuitable for judicial resolution, of which notable examples are discretionary decisions on the allocation of scarce resources or the distribution of risks.' (*Rowling* v. *Takaro Properties Ltd* [1988] AC 473)

The way the distinction works in practice can be illustrated by considering the facts of *Home Office* v. *Dorset Yacht Co Ltd* [1970] AC 1004. The decision of the Home Office to operate an open borstal system was a policy matter and hence unchallengeable in the courts. By way of contrast, however, the carelessness of the borstal officers in going off to bed, leaving their charges to their own devices, contrary to regulations, was an operational matter and it was appropriate to hold the Home Office liable for that carelessness.

While negligence is sufficient to take a public body *ultra vires*, the converse does not hold true. Actions of a public body may be *ultra vires* for a number of reasons which do not connote negligence. This was the case in *Takaro* which considered the question of tortious liability in respect of the decision of the New Zealand Minister of Finance to refuse consent to the issue of shares by an overseas company. This decision had in separate proceedings been held *ultra vires* on the ground that the Minister had taken an irrelevant consideration into account in making his decision. The Privy Council held that the Minister had not been negligent in failing to do so as his error lay in misconstruing a statute, a mistake which anybody, even a judge, could have made. *Takaro* was a case in which the Privy Council considered whether, despite the finding of *ultra vires*, the defendant had in fact exercised reasonable care; in some cases the court will not embark upon such enquiry at all. Had the decision taken in *Takaro* appropriately been classified as a 'policy' decision, then the Minister would have owed no duty of care at all and the question of breach of duty would not have arisen.

8.2   The Police

There is no question that a police officer, like anyone else, may be liable in tort where her negligent acts result in injury to another. By section 48 of the Police Act 1964, the Chief Constable of the area may be vicariously liable for these acts, in which case damages will be paid out of the police fund (see Chapter 22). However, as is the case with other public institutions, the courts have faced problems in dealing with allegedly negligent omissions or policy decisions.

Claims against the police in respect of a negligent omission will succeed if they fall within an established category of liability for omission. Thus, as we have seen (6.2), the police may be liable for failing to protect a suicidal mental patient from herself after she has been taken into custody. Furthermore, by analogy with the *Dorset Yacht* case, they may also be held liable for damage caused in the course of a prisoner's escape from their control. However, the police cannot be held liable to those who suffer harm from criminal activities which they allege the police should have prevented. This conclusion was reached by the House of Lords after considering the issue in a case brought by the mother of the last victim of the so-called 'Yorkshire Ripper', a mass-murderer who conducted a campaign of terror against young women in the north of England from 1975 to 1980 (*Hill* v. *Chief Constable of West Yorkshire* [1989] AC 53). Lord Keith expressed the following policy reasons why this should be so. First, the fear of liability might cause the police to carry out their tasks in a detrimentally defensive frame of mind. (It seems that borstal officers are made of sterner stuff: in the *Dorset Yacht* case, Lord Reid expressly dismissed the argument that officers might be dissuaded from doing their duty by the fear of liability.) Secondly, many cases would concern the exercise of discretion as to the way an investigation should proceed: this could not be called into question by the courts. Thirdly, the time, trouble and expense put into the defence of claims, even those that were totally meritless, would represent a significant diversion of police manpower and attention from their task of suppressing crime.

Even in cases where the plaintiff's injury stems from police actions, rather than omissions, the courts may be unwilling to entertain a claim for fear of interfering with police discretion. Lord Wilberforce's distinction between policy and operational areas of the activities of public bodies is central here. In *Rigby* v. *Chief Constable of Northamptonshire* [1985] 1 WLR 1242, a building owner claimed against the police after they had used inflammable CS gas to smoke out a gunman holed-up in the property, a ploy which achieved its aim but also succeeded in causing serious fire damage to the building. Taylor J relied on Lord Wilberforce's distinction to hold that he could not impugn the police force for equipping itself with inflammable CS gas even though a non-flammable alternative was available: this was a policy decision. However, he did hold the police liable in negligence for failing to have firefighting equipment in attendance at the time they used the gas; this, evidently, was a matter falling within the operational area.

8.3 The Legal Profession

A lawyer, whether barrister or – in these progressive times – solicitor, cannot be sued by her client for negligence in presenting the latter's case in court. This was decided by the House of Lords in the case of *Rondel* v. *Worsley* [1969] 1 AC 191 in which a man convicted of causing grievous bodily harm complained that his barrister had negligently failed to lead evidence that the accused had caused the injuries with his teeth and hands, rather than with a knife. The House of Lords held that on grounds of public policy the case should not be heard. The following reasons for this stance were identified in the speeches.

First, if an advocate were required constantly to look over her shoulder this would hamper the true administration of justice. An advocate owes an overriding duty to the court which, on occasion, may conflict with her duty to her client. She may, for instance, have to clear up a misunderstanding on the part of the judge even though it may be favourable to her client's case. Equally, the judge may rely upon her to pare her client's case down to its bare essentials, rather than allow the client an opportunity to air all her grievances, at the expense of valuable court time, whether they are legally relevant or not. If an advocate were to face the threat of actions for negligence, this might cause her to turn a blind eye to the interests of justice in order to keep her client happy.

Secondly, removing the immunity might have the effect that advocates would begin to pick and choose their clients in order to avoid those whose case is wholly without merit and who seem intent on airing their grievance in whatever forum is open to them. These evasions of the so-called 'cab-rank' rule – that an advocate is bound to provide her services for any client that can pay her fee – would risk injustice, for an unpleasant client with an apparently hopeless case may, after a full and fair hearing, turn out to be in the right.

Last, a suit alleging negligent conduct of a court case would inevitably require a re-trial of the original case. This, according to Lord Morris, would be contrary to public policy. If the action were brought in respect of a criminal conviction, allowing the accused to seek to establish her innocence in a civil court would be to graft on to the criminal appeals system 'a sort of unseemly excrescence'. If it concerned a civil action, the result would be 'litigation upon litigation with the possibility of a recurring chain-like course of litigation'. This would offend against the interest in finality in litigation.

The barrister's immunity only extends to the conduct of litigation and those preliminary matters that are intimately connected with the conduct of the case in court (see *Saif Ali* v. *Sidney Mitchell & Co* [1980] AC 198). By section 62 of the Courts and Legal Services Act 1990, solicitors are entitled to benefit from an immunity of the same extent. In cases that fall outside this immunity, it seems that a solicitor or barrister may be liable for carelessly giving negligent advice or otherwise negligently conducting her client's affairs. This would be the case, for example, where a solicitor negligently fails to draw up a will correctly, with the result that an intended beneficiary loses out on her bequest (see 5.3). The main problem in such cases is that the alleged liability is usually for pure economic loss. However, it is likely that many of them will fall under the principle of *Hedley Byrne* v. *Heller*, particularly in view of the fact that the plaintiff (generally the client) is readily identifiable and the exposure to risk ascertainable.

Summary

8.1 Public bodies may only be held liable for negligence in respect of the exercise of their statutory powers if they have acted both in breach of a duty of care and in an *ultra vires* fashion. Because of concerns as to the limitations of the forensic process, a duty of care may only arise in relation to an 'operational' matter and not in relation to a 'policy' decision. A finding of an 'operational' breach of duty is sufficient to take the conduct of the public body *ultra vires*. The converse is not true: a public body may act in an *ultra vires* fashion without being in breach of a duty of care.
8.2 No duty of care arises in respect of 'policy' decisions by the police. Only in very exceptional circumstances do the police owe potential victims of crime a duty of care to safeguard them from criminal acts.
8.3 Barristers and solicitors owe no duty of care with regards to the conduct of litigation or to preliminary matters which are intimately connected with the conduct of a case in court.

Exercises

8.1 A local authority is empowered by statute to supervise and control the operations of builders with a view to maintaining proper standards of health and safety and has set up an inspectorate to perform this task. One of the inspectors, A, carelessly fails to spot that a certain house is built on defective foundations. The house subsequently falls down and injures its occupier, B. Advise the parties as to their rights and liabilities in tort. Would it make any difference if B's house had not been inspected because (a) for budgetary reasons, the authority had decided to suspend all inspections, or (b) the authority's lawyers had misinterpreted the relevant statute and advised the authority that it was not in fact entitled to carry out on site inspections.

8.2 Assess the strength of the 'overkill' argument in relation to lawyers, the police and public bodies generally.

8.3 In what circumstances is the interest in the finality of litigation considered relevant to an action in negligence? Whose interest is it? What weight should the courts attach to it?

---

9   Breach of the Duty of Care

9.1 Introduction

Under the heading of breach of a duty of care the question is not whether the defendant should be held liable for her negligence (which is the question in relation to duty, causation and remoteness), but whether the defendant was in fact negligent in the first place. Negligence consists in falling below the standard of care required in the circumstances to protect others from the unreasonable risk of harm. This is judged in relation to the position in which the defendant found herself: it is easy to be wise after the event, but a court should not let hindsight influence its judgment as to what the defendant ought to have done in the circumstances. It follows that where knowledge of the risks involved in particular activities has developed over the course of time, the defendant's conduct should be assessed in the light of the state of knowledge at the time she acted, not that at the date of trial. In *Roe* v. *Minister of Health* [1954] 2 QB 66, the plaintiffs had become paralysed after being injected with anaesthetic which had been contaminated by disinfectant. The anaesthetic had been stored in ampoules placed in the disinfectant; this had seeped into the ampoules through invisible cracks. At the date of the injuries, 1947, this was not generally considered possible. In the Court of Appeal, Denning LJ stressed that developments in scientific knowledge should be ignored in assessing the culpability of the defendants: 'We must not look at the 1947 accident with 1954 spectacles.'

9.2 The Objective Standard of Care

In general, the law requires defendants in negligence actions to measure up to an objective standard and declines to accept excuses that are founded on the defendant's inability to measure up to that standard. The question to be asked is, 'What would a reasonable person have done in the circumstances?' rather than 'What could the defendant have done?' As Lord Macmillan put it in the case of *Glasgow Corporation* v. *Muir* [1943] AC 448, the objective standard 'eliminates the personal equation and is independent of the idiosyncrasies of the particular person whose conduct is in question'. The reason for this approach was clearly expressed by the great American judge and jurist, Oliver Wendell Holmes (1881):

'The standards of the law are standards of general application. The law takes no account of the infinite varieties of temperament, intellect and education which make the internal character of a given act so different in different men. It does not attempt to see men as God sees them. [W]hen men live in society, a certain average of conduct, a sacrifice of individual peculiarities going beyond a certain point, is necessary to the general welfare. If, for instance, a man is born hasty and awkward, is always having accidents and hurting himself or his neighbours, no doubt his congenital defects will be allowed for in the courts of Heaven, but his slips are no less troublesome to his neighbours than if they sprang from guilty neglect. His neighbours accordingly require him, at his proper peril, to come up to their standard, and the courts which they establish decline to take his personal equation into account.'

This general rule holds true when we are concerned with those whose lack of skill, experience or intelligence leads them to injure others. In the leading English case, *Nettleship v. Weston* [1971] 2 QB 691, a learner-driver failed to straighten the steering-wheel after turning a corner and ran into a street lamp; her driving instructor was injured. The Court of Appeal held her liable to the instructor, finding that she had fallen below the standard expected of a qualified and experienced driver; it was irrelevant that she as a learner might not be able to attain that standard. However, it may be that abnormal physical characteristics will be taken into account. Though the matter has yet to come before an appellate court, it seems likely that infant defendants in negligence actions will not be judged as if they were adults and will be required to do no more than live up to the standards expected of a child of their age (see *Staley v. Suffolk County Council*, 26 November 1985, unreported). Whether the same approach will be taken to others who might by virtue of their physical characteristics be unable to attain the objective standard is less certain. Consider the case of a deaf driver who causes an accident because she fails to hear the siren of an ambulance. As soundness of hearing is not a prerequisite for driving on English roads, it might be thought unfair to penalise the deaf driver in respect of the unexpected consequences of her disability. However, it may be that a court would be influenced by the fact that the driver would almost certainly carry liability insurance and find her liable, resting content in the knowledge that she would at worst only bear the cost of this liability indirectly.

Where a person holds herself out as possessing a special skill over and above that of reasonable people, then she will of course be expected to live up to the standard she has represented she can attain. It would be no excuse for the surgeon whose piercing of your ears resulted in an infection to say that you were not entitled to demand more in the way of hygiene or competence than you would expect had you visited a jeweller instead. However, a jeweller performing the same service is not to be judged by the standards of a surgeon, for ear-piercing is not an activity that requires surgical skill (see *Philips v. Whiteley (William) Ltd* [1938] 1 All ER 566).

9.3   Application of the Objective Standard

Many commentators have discerned a progressive raising of the objective standard in the course of the last century which they attribute to the spread of liability insurance (see Tunc, 1983). The courts are now inclined to treat inevitable lapses of concentration or judgment as deviations from the standard of the reasonable person, though occasionally a judge will stand against the tide by arguing that not every careless slip can give rise to liability (especially in emergencies and other situations demanding split-second judgements: see *Wooldridge* v. *Sumner* [1963] 2 QB 43). In terms of ease of adjudication, cases involving lapses of concentration or judgment present few problems, for the defendant would be almost bound to admit that she had done something wrong and that she could think of no justification for doing what she did. However, as we move away from simple lapses of attention into the area of accidents that might have been avoided with a bit of foresight, things become more complicated. In these cases, it might be that the defendant can argue that she thought she could not be expected to behave differently to guard against possible injury to the plaintiff. Taking risks with our own and others' personal welfare and property is part of everyday existence. Indeed, life would be impossible if we did not do so. The point was put graphically by Asquith LJ in *Daborn* v. *Bath Tramways* [1946] 2 All ER 333: 'if all the trains in this country were restricted to a speed of 5 miles an hour, there would be fewer accidents, but our national life would be intolerably slowed down'. The question the law of negligence must confront then is: 'Just how much is the law to require us to do in order avoid causing harm to others?'

The precautions we should take to guard against injury to others depend on the circumstances of the case. The more likely injury is to result, and the greater the severity of that injury if it does result, the more we should do to eliminate the risk. On the other hand, if the costs of eliminating the risk exceed the benefits to be gained from doing so, then it might be reasonable to do nothing. This has been expressed as a mathematical formula by the American judge, Learned Hand. Where the probability of injury occurring is P, the extent of the likely loss is L and the burden of taking precautions to eliminate the risk is B, liability will arise if $B < PL$ (in other words if the seriousness of the risk, assessed by looking at the factors on the right-hand side of the equation, outweighs the burden of eliminating it). This is known as the 'Learned Hand formula'.

Whilst English courts might deride such an approach for its veneer of scientific infallibility, the cases show that they attach significance to the same factors as feature in the 'Learned Hand formula', namely (a) probability, (b) the severity of the possible loss, and (c) the burden of eliminating the risk of loss.

Considerations of the degree of *probability* that harm might result from the defendant's activity may explain why, for example, the courts have reached apparently conflicting decisions on the issue of whether a cricket club should be held liable for damage caused by balls hit over the boundary fence. If the likelihood of this occurring was great, the club might be expected to have erected a taller fence or even to have moved to another site (as in *Miller* v. *Jackson* [1977] QB 966). However, if this was likely to be a rare occurrence, the club's conduct might be beyond reproach (as in *Bolton* v. *Stone* [1951] AC 850).

The severity of the likely *loss* or injury was the crucial factor in the decision in *Paris* v. *Stepney Borough Council* [1951] AC 367. In that case, the court found that an employer was negligent in failing to provide safety goggles to a particular employee, blind in one eye, even though there was no need to provide them for all employees: the consequences of losing the sight of one's only good eye were far worse than losing the sight of one of two good eyes.

The *burden* or cost of eliminating the risk of injury was considered in the case of *Latimer* v. *AEC Ltd* [1953] AC 643. In that case, the defendant's factory had been flooded and the water, mixed with oil from channels in the floor, left the floor exceedingly slippery. The trial judge held that in these circumstances the factory should have been shut down until the floor was made safe. The House of Lords overturned this ruling on the grounds that the circumstances did not demand that the employer take such a drastic step. In looking at the cost of eliminating the risk of injury, the court's enquiry may go beyond the consequences for the defendant and look at the consequences for society as a whole. Thus, in *Watt* v. *Hertfordshire County Council* [1954] 1 WLR 835, the Court of Appeal accepted that it might be reasonable for firemen responding to an emergency situation to load a heavy jack on to a lorry not fitted to carry it when the specially adapted lorry was unavailable. Accordingly, a fireman injured when the jack rolled against him in the back of the lorry was unable to obtain compensation.

9.4 Common Practice

The cost-benefit analysis that courts are expected to perform in assessing whether defendants have acted unreasonably may stretch the forensic process to its limits. Many of the issues raised are highly technical and arise in areas in which the courts have no expertise. Recognising this, the courts have shown themselves quite willing to yield to the judgement of those more qualified than themselves. Where those involved in the defendant's activity take certain precautions against the risk of harm as a matter of common practice, then the courts are likely to find the defendant to have been negligent if she failed to take those precautions. In order to escape liability, she would have to produce convincing reasons for why she acted as she did. Conversely, where the defendant does take all the precautions commonly adopted by others in her field of activity, then this on its own will often be sufficient to defeat the plaintiff's claim.

Although common practice may be relevant in asking what the defendant might reasonably have done, it is not decisive. The courts reserve the power to set standards for a field of activity and do not limit themselves merely to reflecting the standards of those engaged in that activity. Thus, in the context of industry, the courts have on occasion declared an industry-wide practice to be negligent and have insisted that standards be raised across the board. A progressive judgment in this respect is that of Mustill J in *Thompson* v. *Smith Shiprepairers Ltd* [1984] QB 405, a case concerning industrial deafness suffered by workers in shipyards. Mustill J proceeded on the basis that 'the defendants simply shared in the indifference and inertia which characterised the industry as a whole', and made it clear that one employer was not exonerated merely by proving that other employers were just as negligent. His view was that there were certain cases in which an employer might be penalised for failing to take the initiative in seeking out developing knowledge of possible risks and precautions. He emphasised, however, that the obligation placed on employers should not be too demanding: 'The employer must keep up to date, but the court must be slow to blame him for not ploughing a lone furrow'.

Where there are conflicting views as to the appropriate practice to adopt, it will generally be sufficient for a plaintiff to show that she acted in a way that a responsible body of those in her field regarded as reasonable. The fact that a contrary view exists will be regarded as irrelevant. This is known as the *Bolam* test, named after the case in which McNair J explained the issue of a doctor's liability in negligence to a jury in substantially those terms (*Bolam* v. *Friern Hospital Management Committee* [1957] 1 WLR 582). The test has now been applied to all professions or callings which require special skill, knowledge or experience.

9.5   Proof of Negligence

Plaintiffs may face an uphill struggle in proving that the defendant's negligence was responsible for the harm they have suffered. Often the scale of the task will be immense. In the litigation arising out of the use of the anti-arthritis drug, Opren (see *Davies* v. *Eli Lilly & Co* (1987) 137 NLJ 1183), the plaintiffs had to hire a team of scientific, medical, pharmaceutical and legal experts to plough through literally millions of documents released to them by the manufacturer of the drug. Furthermore, in many cases the plaintiffs will have to rely on the defendant releasing information to them (e.g., as to the tests to which a new pharmaceutical product was subjected); an unscrupulous defendant might attempt to destroy documents unfavourable to her case rather than comply with a court order for the disclosure of such evidence (known as an order for discovery). The plight of plaintiffs in such cases has prompted innovation on the part of Parliament and the courts to ensure just claims are not defeated by evidential difficulties. In the area of substantive law, legislative reform of the law of product liability was motivated in part by this concern (see Chapter 14). At a procedural level, Parliament has made rules of discovery more stringent over the last century. The response of the courts to the same problem can be seen in the doctrine of *res ipsa loquitur* ('the accident tells its own story').

The classic exposition of the doctrine is that of Erle CJ delivering the judgment of the Court of Exchequer Chamber in the case of *Scott* v. *London and St Katherine Docks Co* (1865) 3 H&C 596. The plaintiff had been injured when struck by six bags of sugar which fell on him from above when he walked under a crane. The crane was being used by the defendants' servant to lower the sugar to the ground from the defendants' warehouse. At trial, the plaintiff gave no explanation of how the accident had happened, with the result that the trial judge directed the jury to find for the defendants on the grounds that there was no evidence of negligence on their part. The plaintiff appealed and the case eventually came before the Court of Exchequer Chamber to determine if there should be a new trial. The court held that there should, applying the following proposition of law:

> 'There must be reasonable evidence of negligence, but, where the thing is shown to be under the management of the defendant, or his servants, and the accident is such as, in the ordinary course of things, does not happen if those who have the management of the machinery use proper care, it affords reasonable evidence, in the absence of explanation by the defendant, that the accident arose from want of care.'

This passage makes it clear that two requirements must be met before the rule comes into operation. In the first place, the thing causing the accident must be 'shown to be under the management of the defendant or his servants'. This would be the case where you were driving your car when it suddenly swerved across the road, colliding with oncoming traffic. However, if the car had been driven by a friend to whom you had lent it, it could not be said to have been under your management and the doctrine could not be raised against you. Erle CJ's second requirement was that 'the accident is such as, in the ordinary course of things, does not happen if those who have the management of the [thing] use proper care'. Whether this requirement is satisfied will depend on all the circumstances. Thus, for example, the inference of negligence where you slip on yoghurt spilt on someone's floor will be stronger where the accident takes place in a supermarket rather than an office block, for in the former case the owners should have known that spillages would not be infrequent and should have taken precautions to deal with them as soon as they occur (compare *Ward* v. *Tesco Stores Ltd* [1976] 1 WLR 810 with *Bell* v. *Department of Health and Social Security* (1989) *The Times*, 13 June).

Views have differed as to the effect of the doctrine of *res ipsa loquitur* and the law on the subject remains murky. Two diametrically opposed positions have attracted the most support (see Atiyah, 1972). One school of thought holds that the proposition lays down no new rule of law but merely reflects the common-sense view that, in some circumstances, the likelihood that an accident was caused by the defendant's negligence is so great that it is not necessary for the plaintiff to explain exactly how the accident came to occur. Accordingly, if Erle CJ's requirements are met, it is permissible for the court to infer from the occurrence of an accident that it was probably caused by the defendant's negligence. The opposing view is that the doctrine of *res ipsa loquitur* is a distinct legal rule which casts the legal burden of proof on the defendant when certain requirements are met. This burden requires the defendant to do one of two things. One course is for her to explain precisely how the accident happened, for once the facts are known the maxim can have no application: it is simply a matter of deciding whether those facts support the allegation of negligence or not. If she cannot do this, she may take the second course of trying to prove that she took all reasonable care irrespective of the cause of the accident. As, on this view, the burden of proof lies with the defendant, the judge must resolve any doubt she has as to whether the defendant's negligence caused the accident in favour of the plaintiff rather than the defendant. The extent of the hurdle facing the defendant can be gauged from *Henderson* v. *Henry E. Jenkins & Sons* [1970] AC 282. Mr Henderson had been killed after the brakes on the defendant's lorry had failed. The defendant firm produced evidence that the lorry had been inspected in accordance with the manufacturer's instructions; however, the House of Lords held that, in order to prove it had exercised all reasonable care, the firm should have produced evidence that the lorry had not been carrying corrosive loads of any kind.

Despite this House of Lords authority that the effect of the doctrine is to reverse the legal burden of proof, the Privy Council has recently expressed a preference for the alternative view in *Ng Chun Pui* v. *Lee Chuen Tat* [1988] RTR 298. This is to be regretted. As Atiyah (1972) has pointed out, there is good reason for allowing an exception to the general rule that it is up to the plaintiff to prove her case on the balance of probabilities in precisely those cases identified by Erle CJ in which the thing causing the accident was under the control or management of the defendant. In such cases, the plaintiff may be in grave difficulties as she will have no information as to the precautions the defendant took in using the thing. A shift in the burden of proof would help to redress this imbalance.

Summary

9.1 'Negligence' or 'breach of duty' consists in falling below the standard of care required in the circumstances to protect others from the unreasonable risk of harm.
9.2 Negligence does not connote personal fault but merely the failure to comply with the standard of conduct to be expected of a reasonable person in the circumstances. This standard is assessed objectively, without regard to the defendant's lack of skill or experience, though it arguably takes account of the defendant's physical characteristics. The defendant is judged according to a higher standard if she holds herself out as possessing particular skills.
9.3 Generally, it will be self-evident whether the defendant's conduct was negligent or not. Where, however, this is open to argument the court will compare the extent of the risk created by the defendant's activities with the cost of eliminating or reducing that risk in order to determine whether the defendant behaved reasonably or not.
9.4 The existence of a common industrial or professional practice creates a standard against which to judge the defendant. However, deviation from that practice is not conclusive of negligence, and neither is compliance conclusive of lack of negligence.
9.5 Where the plaintiff alleges that the defendant was negligent in causing an accident but does not know how the accident occurred, she may be aided by the doctrine of *res ipsa loquitur*. The way the doctrine operates is disputed.

Exercises

9.1 Do you think that the courts approach the question of breach of duty intuitively or scientifically, or does it depend on the case? If your answer is 'It depends', state what it depends upon.

9.2 What does it mean to describe the standard of care as 'objective'? When can the courts take account of factors peculiar to the defendant?

9.3 Is the *ratio* of *Nettleship* v. *Weston* that, although women drivers are unable to match up to the standards of their male counterparts, they should be judged by those standards for the purposes of the tort of negligence? If not, what is the *ratio* of that case? Is it fair?

9.4 What is the 'Learned Hand formula'? Is it employed by the English courts?

9.5 Is it ever legitimate to ignore a very sizeable risk of harming another person? If so, in what sort of case?

9.6 To what extent is the plea 'Well, everybody else does it' sufficient to rebut an allegation of negligence?

9.7 What is the doctrine of *res ipsa loquitur*? Is it a doctrine at all? If so, what effect does it have?

9.8 A owns a medical supplies business and employs a number of van drivers to deliver the supplies to hospitals throughout the country. In the aftermath of a mining disaster in South Wales, she received an emergency request for supplies from a local hospital. Unfortunately, all her regular drivers are away making deliveries in France and, rather than arrange for one of them to be flown back, she reluctantly decides to drive the van herself although it is some time since she has driven. On the way, the brakes of A's van fail and it crashes into a car travelling in the opposite direction. B, the driver of that car, is badly hurt; A escapes unharmed. There is some evidence that a van driver who drove regularly would have been able to control the vehicle and avoid the collision. It seems that the brake failure was caused by a hole in an unusually corroded part of the brake pipe which would only have been visible had the pipe been removed from the lorry. In fact, A, following the practice of other firms, had not done so, though she had complied with the manufacturer's advice that the visible parts of the pipe be inspected regularly. It is not clear whether the van had previously been used to carry any corrosive chemical agents. Advise the parties as to their rights and liabilities in tort.

10 Causation

Causation is a central, but elusive, concept in the law of tort. In the tort of negligence, the plaintiff is required to prove that the defendant's negligence caused her loss, and there is an equivalent causation requirement for most other torts as well. In the vast majority of cases causation presents no problems. In a small minority, however, the questions raised are ones that have bemused lawyers and philosophers for centuries.

10.1 Causal Relevance and the 'But For' Test

If you were to witness a car accident and afterwards note down all the details that you could remember, your list would include some factors that were causally relevant to the accident and some that were not. Amongst the former, you might count the treacherously icy condition of the road, the fact that the driver of one of the cars had evidently been drinking and the failure of a faulty traffic light to turn to red. Conversely, the registration numbers of the vehicles involved, the colour of the victims' hair and the clothes they were wearing could not be treated as causally relevant. The presence of these factors was in no way necessary for the accident to happen.

The notion of a 'necessary condition' is crucial to the issue of causal relevance. When we stipulate that a factor must be a necessary condition of the harm in question, we mean that it must be a necessary member of a set of conditions which together are sufficient to produce that harm. If you were to throw a lighted match into the waste-paper basket, your action would be treated as the cause of the fire: it is plain that what you did was necessary to complete a set of conditions (which also includes the presence of inflammable material in the basket and oxygen in the atmosphere) jointly sufficient to produce the fire.

In seeking to separate causally relevant and irrelevant factors, courts often rely on the so-called 'but for' test. This poses the question: would the plaintiff not have suffered harm but for defendant's negligence (i.e., in the absence of defendant's negligence, would she have suffered the harm anyway?) The case of *Barnett* v. *Chelsea and Kensington Hospital Management* [1969] 1 QB 428 is frequently cited as an example of how the test is applied. In that case, the plaintiff's husband had experienced persistent vomiting after drinking some tea and had gone to the casualty department of a hospital. The duty doctor refused to see him and Mr Barnett subsequently died from arsenical poisoning. The court found that the doctor's refusal to see Mr Barnett, though negligent, was not causally relevant to his death for there was no chance that effective treatment could have been given in time anyway. To put it another way, Mr Barnett's drinking the poisoned tea would have brought about his death whether or not he was treated in hospital.

10.2   Multiple Causation

The 'but for' test is generally a good guide as to whether a given factor was causally relevant or not. However, it is not a perfect guide. As Hart and Honoré (1985) point out, the test's major defect is that it rests on the assumption that there was, at the moment in question, only one set of conditions sufficient to bring about the plaintiff's injury. Where this is not so – in cases of 'multiple causation' – the test will produce misleading answers. Thus, if two raging fires converge and together burn down your house, applying the 'but for' test would lead to the absurd conclusion that neither fire was the cause provided that each was sufficient to cause the damage: whichever one we imagine not to have happened, we could only conclude that the damage would have resulted anyway. In these cases, it is generally accepted that the law puts aside the 'but for' test and addresses the more fundamental matter of whether the factor in question was necessary to complete a set of conditions together sufficient to produce the result. Looked at this way, it is clear that each fire was a cause of your house burning down as each fire, together with other conditions such as the way the wind was blowing and the presence of dry leaves on the ground, was sufficient to bring about the damage that occurred. Accordingly, if each fire was started through the negligence of different people, each of them would be jointly and severally liable for the harm. However, where one fire was attributable to natural causes, it may be that the person who negligently started the other fire could argue that, though her fire was a cause of the harm, she need pay nothing by way of compensation. To justify this contention, she would point to the rule that the aim of an award of damages is to put the plaintiff into the position she would have been in had she not suffered a tort: as your house would have burnt down by virtue of natural causes anyway, you are not entitled to any damages from defendant.

To be distinguished from cases such as that of the converging fires, in which there may be said to be 'additional causes', are cases involving 'pre-empted causes'. An example of this type of case is where a woman about to set out across the desert has a lethal dose of poison put into her water keg by one enemy and the keg emptied by a second; ignorant of this, she sets out on her journey during the course of which she dies. The 'but for' test is no help here: if the keg had not been poisoned, the traveller would have died of thirst while, alternatively, if the keg had not been emptied, she would have died from the poison. However, this is not a case like that of the converging fires where we can say that both factors were a cause, for the traveller in fact died of thirst and not of poison. In cases of this sort, we would say that the plan of the first enemy was 'pre-empted' or 'neutralised' by that of the second. The secret here, as Wright (1985) points out, is to ask what actually happened, not what might have done. Of course, this leaves open the question of the assessment of damages: can the second enemy argue that she need pay no compensation to put the plaintiff into the position she would have been in had she not suffered the tort, on the grounds that the plaintiff would have died on the journey anyway? It would be unjust to let this argument succeed and it might be combated by saying that, in assessing damages, the courts are to ignore any tortious injury the plaintiff would have suffered had it not been pre-empted by defendant's tort.

The issue of pre-empted causes commonly arises where a plaintiff suffers injury from two independent factors, operating successively, each of which would have been sufficient to cause the same injury in the absence of the other factor. In these cases, the approach elaborated above suggests that only the first of the two factors can be treated as a cause of the injury, the latter being pre-empted. In *Performance Cars* v. *Abraham* [1962] 1 QB 33, the plaintiff's Rolls Royce was involved, in the space of two weeks, in two collisions, each of which was caused by the fault of another. Either collision on its own would have necessitated a respray of the car. In an action against the second tortfeasor, the Court of Appeal rejected the owner's claim for the cost of the respray on the grounds that the loss did not flow from the defendant's wrongdoing. Translated into the terminology adopted above, the need for a respray arose from the first collision which pre-empted the second.

Where an action is brought in respect of the first of two successive factors, that factor will be regarded as a cause; however, the assessment of damages will raise tricky problems. In *Baker* v. *Willoughby* [1970] AC 467, the plaintiff was first run down by the defendant's negligent driving, suffering a stiff leg, and then shot in the same leg in a hold-up, after which the leg had to be amputated. With his stiff leg, the plaintiff had suffered a loss of mobility and a consequent reduction in his earning capacity; the loss of the leg, on its own, would have been sufficient to produce that same (and greater) loss of mobility and reduced earning capacity. The House of Lords rejected the argument that the defendant's negligence could only be regarded as the cause of that loss up to the time of the second incident, the second injury 'obliterating' the effect of the first. Consistently with the view adopted here, Lord Reid, speaking for the majority of the court, held that the original injury was still a cause of the disabilities and that the defendant was therefore liable even in respect of the period beyond the shooting (though inconsistently with that view, and surely erroneously, he said that the latter injury was a 'concurrent' cause of the disabilities). He thus treated the issue purely as one of causation and ignored the principle that, in assessing damages, the aim is to put the plaintiff into the position she would have been in had the tort not happened. This aspect of his speech attracted much criticism in the subsequent decision of the House of Lords in *Jobling* v. *Associated*

Dairies [1982] AC 794. This case differed from *Baker* in that the second (pre-empted) factor was the natural onset of a disease and not the tortious conduct of a third party. The defendants had been responsible for injuring the plaintiff's back and thereby reducing his earning capacity. Subsequently, the onset of the disease rendered the plaintiff totally unfit for work. Again the House of Lords had to consider whether the defendants continued to be liable for that reduced earning capacity in respect of the period after the second event, the onset of the disease. This time their Lordships took account of the aim of an award of damages and held that the plaintiff would be overcompensated if able to recover for the continuing loss. Accordingly, the defendants' liability ceased at the time of the onset of the disease. Yet, although the members of the House of Lords criticised the reasoning of Lord Reid in *Baker*, they accepted that that case might be correctly decided on its facts and were not prepared to rule out the possibility that the result reached in *Baker* might be appropriate in cases involving successive tortious injuries. This seems fair: as Lord Keith pointed out in *Jobling*, where two successive tortfeasors are liable to the plaintiff, 'it would be highly unreasonable if the aggregate of both awards were less than the total loss suffered'.

10.3   Proof of Causal Relevance

Where the plaintiff is injured in a car accident, proof of causal relevance is in practice a simple matter. Generally all she would have to do would be to produce witnesses who saw the defendant's car hit her. However, as we move away from this paradigmatic instance of negligence liability, we come across cases in which no number of witnesses could produce evidence that would allow us to come to a firm conclusion as to how the plaintiff was injured. In such cases, all we can do is talk in terms of probabilities. Typical of cases of this sort are those that involve disabilities that arise after medical treatment or exposure to some toxic substance. A example that provoked tremendous political controversy in the USA arose out of the use in the Vietnam War of the chemical Agent Orange, a defoliant employed as part of a modern-day 'scorched earth' policy by the US Army (see *Agent Orange Litigation* 597 F. Supp 740 (1984)). After the war, veterans claimed that exposure to the chemical as it was sprayed over the forests of Vietnam had caused them serious health problems and had produced congenital disabilities in their offspring. They sought to pin responsibility on the various manufacturers of Agent Orange whom they alleged had improperly failed to warn of the risks inherent in the use of the chemical. However, the veterans faced an uphill battle in making out a case for compensation for, although there was evidence that the incidence of health problems of those exposed to Agent Orange was abnormally high, there was no evidence that any individual had suffered those problems as a consequence of that exposure rather than through natural causes. Nor was there evidence as to which company had manufactured the particular quantities of Agent Orange with which each individual came into contact. These difficulties of establishing causation in individual cases forced the veterans to settle out of court for a level of compensation that fell far short of their original expectations.

The Agent Orange case neatly illustrates two different problems that plaintiffs might face in seeking to establish causation (see Fleming, 1988, pp. 252–63). First, there is the problem of the 'indeterminate plaintiff'. This arises in cases where it is not clear whether the plaintiff's injury was caused by negligence or by some other, non-tortious factor. This difficulty faced many of those involved in the Agent Orange litigation, as there was a pre-existing 'background risk' of contracting, without any contact with the chemical at all, many of the conditions from which the plaintiffs suffered. Secondly, there are cases in which the plaintiff's injury was certainly caused by someone's fault but it is not clear whose: these cases raise the problem of the 'indeterminate defendant'. In the Agent Orange litigation there was no evidence available with which to prove that it was one manufacturer rather than another that had produced the particular quantities of Agent Orange to which individual veterans had been exposed.

The normal rules of proof in civil litigation require the plaintiff to prove on the balance of probabilities that she has a good cause of action against the defendant. In cases that raise the problem of the indeterminate plaintiff or defendant, these rules may be thought to deprive the plaintiff of reasonable compensation and to weaken the incentive on the defendant to take due care. Accordingly, efforts have been made to get around the normal rules, either by awarding damages to represent the chance that the defendant caused the plaintiff's injury or by reversing the burden of proof.

In English law, such innovative ideas have as yet only been considered by the courts in the context of the problem of the indeterminate plaintiff. In this context, recent decisions of the House of Lords have rebuffed efforts to suggest that a departure from normal rules is justified (see Fleming, 1989a; Stapleton, 1988b). In *Hotson v. East Berkshire Area Health Authority* [1987] AC 750, the House was confronted with an argument that damages should be awarded to represent the chance that the defendant had caused the plaintiff's injury even though the plaintiff could not prove this on the balance of probabilities. The case concerned a teenage boy who had fallen from a tree in his school playground. He was subsequently taken to hospital where staff negligently failed to appreciate the extent of his injuries, with the result that treatment was delayed for several days. After the incident, the boy was found to be suffering from a permanent disability in his hip joint. Medical evidence suggested that it was likely that this disability would have resulted from the fall anyway, but that there was a 25 per cent chance that the boy would have recovered had he been treated promptly. In view of this evidence, the boy defined his claim as one for the loss of the chance that he might have recovered and sought 25 per cent of the damages that would be awarded in respect of disabilities like his if causation were not in dispute. The House of Lords robustly rejected this attempt to get around the normal rule that you must prove that your personal injury was caused by the defendant's negligence on the balance of probabilities.

In another recent case, *Wilsher* v. *Essex Area Health Authority* [1988] AC 1074, the House of Lords dismissed an argument that in exceptional cases the burden of proof should be placed upon the defendant. This argument was founded on the speech of Lord Wilberforce in *McGhee* v. *National Coal Board* [1973] 1 WLR 1, a case involving industrial dermatitis contracted by a worker in a brick kiln through exposure to brick dust (see Weinrib, 1975). The employers had negligently failed to provide showering facilities at the workplace, and this failure had increased the risk of dermatitis as brick dust was left caked on to the bodies of workers until they got home. However, the risk of contracting dermatitis was part of the job of a kiln worker and there was no evidence that the worker would have remained healthy had showers been installed. Sympathetic to the plaintiff's plight, Lord Wilberforce said that, in cases where the defendant had negligently increased the risk of injury to the plaintiff but there was no evidence that this had actually affected the plaintiff, the burden of proof should be reversed. As the defendant would inevitably be unable to discharge that burden, the loss would fall on her. In *Wilsher*, the House of Lords criticised Lord Wilberforce's speech and stated that he must be regarded as having dissented from the majority in *McGhee*. The House affirmed the rule that, where an injury might have been caused by negligence but might alternatively have been the result of factors for which no one could be held responsible, the plaintiff has the burden of establishing that it was the negligence more likely than not that caused her injury.

The cases cited so far deal with the problem of the indeterminate plaintiff. The problem of the indeterminate defendant, by contrast, has been curiously neglected by English lawyers. (In *Fitzgerald* v. *Lane* [1987] QB 781, the Court of Appeal overlooked the distinction between the two types of case but came to the conclusion advocated below. Deficiencies in its reasoning leave the status of that case questionable.) Where a plaintiff has undoubtedly been injured by another's negligence and the question is simply how, if at all, to allocate responsibility for that loss amongst a number of people who have behaved carelessly, the policy considerations are rather different from those that govern the case where it is by no means clear that the plaintiff has been made worse off by negligence. This observation explains the difference of result in the cases of *Baker* and *Jobling* above. Hence, we should not rule out the possibility that English courts might be prepared to accept innovations in the law of evidence when the problem is that of the indeterminate defendant rather than that of the indeterminate plaintiff. Cases in the USA and Canada have resorted to a reversal in the burden of proof in order to deal with hunting accidents in which there was no evidence as to which of two hunters fired the shot that injured the plaintiff, with the result that the loss was apportioned equally between them both (*Summers* v. *Tice* 199 P. 2d 1

(1948); *Cook* v. *Lewis* [1952] 1 DLR 1). More radically, the Californian Supreme Court was prepared to hold pharmaceutical concerns liable in proportion to their market share when it was not clear which of them was the source of a generic drug that had injured the plaintiff (*Sindell* v. *Abbott Laboratories* 607 P. 2d 924 (1980)). It will be interesting to see the reaction of English courts to such innovations if suggested to them in appropriate cases.

10.4 Selection from amongst Causally Relevant Factors

When we seek to identify the cause of a particular event, we do not ordinarily try to compile a list of all causally relevant factors. What we do is pick out one or other of them as particularly significant. Thus, in the car accident example given above, we might say that the cause of the accident was the icy road surface or drunken driving, but it would not be particularly illuminating to isolate the fact that all cars involved had petrol in their tanks, even though, indisputably, this was a necessary condition for the accident. Not everyone will pick out the same factors: our choice is determined by who we are and what we are trying to prove. This is shown by the following example (see Honoré, 1983): a man lives with his wife in an unhappy marriage, comes home drunk, quarrels with her, takes out a revolver which he possesses without a licence, and shoots her, whereupon she consults a quack who treats her unsuitably and she dies. To a marriage reformer, the cause of her death is the state of divorce law; to a teetotaller, it is drink; to a pacifist, possession of the weapon; to an upholder of medical interests, the activity of the quack. Ordinary people, however, have no time for this arid intellectualism: their response is more instinctive. Headlines in the tabloid press would scream 'Wicked husband brutally murders wife', and millions across the country would nod their heads in agreement. By and large, the law takes the tabloid line.

The 'tabloid line' reflects a highly individualistic political theory which demands that people take full responsibility for their deliberate actions and trusts in their ability to control the physical world around them. Accordingly, in selecting from amongst causally relevant factors, the law grants special status to deliberate human acts. Furthermore, it homes in on the deliberate human act that most closely preceded the outcome in question and will generally look no further for its cause. In doing so, the law assumes that the choice of whether or not to bring about the outcome lay entirely in the hands of the last actor: it refuses to let her 'pass the buck' and will not hold anyone else responsible for her actions. One product of this approach is that the pre-existing susceptibility of the plaintiff to injury of the type suffered is considered immaterial (see the 'thin skull' rule, 11.4). Another is the tendency to treat deliberate interventions by third parties, and deliberate risk-taking by the plaintiff, as intervening acts negating causal connection between the defendant's wrongdoing and the plaintiff's injury.

Of course, not all deliberate acts intervening between a defendant's wrongdoing and the plaintiff's injury will negative causal connection. Acts of irresponsible agents such as infants and those with mental disabilities will rarely do so (see *Kirkham* v. *Chief Constable of Greater Manchester* [1990] 2 QB 283). Even the deliberate acts of a responsible agent will not do so if those acts cannot be regarded as 'voluntary'. Where a pedestrian is knocked down by a car, taken to hospital and given emergency treatment which is known to be highly dangerous, her death in the course of this treatment will still be regarded as a consequence of the accident. The reason for this is that the doctors' actions in administering the emergency treatment cannot truly be said to be voluntary: their choice to pursue that course of action was not free but was forced on them by the circumstances. This will be true in all situations where the intervening act was done either out of self-preservation or out of a praiseworthy desire to save the lives of others (see 7.2).

A case which illustrates this, as well as demonstrating the tendency of the courts to obscure the issue by recourse to bewildering metaphors, is *The Oropesa* [1943] P 32. Two ships, the *Oropesa* and the *Manchester Regiment*, had been involved in a collision at sea for which they were both partly to blame. The weather was rough and, in view of the damage his ship had sustained, the master of the *Manchester Regiment* feared she might not stay afloat. He began to ferry his crew across to the *Oropesa* by boat; on its second trip, with the master and the deceased crew member whose family brought the action on board, the boat overturned and the deceased was drowned. The Court of Appeal had to consider whether the act of setting off in the boat negated causal connection between the negligence of the *Oropesa* and the death of the deceased. In reaching the conclusion that it did not, Lord Wright, who delivered the leading judgment, explained his approach in the following cryptic, but oft-cited, passage: 'To break the chain of causation it must be shown that there is something which I will call ultroneous, something unwarrantable, a new cause which disturbs the sequence of events, something which can be described as either unreasonable or extraneous or extrinsic.' As Hart and Honoré (1985) remark, 'It would have been simpler to say that the acts were done partly for self-preservation and partly in pursuance of what was at least a moral duty to save the lives of those on board.'

It is not only voluntary acts that may intervene to negate causal connection; abnormal acts and events may do so as well. Let us return to our example of a pedestrian knocked down by a car. Suppose now that she died in hospital only because the hospital staff, mistaking her for another patient, gave her the wrong operation. The staff cannot be said to have exposed her to risk any more voluntarily than before: they were still acting under the pressure of the circumstances. Yet the treatment was so wholly wrong that it would be unjust to hold the negligent driver responsible for her death. In cases where something totally out of the ordinary intervenes after the defendant's negligent conduct to bring about the result, we treat that intervention as negating causal connection. This is so whether the intervention is human, as where medical treatment is wholly wrong, or natural, as would be the case where the accident victim was killed when the ambulance ferrying her to hospital was hit by a falling tree. In all cases, the question whether the intervening act or event was sufficiently out of the ordinary to negate causal connection is a matter of degree (compare *Rouse* v. *Squires* [1973] QB 889 with *Knightly* v. *Johns* [1982] 1 WLR 349).

In summary, causal connection between the defendant's negligence and the plaintiff's injury is negated if (a) a third party or the plaintiff voluntarily brings about, or runs the risk of, that injury or (b) an abnormal human act or natural occurrence intervenes to bring it about. This, essentially, is the thesis advanced by Hart and Honoré (1985). The most common attack on this thesis is that it introduces policy considerations into what should be a purely factual concept (see Wright, 1985). However, Hart and Honoré (1985) are surely right in maintaining that the process of selection from amongst causally relevant factors is appropriately termed 'causal', for it merely reflects the distinction we make in ordinary speech between 'mere conditions' and 'the cause' of an event. This, of course, is not to insist that the causal enquiry is value-free. Indeed, as our values change, it may be possible to discern some difference in our, and the law's, use of causal language. Thus it may be that the advance of collective values at the expense of the individualistic values of pre-Welfare State Britain may prompt the law to relax its insistence that deliberate acts negate causal connection, and to hold responsible those who provide the opportunity for others deliberately to cause harm. To some extent, this has already happened with regard to landowners and public authorities (see 6.4 and 8.1).

Summary

10.1 The defendant's negligence will be treated as causally relevant to the plaintiff's injury if it was a necessary element of a set of conditions together sufficient to produce that injury. This requirement is sometimes presented in a simplified form as the 'but for' test.

10.2 The 'but for' test is not able to deal with cases of multiple causation and in such cases we have to employ the more fundamental notion of causal relevance. However, even if the defendant's action is treated as causally relevant, it may be that the policy of the law relating to the assessment of damages requires the court to take account of the fact that the plaintiff's loss would have occurred because of some other (non-tortious) factor anyway.

10.3 The plaintiff must prove, on the balance of probabilities, that her loss was caused by negligence rather than by natural causes. She cannot evade this requirement by framing her claim as one for the loss of a chance.

10.4   Not all causally relevant factors are treated as the cause of the plaintiff's loss. The law will ignore the defendant's causal connection to the plaintiff's injury where a 'voluntary' human act or an abnormal occurrence intervenes in point of time between the two.

Exercises

10.1   What is the 'but for' test? Does it always identify all the factors that may be treated as the cause of the plaintiff's loss? Does it identify them specifically enough or do we need to supplement it with different principles of causation?

10.2   How, if at all, can *Baker* v. *Willoughby* be reconciled with *Jobling* v. *Associated Dairies*?

10.3   Your employer is required to issue you with a safety harness when you work above ground level but has never done so. You are pig-headed and there is a chance that you would have refused to use one even if it was provided. If you were injured in a fall that would have been avoided had you been wearing a harness, how would a court decide if your injury was caused by your employer's neglect?

10.4   Explain the difference between the problem of the indeterminate plaintiff and the problem of the inderterminate defendant. Should the same considerations govern both?

10.5   How do the courts decide if the causal connection between the defendant's negligence and the plaintiff's loss is negated by an intervening act or event?

10.6   Is there sufficient causal connection in the following situations?

    (a)   A hits B and leaves her on the beach where she is drowned by the incoming tide.

    (b)   C hits D and leaves her on the beach where she is murdered by a robber.

    (c)   E crashes her car into a lamp post. A police officer negligently directs traffic around the obstruction and a collision ensues in which F is killed.

    (d)   G carelessly leaves the door of her house unlocked. Thieves walk in, break down a thin partition wall and steal property from H's house next door.

10.7   To what extent do the law's principles of causation reflect matters of policy?

11 Remoteness of Damage

11.1 The *Wagon Mound* Test of Remoteness

In order to recover damages in respect of injury caused by another's negligence, you must establish that injury of that type was a foreseeable consequence of the negligence. This rule – laid down by the Privy Council in the case *Overseas Tankship (UK) Ltd* v. *Morts Dock & Engineering Co Ltd, The Wagon Mound* [1961] AC 388, and subsequently accepted as correct in terms of English law – is one of a number of mechanisms by which the law limits liability for the consequences of one's negligence; most notable amongst the others are the principles concerning selection from amongst causally relevant factors and those concerning the existence and scope of the duty of care.

In the *Wagon Mound*, a fire started in Sydney Harbour had damaged a wharf belonging to the plaintiffs. The fire had begun when oil, which had carelessly been allowed to overflow from the defendant's ship, the *Wagon Mound*, was accidentally set alight. The Privy Council held that, while it was foreseeable that the oil spillage might foul the plaintiff's wharf, it was not foreseeable that the oil would be set alight and cause fire damage to the wharf. The claim in respect of fire damage was disallowed. It was not enough that some damage to the plaintiff's wharf was foreseeable; the plaintiff had to establish that damage *of the type that actually occurred* was foreseeable.

The justification for the rule is that it ensures that the defendant is not penalised excessively for her default. Under the law as it stood before the *Wagon Mound* decision, the defendant was held liable for all the consequences of her negligence so long as they were 'direct'. This requirement, which had been established by the Court of Appeal in the case *Re Polemis* [1921] 3 KB 560, strikes many as obscure and seems to do no more than reiterate the fact that an intervening act or event may negate the causal connection between the defendant's wrongdoing and the plaintiff's loss. In the *Wagon Mound*, Viscount Simonds suggested that the rule in *Re Polemis* might give rise to 'palpable injustice': 'it does not seem consonant with current ideas of justice or morality that, for an act of negligence, however slight or venial, which results in some trivial foreseeable damage, the actor should be liable for all consequences, however unforeseeable and however grave, so long as they can be said to be "direct".'

The *Wagon Mound* rule of remoteness applies elsewhere in the law of tort, for instance in the law of nuisance and, probably, with respect to breach of statutory duty and the rule in *Rylands* v. *Fletcher* (186) LR 1

Exch 265. However, it does not apply where the defendant intends to inflict injury on the plaintiff: in torts such as deceit and the economic torts, in which intentional injury is the gist of the tort, the plaintiff can recover in respect of all the direct consequences of the defendant's wrong under the rule in *Re Polemis* (see *Doyle* v. *OUay (Ironmongers) Ltd* [1969] 2 QB 158).

11.2   The Concept of Foreseeability Examined

Foreseeability in the context of the *Wagon Mound* rule of remoteness plays a rather different role from when it is employed in order to determine whether a defendant was negligent (in breach of duty). Its place in the latter enquiry is as one of a number of factors – others being the gravity of the possible injury and the burden of guarding against it – which must be considered before we can say whether certain behaviour was reasonable or not. The degree of foreseeability required before the defendant is branded negligent varies in relation to those other factors: running a risk of a certain probability will be reasonable in some circumstances but not in others. In contrast, the stipulation that the harm the plaintiff has suffered must be of a type that was foreseeable requires a court to look at the issue of foreseeability in isolation and to demand the same degree of foreseeability whatever the circumstances of the case.

That foreseeability is used in different senses in these two contexts is established by the case of *Overseas Tankship (UK) Ltd* v. *The Miller Steamship Co, The Wagon Mound (No 2)* [1967] 1 AC 617. This arose out of the same set of circumstances as the first *Wagon Mound* decision, but dealt with a claim by a different plaintiff. The fire in Sydney Harbour damaged not only the wharf belonging to Morts Dock, the plaintiffs in the first action, but also ships belonging to The Miller Steamship Co, the plaintiffs in the second. As we have seen, the Privy Council held in the first case that it was not foreseeable that the oil would be set alight and cause fire damage to the wharf. In the second case, different evidence was led, causing the trial judge to take a different view of the facts of the case. He held that it was in fact foreseeable that the oil might catch fire and the Privy Council held that he was perfectly entitled so to do. The trial judge went wrong, however, in going on to hold that this risk was too small to attract liability. This was an error because, once it had been decided that fire damage was a foreseeable possibility, the question was whether a reasonable person would have run that risk. In determining this, the degree of risk could not be looked at in isolation but had to be considered in the light of other factors such as the cost of averting the danger. The trial judge had not appreciated this and, while he had correctly analysed foreseeability in the remoteness context, he had fallen into error when it came to looking at it from the point of view of breach of duty. On the facts of the case, as the risk was not far-fetched, and as it could have been eliminated without expense simply by stopping the discharge, the Privy Council held the defendant ship-owners liable (see Dias, 1967).

11.3   The 'Type of Loss' Requirement

As we have seen, the plaintiff must show that the type of loss she suffered was foreseeable. It was for this reason that the plaintiffs in the first *Wagon Mound* case failed: their actual loss (the fire damage to the wharf) was of a different type from that which was foreseeable (damage by oil fouling). However, while the plaintiff must prove that loss of the type she suffered was foreseeable, she need not prove that loss of the same extent was foreseeable. Neither need she prove that the exact chain of events leading to her loss was foreseeable. The leading case is *Hughes* v. *Lord Advocate* [1963] AC 837. Road works being carried out by the Post Office were left unattended during a teabreak. There were paraffin lights around the site. Two boys sneaked on to the site to play. One of them knocked over a lamp which fell into a manhole and caused a violent explosion; the boy was badly burnt. The House of Lords accepted that the explosion had been unforeseeable but held that the boy's injury was not too remote as it was foreseeable that he might have been burnt by the oil in the lamp. The foreseeable risk that did not eventuate and the unforeseeable risk that did were both of the same type. As Lord Guest remarked, 'I cannot see that these are two different types of accident. They are both burning accidents and in both cases the injuries would be burning injuries.'

Although some parts of their Lordships' speeches in *Hughes* seem to indicate the contrary, it seems that injuries might be regarded as too remote on the grounds that the chain of events leading to them was not of a type that might be anticipated. This would be so even where the injuries suffered were foreseeable. This is the premise of the Court of Appeal decision in *Doughty* v. *Turner Manufacturing Co Ltd* [1964] 1 QB 518. The case concerned an accident at work in which the plaintiff had suffered burns. The accident occurred when the cover of a cauldron of molten liquid was inadvertently knocked into the cauldron. The cover reacted with the molten liquid and caused an explosion in which the plaintiff was injured. The court held that, while it was foreseeable that an employee might be burnt by the splashing when the cover fell in the cauldron, the actual events that occurred were wholly unforeseeable and hence too remote from the original inadvertence.

The application of the *Wagon Mound* remoteness test requires the courts to make fine distinctions of fact and degree. Sometimes they have bent over backwards to ensure a deserving plaintiff is compensated (as in *Hughes* v. *Lord Advocate*); on other occasions, their application of the test seems inequitably restrictive in view of the plaintiff's injury and the defendant's negligence. A notable example of the restrictive approach is to be found in the case of *Tremain* v. *Pike* [1969] 1 WLR 1556. Tremain was a herdsman at the defendants' farm. The farm was overrun with rats and, through coming into contact with rats' urine in the course of his employment, Tremain contracted Weil's disease. Payne J held that the defendants ought to have foreseen the possibility of some illness or infection arising from the infestation but decided that the contraction of Weil's disease was unforeseeable and therefore too remote to be recoverable. Other examples in which the courts have taken a generous or restrictive view of the facts could be given. However, these cases seldom raise interesting points of law and an exhaustive look at them would be unwarranted. (For criticism of *Doughty* and *Tremain*, and for an ambitious attempt to impose order on the cases in this field, see Clerk and Lindsell, 1989, paras 10–151 to 10–157).

11.4   The 'Thin Skull' Rule

The 'thin skull' rule is a major exception to the requirement that the type of harm suffered by the plaintiff must have been foreseeable. Where the plaintiff suffers foreseeable injury as the result of the defendant's negligence and this triggers off an unforeseeable reaction which is attributable to the plaintiff's pre-existing susceptibility, the plaintiff can recover in respect of both foreseeable and unforeseeable consequences of the negligence. In such cases, the principle enunciated by Lord Parker CJ in the leading case of *Smith* v. *Leech Brain & Co Ltd* [1962] 2 QB 405 is that 'a tortfeasor takes his victim as he finds him'. The case concerned an accident at the defendant's iron works in which Mr Smith was hit on the lip and burnt by a piece of molten metal. As he had a premalignant condition, he was abnormally susceptible to cancer; shortly afterwards a cancerous growth, which proved to be fatal, formed at the site of the burn. The court allowed Mr Smith's wife to recover damages in respect of his death regardless of the unforeseeable nature of his fatal cancer; it was sufficient that the burn he had suffered was foreseeable. In the view of the court, the Privy Council in the *Wagon Mound* did not have any intention of making inroads into this 'thin skull' doctrine.

The effect of the thin skull rule is limited by the requirement that the injury that triggers off the defendant's susceptibility must be foreseeable. This can be illustrated with reference to the law on nervous shock. One who, lacking what Lord Porter in *Bourhill* v. *Young* [1943] AC 92 called the 'customary phlegm', is prone to psychiatric injury cannot recover for such injury unless a person of reasonable fortitude would suffer some such injury; however, if this is established, the thin skull rule operates to allow that person to recover even if the psychiatric injury she suffers is unforeseeably severe (*Brice* v. *Brown* [1984] 1 WLR 997).

11.5   Impecuniosity

The 'thin skull' rule does not apply to those whose loss is attributable to their abnormal lack of financial resources. In *Liesbosch Dredger (Owners)* v. *Edison (Owners)* [1933] AC 449, a vessel called the *Edison* negligently caused the loss of a dredger known as the *Liesbosch*. The *Liesbosch* was under contract to carry out certain work and, in order to complete these contracts, the owners of the *Liebosch* were obliged to secure the use of a substitute dredger. In the long run, it would have been cheaper to buy the substitute rather than hire it, but the financial position in which the owners found themselves precluded this. The House of Lords declined to allow the owners to recover the hire charges in full, limiting their damages to the cost of a replacement dredger. In doing so, their Lordships sharply distinguished cases that fell under the thin skull rule from those, like that before them, in which loss was attributable to the plaintiff's impecuniosity.

The harsh effects of this rule may, however, be avoided if it can be said that extra expense incurred by the plaintiff was not due solely to impecuniosity but, more generally, to 'commercial good sense'. In *Dodds Properties (Kent) Ltd* v. *Canterbury City Council* [1980] 1 WLR 433, the plaintiffs sought compensation in respect of damage caused to their garage by the defendants' building operations nearby. The damage was suffered in 1970 but the plaintiffs postponed carrying out repairs until after judgment had been given against the defendants in 1978, by which time the cost had soared. One of the reasons for this delay was the fact that the plaintiffs were very short of cash. The trial judge followed *Edison* in holding that the delay was due to the plaintiffs' impecuniosity, and therefore they could only recover the cost of repairs as they would have been in 1970. The Court of Appeal reversed this ruling, Megaw LJ distinguishing *Edison* on the grounds that '[t]he 'financial stringency' which would have been created by carrying out the repairs was merely one factor among a number of factors which together produced the result that commercial good sense pointed towards deferment of the repairs'. Amongst the other factors was the concern that, if the defendants were not found liable, the plaintiffs, limited resources might be better spent on another project.

Summary

11.1 The plaintiff must establish that the harm she suffered was the foreseeable consequence of the defendant's negligence. This is known as the *Wagon Mound* rule of remoteness.

11.2 The use of the concept of foreseeability in this context is rather different from its use as one of the factors determining whether the defendant was in breach of duty.

11.3 It is not enough that *some* loss to the plaintiff was the foreseeable consequence of the defendant's negligence: the same *type* of loss as that suffered by the plaintiff must have been foreseeable.

11.4. The 'thin skull' rule applies to allow the plaintiff to recover in respect of the unforeseeable consequences of the defendant's negligence when those consequences were attributable to the plaintiff's pre-existing susceptibility.

11.5 The 'thin skull' rule does not apply to those whose loss is attributable to their impecuniosity. The courts must take care to distinguish those who incur losses because of impecuniosity from those whose losses stem from reasonable caution in commercial affairs.

Exercises

11.1   What is the difference between the *Wagon Mound* and *Polemis* test of remoteness? Which torts take which test?

11.2   How does the role of the concept of foreseeability in the context of remoteness of damage differ from its role in the context of breach of duty?

11.3   According to what criteria do the courts decide if the harm that eventuates is of the same type as that which was foreseeable?

11.4   What is the 'thin skill' rule and how does it relate to the law dealing with the impecunious plaintiff?

---

12 Defences

12.1 Voluntary Assumption of Risk: Introduction

A plaintiff may be precluded absolutely from recovering damages for loss caused by someone else's carelessness on the grounds that she voluntarily assumed the risk of being injured in that way. This can mean either that she agreed in advance to give up any claim for compensation or that her conduct was so unreasonable that it would be wrong to allow her to recover (if you play with fire, you cannot complain if you get your fingers burnt). The next two sections of this chapter accordingly consider voluntary assumption of risk by agreement and voluntary assumption of risk by conduct in turn (12.2–3).

When faced with cases of this sort, the courts have adopted a pragmatic approach, preferring to reach a fair result on the facts rather than to seek a coherent doctrinal basis for their decision. They dispose of cases by reference to various legal concepts which they rarely seek to differentiate and which they seem prepared to use interchangeably. Chief amongst these concepts is the principle expressed by the Latin phrase *volenti non fit iniuria*. This is generally, if rather clumsily, translated into English by saying that one who voluntarily assumes the risk of injury through another's negligence cannot complain if that risk eventuates. The *volenti* principle is sometimes said to rest upon the plaintiff's *consent* to the risk in question. Such an analysis is hard to reconcile with the recourse made to the principle in cases of 'playing with fire' in which there is no express agreement, and its advocates are forced to adopt the tortuous argument that the plaintiff's consent in such cases can be *implied* from her conduct. This imports fiction into the law, and it is better to recognise that the real reason for denying the plaintiff redress in such cases is her unreasonable conduct. The position adopted here is that principles of voluntary assumption of risk are appropriate in both 'agreement' and 'conduct' cases. In the former, the language of exclusion and disclaimer of liability is often employed in preference to the language of *volenti*. In the latter, there is some overlap with the law relating to causation, for, where the plaintiff's unreasonable conduct intervened between her injury and the defendant's negligence, the courts may say either that the plaintiff voluntarily assumed the risk of injury in such cases or that the plaintiff was the author of her own misfortune, her conduct negating any causal connection with the defendant's negligence (see *McKew* v. *Holland & Hannan & Cubitts (Scotland) Ltd* [1969] 3 All ER 1621). For an attempt to rationalise the terminology employed, see Jaffey (1985).

It is important to bear in mind in this area that the question of whether the defendant has been careless at all must be considered prior to the question whether the plaintiff, by reason of her agreement or conduct, should be precluded from recovering compensation for the consequences of any carelessness. This has not always been appreciated by the courts who, on occasion, have made erroneous use of the principles of voluntary assumption of risk. This fault is particularly evident in cases which deal with injuries suffered by participants in, or spectators at, sporting events. The issue was fully discussed in *Wooldridge* v. *Sumner* [1963] 2 QB 43, in which a professional photographer covering the National Horse Show sought to recover damages after being knocked down by the defendant's horse; the horse had been taken too fast into a corner by its rider and had careered into a seating area. The Court of Appeal denied that principles of voluntary assumption of risk had any application in the case: the only question was whether the rider had taken reasonable care in the circumstances. As the circumstances were those of a fast-moving competition, not every error of judgment or lapse of skill would amount to a departure from the standard of the reasonable participant. Something akin to a reckless disregard of the spectator's safety was required and the rider's conduct fell far short of this. The practical reason for analysing these cases in terms of breach of duty rather than voluntary assumption of responsibility is to prevent the result depending on the identity of the plaintiff. The *volenti* principle can only be employed against responsible agents with knowledge of the risk in question: where does this leave the infant spectator struck in the face by the football or the passer-by outside the ground hit when the ball is kicked over the fence? If liability to such plaintiffs is to be denied, it can only be on the basis that the defendant did nothing wrong rather than that the plaintiff voluntarily assumed the risk.

Principles of voluntary assumption of risk have played a significant role in the history of tort law, though that role has decreased in recent times (see Cornish and Clark, 1989, pp. 499–500, 509–10). The product of an earlier and more individualistic age, the principles were used to shield entrepreneurs in post-Industrial Revolution Britain from claims by the victims of increasing industrialisation. Employees injured as a result of dangerous conditions at work were held to have voluntarily assumed the risk of that injury on the grounds that they were aware of the dangers; no heed was paid to the economic pressures that forced them to endure those conditions. The railway companies protected themselves against claims from passengers hurt in train crashes by issuing tickets only on terms that the companies were not to be liable for such injury. Gradually, however, the tide turned. The courts realised the harsh social consequences of regarding employees as having 'volunteered' to work in dangerous conditions: this could only be true if the employees had accepted additional wages as 'danger money' (see *Bowater* v. *Rowley Regis BC* [1944] KB 476). Futhermore, once the defence of contributory negligence was reformed in 1945, the courts were quick to have recourse to it where before they might have found a voluntary assumption of risk. The attraction of the reformed defence is that it allows the courts greater flexibility to apportion responsibility for harm suffered between plaintiff and defendant: whereas voluntary assumption of risk operates on an 'all-or-nothing' basis, as did the defence of contributory negligence up to 1945, the latter now empowers the court merely to reduce the defendant's liability by a proportion it thinks fair. These changes in judicial attitude were followed by significant statutory restrictions on the operation of the principle: successive Road Traffic Acts and the Unfair Contract Terms Act 1977 prevented defendants from relying on voluntary assumption of risk in cases involving, respectively, passengers in motor vehicles and some forms of 'business liability' (see 12.4).

12.2 Voluntary Assumption of Risk by Agreement

A person may voluntarily assume the risk of harm by agreeing in advance with the person responsible for the risk that she will not sue if the risk eventuates. Often this agreement will be enshrined in a contract as an exclusion clause: one only has to think of the small print on airline tickets or car-hire forms for examples of this. However, there need not be any contract and it will be sufficient that the plaintiff freely exposes herself to the risk after being informed that the defendant takes no responsibility for any harm that occurs. Thus, if the plaintiff enters premises after seeing a notice to that effect or, as in *Hedley Byrne* v. *Heller* (see 5.5), takes an economic stake in the success of a company after being told that assurances given about the company finances were made 'without responsibility', then she will be denied compensation if she is injured on those premises or loses money when the company fails (subject to the operation of the Unfair Contract Terms Act, below). The reason for giving effect to these non-contractual provisions is that the defendant might have relied on the plaintiff's agreement to those terms in placing herself in a position of potential liability (see Jaffey, 1985). Had she known that the plaintiff would ignore those provisions, she might have chosen not to let the plaintiff on to her premises or not to give her financial advice.

Where parties are linked together by a chain of contracts and sub-contracts, the principle of voluntary assumption of risk may allow the defendant to defeat the doctrine of privity of contract by allowing her to rely upon an exclusion clause accepted by the plaintiff in a contract to which the defendant was not a party. In such cases, the rules of contract law cause commercial inconvenience and attempts to evade them have created their own problems (see McKendrick, 1990, section 7.6). The way the principle of voluntary assumption of risk would operate in this area can be illustrated by considering a *Smith* v. *Eric S Bush*-type situation (see 5.7): you buy a house, trusting that the valuation survey commissioned by your building society mortgagee would have uncovered any structural unsoundness; the valuation report, submitted to the building society by an independent surveyor and passed on to you, is headed with the words 'without responsibility'. According to a strict contractual analysis, no clause in the contract between surveyor and building society could affect your rights or liabilities as you were not party to that contract. However, because the surveyor's exclusion was brought to your attention, you will be unable to sue unless the notice can be disregarded by virtue of the provisions of the Unfair Contract Terms Act (see further *Norwich City Council* v. *Harvey* [1989] 1 All ER 1180).

12.3   Voluntary Assumption of Risk by Conduct

Where a plaintiff exposes herself to a known risk, it is said that she will be barred from recovering if she did so 'voluntarily'. In this context, the concept of voluntariness is given a narrower definition than it is in the criminal law: many acts are regarded as non-voluntary even though the actor is in full possession of her senses and full control of her muscular movements. *Haynes* v. *Harwood* [1935] 1 KB 146, along with other so-called 'rescuer' cases, is a good example of this. In *Haynes*, considered above, horses, left unattended in a public place by the defendant's servant, were startled and ran off down a crowded street. The plaintiff police constable saw that people in the street were in considerable danger and averted that danger by grabbing hold of the horses and bringing them to a stop. In the course of this 'rescue', he was injured. The court ordered the defendant to pay him compensation, declining to find that the police constable had voluntarily exposed himself to the risk of harm.

The rescuer cases suggest that a plaintiff will not be barred from recovering where she exposes herself to risk only in order to avert injury to herself or to others. However, the circumstances in which the law will allow a claim for damages even though the plaintiff has knowingly exposed herself to risk go far beyond that sort of case. Thus, as we have noted, workers are rarely said voluntarily to have assumed the risk of injury suffered as a result of their dangerous employment. In hard cases, the notion of voluntariness provides little assistance as we try to decide whether the plaintiff should succeed or not; ultimately everything turns on the reasonableness of the defendant's actions. Suppose you are an aeroplane instructor. You take a novice on her first flight; her inexperience leads her to crash the plane on take-off and you are injured. In such a case, it seems that you would be able to recover damages from the novice (see *Nettleship* v. *Weston* [1971] 2 QB 691). But what if you had been injured after getting into a plane with a pilot whom you knew to be drunk? Your lack of any good reason for exposing yourself to the risk of injury might well cause a court to bar your claim for compensation (see *Morris* v. *Murray* [1991] 2 QB 6).

As contributory negligence is now the judges' favoured device for taking account of a plaintiff's unreasonable exposure of herself to risk, the circumstances in which a claim will be defeated by this branch of the defence of voluntary assumption of risk will be rare. The defence is most likely to arise when contributory negligence rules seem to be too generous towards a foolhardy plaintiff. This may be the case where the defendant has been just as negligent as the plaintiff, for the rules of contributory negligence require that the proportion deducted from the plaintiff's damages reflect her 'share in the responsibility for the damage' (Law Reform (Contributory Negligence) Act 1945, s. 1(1)). The word 'share' precludes the court from finding an extremely foolhardy plaintiff 100 per cent contributorily negligent, for then responsibility for the accident would be assigned to the plaintiff alone and not shared at all. However, the court can reach the same result by allowing a defence of voluntary assumption of risk. In his candid judgment in *Imperial Chemicals Industries Ltd* v. *Shatwell* [1965] AC 656, Lord Reid admits to having been influenced by these considerations. The case concerned two brothers, George and James Shatwell, who were employed by ICI as shotfirers, whose job it was to detonate explosives at a quarry belonging to the company. One day, when testing a series of some 50 explosives wired together, they found that one of the detonators in the circuit must have been a dud. They decided to test the detonators by passing an electrical current through each of them in turn. The law's mythical 'reasonable man' might have thought it safer to retreat some distance before doing this; however, reasonableness, on this evidence of this incident, was in rather short supply in the Shatwell family. George and James, acting contrary to company regulations, carried out the testing from close at hand. The predictable result was an explosion in which both men were injured. George commenced legal proceedings against ICI, alleging the company was vicariously liable for James's negligence. The House of Lords ruled that George had voluntarily assumed the risk of injury and hence could recover nothing. Lord Reid drew particular attention to the interplay between the rules of voluntary assumption of risk and those of contributory negligence. Noting that a finding of 100 per cent contributory negligence was impossible in the case before him, he said that, in view of the brothers' deliberate disobedience of the company rules and of their knowledge of the risk involved, it was appropriate to employ the complete defence of voluntary assumption rather than the partial defence of contributory negligence.

12.4 Statutory Restrictions on the Defence of Voluntary Assumption of Responsibility

Two major pieces of legislation restrict the scope of the defence of voluntary assumption of responsibility. The first of these to be introduced was a predecessor of the current Road Traffic Act 1988. Section 149 of this Act provides that no defence of voluntary assumption of responsibility can defeat the claim of a passenger in a compulsorily-insured vehicle against the driver of that vehicle. The section makes it clear that this rule applies to voluntary assumption of risk both by agreement and by conduct. So accepting a lift from a driver who is clearly drunk can never deprive the passenger of a claim against the driver in the event of a crash, though the passenger would undoubtedly be regarded as contributorily negligent. As such a claim would be met out of the considerable resources of an insurance company, it would be unduly harsh to decline to let even an extremely foolhardy passenger recover nothing at all.

The second, and more general, piece of legislation to restrict the defence of voluntary assumption of risk is the Unfair Contract Terms Act 1977. This Act applies to liabilities in tort as well as in contract, and casts its net over non-contractual provisions such as notices which attempt to limit liability, as well as over contract terms. Two questions concern us here: when does that Act apply and what is its effect when it does apply.

In the context of the law of tort, the range of application of the Act can be put shortly as follows: the Act applies to all attempts to exclude or limit business liability for negligence. This short definition has three elements which we shall consider in turn: exclusions and limitations, business liability, and negligence.

Exclusions and Limitations

A defendant might attempt to exclude or limit her liability in various ways. In many cases, the most prudent course would be to make it an express term of a contract with the plaintiff that she should agree to waive any rights against the defendant in the event that she is injured by the defendant's fault. If contracting with the plaintiff is not practicable, then the defendant might put up a notice to the same effect where it will be seen by the plaintiff. For instance, a landowner might put a sign at the entrance to her grounds making it clear that those coming on to her land do so at their own risk. These are obvious attempts to exclude liability; less obvious are ingenious efforts to avoid the operation of the Act by trying to prevent any duty of care coming into existence at all rather than by seeking to exclude liability in respect of an admitted breach of duty. You will recall that liability under the rule in *Hedley Byrne* v. *Heller* has often been said to depend on an 'assumption of responsibility' by the defendant towards a plaintiff. Could all those facing possible *Hedley Byrne*-type liabilities escape the operation of the Act by the simple expedient of telling those who might rely on their advice 'I assume no responsibility towards you'? The answer – it is now clear – is 'No'. In *Smith* v. *Eric S Bush*, the surveyor who prepared the valuation report that Mrs Smith relied on in purchasing her house put words to that very effect on the front of his report; the House of Lords declined to accept the argument that the Unfair Contract Terms Act could not bite on such a provision. Their Lordships took the view that, if the effect of a provision was to exclude or limit liability, it did not matter one jot how that provision was phrased.

Business Liability

The scope of the Act, in so far as it applies to liabilities in negligence, is restricted to cases of 'business liability'. This phrase is given a technical definition in section 1(3) of the Act. Originally, the Act applied to all liabilities arising out of business activities or from the occupation of premises used for business purposes of the occupier, with 'business' referring not only to commercial ventures but also to the activities of public bodies. In 1984, the reference to liabilities arising out of the occupation of 'business premises' was amended to take account of the objections of farmers who thought it unfair that they should not be entitled to exclude their liabilities towards members of the public strolling across their fields and who threatened to restrict access to their land in response. Section 1(3) was accordingly amended, by the Occupiers' Liability Act 1984, so as to ensure that those injured on account of the dangerous state of land they had entered for recreational or educational purposes might be prevented from suing the landowner by an appropriate notice: liability in such circumstances would no longer be regarded as a 'business liability'. However, the amendment makes it clear that, where granting access to land for recreational or educational use falls within the business purposes of the occupier, the Act still applies. Hence, while Farmer Giles is free to exclude his liability towards those who wander through his fields without worrying about the provisions of the Act, Lord Fauntleroy cannot do the same to those who pay an entrance fee to stroll through his ornamental gardens.

Negligence

A brief glance at the Act gives the impression that it only prevents the exclusion or limitation of liabilities in the tort of negligence. This is somewhat misleading, for section 1(1) of the Act gives an extended definition of the word 'negligence'. As well as covering liabilities in the tort of negligence, the word also refers to breach of all other common law duties to take reasonable care as well as to breach of the common duty of care imposed by the Occupiers' Liability Act 1957. Curiously, 'negligence' is not said to cover breach of the duty owed to trespassers imposed by the Occupiers' Liability Act 1984. Perhaps this is because this duty is a legal minimum that cannot ever be restricted at all (see 14.8).

Having considered the circumstances in which the Act will apply, let us turn now to look at what effect the Act has in such circumstances. This can be dealt with briefly. Everything depends on the type of loss of which the plaintiff complains. Where that loss is death or personal injury, the Act prevents any exclusion or limitation of liability at all (s.2(1)). Where the plaintiff merely suffers property damage or pure economic loss, then section 2(2) allows the defendant to exclude or restrict her liability in so far as the contractual term or notice in question is reasonable. It is not possible exhaustively to catalogue all the factors that may be taken into account in assessing the reasonableness of an exclusion or restriction of liability: different factors will be relevant depending on the circumstances. An example of how this enquiry is carried out can be found in *Smith* v. *Eric S Bush*, in which the House of Lords considered the reasonableness of the surveyors' attempted exclusion of liability. In deciding that the notice was not reasonable, their Lordships took account of the inequality of bargaining power favouring the surveyors, the 'low risk' nature of the task they were performing and the ease with which they could obtain liability insurance. Had the property been destined for commercial use, however, their Lordships felt that the result might have been different.

12.5 Contributory Negligence

Until 1945, contributory negligence operated like voluntary assumption of risk to bar a plaintiff's claim completely. This rule, which operated no matter how trivial the plaintiff's fault, came to be regarded as unduly repressive and the courts devoted considerable ingenuity to defeating its effect. Pressure for reform was met with the introduction – in the Law Reform (Contributory Negligence) Act 1945 – of a new regime which gave a court freedom to reduce an award of damages 'to such an extent as the court thinks just and equitable having regard to the claimant's share in the responsibility for the damage' (section 1(1)). As we have seen (12.3), the word 'share' prevents the plaintiff being found 100 per cent contributory negligent.

The defence does not depend on the plaintiff owing the defendant a duty of care: the only question is whether the plaintiff had taken due care in ensuring her own safety. This is assessed according to an objective standard, attaching weight to much the same factors as determine whether a defendant was in breach of duty. Hence, the degree of care demanded of someone placed in an emergency situation by the defendant's negligence is lower than that demanded of one who can respond in a considered fashion (see *Jones* v. *Boyce* (1816) 1 Stark 493). The words of the statute make it clear that the rules of contributory negligence only operate where there is some causal link between the plaintiff's conduct and the harm she suffers: if she is injured in a head-on car crash, it would be no defence for the negligent driver of the other vehicle to point to the fact that she had been driving without brake lights.

The defence of contributory negligence represents a powerful weapon in the hands of defence lawyers during the out-of-court settlement process (see 23.5). As judges are left with a great deal of discretion as to the appropriate level of deduction to make in individual cases, raising the defence may contribute to the uncertainty playing on the plaintiff's mind and induce her to accept an early, and hence low, offer of settlement. Plaintiffs are fearful of the risks inherent in personal injuries litigation. Their concern is not only that they might lose their case, but also that they might not win it handsomely enough. If the defendant has made a payment of an offer of settlement into court, and if the damages eventually awarded to the plaintiff are lower than that payment, then the court will penalise the plaintiff for continuing with her case by declining to make the usual order for costs against the losing defendant. In such circumstances, the more uncertainty surrounding the plaintiff's prospects of success, the greater the 'downside risk' will weigh in her mind. Things are improved somewhat by the courts' willingness to lay down fixed percentage reductions in certain frequently occurring types of case, a practice first approved by the Court of Appeal in *Froom* v. *Butcher* [1976] QB 286. For instance, the standard deduction where a car driver injured in a crash would have escaped injury had she been wearing a seat-belt is 25 per cent. Use of these fixed percentage reductions makes it more difficult for defence lawyers to 'bully' injured plaintiffs into accepting a low offer of settlement.

12.6 Illegality

The English law of tort recognises a defence of illegality. It would undermine the authority of law if unlawful activity were condoned by the award of damages to those who break the law. Furthermore, depriving law-breakers of a remedy in damages might serve to make them think twice about pursuing their wrongful conduct. Yet the law does not go so far as to brand all those who have in the past engaged in unlawful conduct, or even those engaging in unlawful conduct at the time of their loss, as 'outlaws' for the purposes of tortious compensation. It would be Draconian, for instance, wholly to disallow a claim for damages following a traffic accident just because the plaintiff was breaking the speed limit at the time the defendant negligently veered into her path. Sometimes illegality will defeat a claim and sometimes it will not, and the question of when precisely it will do so has provoked much controversy.

The English courts have varied between two approaches: some have applied a 'public conscience' test, asking whether allowing recovery would be an affront to the public conscience; others have declared it impossible to determine an appropriate standard of care where two parties to a joint illegal enterprise have absolved each other from acting according to normal standards (the 'adjudication is impossible' approach). The latter approach can be illustrated by reference to a popular imaginary example in which two safeblowers set out to burgle a house, only for one of them to detonate the explosives too soon, injuring the other. In such a case, it is alleged, it would be impossible for a court to prescribe what precautions the burglars should have taken for they have no way of knowing how burglars might respond to the exigencies of the situation (footsteps upstairs, police sirens wailing in the distance, etc). It seems that this approach is in the ascendant. In *Pitts* v. *Hunt* [1991] 1 QB 24, the plaintiff, Pitts, and his friend, Hunt, had spent the night drinking at a disco before setting off home on a motorcycle, driven by Hunt with Pitts riding pillion. Encouraged by Pitts, Hunt drove in a dangerous manner designed to frighten other road users. The motorcycle crashed: Hunt was killed and Pitts was injured. The Court of Appeal held that Pitts's claim for damages against Hunt's estate was barred by the defence of illegality. The majority of the court based its decision on the fact that it was impossible to set a standard of care for a course of criminal conduct, Dillon LJ expressly rejecting the public conscience test. In his view, that test was unsatisfactory because the reaction of the public to the compensation of wrongdoing plaintiffs might be affected by irrational considerations (such as factors of an emotional nature) and because it would be impossible to draw a graph of moral turpitude that would separate those plaintiffs who should succeed from those who should not. The 'adjudication is impossible' approach of the majority, however, is flawed (see the powerful arguments of Brennan J in *Gala* v. *Preston* (1991) 172 CLR 243). It is a fiction to say that it is impossible to determine a standard of care for those involved in unlawful ventures: even if we take the case of the safe-blowing burglars, it is not hard to see that, by any standard, it is careless for the burglar with the plunger to detonate the charge while the other is attaching gelignite to the safe. Furthermore, the courts are well used to altering their view of the conduct required of the defendant in the light of the exigencies of her situation: a police officer engaged in a high-speed car chase need not obey the same rules of the road as ordinary drivers. In any case, this approach can have no application where only the plaintiff, and not the defendant, was involved in a criminal venture (for instance, the cat-burglar who plunges to the ground when the tiles of the defendant's roof give way).

In truth, the courts have responded to the problem of the wrongdoing plaintiff in a way that is more intuitive than reasoned. Their approach is thus more akin to the 'public conscience' test. Where the plaintiff's wrongdoing consists in a breach of a law passed for her own benefit, the court is unlikely to deprive her totally of her remedy. This argument is most likely to succeed in the context of workplace accidents arising out of an agreement between employer and employee to 'cut corners' in breach of the law relating to health and safety at work (see *Progress and Properties* v. *Craft* (1976) 135 CLR 651). Where the law cannot be said to have been passed for the plaintiff's benefit, the court will attach importance to the seriousness of the offence and also to the closeness of the link between the plaintiff's injury and her unlawful conduct. In our safe-blowing burglars example, the injured party would be unable to recover if she was blown up by her colleague: her injury would have been sustained in the course of criminal conduct. Neither would she get compensation if she sustained her injury in a crash which brought to an end their high-speed getaway: this was a risk that she brought upon herself (see *Ashton* v. *Turner* [1981] QB 137). However, she would probably succeed in a suit against her accomplice if the latter crashed the getaway car well away from the scene of the crime when there was no longer any imediate pressure to avoid detection: in this case, her injury would be merely coincidental to her wrongdoing.

So far we have looked at cases in which illegality bars the plaintiff's claim in its entirety. In other cases, the courts have ruled out only part of the plaintiff's claim on the grounds that it would offend public policy to allow recovery of particular heads of damage (for instance, where the plaintiff requests damages for loss of earnings derived from her career as a burglar: see *Burns* v. *Edman* [1970] 2 QB 541). The courts would describe their approach to this sort of case as pragmatic, though others would regard it as merely arbitrary. A striking example is *Meah* v. *McCreamer* [1985] 1 All ER 367, [1986] 1 All ER 943. The litigation arose out of a car crash caused by McCreamer's negligence, in which Meah suffered brain damage which brought on a change in personality. Some years later, Meah perpetrated a number of violent sexual attacks, for which he was convicted and imprisoned; he was also successfully sued by two of the victims of the assaults. In two successive cases against McCreamer, he sought damages first in respect of the time he spent in prison and then in respect of the compensation he was required to pay his victims. Although both claims were founded on the same criminal conduct, Woolf J allowed only the first, arbitrarily disqualifying the second as offensive to public policy.

Summary

12.1 The defence of voluntary assumption of responsibility operates as a total bar to the recovery of damages. It only comes into play if the defendant was in fact careless, and care should be taken not to invoke the defence unnecessarily in cases where the defendant has done nothing wrong. The role of the defence has diminished as a result of legislative changes.

12.2 A plaintiff voluntarily assumes the risk of injury if she agrees to a contractual exclusion clause or a non-contractual disclaimer of liability.

12.3 A plaintiff may also voluntarily assume the risk of injury if her conduct was so foolhardy that it would be wrong to allow her to recover damages.

12.4 The ability of the defendant to make out the defence of voluntary assumption of risk has been restricted by statute. The defence will not operate against passengers in motor vehicles; neither will it be effective in many cases of business liability.

12.5 Since 1945, the defence of contributory negligence has operated to reduce, by an amount considered just by the court, the damages recovered by a plaintiff who shared responsibility for her injury.

12.6 Where the plaintiff was engaged in unlawful activity at the time of her injury, she may be barred from recovering damages by the defence of illegality, though certain unlawful acts may be deemed insignificant.

Exercises

12.1 In what circumstances will the defence of voluntary assumption of risk arise? Is the defence based exclusively on agreement?

12.2 Do you agree with Lord Reid (in *ICI* v. *Shatwell*) that voluntary assumption of risk is 'a dead or dying defence'? If so, why is this the case?

12.3 Would the case of *Hedley Byrne* v. *Heller* (see 5.5) still be decided the same way now that the Unfair Contract Terms Act 1977 has come into force?

12.4. What advantages are there in developing a set of tariffs to deal with commonly recurring types of contributory negligence?

12.5 When will the fact that the plaintiff has engaged in illegal activities be relevant in a tort action?

12.6 F and G, both aged 14, decide to go cycling on their tandem one afternoon. After cycling for a while, they decide to stop for some liquid refreshment and go into an off-licence where they are served by H. F asks for a six-pack of Lodgers Extra Strength lager for each of them, adding jokingly that 'Cycling up the hills should be a good deal easier after drinking that lot.' H sells them the lager. F and G get back on their tandem and cycle several more miles, drinking as they go. Rather the worse for alcohol, they decide to start a 'Mexican wave', which involves each of them in turn standing up on the pedals and waving her hands in the air. As they are doing this, F, who is steering, loses control of the tandem and both are involved in a head-on collision with J. J's car is dented and one of the tyres is punctured. Nevertheless, J decides to drive F and G to the hospital. However, on the way, she loses control of the car because of the punctured tyre. The car crashes into a ditch, causing extensive damage to the bodywork but no further injury to those in the car. J asks her neighbour K, who is a keen DIY car-repairer, if she would fix the bodywork on her car. K replies that she 'will have a go'. K makes a mess of the job and J has to have the car repaired professionally at considerably greater cost than would have been necessary before K had done any work on it. Advise the parties as to their rights and liabilities in tort.

Part II

Interference with the Person and Personal Property

13 Interference with the Person and Personal Property

13.1 Overview

Having considered the tort of negligence, we begin now our discussion of the remaining torts that feature on the typical tort syllabus. As we stated above, these are to be grouped according to the interests they may be said primarily to protect (see 1.3). Here we deal with torts which protect against interference with the person and personal property. Subsequent parts of the book deal with interest in land (Part III) and interests in reputation and privacy (Part IV). In each of these areas, we consider the impact made by the tort of negligence and the distinctive contribution made by other tortious causes of action.

In the context of interference with the person and with personal property, the tort of negligence has had a significant impact. As a practical matter, it has tended to marginalise the older common law torts. As a matter of strict law, it has led the courts to regard the distinctive features of other torts as anomalous, and consequently to eliminate those features. However, a number of older common law torts continue to play a valuable role in the law today. The most important of these are listed below:

Trespass to the person is the label affixed to a group of torts, actionable without proof of damage, which deal with 'direct' violations of the person or of personal liberty. The group consists of *assault*, *battery* and *false imprisonment*. These are considered in Chapter 17.

Wrongful interference with goods (not considered elsewhere in this book) is also a name given to a group of torts, this time dealing with injury to personal property rather than to the person. Amongst them are *trespass to goods*, which consists in any unjustified 'direct' interference with goods (e.g., snatching your wallet, kicking your dog or ramming your car) and *conversion*, which consists in unjustified and wilful taking away, detention, disposal or destruction of goods in a manner inconsistent with the rights of another. If nothing done to the goods is inconsistent with another's rights, the only action is in trespass. Thus my stealing your ball is both a trespass and conversion, but my grabbing your ball to throw it at someone else is only a trespass, for I am not questioning your rights over it.

Liability for animals, an example of strict liability (i.e. liability without fault), developed in the early days of the common law. It was expressed in two common law rules, the first concerning *cattle trespass*, the second dealing with the infliction of harm by dangerous animals whose vicious propensity was known – actually or imputedly – by their keeper (the *scienter* action). The common law actions were abolished, and the principles of strict liability in relation to the keeping of animals codified, by the Animals Act 1971.

The emergence of the tort of negligence, and of the ideology that underpins it, has influenced the legal development of the other torts and led to their marginalisation in practice. These processes are evident when we consider the relationship between negligence and trespass to the person. The influx of notions of negligence into the legal definition of trespass is traced below (see 17.1). As trespass became increasingly assimilated to negligence, it was tempting to regard as anomalous those exceptional cases in which liability might arise in the former but not in the latter (e.g. where the plaintiff suffers no damage). The result has been an attempt to eradicate those anomalies by treating unintentional interference with the person as giving rise to liability in negligence alone (*Letang* v. *Cooper* [1965] 1 QB 232; see 17.2) As a matter of practice, however, negligence had long since supplanted trespass as the principal action for personal injuries. Although negligence could not be regarded as a comprehensive and self-contained tort until *Donoghue* v. *Stevenson*, liability for negligence in various contexts was established centuries before. In such contexts (e.g. running-down cases on the highway), it was preferable for plaintiffs to frame their actions in negligence, as the scope of the action of trespass was limited and uncertain. Crucially, there were doubts as to whether the requirement of trespass that the interference be caused by 'direct' means was satisfied where a collision on the highway was caused by negligence rather than by wilful conduct (see Baker, 1990, pp. 466–7). By way of contrast, actions for negligence came to be allowed in respect of both 'direct' and 'indirect' damage (see *Williams* v. *Holland* (1833) 10 Bing 112) and so the risk of losing one's case on the pleadings was reduced.

Weir (1992) has noted wryly that 'Negligence is always trying to edge out the other torts. . . [but]. . . a few torts have managed to survive the competition' (p. 313). The torts considered in the subsequent chapters of this part of the book may be numbered amongst them. They are not mere historical relics. The various forms of trespass to the person (see Chapter 17) retain a practical importance in the protection of civil liberties and the vindication of individual rights. Furthermore, various statutory torts provide a more satisfactory remedy than the tort of negligence. One reason for this is that the availability of an action in negligence may be limited by restrictions on the scope of the duty of care (as was the case in relation to occupiers' liability: see Chapter 14). Another reason is that a number of statutes impose liability that is 'strict', in the sense that negligence on the part of the defendant need not be established (see Chapters 15 and 16).

13.2 Fault-Based and Strict Liability

When considering the role of fault in tort liability throughout history, three phases can be distinguished.

1. Early tort actions seem little concerned with fault. This was probably because the age was unmechanical and it was difficult for people at the time to conceive of harm being caused other than intentionally. If the fact that the defendant took all reasonable care was recognised as an excuse, this does not appear in the law reports of the time (see Baker, 1990, pp. 456–9).

2. With increasing industrialisation all this changed. Accidents at the workplace and on the roads, railways and shipping routes became frighteningly common. Infant industry, its existence still precarious, feared being crippled by liabilities imposed by the law of tort. To limit these liabilities, it adopted the standard 'No liability without fault'. Where industry was not threatened, by contrast, liability might well be recognised as strict, as was the case with the *scienter* action.

3. The advent first of workers' compensation schemes (1897) and then of the social welfare state (1946) reflected a change in society's attitudes to its responsibilities for the unfortunate. Industry was now established and producing enough wealth to safeguard its future even if it were exposed to an increased level of tortious liabilities. Many people came to feel that industry had a responsibility towards those who were injured by its activities, irrespective of whether anyone was at fault. In a startling piece of judicial innovation, the courts in *Rylands* v. *Fletcher* recognised strict liability in respect of damage caused by the escape of water from a reservoir used to power the defendant's mill (see Chapter 20). The courts also began to recognise liability for the breach of strict statutory duties imposed upon employers and others, even when no statutory remedy was prescribed (see Chapter 16). The spirit of reform has enveloped the legislature as well, notably in the field of product liability (see Chapter 15).

The rationale of strict liability is that it is unfair for the community at large to benefit at the expense of the individual. The community benefits from risky activities carried out in industrial and other spheres, activities which have their inevitable cost in the injuries suffered by employees, consumers and others. The wealth generated by industry could well be employed to provide compensation for the victims of the machine age. The rationale of strict liability can be contrasted with that of negligence liability. Whereas the latter focuses upon the defendant's wrong and treats that as the reason for requiring him to compensate the victim, strict liability assumes that the defendant's conduct was blameless but nonetheless requires him to compensate the victim as the price of pursuing his activities. The compensation paid may be viewed as a tax on, or license fee for, those activities.

13.3 Compensation for Personal Injuries

As we have just seen, a more general response to increasing welfarism than the recognition of strict liability in certain areas was the introduction of workers' compensation schemes and subsequently of social security benefits. Once the principle of compensation out of public funds and irrespective of fault became established, a collision of ideals between the social welfare state and the common law of tort was inevitable. The continuing relevance of the law of tort as a means of providing compensation for personal injuries was now open to doubt.

The centrepiece of any discussion of the role of tort law in compensation for personal injury is the report of a Royal Commission on Civil Liability and Compensation for Personal Injury, chaired by Lord Pearson, which was presented to Parliament in 1978. The Commission had been set up in 1972 amid public concern about the Thalidomide cases. These cases had fuelled debate about the place of tort law in modern society and had stimulated a number of calls for tort law's abolition. Providing ammunition for those making such calls were the reports of government-appointed teams of enquiry in New Zealand (1967) and Australia (1974), both chaired by Mr Justice Woodhouse. The reports concluded that tort claims in respect of personal injury should be abolished and replaced by comprehensive schemes providing compensation irrespective of whether anyone else could be proved to be responsible for the injury. These factors generated the expectation that the Pearson Commission would recommend the abolition of the tort system in respect of accidental injury. However, this was not to be.

The Pearson Commission took the view that its terms of reference precluded it from considering whether tort should be abolished. It had been directed to consider when and how compensation should be paid in respect of death or personal injury caused at work, on the roads, by defective products or services, on other people's premises or otherwise through the acts or omission of another. As a large proportion of injuries, notably many of those suffered in the home, fell outside these terms, the Commission felt unable to recommend a comprehensive scheme dealing with all personal injury. Having reached this controversial conclusion, it was inevitable that the Commission would base its detailed recommendations on the assumption that tort should continue to have a major role in any accident compensation strategy. As the Commission pointed out, unless a comprehensive compensation scheme were in operation, 'the abolition of tort for personal injury would deprive many injured people of a potential source of compensation, without putting anything in its place'. Accordingly, the Pearson Commission recommended the retention of a 'mixed system' of accident compensation.

13.4 The Mixed System of Accident Compensation

The mixed system that the Pearson Commission wished to perpetuate was and is one in which social security is the primary method of providing compensation and the role of tort law is supplementary. As a system of compensation, tort law suffers from a number of drawbacks in comparison with social security, being of limited scope, costly and prone to delay. In terms of the scope of its coverage, it is social security which ensures that the needs of the vast majority of those who have been injured are met. The Pearson Commission found that, whereas over 1.5 million of those suffering personal injury receive social security payments, only 215 000 (6.5 per cent) of them obtain tort damages. Those whose condition stems from illness rather than accident are particularly unlikely to recover in tort. As Stapleton (1986a) points out, even those who suffer from 'manmade disease', and who are therefore potential tort claimants in that they at least have a defendant to pursue, may find their case runs up against insurmountable obstacles. In particular, it may prove impossible to establish more than the fact that exposure to a certain substance may cause injuries of the sort suffered by the claimant, which is not sufficient to satisfy the causal requirement that the plaintiff was in fact injured in a certain manner (see 10.3).

In terms of cost, tort again suffers in comparison: lawyers charge breathtaking fees, insurance companies devote considerable resources to handling claims and valuable court time is taken up with determining liability and assessing damages. Taking all such factors into account, the Pearson Commission estimated that the operating costs of the tort system amount to about 85 per cent of the value of tort compensation payments; the equivalent figure for social security was about 10 per cent. These costs suggest that tort law is an inefficient means of channelling compensation to accident victims. The same story emerges from a consideration of the length of time it takes for accident victims to receive compensation. Although, according to the Pearson Commission, almost half of all tort claims are settled within a year, those alleging substantial losses often take considerably longer (sometimes over five years). A long delay before receiving compensation may place considerable demands on the resources of the victim, especially as he may be in no condition to work, may detrimentally affect his quality of life. This is exacerbated in the case of those whose condition may actually require them to spend money: someone who is crippled after an accident, for instance, may have to make alterations to his house in order to get about it freely. By way of contrast with the law of tort, victims of accidents or illness begin to receive social security benefits as soon as they need them.

Advocates of the tort system would argue, however, that the expense of running the system is justified. Adherents to notions of corrective justice, for example, maintain that those injured by another's fault have a claim to greater compensation than the bare minimum support provided by the social security system, even if their injuries are similar to those of people who have to make to without such support. (This view seems to underpin much of the Pearson Commission's thinking; contrast Atiyah, 1987, Ch. 19.) A different school of thought holds that the expense of the tort system is warranted on the grounds that the threat of liability serves to deter wrongdoing and leads to the most efficient utilisation of society's resources (see Posner, 19). For a comprehensive analysis of the competing theories, see Atiyah (1987, Chapters 22–24).

13.5   The Pearson Commission Proposals

As the Pearson Commission thought that recommending a comprehensive compensation system was beyond its remit and was committed to the continuation of a mixed system, its proposals for reform were rather limited. They amount to an effort to tinker with the tort system rather than a major overhaul. The Commission's aims were fourfold: (a) to make sure that tort compensation did not overlap with social security payments; (b) to give priority within the tort system to the most seriously injured and ensure that their interests were adequately looked after; (c) to introduce pockets of strict liability; and (d) to consolidate or extend 'no-fault' schemes of limited scope in certain areas.

(a)   The Prevention of 'Overlap'

In a mixed system of compensation, there is a danger that benefits from one source will simply duplicate those from another. The result is overcompensation. To guard against the possibility of overlap between the two partners in the mixed system of compensation approved by the Pearson Commission, the Commission made a number of recommendations: the value of social security payments should be deducted in full from damages awards (implemented in part by the Social Security Act 1989; see 23.10); private medical expenses should only be recoverable where the plaintiff could show that for medical reasons it was reasonable to incur them (not implemented); and the value of being maintained by the NHS (the 'hotel element') should be taken into account in the assessment of damages (implemented by Administration of Justice Act 1982,. s.5; see 23.8).

(b)   Prioritising the Most Serious Cases

The Pearson Commission aimed to give priority within the tort system to those who would need it most by making radical changes to the law relating to the assessment of damages (see Chapter 23). First, many minor cases were to be removed from the system altogether by imposing a threshold in relation to non-financial loss. The Commission recommended that no damages should be recoverable for non-financial loss suffered during the first three months after the date of injury. Its rationale for this restriction was that it would leave the tort system free to concentrate on serious and continuing losses. Secondly, the Commission recommended that no damages for non-financial loss should be recoverable for permanent unconsciousness: the award of such damages could perform no useful purpose as the plaintiff would not be able to derive enjoyment from their use. Thirdly, the Commission proposed that, in cases of death or serious and lasting injury, compensation for post-trial financial losses should be paid on a periodic basis rather than in a single lump sum. The extra expense which would result from the operation of a system of periodic payments would be justified by the fact that the plaintiff would be more accurately compensated for what he had lost, namely his income, and better protected in the event of a change in his circumstances. None of these proposals has as yet been implemented.

(c) Strict Liability

The Pearson Commission considered that, in general, negligence should remain as the basis of liability in tort. However, the Commission recommended the introduction of strict liability regimes in respect of rail transport, defective products, vaccine damage, and things and activities involving exceptional risks (see Atiyah, 1987, pp. 143–9). The rationale behind this piecemeal approach is unclear; certainly, it was never fully explained by the Commission. Its reasons for emphasising the role of 'fault' as a precondition of tort liability seem largely sentimental and amount to little more than a repeated assertion that it would be unfair to hold those who cause accidents innocently liable to their victims. This ignores both the justifications for the imposition of strict liability (see 13.2) and the fact that much tort liability is already strict (e.g. breach of statutory duty: Chapter 16; vicarious liability: see Chapter 22). Even the tort of negligence manifests some characteristics of strict liability, for the standard of care it demands is that of the reasonable person and this may result in the imposition of liability even though there was nothing a particular defendant could have done to prevent the injury in question (see 9.2).

The only area in which the Pearson Commission's proposals on strict liability have properly been implemented is that of product liability, on which the UK was required to act as a matter of EC law (see Chapter 15). In relation to vaccine damage, the government, on which the strict liability was to fall, pre-empted the Commission's proposals by announcing that, subject to certain qualifications, severely vaccine-damaged children would be given lump sum payments of £10 000 (now increased to £20 000). Atiyah (1987), commenting on the preferential treatment of vaccine-damaged children as compared with other disabled children, concludes:

'One is left with the uncomfortable feeling that vaccine-damaged children are to be given more generous financial treatment because their parents have been able to mount an effective campaign, and for no other reason. There are signs that this sort of ad hoc, politically-motivated approach to compensation issues is common.' (p. 149)

(d) 'No Fault' Compensation Schemes

The Pearson Commission advocated the consolidation or extension of 'no fault' compensation schemes in three areas. No fault schemes provide accident victims with compensation regardless of whether their injuries were the result of anyone else's fault. In this, it resembles strict liability. It differs from strict liability, however, in that the money paid as compensation comes from a central fund rather than directly from the person who caused the accident. The Pearson Commission approved the basic structure of the existing industrial injuries scheme, although it recommended some improvements (the benefits are now payable as Statutory Sick Pay). It suggested that a new scheme be introduced for those injured on the roads. This has not been done, although the issue is currently under consideration in the Lord Chancellor's Department following a recommendation in the *Civil Justice Review*. Finally, the Pearson Commission submitted that a new social security benefit should be introduced for severely handicapped children (not implemented). In each of these areas, injured people were to retain their rights to tort compensation.

13.6   Comprehensive Compensation Schemes

The piecemeal approach of the Pearson Commission to the institution of no fault compensation schemes contrasts with efforts to implement comprehensive schemes elsewhere. As we have noted, the introduction of such schemes was first seriously considered in the common law world in New Zealand and Australia. The New Zealand accident compensation scheme was introduced in 1974 by legislation which at the same time abolished any claim to compensatory damages in tort for accidental personal injury; proposals to introduce a similar scheme in Australia were scuppered shortly afterwards as a result of a change in government.

The New Zealand scheme set out to achieve compensation and deterrence objectives (see 2.5) more effectively than under a mixed system. Its fundamental precept was that of comprehensive entitlement to compensation. Compensation was to be paid to all those suffering 'personal injury by accident'. This phrase included injuries suffered because of medical misadventure as well as occupational disease, though not ill health generally. The compensation provided by the scheme was to be paid on a periodic basis and was to be earnings-related. However, a limit was set to awards in respect of lost income at 80 per cent of pre-accident earnings subject to an overall maximum figure; the scheme's focus upon pre-accident earnings meant that no allowance could be made for prospects of promotion or other contingencies. Provision was made for the award of lump sums up to specified maximums in respect of non-financial losses. The scheme was to be paid for by levies on employers, the self-employed and vehicle licence holders, as well as out of general taxation. This allowed a deterrence element to be built into the scheme. Employers with good safety records could have a proportion of their contributions to the scheme refunded, while those with bad safety records might incur penalty rates (though some remain sceptical about the significance of these provisions).

The scheme became the envy of many in other countries. Its combination of the principle of comprehensive entitlement with administrative costs that proved to be very low (around 6 per cent of the sums paid out) led to it being treated as a model of enlightened reform. In so far as the scheme attracted criticism, it was for failing to go far enough, and many pressed for its extension to all cases of disease as well as accidental injury. Such calls ignored the financial strains that the burden of ensuring comprehensive compensation was already imposing on the scheme. These strains were such that major changes in the scheme became necessary. The Accident Rehabilitation and Compensation Insurance Act 1992, described in its preamble as '[a]n Act to establish an insurance-based scheme to rehabilitate and compensate in an equitable and financially affordable manner those persons who suffer personal injury', made several significant reforms in an effort to cut costs. First, it abolished the right to recover a lump sum in respect of non-pecuniary losses, replacing it with a weekly independence allowance for those left with significant disabilities. Secondly, it gives a restricted definition to the concept of 'medical misadventure' which, under the original scheme, had been viewed expansively by the courts. In many cases, it will now be necessary to prove that the misadventure was attributable to negligence in order to make a claim on the compensation fund. Last, the new scheme will be financed by premiums levied upon health care professionals as well as upon those who subsidised the original scheme; these premiums will be 'experience rated' in order to promote the deterrence objectives of the scheme.

The troubles of the New Zealand scheme have come as a rude shock to those who viewed it as a model for reform elsewhere. They throw considerable doubt upon the financial feasibility of operating such a scheme. Only time will tell whether comprehensive entitlement to compensation is a realistic goal for a legal system to pursue.

Summary

13.1 The emergence of the tort of negligence has put other torts concerned with interference with the person and personal property into the shade. Many of the latter have been assimilated to negligence in some measure. Nevertheless, they retain practical importance in some fields (e.g. the protection of civil liberties). Furthermore, tort liabilities imposed by statute may be more stringent than those in negligence.

13.2 Although the ideology expressed by the tort of negligence has dominated legal thinking since the time of the industrial revolution, the welfare values of the last hundred years or so have questioned whether fault should be a prerequisite of liability. The result has been the judicial recognition and legislative creation of pockets of strict liability.

13.3 Increasing welfarism has also focused attention on the way accident victims are dealt with by society. The role of tort law in providing compensation for personal injury, and its relationship with social security, was considered by the Pearson Commission.

13.4   The Pearson Commission recommended the retention of a mixed system of compensation for personal injuries in which social security would play the major role, but tort law would continue to provide – at a cost – higher levels of compensation for the privileged few.

13.5   The reforms proposed by the Pearson Commission were designed to ensure there was no overlap between tort damages and social security benefits, to prioritise the most serious cases in the tort system and to introduce areas of strict liability and no fault compensation. Many of these proposals have yet to be implemented.

13.6   A more radical solution to that found in the Pearson Report would be the institution of a comprehensive no fault compensation scheme. In such a scheme, an example of which exists in New Zealand, the entitlement to compensation would be available even to those whose injuries were not caused by fault and the awards would be paid from public funds. The extent of the financial burden imposed by such a scheme is evident from the New Zealand experience.

Exercises

13.1   What is strict liability? Can its imposition ever be justified?

13.2   What was the Pearson Commission? What were the principal recommendations that it made? Did these recommendations go far enough?

13.3   What is meant by talk of the 'mixed system' for compensation for personal injuries? Does every part of that system perform the task of compensating the needy satisfactorily? Does any part of that system perform any other tasks (please specify)?

13.4   What reforms would you advocate for the system of compensation for personal injuries?

---

14 Occupier's Liability

14.1 Introduction

This chapter is concerned with the liability of an occupier of premises for injury caused or damage done to persons or their property whilst on the premises. The law in this area is now statutory and is governed by the 1957 and 1984 Occupiers' Liability Acts. This chapter does not deal with the situation where things done on the occupiers' premises affect other premises; this is the province of the law of 'nuisance' and *Rylands* v. *Fletcher* (1868) L.R. 3 H.L. 330 (see Chapters 19 and 20). The 1957 and 1984 Acts replaced a somewhat complex regime of common law, distinct from that developed from *Donoghue* v. *Stevenson*, under which an occupier owed different standards of duty depending on the status of the person who came on to his land. Those entering under a contract were owed the highest duty, while progressively lower duties were owed to those entrants the law classified as invitees, licencees or trespassers. The position today is that the Occupiers' Liability Act 1957 governs liability to lawful visitors and the 1984 Act governs the duty owed to those entrants loosely referred to as 'trespassers'. In the first part of this chapter we will look at the Occupiers' Liability Act 1957.

14.2 Scope of the Occupiers' Liability Act 1957

The Act abolishes the fine distinctions drawn by the common law between invitees and licencees and treats them alike by substituting a single 'common duty of care'. This duty is owed by an occupier to all lawful visitors (including those entering under a contract) in respect of dangers due to the state of the premises and to things done or omitted to be done on them.

A number of general points as to the scope of the Act need to be made. First, premises are given a broad definition by section 1(3)(a) to include 'any fixed or moveable structure, including any vessel, vehicle or aircraft'. Along with land, houses and factories, such things as ladders, scaffolding, diving boards and even chairs have been held by the courts to be premises for the purpose of the Act. Secondly, the Act, by virtue of section 1(3)(b), extends to cover property damage incurred on the premises, whether the property be that of the visitor or of a person who is not a visitor. Thirdly, liability under the Act may also, by virtue of section 1(1), arise in respect of omissions. Thus in the recent case of *Stimpson* v. *Wolverhampton Metropolitan Borough Council* (Lexis 1990), owners of a public park, who knew that golf balls were regularly hit in the park and did nothing to stop it, were held liable to a visitor to the park injured by a golf ball struck by a third party. Finally, there has been some academic debate as to whether the Act gives rise to liability for injuries sustained due to activities carried out on the land as well as injuries sustained due to a defect in the state of the premises. The better view is that the Act can cover the former situation and such a view finds support in the judgment of Lord Keith in *Ferguson* v. *Welsh* [1987] 3 All ER 777, where he said,

> 'it may therefore be inferred that an occupier might in certain circumstances be liable for something done or omitted to be done on his premises by an independent contractor if he did not take steps to satisfy himself that the contractor was competent and that the work was being done properly.'

For most practical purposes this should not be of any importance because, even if injuries caused by activities are not covered by the Act, an action will in any event lie for negligence under the common law where, in effect, the same duty is owed.

14.3   Who is an Occupier?

The Act does not attempt a definition of 'occupier', but instead, in section 1(2), provides that an occupier is a person who would have been treated as such at common law. The leading case on the definition of an occupier is *Wheat* v. *Lacon* [1966] AC 552. In that case the defendants were owners of a public house, the management of which they entrusted to a manager. By virtue of the service agreement, the manager was entitled to live in a flat above the public house and to take in paying guests. There was no direct access between the pub and the flat, both parts having separate entrances. W and his wife were paying guests of the manager. W was fatally injured when he fell down an unlit and defective staircase in the flat. W's wife sued the defendants and the main issue was who was in occupation of the flat. The House of Lords held that, in determining who the occupier was, the important question was who had sufficient degree of control over the premises such that he ought to be under a duty of care to those who come lawfully on to the premises. Applying this test they said that the defendants were to be treated as occupiers for the purposes of the Act.

Although it is clear that the important question is one of control, it is more difficult to determine what is a sufficient degree of control for the purposes of the Act. Whilst an owner in occupation would no doubt have sufficient control, *Wheat* v. *Lacon* makes clear that an absentee owner may also retain sufficient control to be an occupier. In Lord Denning's speech in *Wheat* v. *Lacon*, he said that the defendants, although not in actual occupation, retained sufficient control because they had only granted a contractual licence to the manager to occupy the flat and had retained a right to enter to do repairs. This right was enough to make them occupiers.

On the other hand, if the defendants had let the flat to the manager, granting him a right of exclusive occupation, they would not have been occupiers for the purposes of the Act. In such circumstances the defendants would be treated as having parted with all control over the premises.

Wheat v. *Lacon* makes a further point clear. It is possible for two or more persons to be in occupation, for the purposes of the Act, at the same time. Thus, if the plaintiff had sued the manager it seems from the speeches of Lords Denning, Morris and Pearson that they would have held the manager also to be in occupation for the purposes of the Act.

To conclude, the question of occupation is to be decided in each case on the particular facts, having regard specifically to the degree of control exercised by the defendant over the premises. As has been seen, particular legal relationships or the fact of absentee ownership cannot be conclusive one way or the other, but are no doubt factors to be taken into account.

14.4 Who is a Visitor?

The occupiers' duty under the 1957 Act is only owed to lawful visitors. The Act does not define visitors but provides in section 1(2) that a visitor is a person who would at common law have been treated as an invitee or licensee. These two categories cover a wide range of entrants and essentially encompass all those who enter with the express or implied permission of the occupier.

Whilst this group is very wide, the Act also makes specific provision for other classes of entrant who were not invitees or licensees at common law and these deserve some mention. First, at common law, those entering under a contract (such as hotel guests or workmen carrying out building work), although not classified as invitees or licensees, were nevertheless afforded a high degree of protection. Section 5(1) of the 1957 Act now provides that in the absence of a specific term of the contract dealing with the duty owed to the contractual entrant, there will be implied a term that he is owed the common duty of care. The parties are, however, free to negotiate different terms which may provide that a more or even less onerous duty is owed.

Secondly, by virtue of section 2(6), those who enter premises for any purpose in the exercise of a right conferred by law, are treated as permitted to be there for that purpose and are thereby owed the common duty of care, whether or not they have the permission of the occupier. A policeman entering a house in execution of a search warrant or firemen entering to fight a fire are examples of such visitors. Persons using a public (*Greenhalgh* v. *B.R.B* [1969] 2 QB 286)) or private (*Holden* v. *White* [1982] 2 WLR 1030) right of way are not visitors for the purposes of the Act, although those exercising a private right of way are owed a duty of care under the Occupiers' Liability Act 1984.

As already mentioned, invitees and licensees were those people who entered with the express or implied permission of the occupier. Where the occupier expressly invites a person on to his premises, it is generally clear that that person is a lawful visitor for the purposes of the Act. Significant problems may, however, arise in determining whether a person has the implied permission of the occupier to be on the occupier's premises.

It is a question of fact whether or not a person's entry has been impliedly permitted and the onus of proving this rests on the person who asserts it. To take a simple example, a person who walks up an occupier's front path with the intention of paying a social visit, or of trying to sell something to the occupier, will be treated as having the occupier's implied permission to be there (*Robson* v. *Hallet* [1967] 2 QB 939). It may be that even where he enters for his own purposes (for example if his hat is blown off into the occupier's front garden and he enters to retrieve it) he will still be held to be a visitor. However, it is clear that a licence can be withdrawn provided this is done clearly and that the licensee is given a reasonable time to leave the premises.

Apart from these examples, it is somewhat more difficult to discern when the courts will hold that a person's entry has been impliedly permitted. The courts have on a number of occasions made it clear that such permission should not be implied lightly. Thus, mere knowledge that persons are entering the occupiers' premises will not generally be enough (*Edwards* v. *Railway Executive* [1952] AC 737). What must be shown is that in spite of this knowledge the occupier took no steps, or took insufficient steps to keep the visitor out. This can be illustrated by the case of *Lowery* v. *Walker* [1911] AC 10. People were in the habit of using the defendant's field as a shortcut on their way to the railway station. Although the defendant gave them no express permission to do so, he knew they used it as such and he took no steps to stop them. The defendant, without any warning, put a savage horse into the field which attacked and injured the plaintiff. On the facts the House of Lords held that the plaintiff was a lawful visitor.

In spite of these judicial warnings against being too ready to imply permission, the courts have in the past been unwilling to classify children as trespassers in circumstances where there seems little doubt that if the injured person had been an adult he would have been so classified. This has particularly been the case where a child has been injured on, or by, what to the child would appear a particularly attractive plaything (e.g., a railway turn-table in *Cooke* v. *Midland Great Western Railway* [1909] AC 229 or poisonous berries in *Glasgow Corporation* v. *Taylor* [1922] 1 AC 44). This willingness of the courts in such cases to imply a licence can probably be attributed to two factors: first, until recently trespassers were very harshly treated by the law, and secondly, most children would appear as very meritorious plaintiffs whom the courts would if possible wish to compensate. However, since the enactment of the Occupiers' Liability Act 1984, which substantially raises the duty owed to trespassers, the courts may well be less willing to imply permission in such circumstances.

Two further problems in relation to implied permission deserve mention. The first arises where, in contravention of an express prohibition by an employer in occupation of certain premises, an employee or independent contractor invites on to the premises a person who is then injured. This situation arose in *Ferguson* v. *Welsh* where the House of Lords held that in such circumstances the injured person would be a lawful visitor *vis-à-vis* the employer provided he honestly and reasonably believed that the employee or independent contractor was entitled to invite him on to the premises. In *Ferguson* v. *Welsh*. a local council engaged S to do some demolition work. The contract between them expressly prohibited S from sub-contracting the work. In breach of this, S arranged with W. Bros to do the work. The plaintiff who was working for W. Bros was injured as a result of unsafe working practices being adopted. One of the issues considered by their Lordships was whether, *vis-à-vis* the council, the plaintiff was a lawful visitor. The House of Lords held that he was. The plaintiff had no reason to know anything about the details of the contract between the Council and S, and thus it was reasonable for him to believe that both S and W. Bros were entitled to invite him on to the premises.

Secondly, even where a person has the permission of an occupier to enter premises such permission may be limited by time, space or circumstance. As Scrutton LJ said in *The Calgarth* [1927] p. 93, at p. 110, 'when you invite a person into your house to use the stairs, you do not invite him to slide down the bannisters'. However, this question of limitation is approached by the courts in their usual pragmatic way. Consider, for example, if a customer in a public house should wander into a private part of the building, in search of a lavatory, and in so doing should suffer injury. Provided he was not behaving unreasonably in searching where he was searching, even though he had no express permission to be there, he is likely to remain a lawful visitor (*Gould* v. *McAuliffe* [1941] 2 All ER 527n).

14.5 The Common Duty of Care

Section 2(1) of the Occupiers' Liability Act 1957 provides that the duty which an occupier owes his visitor is the common duty of care. This is defined in section 2(2) as 'a duty to take such care as in all the circumstances is reasonable to see that the visitor will be reasonably safe in using the premises for the purposes for which he is invited or permitted by the occupier to be there'. This duty, as Lord Denning pointed out in *Roles* v. *Nathan* [1963] 2 All ER 908, is really the same as the ordinary duty of care in negligence and thus the factors mentioned in the chapter on breach of duty (Chapter 9), such as the nature of the danger, the length of time the danger was in existence, the steps necessary to remove the danger and the likelihood or otherwise of an injury being caused, are equally relevant here. However, the Act also draws attention to two specific matters which are to be taken into account when considering the degree of care required.

First, section 2(3)(a) provides that 'an occupier must be prepared for children to be less careful than adults'. This gives statutory recognition to a fact of life which the courts have always taken into account: namely, that what may not be a danger to adults may nevertheless be a danger to a child. Thus the courts have held that it is careless for a local authority to plant a shrub with poisonous berries in a public park to which children have access, because it is known that children are attracted by bright berries and may try to eat them (*Glasgow Corporation* v. *Taylor*). Were an adult to eat one of the berries it is unlikely that the court would allow recovery because it is simply not foreseeable that an adult would be so foolhardy as to eat one. Whether or not something is likely to attract a child and therefore become a danger in circumstances where it would not be a danger to an adult is a question of fact to be decided in the light of all the circumstances. What needs to be emphasised is that where an occupier knows that children are in the habit of frequenting a particular place he must take account of that fact, and may be required to take greater care than he would do if children did not have access. Having said that, the courts have made it clear that occupiers may in some circumstances be entitled to rely on children being supervised by their parent. Thus, while it may be expected that children will be left unaccompanied in designated play areas, the same cannot be said of wasteland or building sites (*Phipps* v. *Rochester Corporation* [1955] 1 QB 450). As Devlin J said in that case:

> 'the responsibility for the safety of little children must rest primarily on the parents; it is their duty to see that such children are not allowed to wander about by themselves, or at least to satisfy themselves that the places to which they do allow their children to go unaccompanied are safe for them to go to. It would not be socially desirable if parents were, as a matter of course, able to shift the burden of looking after their children from their own shoulders to those of persons who happen to have accessible bits of land.'

The second specific matter highlighted in the Act is found in section 2(3)(b), which provides that 'an occupier may expect that a person in the exercise of his calling will appreciate and guard against any special risks ordinary incident to it, so far as the occupier leaves him free to do so'. This sub-section was extensively considered by the Court of Appeal in *Roles* v. *Nathan* [1963] 2 All ER 908. A central heating boiler produced a great deal of smoke when lit. On the advice of a heating engineer, two chimney sweeps were engaged to clean the flues. The engineer warned the sweeps of the dangers presented by fumes when the boiler was lit and told them not to clean the flues at such a time. The sweeps, however, disregarded this warning and were subsequently killed by the fumes given off. The action brought by their widows failed because, as Lord Denning put it, 'the householder could reasonably expect the sweeps to take care of themselves so far as any dangers from the fumes are concerned'. This was a special risk ordinarily incident to the work of a sweep. Conversely, if a sweep suffered injury as a result of a risk that was not special to his trade, (e.g., if a defective chair on which he was sitting having a coffee break had given way causing him to fall) the occupier could well be liable. The risk of a chair breaking is not such a risk as may be considered to be a special risk ordinarily incident to a sweep's work.

Section 2(3)(b) will not automatically absolve the occupier from liability. This is illustrated by its application to cases where firemen have suffered injury while fighting a fire on the defendant's premises. In *Salmon* v. *Seafarer Restaurants* [1983] 1 WLR 1264, firemen were injured at a fire negligently started by the occupier in his fish and chip shop. The defendants sought to argue that there is always some risk involved in firefighting and that they should only be liable where they failed to warn the firemen of some exceptional risk not ordinarily incident to the job. Woolf J, however, rejected this argument and stated that an occupier would be liable where 'it can be foreseen that the fire which is negligently started is of a type which could first require firemen to extinguish the fire and where because of the nature of the fire they will be at risk even though they exercise all the skill of their calling'.

In considering whether the occupier has discharged the common duty of care, section 2(4) of the Act lists two further matters to be taken into account. First, section 2(4)(a) provides that 'where damage is caused to a visitor by a danger of which he has been warned by the occupier, the warning is not to be treated without more as absolving the occupier from liability, unless in all the circumstances it was enough to enable the visitor to be reasonably safe'. Clearly if a notice is illegible or unintelligible it will not be enough and, in considering this, account must be taken of the capabilities of those whom the occupier knows or ought to know are likely to see or hear the warning. Even if the warning is clear, this may not be enough to comply with the duty which, after all, is to make the premises reasonably safe. For example, if to reach the occupier's front door I have to cross a bridge over a river on the occupier's land and the bridge is rotten, the occupier is unlikely to be absolved from liability by putting up a notice warning that the bridge is rotten. This does not enable me to be reasonably safe if it is the only way to get to the front door. Conversely, if there are two bridges, only one of which is safe, and a notice which says 'this bridge is dangerous, use the other one', the occupier will not be in breach of his duty towards me because the warning enables me to be reasonably safe (*Roles* v. *Nathan*, per Lord Denning MR).

Secondly, section 2(4)(b) provides:

'where damage is caused to a visitor by a danger due to the faulty execution of any work of construction, maintenance or repair by an independent contractor employed by the occupier, the occupier is not to be treated without more as answerable for the danger if in all the circumstances he had acted reasonably in entrusting the work to an independent contractor and had taken such steps (if any) as he reasonably ought in order to satisfy himself that the contractor was competent and that the work had been properly done.'

This section was considered by the House of Lords in *Ferguson* v. *Welsh* where their Lordships rejected the plaintiff's argument that, having regard to section 2(4)(b), the council had failed to discharge the common duty of care which they owed to him. In so doing, their Lordships considered a number of problems concerning the interpretation of that section. First, the plaintiff had argued that the council should not be able to rely on the section because the work it had engaged S to do was 'demolition' and this was not within the ambit of the section which refers to 'any work of construction, maintenance or repair'. In rejecting this argument the House of Lords held that 'a broad and purposive' approach should be taken to the meaning of these words, and that 'demolition' was embraced by the word 'construction'. Secondly, it was argued that an occupier did not discharge the common duty of care where he employed someone he knew or ought to have known was incompetent. Whilst this argument was accepted as correct in principle, it was rejected on the facts of the case. There was not enough evidence to suggest that the council ought reasonably to have doubted the honesty or competence of S. Had the council known that S was in the habit of adopting dangerous working practices, it is unlikely that it would have been held to have discharged the common duty of care. Finally, it was argued that the council ought to have supervised the conduct of the work. Again, this was rejected on the facts. The council did not have any reasonable grounds to suspect S was anything other than competent and this was not the type of work where supervision would ordinarily be required. However, certain work may be of such technical difficulty that the occupier's common duty of care will not be discharged unless a specialist is employed to supervise the work and to make sure that it is completed properly.

14.6 Defences

The area of defences generally is dealt with in Chapter 12 and as a result only matters specifically relevant to the liability of occupiers will be mentioned here.

First, by section 2(5), the Act expressly preserves the general defence of *volenti non fit iniuria*. Secondly, the Act does not specifically mention whether a visitor's own lack of care can be taken into account in reducing damages. However, the courts have in a number of cases applied the Law Reform (Contributory Negligence) Act 1945 to reduce damages. Thus, it seems clear the defence of contributory negligence is available to an occupier. Finally, section 2(1) of the Act specifically allows an occupier the freedom 'to extend, restrict, modify or exclude his duty to any visitor or visitors by agreement or otherwise'. However, such freedom is limited in two important ways. The first, and most important limitation is by the

Unfair Contract Terms Act (see 12.4). The second limitation is found in section 3(1) of the Occupiers' Liability Act 1957 which provides that, where an occupier is bound by contract to permit persons who are strangers to the contract to enter or use the premises, he owes them the common duty of care and the occupier cannot by that contract restrict or exclude this duty. Thus, if I put K up as a lodger in my flat, I cannot stipulate that I will not be liable for any injury suffered by any person visiting K as a consequence of a defect in the premises.

14.7 Liability to Trespassers

The law governing the duty of care owed by an occupier to a trespasser was left unaltered by the 1957 Act and, until the House of Lords' decision in *B.R.B* v. *Herrington* [1972] AC 877, the law was as laid down in *Robert Addie & Sons (Collieries)* v. *Dumbreck* [1929] AC 358. In *Addie*, it was held that the occupier had to do some act either deliberately intending to harm the trespasser, or at least with reckless disregard for his safety, before a trespasser could succeed in an action against him. The harshness of this principle was to a large extent alleviated by the House of Lords in *B.R.B.* v. *Herrington*, where it was held that trespassers were owed the 'common duty of humanity'. Their Lordships did not, however, make clear precisely what they meant by this and in particular how it differed from the ordinary duty of care in negligence or that arising under the 1957 Act. Subsequent cases indicated that the duty was somewhat higher than the old common law duty, but lower than the ordinary duty of care in negligence. At least initially, much dissatisfaction was expressed about the uncertainty of the principle. As a result, in 1972 the Lord Chancellor, Lord Hailsham, asked the Law Commission to consider 'in the light of the decision of the House of Lords in *B.R.B.* v. *Herrington*, the law relating to liability for damage or injury suffered by trespassers'. The Law Commission recommended that legislation was needed to clear up the uncertainty. As a result the Occupiers' Liability Act 1984 was passed some 12 years later.

14.8 The Occupiers' Liability Act 1984

The Act replaces the common law as laid down in *Herrington*. It places occupiers, the word 'occupier' being given the same meaning as it had in the 1957 Act, under a duty to 'trespassers', to take such care as is reasonable in all the circumstances to see that they do not suffer injury on the premises, provided certain criteria are satisfied.

The word 'trespasser', which is usually taken to refer to someone who enters land without express or implied permission, will be used here because it is a convenient shorthand and because in practice most non-visitors are trespassers. However, the Act in fact provides in section

1(1)(a) that the duty is owed by an occupier to 'persons other than his visitors'. Such a definition encompasses those using a private right of way and those exercising rights under national parks legislation as well as trespassers and is thus wider than the definition of 'trespasser'.

As with the 1957 Act, the duty is owed in respect of dangers due to the state of the premises or to things done or omitted to be done on them. However, unlike the earlier Act, the 1984 Act does not cover damage to an entrant's property (section 1(8)). Thus, if I enter your land as a trespasser, riding my scrambling bike, and due to a danger on your land I fall off, I may be able to recover for any personal injury I suffer, but I will not be able to recover for any damage done to my bike.

The Act provides in section 1(3) that a duty is owed by an occupier to a trespasser provided:

> '(a) he is aware of the danger or has reasonable grounds to believe it exists;
> (b) he knows or has reasonable grounds to believe that the other is in the vicinity of the danger concerned or that he may come into the vicinity of the danger; and
> (c) the risk is one which in all the circumstances of the case he may reasonably be expected to guard against.'

The phrasing of sections 1(3)(a) and 1(3)(b) creates some difficulty. Are we to say that a duty will only arise if the occupier had actual knowledge of the existence of the danger and a similar knowledge of the presence or likely presence of the trespasser? Or is it enough that a reasonable man would have or ought to have such knowledge? The language used is unclear, providing as it does that the occupier must know or be aware or 'have reasonable grounds to believe' that the danger exists and that the trespasser is in the vicinity or is likely to come into the vicinity. The better view is that the occupier must either have actual knowledge of the danger or that he must have actual knowledge of facts from which a reasonable man would draw the inference that the danger existed and that the person was in the vicinity or was likely to come into it. This is not the same as saying that it is enough that a reasonable man ought to know of the danger and likely presence of the trespasser.

This view is supported by the decision of the Court of Appeal in *White* v. *St Alban's City Council* (1990) *The Times* 12 March. The plaintiff was injured while taking a short cut to get to his car, which was parked in the defendants' car park. Although the defendants were aware of the danger and had taken steps to prevent any injury arising from it by blocking off access to the short cut, they had no evidence that the short cut was ever used to get to the car park. The court held that section 1(3)(b) was as a result not satisfied. This would have been the case even if a reasonable man in the position of the occupier would have been aware that the short cut was in fact used.

The content of the duty owed under the 1984 Act is governed by section 1(4). This provides that the occupier owes a duty to 'take such care as is reasonable in all the circumstances of the case to see that the trespasser does not suffer injury on the premises by reason of the danger concerned'. The duty owed is akin to the ordinary duty of care in negligence and as a result, unlike under *B.R.B* v. *Herrington*, questions of the resources of the individual defendant will be irrelevant. However, in considering whether the duty has been breached, it is to be remembered that what constitutes reasonable care will vary according to the circumstances. Thus, for example, the duty will be less easily breached with respect to a burglar than with respect to a child who wanders into an occupier's garden to have a look at the fish in a pond.

By virtue of section 1(5), the duty owed may be discharged when warning of a danger is given. As is the case under the 1957 Act, a warning will not in every case be sufficient to discharge the duty owed by an occupier. However, it is more likely to be effective to discharge the duty owed to a trespasser than to a lawful visitor. The reason for this is that whereas a lawful visitor may have no choice but to run the risk of being injured on the premises, the trespasser will usually have that choice.

Finally, it should be noticed that the Act makes no provision as to whether the duty owed to trespassers can be excluded. As a matter of policy it could be argued that the duty imposed by the Occupiers' Liability Act 1984 should be seen as an irreducible minimum imposed by the law which cannot be excluded. The problem with such an argument is that in certain circumstances, it would leave a lawful visitor, to whom the duty has been properly excluded in a worse position than a trespasser. This may lead lawful visitors, where there is an exclusion clause, to seek to argue that they are trespassers. The courts could deal with this problem either by holding that the duty under the 1984 Act can be excluded, or (and this, it is argued, is the better solution) by holding that the 1984 Act provides an irreducible minimum duty which cannot be excluded as against either visitors or trespassers.

Summary

14.1 The law relating to the liability of an occupier of premises for injury caused or damage done to persons or their property whilst on the occupier's premises, is governed by the Occupiers' Liability Acts 1957 and 1984. These Acts replace a complex regime of common law rules distinct from that developed from *Donoghue* v. *Stevenson*.

14.2 The Occupiers' Liability Act 1957 governs the liability of occupiers to their lawful visitors and certain other entrants in respect of dangers due to the state of the premises and to things done or omitted to be done on them.

14.3 An occupier is a person who has sufficient degree of control over the premises such that he ought to be under a duty of care to those who come on to the

premises. It is possible for more than one person to be an occupier. An occupier need not live in the premises of which, for the purposes of the Act, he is an occupier.
14.4 A 'lawful visitor' is a person who enters with the express or implied permission of the occupier. The Act also expressly provides that persons entering premises under a contract and those entering as of right are afforded the same protection as lawful visitors. An occupier may limit permission to enter.
14.5 The duty owed by an occupier to his lawful visitors is the common duty of care. This is very similar to the ordinary duty of care in negligence. The Act requires two specific matters to be taken into account when considering the standard of care required. These are, first, that children may be less careful than adults and, secondly, that a person should guard against risks ordinarily incident to his calling. In considering whether the duty has been discharged, regard is to be had to any warning given. Furthermore, in considering whether an occupier is to be held liable for acts of an independent contractor, regard must be had to his selection and supervision of the independent contractor.
14.6 The same general defences available in an action under the ordinary law of negligence apply with regard to the Occupiers' Liability Act 1957. An occupier may extend, restrict, exclude or modify his liability to a lawful visitor, to the extent that the law leaves him free to do so. The Unfair Contract Terms Act and section 3 (1) of the 1957 Act substantially curtail this freedom.
14.7 The law relating to the liability owed to trespassers is now governed by the Occupiers' Liability Act 1984. The Act replaces the common law test as laid down by the House of Lords in *B.R.B* v. *Herrington*.
14.8 Occupiers owe a duty of care to trespassers and certain other entrants in respect of dangers due to the state of the premises and to things done or omitted to be done on them. The duty is only owed to a trespasser if the criteria set out in section 1 (3) are satisfied. The standard of care imposed is to take reasonable care to see that the trespasser does not suffer injury while on the premises.

Exercises

14.1 Who is an occupier for the purposes of the Occupiers' Liability Acts 1957 and 1984?

14.2 Would an action against the manager have succeeded in *Wheat* v. *Lacon*?

14.3 Are all their Lordships in *Wheat* v. *Lacon* agreed on the basis on which the defendants were occupiers *vis-à-vis* the plaintiff's husband?

14.4 Who is a lawful visitor for the purposes of the 1957 Act? Why are those persons exercising a public or private right of way not lawful visitors?

14.5 In what circumstances will the courts hold that an entrant has the implied permission of the occupier to be there? Why are the courts more ready to find such permission exists in the case of children than in the case of adults?

14.6 What factors, along with those specifically mentioned in the Act, will the courts take into account when considering whether or not the common duty of care has been broken?

14.7 Was it fair in *Phipps* v. *Rochester Corporation* to refuse to allow the child to recover anything? Would a different approach have been fairer?

14.8 A fireman is injured at a fire negligently started by the occupier, what factors will be relevant in deciding whether or not the occupier is liable?

14.9 In what circumstances would it be unreasonable (a) for an occupier to entrust work to an independent contractor, and (b) for an occupier not to supervise an independent contractor?

14.10 Is property damage recoverable under the 1984 Act? If it is not recoverable under the Act, would an action succeed at common law?

14.11 What degree of 'knowledge' must be possessed by the occupier before a duty will be owed to a trespasser?

14.12 Is it possible to exclude the duty imposed upon an occupier by the 1984 Act?

15 Product Liability

15.1 Product Liability at Common Law

The most famous product liability case of all is perhaps the most famous in all of the law of tort: no defective product has ever since achieved the notoriety of Mrs Donoghue's bottle of ginger beer and its alleged contents, the decaying remnants of a snail. In deciding that case, Lord Atkin laid down the following test for liability for products in the common law of negligence:

> '[A] manufacturer of products which he sells in such a form as to show he intends them to reach the ultimate consumer in the form in which they left him, with no reasonable possibility of intermediate examination, and with the knowledge that absence of reasonable care in the preparation or putting up of the products will result in injury to the consumer's life or property, owes a duty to that consumer to take that reasonable care.' (*Donoghue* v. *Stevenson* [1932] AC 562)

The case allowed consumers rights against manufacturers of defective products that they lacked under the law of contract. Contract law provided consumer plaintiffs with very powerful remedies against those defendants with whom they could establish privity of contract. Most significantly, contractual remedies were available even where the defendant was in no way at fault as liability for breach of contract is, in general, strict. The common law of contract was buttressed by the Sale of Goods Act (now of 1979) which implied terms into contracts of sale that the goods sold were of 'merchantable quality' and reasonably fit for any purposes made known by the buyer to the seller (ss.14–15). However, the doctrine of privity of contract limited the value of contractual remedies in two respects. In the first place, liability could only arise in favour of someone who had 'bargained for' the goods. That is why Mrs Donoghue was unable to sue in contract: her bottle of ginger beer had been bought for her by a friend. Secondly, it is the seller of the good, not the manufacturer, who is held liable to the consumer in the law of contract. Had Mrs Donoghue bought the bottle of ginger beer herself, it would have been Minchella, the cafe-owner, and not the manufacturer, who would have had to compensate her. The cafe-owner would then have had to sue his supplier, initiating a series of actions for breach of contract which would continue until the 'contractual chain' led to the manufacturer. This is at best a clumsy way of fixing liability on the manufacturer and is unfair to any seller who cannot identify his supplier or whose supplier has gone out of business. The tort of negligence avoids both these problems.

The development of the tort of negligence served the interests of consumers well. Although in theory the burden of establishing fault lay on the consumer, in practice the presence of a defect in a product gave rise to an inference of negligence. Furthermore, it was no excuse for a manufacturer to say that his quality control system was as good as could be and the defect could only be the result of human error: through the doctrine of vicarious liability, the manufacturer would be liable for the errors of his employees. These principles were relied upon in the Australian case of *Grant* v. *Australian Knitting Mills* [1936] AC 85, which went on appeal to the Privy Council. Mr Grant had suffered a severe skin complaint after wearing a new pair of woollen underpants and he sued the manufacturer, alleging that traces of chemicals used in the manufacturing process had been left in the wool. The Privy Council found that Mr Grant was entitled to damages and Lord Wright, who delivered the advice of the Privy Council, described how the case was approached:

'If excess sulphites were left in the garment, that could only be because someone was at fault. The appellant is not required to lay his finger on the exact person in all the chain who was responsible, or to specify what he did wrong. Negligence is found as a matter of inference from the existence of the defects taken in connection with all the known circumstances.'

The 50 or so years since that decision have shown that the courts have preferred to uphold the spirit of Lord Atkin's 'neighbour principle' rather than seek a literal application of his words quoted above. Failure to fit in with Lord Atkin's precise words has not resulted in a total denial of liability: courts have assured themselves of a degree of flexibility to meet the circumstances of each case. Hence the possibility of intermediate inspection, for example, will not prevent a duty of care from arising, although it may cause the harm caused by a product to be regarded as too remote (see *Aswan Engineering Establishment Co* v. *Lupdine Ltd* [1987] 1 WLR 1).

15.2   Reform: The Consumer Protection Act 1987

Despite these developments, well-publicised tragedies arising from the use of defective products stimulated pressure for legislative reform. In particular, the Thalidomide tragedy of the late 1960s and early 1970s, in which hundreds of babies were born without limbs as the result of an unforeseen side-effect of a drug their mothers had taken during pregnancy, gave rise to public concern and prompted consideration of the issue by law-review bodies. Ultimately, reform was accomplished as part of EC law. A 'Products Liability' Directive (85/374/EEC) was adopted in

1985, obliging member states to implement its provisions in their domestic legislation. This was done in the UK by Part I of the Consumer Protection Act 1987.

The goals of the new statutory products liability regime were spelled out in the recital to the European Directive: '[l]iability without fault on the part of the producer is the only way of solving the problem, peculiar to our age of increasing technicality, of a fair apportionment of the risks inherent in modern technological production'. However, sceptics predict that, in terms of consumer protection, the new scheme is flawed because it will be no easier to prove that a product is defective than that it was negligently manufactured (especially when the effect of the development risks defence is considered as well; see 15.7 and Stapleton, 1986b). On the other hand, proponents of the reform claim that the new scheme provides a speedier and therefore cheaper remedy for consumers (see Jolowicz, 1987). In any case, the consumer will be left no worse off than before: the statutory remedy exists alongside the existing remedies in contract and tort. Thus, those injured by a product they themselves have bought, for example, will still be able to sue for breach of the implied warranty of merchantability in the contract of sale.

One final introductory point to note about the Consumer Protection Act is that, under EC law, it must fully implement all the provisions of the Directive. Should it not do so, the European Court of Justice might call upon the UK to amend its legislation. The UK has sought to avoid this by inserting an 'interpretation clause' in the Act: section 1(1) states that Part I of the Act shall be construed 'as is necessary in order to comply with the product liability Directive'. This clause was intended to allow courts to comply with EC law by adopting a generous interpretation of any provision in the statute that appears, on its face, to be too narrow. It might also have an unintended effect: a court may well decide that the Act shall not be construed as providing any remedy that is not necessary in order to comply with the Directive, thus precluding it from interpreting the statute as being more radical in effect than the Directive.

15.3   Meaning of 'Product'

The basic definition of a product is found in section 1(2) of the Act: "product" means any goods or electricity and . . . includes a product which is comprised in another product'. This last limb of the definition encompasses the component parts of larger products as well as the raw materials of which products are made: if you were to buy a car, the engine and tyres would be regarded as products no less than the car as a whole, and you would be able to sue the manufacturers of these component parts if the parts were defective and caused you injury. The same would be true with regard to the manufacturers of the metal and tyre rubber used as raw materials if the defect were traced to them.

'Goods', in turn, is defined in the Act: section 45(1) says the term is to include 'substances, growing crops and things comprised in land by virtue of being attached to it and any ship aircraft or vehicle'. The precise limits of the definition of 'goods', and therefore of the definition of 'products', will be hard to determine. Take, first of all, the case of buildings and building materials. On its face, the definition of 'goods' seems to encompass these things on the basis that a building is a thing attached to land. However, it is arguable that a building is better regarded as 'land' itself, rather than a thing 'attached to land'. This interpretation is supported by the Directive, Article 2 of which defines 'products' as meaning all moveables, which it contrasts with immoveables, although it allows that moveables remain products even if incorporated into an immoveable. From this, it appears that the building materials (the bricks, beams, tiles, etc.) that are used in constructing a building were, being moveables, meant to be covered by the Directive, even where incorporated into a building. Conversely, the building itself, being an immoveable, falls outside the scope of the Directive, and therefore of the Consumer Protection Act.

A second hard case concerns the information contained in goods like books and computer software (see Whittaker, 1989). Suppose you buy a chemistry text book which contains details of a particular experiment. You are directed to mix two chemicals together in a certain proportion. You follow the instructions to the letter but, because of a misprint, you mix the wrong chemicals and cause an explosion. Can you claim that the textbook was a defective product because of the misprinted information it contained and therefore sue for any injuries you suffered? It seems widely accepted that the answer to this question is 'Yes'. Any doubts about this must surely be laid to rest by consideration of the following example: a traffic light is wired up incorrectly so that it shows red when vehicles should go and green when they should stop; an accident is the result. No one would deny that the traffic light was a defective product. Far removed as this example may seem from the case of a chemistry experiment detailed in a textbook, it is in fact indistinguishable in principle: in both cases, the product is the source of information (how to conduct an experiment, when to cross an intersection) upon which people place reliance.

15.4 Meaning of 'Defective'

The Consumer Protection Act does not hold a producer liable for all the harm caused by his products: he may only be liable if his product is defective. It is more accurate to speak of liability under the Act as 'defect liability' rather than 'strict liability'. The test of defectiveness is found in section 3(1): 'there is a defect in a product . . . if the safety of the product is not such as persons generally are entitled to expect'. Three preliminary points should be noted. In the first place, the test refers to the safety of a product, not to its usefulness. The Consumer Protection Act gives no remedy in respect of products that simply do not work: for this, the consumer must look to the law of contract. Secondly, the test is framed in terms of consumer expectations rather than in terms of whether the producer exercised reasonable care and skill (the test in negligence). It is perfectly possible for a product to be regarded as defective even though the producer took all reasonable steps to ensure its safety. Finally, the court must consider what consumers are *entitled* to expect: the test is one of *legitimate* expectations, which are not necessarily the same as *actual* expectations.

In determining what consumers are entitled to expect about the safety of a product, 'all the circumstances shall be taken into account'. This is the phrase used in section 3(2), which goes on to list certain of those circumstances. In paragraph (a), there is a list of a number of factors which relate to the way the product is marketed or presented (see Schlechtriem, 1989). It seems that the way a product is advertised may be held to affect the legitimate expectations of consumers. If, for example, a car of a particular model is marketed as having advanced anti-locking brakes, it might be regarded as defective if its brakes were in fact no better than those in the standard model. This paragraph also requires regard to be had to any instructions or warnings accompanying the product: a product that is potentially dangerous may be perfectly safe if used correctly. For instance, many drugs are lethal if taken in large quanti- ties: these would not be regarded as defective if the correct dose were clearly stated and a warning against exceeding that dose prominently displayed. Paragraph (b) refers to the use one might reasonably expect the product to be put to. The wording of this paragraph makes it clear that a product may be regarded as defective because its *misuse* was predictable. Hence, bottles of drugs might be declared defective if not fitted with child- proof tops. Finally, paragraph (c) requires the court to look at the time the product was supplied by the producer: the fact that products supplied more recently have additional safety features built in as standard does not require the court to hold an old product to be defective simply because it lacks those features. If a car were marketed today with no safety belts, it would undoubtedly be regarded as defective; however, a vintage car would not be so regarded as the importance of safety belts was not recognised at the time the car was supplied by its manufacturer.

The new statutory scheme has been criticised by some as being little more effective as a consumer remedy than the law of negligence. These critics draw particular attention to the deficiencies of the consumer expectations test when it comes to dealing with design defects as opposed to production errors. In the case of a production error (where something goes wrong during the manufacturing process so that the product does not end up as intended), the law of negligence afforded consumers adequate protection since the mere presence of such an error suggested an inadequate sysytem of quality control or human error (see 15.1). However, the law of negligence was not an effective weapon against products that were dangerous because, although they ended up as intended, the original design was unsafe; in other words, they suffered from a design defect. Such cases present courts with very difficult choices. Suppose a drug company discovers a cure for cancer. This new wonder drug is effective in many cases, but a small proportion of those who use the drug suffers severe side-effects. What right has the judge to say that the harm to the few outweighs the benefit to the many? By and large, courts have viewed the imposition of liability in cases like this as the task of Parliament; they do not have the time and money to look at all the possible ramifications of such a decision, while the adversarial system prevents them from listening to all interested parties. This problem will surface under the new statutory scheme as well for, in determining the safety consumers are entitled to expect from a product, courts will have to consider whether the benefits of that product outweigh its costs. Critics of the new scheme believe, probably correctly, that judges will be no more willing to hold producers liable for deliberate design decisions than they were under the common law, and that consumers will suffer as a result. In truth, really effective consumer protection requires strict liability, not merely defect liability, for the manufacturers of products (see Stapleton, 1986).

15.5   Who can be Liable under the Act?

The primary liability under the Act is upon the producer of a product. 'Producer' is defined in section 1(2) as one who manufactures a product, or wins or abstracts it, or carries out any process upon it to which essential characteristics of the product are attributable. This definition gives rise to a number of complexities which centre around the crucial distinction drawn in section 1(2) between products which have been 'manufactured, won or abstracted' and those which have not. In the case of products not 'manufactured, won or abstracted', liability under the Act will only arise if 'essential characteristics' of that product are attributable to any process which has been carried out on it. This leaves us with a three stage inquiry. First, we have to ask whether the product we are concerned with has been manufactured, won or abstracted. Secondly, if the answer to that question is 'No', we have to determine whether any 'process' has been carried out upon the product. Last, in such cases we have to decide whether that process has given the product certain 'essential characteristics'.

To conduct the first part of our enquiry, we have to know what the words 'manufactured, won or abstracted' mean. Clearly anything which is man-made comes within the meaning of 'manufactured': the word itself means, literally, 'made by hand' but clearly extends to things made by machine. It seems equally clear that substances like coal which are mined come within the definition of those that are 'won or abstracted'. On the other side of the line come agricultural products which appear in section 1(2) as an example of products that are not 'manufactured, won or abstracted'. Beyond these paradigm cases, there is considerable doubt as to where to draw the line between those products which are, and those which are not, 'manufactured, won or abstracted'. In order to ensure effective consumer protection, courts should be encouraged to take a broad view of this phrase so that, for example, blood taken for transfusion should be treated as 'abstracted' from the blood donor.

Passing over these difficulties, we discover more obscurity when we come to the second stage of our enquiry. At this stage we have to ask whether a product which has not been 'manufactured, won or abstracted' has had any process carried out on it. Shells washed up on the seashore are certainly not 'manufactured, won or abstracted': if they are polished, can they be said to have undergone a process? Again, courts should be encouraged to adopt a generous interpretation: anything that is done deliberately to a product, in an attempt to adapt it for some use, should count as a process.

A further complexity is added by section 2(4) of the Act. Where the product in question is game or agricultural produce, the process must be one that can be described as an industrial process if liability is to arise. The word 'industrial' suggests that the process must be on a large and continuous scale and involve the use of machinery. It would, for instance, exclude the making of a few pots of home-made jam in a domestic kitchen. However, in requiring that the process be industrial, the Act might be narrower than the Directive, which speaks only of an 'initial process'. This seems to refer to whatever process is first carried out on a product, be it industrial or not. An English court might feel entitled to ignore the word 'industrial' in order to give effect to the Directive.

The third issue is whether the process carried out on the product has given it 'essential characteristics'. This phrase gives rise to enormous problems of definition. Take the simple example of a carrot. Is it an essential characteristic of a carrot bought from the supermarket that it has had its leaves removed and all the dirt shaken off it? What if it has been sorted into a selection of carrots of the same size and put in a plastic bag? Or if it has been peeled and washed? Or grated? Our intuition tells us that the fact that carrots have been grated is an essential characteristic of those carrots. Equally, we are inclined to view a carrot bought from the supermarket as just a carrot unless we have paid more for it because it has, for instance, been peeled and washed. However, when it comes to formulating a rule to distinguish these cases, and to apply to borderline cases, we come unstuck. It seems likely the courts will address this issue in a very impressionistic way, relying on the notorious 'elephant test': 'Don't ask me to describe it, but I know one when I see one.'

The justification for 'channelling' liability to the producer of the products is that he is best placed both to absorb the loss (typically by taking out insurance) and to do something about the defect by making his product safer. However, a number of other people may, depending on the circumstances, be treated as equivalent to the actual producer of a product and be held liable under the Act. These are anyone who 'has held himself out to be the producer of the product' (e.g. supermarkets who sell 'own-branded' goods), anyone who imported the product in question into the EC ('the importer'), and anyone who has at any time supplied the defective product to another. In the case of suppliers, liability will only arise if they are unable to identify their supplier or, alternatively, the importer or actual producer of the product. These provisions are found in section 2(2),(3) of the Act.

15.6 Who can Recover under the Act?

As a general rule, anyone who suffers personal injuries or property damage which is caused by a defective product may recover to the full extent of his loss. The Act makes no distinction between those who are injured while using the product and those who are mere bystanders injured by someone else's use of the product. The main restrictions on the right to recover relate to property damage. No compensation may be awarded in respect of property damage in three cases. The first case is given in section 5(2): where the damage is to the product itself or to any product supplied with the product in question comprised in it, no liability arises under the Act. This provision means that, if you buy a car which is fitted with a faulty engine that blows up, you cannot claim under the Act for the cost of a replacement engine: the engine is 'the product itself'. Neither can you recover for the cost of repairing the bodywork should that be damaged by the explosion: this is damage to a product (the car) which was supplied with the defective product (the engine) 'comprised in it'. This corresponds to the rule in the common law of negligence that damage to the product itself is pure economic loss and not recoverable (though note the possibility that at common law certain things might be regarded as 'complex structures' so that damage to one part of the structure, even though caused by another part of the same structure, would still be regarded as damage to 'other property': see 5.2). The second case in which property damage gives rise to no liability is where the damaged item is not both of a type that is ordinarily intended for private use and intended by the plaintiff mainly for his own private use (s. 5(3)). Hence, a barrister has no claim under the Act if a leaky pen damages his courtroom attire, but he would have if the pen were to damage the clothes he uses for lazing about the house. The final case is where the total property damage complained of is valued at no more than £275. This case is dealt with by section 5(4) of the Act, the purpose being to cut out trivial claims for property damage.

The simple word 'cause', of course, obscures a great many complicated issues (see Chapter 10). Of particular note in the present context is its use in Civil Law countries, in which it encompasses rules of remoteness or 'legal cause'. It would seem to be possible for an English court to justify applying the *Wagon Mound* foreseeability rule in cases under the Act, and perhaps the principle of *volenti non fit iniuria* too, on the grounds that these rules are entailed by the word 'cause' (see Chapter 11–12).

15.7 Defences

The Act lists a number of specific defences in section 4(1)(a) to (f):

(a) 'the defect is attributable to compliance with any requirement imposed by or under any enactment or with any Community obligation'

Suppose statute requires children's toys to be coated with a certain flame-resistant substance. Many children prove allergic to the substance and suffer severe rashes. The manufacturer would have a defence under this paragraph. However, if the statute did not require, but merely permitted, him to use that substance, the defence would avail him. The statutory permission would, however, almost certainly be conclusive proof that the product was not defective.

(b) 'the person proceeded against did not at any time supply the product to another'

This paragraph effectively excludes waste products from the operation of the Act. A manufacturer cannot be liable under the Act for harm resulting from his discharge of waste into a river. However, should a manufacturer sell his waste products, or even give them away, then he will fall within the definition of supply in section 46(1) and may be liable for any harm that they cause.

(c) the supply was not with any business motive falling within section 4(1)(c)

Liability only attaches to those who produce products with what might loosely be called a business motive. This result is ensured by section 4(1)(c) which allows a defendant a defence that he at no time supplied the product in the course of business or with a view to profit. Thus, if you give your home-made jam to be sold off for charity in the local church fete, you will not be liable under the Act if it makes those who eat it sick, though you may still be liable in the common law of negligence. Equally, if you bring back souvenirs from your holiday in Australia which you give to your relatives, you will face no liability under the Act if they prove to be dangerous even though you have imported and supplied the goods.

(d) the defect did not exist in the product at the time it was supplied by the defendant

This defence protects a manufacturer whose product has become danger-ous because it has been interfered with after it has left his control. However, certain products should be designed so they cannot be interfered with (e.g. containers for prescription drugs should have child-proof tops) and a product might be regarded as defective because it lacks this design feature.

(e) 'the state of scientific and technical knowledge at the [time the product was supplied by the producer] was not such that a producer of products of the same description as the product in question might be expected to have discovered the defect if it had existed in his products while they were under his control'

Suppose a pharmaceutical firm admits that one of its drugs it has now taken off the market has been discovered to have serious side-effects, but claims that no one could have predicted those side-effects at the time the drug was put on the market. Even if the drug could be regarded as defective because the risk of the side-effects out-weighed the benefits of the drug, the manufacturer might still escape liability by arguing that the state of scientific knowledge at the time the drug was marketed just did not allow that risk to be detected. This defence, contained in section 4(1)(e) of the Act, is often known as the 'development risks' or 'state of the art' defence (see Newdick, 1988).

The defence was included in the Directive after enormous pressure from manufacturers, particularly in the pharmaceutical industry. They alleged it would be unfair to hold them liable for risks they could not be expected to detect, and that to do so would impede technological innovation. Member states were left to choose whether or not they would include this defence in their domestic legislation; the UK was among those countries that did. However, the form in which the defence appears in the Consumer Protection Act seems more generous to producers than the directive would allow. Whereas the Directive stipulates that the defence will only avail a producer where 'the state of scientific and technical knowledge at the time when he put the product into circulation was not such as to enable the existence of the defect of the defect to be discovered' (Art. 7), the defence in section 4(1)(e) of the Act requires only that the state of knowledge was such that 'a producer of products of the same description as the product in question might be expected to have discovered the defect'. This is more generous than the Directive in that it asks what might reasonably be expected of producers of a particular product rather than what was *possible* given the state of scientific knowledge. This difference between Act and Directive leaves the UK at risk of prosecution in the European Court for failing properly to implement the Directive.

(f) the defect in the product is wholly attributable to the design of another product in which it was comprised or to compliance with instructions given by the producer of that other product

Note that, even though a manufacturer who supplies component parts or raw materials to another to be incorporated into a more complex product may escape liability under the Act by virtue of this defence, he may yet be liable under the common law. This may be so if he should have known better than the subsequent producer and pointed out the errors of his ways.

Outside the section 4 defences, the defendant may rely on the defence of contributory negligence. Express reference is made to this defence in section 5(4). Yet the defence of *volenti non fit iniuria*, which often arises on the same facts, is not mentioned at all in the Act: it may be that it is encompassed by the concept of 'legal cause'. One defence is expressly ruled out by the Act: by virtue of section 7, the defendant cannot rely on any provision that purports to exclude or limit liability under the Act.

Summary

15.1 At common law, consumers have remedies in respect of harm caused by defective products under the law of contract (within the constraints imposed by the doctrine of privity) and the tort of negligence.
15.2 The Consumer Protection Act 1987 was enacted in order to comply with the European 'Products Liability' Directive which was a response to public concern after disasters such as the thalidomide tragedy. Its most notable feature is that it removes the need for those injured by a product to establish fault on the part of the producer. The extent to which the Act will in practice improve on the common law of negligence is, however, disputed.
15.3 Under the Act, 'product' means any goods or electricity, including component parts and raw materials. The term 'goods' probably includes building materials (but not the buildings into which they are incorporated) and sources of information such as books and computer software.
15.4 The test of defectiveness under the Act is whether the product is as safe as persons generally are entitled to expect (the 'consumer expectations' test). This test is the source of many criticisms of the Act which allege it is insufficiently radical. Such criticisms have most force in the context of design defects.
15.5 The primary liability under the Act is upon the producer of a product, though 'own-branders', importers and suppliers (in some circumstances) may be held liable.
15.6 Anyone who suffers injury or property damage caused by a defective product can recover under the Act, though there are some limitations on the recovery of property damage.
15.7 The Act lists a number of specific defences, of which the most important and controversial is the 'development risks' defence. The exclusion of liability under the act is prohibited.

Exercises

15.1 What are the comparative advantages and disadvantages of the law of contract and the tort of negligence as remedies in respect of defective products?

15.2 Does the Consumer Protection Act 1987 actually advance the interests of consumers?

15.3 What problems does the definition of 'product' under the Act give rise to?

15.4 Explain how design defects differ from production errors. Do the courts approach them in the same way? If not, why not?

15.5 What goals were the framers of the legislation trying to achieve in selecting those who could be liable under the new products liability regime?

15.6 What do the limitations imposed on the recovery of property damage under the Act tell us about the interests that the law is trying to protect?

15.7 What is the 'development risks' defence? Should it be allowed?

15.8 What improvements, if any, could still be made to the law of product liability?

16 Breach of Statutory Duty

16.1 Introduction

Each year Parliament enacts a substantial number of statutes which impose duties on public bodies, private individuals and others. Some of these statutes specifically create a detailed scheme of civil liability of a tortious nature. The Occupiers' Liability Acts of 1957 and 1984, the Animals Act of 1971 and the Consumer Protection Act of 1987 are all examples. Claims brought under these statutes are often described as actions for breach of statutory duty. Whilst there is nothing inherently wrong with this description, claims under these statutes do not create any of the problems normally associated with the tort of breach of statutory duty. The creation of an express tortious action in these cases is clear and the person who has suffered loss has his remedy in the statute.

Our concern in this chapter is with those statutes which impose duties but which either are silent on the question of whether Parliament intended a civil action to lie for breach of that duty or may impose some criminal penalty for such a breach. Does Parliament intend there to be a civil remedy for breach of that duty? A tortious remedy is obviously available where Parliament has made express provision for it, but it does not follow from the fact that Parliament has included no provision for such a remedy that none exists.

It may be thought that, given the enormous volume of legislation now produced by Parliament, covering as it does many disparate areas of human activity, Parliament would articulate clearly whether or not it intends there to be a civil remedy. Unfortunately, this is not the case. Each year a vast amount of legislation is enacted which makes no express provision either in favour or against the provision of a civil remedy. The courts are, therefore, frequently faced with the problem of determining Parliament's intention. Undoubtedly, this is an extremely difficult task in many cases. Indeed, in one case Lord Denning MR protested that, '[t]he dividing line between the pro-cases and the contra-cases is so blurred and so ill-defined that you might as well toss a coin to decide it' *(Ex Parte Island Records Ltd* [1978] 1 Ch. 122, at 135). Nevertheless, it is a task which the courts have to undertake and this chapter will be predominantly concerned with the judicial approach to the problem.

16.2 Inferring the Existence of the Tort

The problem which the courts face in any case where the statute is silent on whether or not a civil remedy was intended is to discern the intention of Parliament on a matter which has not been expressly resolved by the language of the statute. The prevailing approach of the English courts is to seek assistance from a number of presumptions. The courts apply these presumptions to the statute in question to determine whether a civil action was intended. This approach seeks to bring some order and consistency to the problem of whether or not a civil remedy was intended.

Some judges have taken the (perhaps more realistic) view that it is simply impossible to bring any order or consistency to this area of law. Lord Denning MR's judgment in *Ex Parte Island Records* is a good example of this approach. His view was that the courts, in the light of the difficulties with which they are faced, should be left free to exercise their own assessment of Parliament's intention in the light of the statutory language and the pre-existing law without being constrained by any presumptions. Applying the presumptions was unhelpful, he said, because they so often conflict. Whilst this view may have some attraction, it has not gained much judicial support. The presumption approach is now well established and has received the approval of the House of Lords in one of the leading cases in this area, *Lonrho Ltd* v. *Shell Petroleum Co Ltd* [1982] AC 173.

The use of presumptions in this area is unsurprising. By articulating a number of them, the courts let Parliament know that a particular result will ensue unless the contrary is expressly provided for. Parliament is presumed to know the relevant presumptions and how the judges will respond to the use of different legislative drafting techniques. By this method, it is argued, some consistency is achieved. However, this is not to say the presumption approach always achieves satisfactory results. Lord Denning was correct to point out that, on the facts of any given case, the presumptions may point in conflicting directions. Nevertheless, in the light of continued judicial support, consideration must now be given to this approach.

16.3   The Modern Approach

A number of early cases on breach of statutory duty go so far as to hold that where Parliament has created a duty by statute, the common law should provide a remedy to a person injured by breach of it. However, this view can no longer be supported. The modern approach is based on the application of two presumptions which were first stated by Lord Tenterden CJ in *Doe dem. Murray, Lord Bishop of Rochester* v. *Bridges* (1854) 1 B & AD 847. There he said (at 859):

'and where an Act creates an obligation, and enforces the performance in a specified manner, we take it as a general rule that performance cannot be enforced in any other manner. If the obligation is created, but no mode of enforcing its performance is ordained, the common law may, in general, find a mode suited to the particular nature of the case.'

Modern support can be found for this approach in *Lonrho Ltd* v. *Shell Petroleum Co Ltd*. However, in *Lonrho* Lord Diplock, with whom the other Lords agreed, articulated two exceptions to the presumption against actionability where the statute provides a specific mode of enforcement (e.g, through a criminal penalty): first, where the obligation imposed by the Act was passed for the benefit or protection of a particular class of individuals and second, where the statute creates a public right, which he defines as 'a right to be enjoyed by all those of Her Majesty's subjects who wish to avail themselves of it', and a particular member of the public suffers 'special' damage different from that which was common to the rest of the public. In both these cases the presumption against actionability may be rebutted. Having identified the main presumptions articulated by the courts it is now proposed to consider how they have been applied.

Where the Statute is Silent as to the Method of Enforcement

The general presumption in those cases where a statute creates a duty but makes no provision as to the method of enforcement is that a tortious remedy for breach of statutory duty is intended. An example of this can be seen in the case of *Dawson* v. *Bingley UDC* [1911] 2 KB 438. By section 66 of the Public Health Act 1875, every urban authority was required to provide fire-plugs and to identify clearly their position in some way. No penalty or other remedy was provided for breach of this section. The defendants put up a notice which failed to indicate the true position of the fire-plug. A fire broke out at the plaintiff's premises to which the fire brigade were called. They spent some considerable time trying to locate the fire-plug and as a result the plaintiff's property suffered greater damage than it would otherwise have done. The Court of Appeal held that the plaintiff's action for damages for breach of statutory duty should succeed. Where, as here, the statute was silent as to the mode of enforcement, 'the legislature is to be taken as intending the ordinary result; and the proper remedy for breach of a statute is an action for damages'.

Although the Court of Appeal in the *Dawson* case had little difficulty in deciding on the facts that Parliament had intended there to be an action for breach of statutory duty, difficulties may arise where, although the statute provides no method of enforcement, there is already an existing common law remedy, whether of a private or public law nature. In such cases is there still a presumption of actionability? The prevailing view seems to be that where there is an available private law remedy, Parliament cannot have intended to provide an action for breach of statutory duty. This appears to be a sensible enough conclusion. Where the common law already provides a remedy in damages it is unlikely that Parliament intended to duplicate that remedy.

Where the only remedy is a 'public law' one obtainable by means of an application for judicial review the cases are less consistent. In *Hague* v. *Deputy Governor of Parkhurst Prison* [1991] 3 All ER 733 Lord Jauncey considered the existence of a public law remedy was relevant, though by no means conclusive, to the question of whether an action for breach of statutory duty was intended, and refused to find that the breach of the Prison Rules was actionable at the instance of the plaintiff. However, in other cases the existence of the general remedy of judicial review has not deterred the courts from finding that a statute was intended to give rise to an action for damages. The approach in *Hague* is to be preferred. Parliament must surely be presumed to know of *all* existing remedies, whether of a private or public law nature. It seems unsatisfactory to ignore the existence of such rights in considering whether or not Parliament intended there to be an action for breach of statutory duty.

A further problem may arise where the duty imposed is of a very broad nature, giving a large measure of discretion to the person on whom the duty is imposed. Take the example given by Stanton (1986) of section 1(2) of the Employment Protection Act 1975. This places the Advisory Conciliation and Arbitration Service (ACAS) under 'the general duty of promoting the improvement of industrial relations, and in particular of encouraging the extension of collective bargaining and the development and, where necessary, reform of the collective bargaining machinery'. No method of enforcement of this section is provided by the Act. Can it really have been intended by Parliament that breach of this duty should be actionable at the suit of an individual? The duty created is essentially a political one and it must surely be the case that any remedy must therefore be political. It should not be for the courts to second guess what are in effect political decisions of ACAS.

Where the Statute Provides an Alternative Method of Enforcement

Where a statute provides for a penalty to be paid for a breach of the duty a presumption will arise that this was the only remedy. In *Atkinson* v. *The Newcastle and Gateshead Waterworks Co* (1877) LR 2 Ex.D 441 the defendants were, by section 42 of the Waterworks Clauses Act 1847, under a duty to keep water in their pipes under a certain pressure. Failure to comply with this section subjected the defendants to a penalty of £10. In breach of the section the defendants failed to maintain this pressure, as a result of which firemen were unable to save the plaintiff's house from being gutted by fire. The plaintiff brought an action for damages for breach of the section. The Court of Appeal held that the plaintiff's action failed since the penalty was intended to be exclusive. It cannot have been the case, according to the court, that Parliament intended the defendants to become 'gratuitous insurers of the safety from fire . . . of all the houses within the district over which their powers were to extend'.

As Lord Diplock made clear in the *Lonrho* case, this presumption of non-actionability where the statute provides an alternative method of enforcement is subject to two exceptions. We will now consider these exceptions in more detail.

16.4   Exceptions to the Presumption against Actionability where the Statute Provides an Alternative Remedy

Where the Statute is Passed for the Benefit of a Particular Class of Persons

Where the provision was passed for the benefit of a particular class of persons there is a presumption that an action for breach of statutory duty will lie. In *Groves* v. *Lord Wimborne* [1898] 2 QB 402, a workman was injured because of a failure to fence a dangerous piece of machinery. The Court of Appeal held an action would lie for damages despite the fact that the statute provided only for a penalty. Section 5(3) of the Factory and Workshop Act 1891 (now section 14 of the Factories Act 1961) provided that, 'all dangerous parts of the machinery. . . shall either be securely fenced, or be in such position or of such construction as to be equally safe to every person employed in the factory as it would be if it were securely fenced'. This section, the court said, was passed for the benefit and protection of a specified group, namely employees. In the words of Vaughan Williams LJ,

> 'where a statute provides for the performance by certain persons of a particular duty, and someone belonging to a class of persons for whose benefit and protection the statute imposes the duty is injured by failure to perform it, prima facie, and, if there be nothing to the contrary, an action by the person so injured will lie against the person who has failed to perform the duty.'

So also in *Ex Parte Island Records Ltd,* a majority of the Court of Appeal held that musicians had a right of action for breach of section 1 of the Dramatic and Musical Performers' Protection Act 1958. Section 1 provides, 'if a person knowingly- (a) makes a record, directly or indirectly from or by means of the performance of a dramatic or musical work without the consent in writing of the performers. . . he shall be guilty of an offence under this Act'. Although the only remedy provided by the Act was a criminal penalty, the Court held that the Act was passed for the protection of a particular class of individuals – namely, musical performers – and therefore an action would lie for breach of statutory duty.

Where, however, the Act imposes a penalty for breach of the section but imposes no duty towards a special class, an action will not generally lie. In *Atkinson* v. *The Newcastle and Gateshead Waterworks Co*, for example, the obligation to maintain the water in the pipes at a certain pressure was held to be owed to the public in general and not to any member of the public whose property was damaged as a result of the breach. One of the leading cases on this point is *Cutler* v. *Wandsworth Stadium Ltd* [1949] A.C. 398, which raised the question whether an action for breach of statutory duty lay in respect of breach of section 11(2)(b) of the Betting and Lotteries Act 1934. This section provided that, 'the occupier of a licensed track. . . (b) shall take such steps as are necessary to secure that. . . there is available for bookmakers space on the track where they can conveniently carry on bookmaking in connection with dog races run on the track'. The appellant, a bookmaker, claimed injunctions prohibiting the respondents from excluding him from the track and also requiring them to secure a space for him where he could conveniently carry on bookmaking. The House of Lords refused to grant the injunctions. The purpose of the Act was to protect the public interest by regulating the operation of betting at dog tracks. Any benefit which accrued to bookmakers was wholly incidental to this purpose. The Act was not intended to confer a right upon an individual bookmaker who presented himself at the stadium to demand a place on the track.

While the question whether a statute was passed for the benefit of a particular class of persons is undoubtedly treated by the courts as a relevant factor in deciding whether a civil action for breach of statutory duty was intended, it is important not to place too much emphasis on this question. Whether or not a statute is held to have been passed for the benefit of a particular class of persons or the public at large is inevitably a question of impression. In *Cutler*, for example, was it not strongly arguable that the Act had been passed for the benefit of, among others, bookmakers? It could legitimately be said that bookmakers constituted a sufficiently identifiable group and possessed sufficiently common interests to constitute a defined group. Similarly, it appears from *Hague* v. *Deputy Governor of Parkhurst Prison* that even if a court is prepared to accept that legislation (in this case the Prison Rules) was passed in order to benefit a particular class, this does not necessarily mean that a civil action for breach of statutory duty will lie.

The real issue in all these cases is whether Parliament *intended* to confer on the particular plaintiff a cause of action for breach of statutory duty. As Lord Bridge (at p. 741) said in *Hague*:

'[I] do not think one escapes . . . from the fundamental question: "did the legislature intend to confer on the plaintiff a cause of action for breach of statutory duty?" by transposing it into the question "did the legislature intend to confer on the plaintiff protection for damage of a kind for which, if the protection is not effectively provided, the common law will offer a monetary remedy?"'

The answer to this question is rarely clear from the words of the statute themselves. The fact of the matter is that Parliament has chosen not to say anything or has simply not considered the matter. As with the duty of care issue in the tort of negligence, whether an action lies for breach of statutory duty will depend upon considerations of policy.

A number of policy considerations can be identified. Where a penal statute enacts a safety standard to protect against personal injury, the courts have shown themselves willing to infer the existence of the tort (see, e.g., *Groves* v. *Lord Wimborne*). The willingness of the courts to allow an action in the case of industrial safety legislation probably stems, at least in part, from a desire to give monetary compensation to an injured workman and to ensure that employers do not evade safety standards imposed by statute. Whatever the reason, most industrial safety legislation has been interpreted to give rise to an action for the tort of breach of statutory duty. Where, on the other hand, the effect of allowing an action for breach of statutory duty would be to protect the plaintiff against an economic loss, the courts have been markedly less willing to find that a civil action was intended. In *Cutler*, for example, to have given bookmakers a right of action would have protected the bookmaker against an economic loss (i.e., the loss of business as a result of being excluded from the track).

The courts have also taken account of the insurance position. In *Atkinson*, for example, the Court of Appeal was clearly influenced by the burden that would be imposed on the defendant if it were to allow an action for breach of statutory duty to lie. The effect of allowing such an action would be to make the defendant gratuitous insurers against fire of all the houses in their area. In this situation it was thought that the householder was a better loss bearer than the defendants because he is more likely to have insurance and to be able to obtain it more cheaply to cover such an eventuality. Similarly, the courts have generally been unwilling to allow a civil action for breach of any road traffic legislation. This unwillingness reflects the view that to allow an action in such cases may be too harsh on the defendant. For example, having a defective rear light is an offence under road traffic legislation. This is the case even where the light has gone out while the defendant is driving the motor vehicle and had no way of knowing that the light was no longer functioning. This refusal to allow an action in such cases may also reflect the view that the plaintiff can easily acquire insurance to protect himself against non-negligent accidents and the loss should, therefore, fall on him.

On the other hand, it might be argued that the defendant will be, or should be, insured and as he is also the cause of the loss, is the better loss-bearer. This view can be seen reflected in *Monk* v. *Warbey* [1935] 1 KB 75. The plaintiff claimed damages for personal injuries sustained as the result of a collision with a car owned by the defendant. The car had been lent by the defendant to a third party without the benefit of a policy of insurance in respect of third-party risks. This was an offence under section 35(1) of the Road Traffic Act 1930. The Court of Appeal held that this failure was actionable in tort and their decision is surely justifiable on the basis that the very purpose of the section was to ensure that third-party insurance was available to protect accident victims. Where, as here, that insurance had not been taken out, the court were justified in giving the victim the additional protection of an action against the owner of the vehicle. *Monk* v. *Warbey* is, however, almost the only case where a breach of road traffic legislation has been held to give rise to a tortious action, and it seems unlikely that such actions will be extended any further.

Where the Statute Creates a Public Right and the Plaintiff Suffers Special Damage

In *Lonrho* Lord Diplock recognised a second exception to the presumption of non-actionability where the statute provides a penalty. This arises where the statute creates a public right and a particular member of the public suffers 'special' damage. It is not, however, altogether clear in what circumstances this exception is to apply. The widest view would treat all criminal and administrative law duties as creating public rights, any violation of which causing special damage would be actionable by the individual affected. The actual decision in *Lonrho* shows that this is too broad an interpretation of Lord Diplock's words. An Order in Council had been made making it a criminal offence to supply oil to what was then known as Southern Rhodesia. It was alleged by the plaintiffs that, in breach of this Order, the defendants had supplied oil to Southern Rhodesia. The plaintiffs argued that as a result of this they had suffered loss and claimed damages in respect of the breach. The House of Lords held that the plaintiffs had no civil action for breach of this Order. Lord Diplock, delivering a speech with which the other Lords agreed, held that no public right was created. The whole purpose of the Order was to withdraw a pre-existing right (i.e., to trade with Southern Rhodesia) and not to create a right to be enjoyed by the general public.

Although the House of Lords rejected the widest possible interpretation of this exception, its ambit remains in doubt. Little indication was, given however, that this exception should have a particularly wide import. More detailed discussion of this point should be sought in specialist texts: see Stanton (1986).

16.5 Elements of the Tort

Persons Protected and Risk Covered

Once it has been determined that an action for breach of statutory duty lies the court must decide whether the damage suffered is recognised by the statute in question and whether the person is intended to be with the protection of the section. This is a question of judicial interpretation. An example of a case dealing with the former question is *Gorris* v. *Scott* (1874) 9 Exch 125. An Order was made in pursuance of the Contagious Diseases (Animals) Act 1869 requiring sheep or cattle being transported by ship from any foreign ports to ports in Great Britain to be put in pens of certain dimensions. The defendant did not have any such pens on board his ship and the plaintiff's sheep were washed overboard in a storm and drowned. The plaintiff brought an action for damages for breach of the Order. The court held that the plaintiff's action should fail. The statute had been passed, according to the judges, merely for 'sanitary purposes, in order to prevent animals in a state of infectious disease from communicating it to other animals with which they might come into contact'. The purpose of the statute was not to prevent them being drowned.

The Duty Imposed

Secondly, it must be considered what the content of the duty imposed is. The answer to this question depends upon an interpretation of the statutory language used. The wide variety of language used in different statutes has meant that a variety of different standards have been imposed. Some statutes do impose strict or even absolute duties, others, however, impose more qualified 'negligence' duties. There is no rule of thumb used to determine which duty has been imposed. Each statute must be construed carefully to determine what the standard imposed is. Some cases will be given to illustrate the different standards imposed.

Statutes imposing absolute standards are rare. However, an example of an absolute duty can be seen in the case of *Galashiels Gas Co Ltd* v. *Millar* [1949] A.C. 275 (H.L., Sc). By section 22(1) of the Factories Act 1937 it was provided that, 'every hoist or lift shall be properly maintained'. The House of Lords held that the section imposed an absolute duty to maintain a lift in an efficient state. Proof of any failure in a lift mechanism, therefore, established a breach of duty, even if it was impossible to foresee the failure before the event or explain it afterwards. Here liability is truly independent of fault.

More often a statute will impose a qualified duty. For example, section 29(1) of the Factories Act 1961 provides, 'there shall, so far as is reasonably practicable, be provided and maintained safe means of access to every place at which any person has at any time to work'. There are many reported cases which interpret qualified standards of this type. Space considerations, however, preclude full consideration being given to these. The point which must be recognised is that it is always necessary to turn to the statute to discover what the content of the duty imposed on the defendant is. One case may be cited by way of illustration. In *McCarthy* v. *Coldair Ltd* [1951] 2 TLR 1226 an employee fell when a short ladder he was ascending slipped. He claimed that his employer was in breach of what is now section 29(1) of the Factories Act 1961. The employer was held to be in breach of his duty. It was accepted by the court that it would not ordinarily be reasonably practicable to station a man at the foot of a short ladder as this would be a disproportionately expensive way of avoiding a small risk. However, in light of the fact that the ladder was being used on a semi-glazed floor which had been splashed by paint, the court felt that the risk was greatly increased, such that it would be reasonably practicable to take the steps suggested by the worker.

16.6 Reform

As has been shown the English courts, when deciding whether or not an action lies for breach of statutory duty, seek to elucidate Parliament's intention through the use of presumptions. Such an approach has not been without its critics. A number of problems have been identified. First, adoption of a presumption-based approach to determine Parliament's intention is misguided because in most cases the silence of the statute on the question of civil liability points to the conclusion that Parliament either did not have the problem in mind or that it deliberately omitted to provide for it. Secondly, the presumptions are unhelpful in that in many cases their application produces no clear result. The courts are thus left with considerable discretion as to whether liability should be imposed. Thirdly, the presumptions are themselves flawed. For example, why should it be the case that an action should be presumed where a duty is owed to a particular class but not where it is owed to the general public? It is surely strange that a duty which Parliament considers to be so important that it provides that it should be owed to the public at large will generally not give rise to an action, whereas a less important duty owed to a particular class will, prima facie at least, be presumed to give rise to an action.

As a result of this dissatisfaction various alternatives have been suggested. The Law Commission has argued for a statutory presumption that an action will lie unless express provision to the contrary is made in the statute (Law Commission, 1969). This suggestion attracted severe criticism when placed before Parliament and seems unlikely to be adopted. It does at least have the merit of introducing clarity into a notoriously unclear area but it does so, according to its critics, by imposing unacceptably wide liability. The main criticism was that the suggested presumption of actionability pays no attention to the areas in which it would operate. Rights and duties should only be imposed where they are shown to be required. The Law Commission proposal ignores this. It might be argued, however, that it would at least have the merit of focusing Parliament's attention on the question of actionability and would also answer the criticism that Parliament's intention was being frustrated.

An alternative approach is to regard breach of statutory duty as a particular species of negligence. Any breach of such a duty should be treated either as negligence *per se* or as evidence of negligence. Under this approach breach of statutory duty is no longer considered a nominate tort, but is instead subsumed under the tort of negligence. This is the approach favoured by the American courts (where the view adopted by the majority of States is that breach of a statutory duty is *per se* negligence) and the Canadian courts (evidence of negligence only). Perhaps the strongest argument in favour of the 'statutory negligence' approach, in either of its forms, is that it gets rid of the necessity for the courts to ascertain what was Parliament's intention. English courts would no longer be able, were such an approach to be adopted, to shield their decisions from public scrutiny behind the presumptions. At present, however, it seems unlikely that this approach will be adopted.

Summary

16.1 In this chapter we sought to answer the question when statutes which impose duties but either are silent as to whether a civil action should lie for breach or impose some other form of liability for breach give rise to a civil action for breach of statutory duty.

16.2 In determining whether a statute gives rise to a civil action for breach of statutory duty, the courts seek to determine whether Parliament intended there to be an action. In ascertaining the intention of Parliament the courts apply a number of presumptions.

16.3 The two main presumptions are: (a) where the statute is silent as to the method of enforcement there is a presumption that a tortious remedy for breach of statutory duty is intended; and (b) where the statute provides an alternative remedy for breach of the statute, a presumption arises that this is the only remedy intended, and therefore no action for breach of statutory duty lies.

16.4 The presumption of non-actionability in the case of statutes which provide for an alternative remedy can be rebutted either where the statute is passed for the benefit of, or to protect, a particular class of persons, or where the statute creates a public right and a particular member of the public suffers 'special' damage. In considering whether a statute is passed for the benefit of a particular class of persons the courts take into account a number of policy factors.

16.5 Once it has been determined that an action for breach of statutory duty lies, the court must decide whether the damage suffered is recognised by the statute in question. The court must also determine what the content of the duty imposed is.

16.6 A number of proposals have been made to reform the law relating to breach of statutory duty. They have involved either the replacement of the existing presumptions with a new one (Law Commission) or treating breach of statutory duty as a particular species of negligence.

Exercises

16.1 I'm the Parliamentary Draftsman,
I compose the country's laws,
And of half the litigation
I'm undoubtedly the cause. (J.P.C., Poetic Justice, 1947)
Is this true? (See Williams (1960) from where this 'poem' is taken).

16.2 Is the preferable approach to determining whether a statute gives rise to a breach of statutory duty that of Lord Denning in *Ex Parte Island Records* or that taken by the House of Lords in *Lonrho* v. *Shell Petroleum Co Ltd*?

16.3 What are the main presumptions applied by the court for determining whether an action for breach of statutory duty lies?

16.4 What effect does the existence of a private or public law remedy have on the question of whether Parliament intended there to be a civil action?

16.5 What policy considerations, if any, do the courts take into account in considering whether a statute was passed for the benefit of a particular class of persons? Does the fact that a statute was passed to benefit a particular class of persons mean that an action will always lie?

16.6 Why have the courts not imposed a civil liability for breach of statutory duty in the area of motor vehicles?

16.7 What proposals for reform have been suggested? Which do you prefer?

17 Trespass to the Person

17.1 Introduction

In most societies, protection of an individual's bodily integrity is likely to rank high on the agenda of interests considered worth protecting. It is perhaps understandable, therefore, that one of the earliest remedies provided by English law was for forcible wrongs against the person. Such wrongs were remediable by commencing an action using a writ of trespass. The writ of trespass emerged in the thirteenth century. It originally existed in a semi-criminal form; if the defendant did not appear to answer the writ he would be outlawed while, if convicted, he was liable to a fine or imprisonment in addition to being liable to the plaintiff in damages. However, by the end of the medieval period the tort action had shed its criminal characteristics. In the civil law the writ of trespass dealt with direct interference with the person in three types of case which correspond to the modern torts of assault, battery and false imprisonment.

By the eighteenth century trespass was differentiated from the other main writ providing a remedy for tortious misconduct, namely, the action of trespass on the case (later simply called case), by its requirement that the harm be directly caused. Case provided a remedy where the harm was indirectly caused. The tendency in later years, however, has been to associate case with negligently caused harm and trespass with intentional wrongs. The main cause of this belief is the fact that the modern law of negligence is derived from the action on the case. As case was associated with negligence, so trespass came to be seen as a tort of intention. However, unlike negligence which provides a remedy for both indirectly and directly caused harm, trespass has still retained the requirement that the harm must be directly caused.

17.2 Trespass and Negligence

The essence of trespass to the person is that it affords a plaintiff protection against direct invasions of his bodily integrity. In this regard the early common law imposed a very strict responsibility on the defendant. Although it is doubtful that a person would ever have been liable in trespass where he was totally without fault, it was certainly once true that where the plaintiff had established a direct interference the defendant would be liable unless he could establish some justification or excuse. However, in 1959 it was clearly established that in order to succeed in trespass it was not enough for the plaintiff simply to prove a direct invasion of his bodily integrity. In *Fowler* v. *Lanning* [1959] 1 QB 426, the plaintiff's statement of claim alleged simply that on a certain date and at a certain place 'the defendant shot the plaintiff' and that by reason thereof the plaintiff suffered injury. The defendant objected that this statement of claim disclosed no cause of action in that it did not allege that the shooting was intentional or negligent. Diplock J held that to succeed in trespass it was not enough to prove a direct act (the defendant shot me); the plaintiff had in addition to prove that the direct act was done intentionally or negligently.

The result of *Fowler* v. *Lanning* is that where the injury is unintended, whether it is a direct or indirect consequence of the defendant's act, the plaintiff will only succeed where he can show that the defendant's conduct was unreasonable (i.e., negligent). Thus, in most cases of unintentional injury, the plaintiff will bring his action in negligence rather than trespass because there is no need in negligence, unlike trespass, to prove that the injury was a direct consequence of the act. To a large extent, therefore, the rules of negligence have overtaken those of trespass where the defendant's act was unintentional.

Difficulties, however, remain in determining the true relationship between trespass and negligence. Can an action for trespass still be brought where the defendant's act was unintentional? This question is important in cases where the plaintiff suffers no damage because, unlike negligence where *damage* is the gist of the action, the tort of trespass is actionable *per se* (i.e., without proof of damage). The point was considered by the Court of Appeal in *Letang* v. *Cooper* [1965] 1 QB 232. The defendant negligently drove his Jaguar over the legs of the plaintiff, who was sunbathing in a car park. More than three years after the accident the plaintiff sued the defendant in negligence and trespass. The plaintiff admitted that her action in negligence was time-barred by the (then) Limitation Act 1939 but argued that her alternative claim in trespass was not. Her argument succeeded at first instance, but was rejected by the Court of Appeal. One reason given was that an action for trespass fell within the terms of the Act. However, the court went considerably further than that. Lord Denning MR, with whom Danckwerts LJ agreed, held that where the defendant inflicts the injury unintentionally no action would lie for trespass. He agreed with the judgment of Diplock J in *Fowler* v. *Lanning*, but said (at p. 240): 'I would go this one step further: when the injury is not inflicted intentionally, but negligently, I would say that the only cause of action is negligence and not trespass. If it were trespass, it would be actionable without proof of damage; and that is not the law today.' In Lord Denning's opinion, therefore, trespass is truly an intentional tort in that only the intentional application of force can give rise to an action in trespass. Where the act is unintentional, the correct and only cause of action is negligence.

Lord Denning's opinion that a cause of action will only lie in trespass where a person intentionally applies force directly to another has not found universal support. For example, Diplock LJ in *Letang* v. *Cooper* accepted that trespass could be committed negligently but thought that there were no significant differences between an action for unintentional (but negligent) trespass and an action in negligence. Also, in Canada and Australia support still exists for the view that there may be a negligent trespass. While the point still remains open, the better view is that expressed by Lord Denning. In the first place little is lost to the plaintiff by depriving him of a right to sue in trespass where the application of force was unintentional. If damage was suffered he has an action in negligence. Where no damage has been suffered it is almost inconceivable that he would want to bring an action. In the second place, Lord Denning's view achieves a welcome clarification of the law classifying liability according to the mental state of the defendant.

17.3   Assault and Battery

Where a person intentionally and unlawfully applies force directly to another, this constitutes a battery. Where a person intentionally and unlawfully makes a threat which causes the plaintiff reasonably to apprehend the immediate infliction of a battery on him, that is an assault. It should be noted that in some of the cases courts use the word *assault* to describe what is in essence a *battery*. The reason for this is because most assaults end in a battery and the result is often described as an assault and battery or just an assault. Despite this terminological confusion, the distinction between the two torts is fairly clear. Thus it is an assault for A to point a loaded gun at B who fears being shot, but if A fires the gun and the bullet hits B that is a battery. It is an assault for A to drive a car at B such that B fears being hit, but it is a battery to hit him. Often battery and assault go together; however, they need not. For example, if A sneaks up behind B without B hearing him and hits him over the head there is a battery but no assault. Similarly, if A shakes his fist at B that is an assault but not a battery.

Battery

In relation to battery there is no requirement that the defendant intended to cause *harm*. All that the plaintiff need show is that the defendant intended to touch the body of the plaintiff. It is the touching and not its consequences which must be intended. This might be thought to give rise to intolerable difficulties. Is it, for example, a battery if I shake your hand in greeting or if I slap you on the back in congratulations when you tell me your examination results? An early attempt to distinguish acceptable from unacceptable touchings was made by Holt CJ in *Cole* v. *Turner* (1704) 6 Mod 149 where he said, 'the least touching of another in anger is a battery'. Whilst there is nothing inherently wrong with this statement in that if A touches B in anger his act will be a battery, some behaviour not committed in anger will still be a battery. Examples of such behaviour might include an unwanted kiss or, as was the case in *Collins* v. *Wilcock* [1984] 3 All ER 374, restraining someone in order to speak to them. Despite the insufficiency of this test as an explanation of those cases likely to be classified as batteries, Holt CJ's words were held to set out the appropriate criterion by the Court of Appeal in *Wilson* v. *Pringle* [1986] 2 All ER 440. Croom Johnson LJ held that for there to be a battery there must be 'something in the nature of overt hostility' (p. 445). Hostility, he said should not be equated with ill-will or malevolence: an act can be 'hostile' even if not committed in anger. Instead he appears to suggest that it means little more than an objectionable touching. This, it is suggested, is not a very helpful test as in essence all it does is restate the very question which needs to be answered.

A better approach was that suggested by Robert Goff LJ in *Collins* v. *Wilcock*. There, he said that a touching will only amount to a battery where it does not fall within the category of physical contacts 'generally acceptable in the ordinary conduct of general life'. Thus being jostled in the underground during the rush-hour would not be a battery, whereas an unwanted kiss or perhaps an overexuberant slap on the back would be. Although this approach was thought impracticable by Croom Johnson LJ in *Wilson* v. *Pringle*, Lord Goff (as he has become) has reiterated his views in the House of Lords in *Re: F* [1990] 2 AC 1, 73 where he explicitly rejected any requirement of 'hostility' as unnecessary. It is likely, therefore, that this will be the approach adopted in future cases.

Historically, a cause of action in trespass only lay where the touching was the direct or immediate result of the plaintiff's act. This requirement was succinctly stated by Blackstone J in *Scott* v. *Shepherd* (1773) 2 Black.W. 892 where he said, 'where the injury is immediate, an action in trespass will lie; where it is only consequential, it must be an action on the case'. Thus, it has been said that where a person throws a log of timber on to the highway and another person falls over it and is injured, this injury is only consequential and an action for trespass will not lie. By way of contrast, if the log were to hit someone that would give rise to an action in trespass because the contact would be direct and immediate. In the modern law the plaintiff is still required to show that the touching was the direct result of the defendant's act, but the courts have stretched the concept of directness so far that it is doubtful whether today this requirement provides a substantial hurdle for many plaintiffs. The facts of *Scott* v. *Shepherd* illustrate the broad nature of the concept. The defendant threw a lighted squib made of gun-powder into a covered market where a large number of people were collected. The squib fell on to B's stall and he picked it up and threw it on to C's stall, who likewise threw it away and in so doing hit the plaintiff. The court, by a majority, held that an action for trespass would lie. The intermediate acts of B and C were, somewhat surprisingly, found not to have broken the chain of directness between the defendant and the plaintiff.

In the more recent case of *D.P.P.* v. *K* [1990] 1 WLR 1067, K, a 15-year old schoolboy, took some concentrated sulphuric acid out of a chemistry lesson and took it to the lavatory. On hearing footsteps outside the lavatory door he poured the acid into a hand and face drier. Another pupil turned the drier on and was badly burnt when acid spurted out. K was convicted of assault occasioning actual bodily harm. Although the case has subsequently been said to be wrongly decided on another ground, it is nonetheless interesting from our point of view as it appears to have been assumed that the contact was the direct, as opposed to consequential, result of the defendant's act. Surely this is a case where the touching was consequential on the act of the plaintiff in putting the acid into the drier. If the case is correctly decided on this point then the abandoning of a log on the highway over which someone falls should also be seen as the direct cause of the plaintiff's harm, as should the setting of a trap for the plaintiff. While other, generally older, cases have taken a narrower view as to the meaning to be ascribed to direct, the requirement no longer appears to be a serious bar to recovery and could be abandoned.

Assault

The essence of an assault is the making of a threat which places the plaintiff in reasonable apprehension of an immediate battery to himself. It is not every threat, however, that will suffice to give rise to liability. Clearly, if A points a loaded gun at B, the pointing of the gun will suffice. In such a case, by virtue of the pointing of the gun the plaintiff reasonably apprehends the infliction of an immediate battery. Would the position be any different if A, without a gun, had said, 'I am going to shoot you dead'? In other words can the speaking of words amount to an assault? Although there are authorities going both ways, the view most often cited is that of Holroyd J in *Mead's and Belt's Case* (1823) 1 Lewin 184. He said there that, 'no words or singing are equivalent to an assault'. This view reflects the fact that in many cases the uttering of mere words will not give rise to fear of an *immediate* battery. In our example, the speaking of the words 'I am going to shoot you dead' by a person without a gun would probably lack immediacy. The speaker would presumably have to go away, find a gun and then return before he could put the threat into effect.

The fact that mere words are used should not, however, mean that in every situation there will be no assault. For example, if a mugger were to say to his victim, 'Your money, or I will beat you up' this could amount to an assault even in the absence of any threatening gestures by the mugger. Similarly, if the defendant, who was engaged in beating up A, were to say to the plaintiff, 'You are next', this too could amount to an assault. The requirement of immediacy would be satisfied. What is important, therefore, is not how the threat is conveyed but whether what is conveyed is enough to place the plaintiff in *reasonable apprehension* of an immediate battery.

Words may not only amount to an assault: they may also have the effect of neutralising a threat made by a gesture. In *Tuberville* v. *Savage* (1669) 1 Mod 3, T put his hand on his sword and said to S, 'If it were not assize-time I would not take such language from you.' These words were held to prevent the gesture from amounting to an assault. For there to be an assault the plaintiff must reasonably *anticipate* the infliction of a battery. Thus, where the plaintiff has no knowledge of the threat there can be no assault. However, there will be an assault if the plaintiff reasonably anticipates the infliction of a battery even if he is not in fact put in a state of fear or terror. It is the plaintiff's knowledge that is important, and not the effect that this knowledge has on his mind. A related, though distinct, question is whether there is an assault where, although the plaintiff thinks that the defendant is about to inflict a battery on him, the defendant does not in fact have the necessary means to do so? For example, if a person points an unloaded gun at another, does this amount to an assault? In *Stephens* v. *Myers* (1830) 4 Car & P 350 Tindal CJ said, 'it is not every threat, when there is no actual personal violence that constitutes an assault there must be, in all cases the means of carrying the threat into effect'. This approach finds support in *Blake* v. *Burnard* (1840) 9 Car & P 626 where Lord Abinger CB held that it was not an assault to point an unloaded pistol at another. However, while these cases have not been overruled, other cases (such as *R* v. *St George* (1840) 9 Car & P 483) have held that such an act can amount to an assault. In principle, the better view is that expressed in *R* v. *St George*. Where a battery is, in all the circumstances, *reasonably* apprehended this should be enough to constitute an assault.

17.4 False Imprisonment

The tort of false imprisonment is committed when the defendant intentionally and without lawful justification restrains a person's liberty within an area delimited by the defendant. It is not necessary in order to establish the tort that a person be locked up in a prison. As was said in the *Termes de la Ley*:

'imprisonment is no other thing but the restraint of a man's liberty whether it bee in the openfield, or in the stocks or in the cage in the street or in a man's own house, as well as in the common gaole; and in all the places the party so restrained is said to be a prisoner so long as he hath not his liberty freely to goe at all times to all places wither he will without baile or mainprise or otherwise.'

Thus, restraining a person from leaving his own house, casting him adrift in a boat or taking hold of him in the street can amount to false imprisonments.

In order for there to be a false imprisonment the restraint must be total. In *Bird* v. *Jones* (1845) 7 QB 742 the defendants enclosed part of Hammersmith Bridge and put seats in the enclosure for the use of paying spectators of a regatta. The plaintiff insisted on passing along the bridge through the enclosure and climbed over the fence of the enclosure without paying the charge. The defendants then refused to let the plaintiff go forward in the direction he wished to go but told him that he could go back and cross the bridge although not through the enclosure. The court held that this was no false imprisonment. In reaching this conclusion, Patteson J said (at pp. 751–2) that there was no imprisonment where 'one man merely obstructs the passage of another in a particular direction, whether by threat of personal violence or otherwise, leaving him at liberty to stay where he is or to go in any other direction if he pleases'.

A difficult decision which at first sight appears to conflict with the decision in *Bird* v. *Jones* is that of *Robinson* v. *Balmain New Ferry Co Ltd* [1910] AC 295. The respondents operated a ferry service between Sydney and Balmain. On the Sydney side a turnstile with an exit and entrance was set up, and a notice displayed stating that a penny had to be paid on entering and leaving the wharf. The appellant paid his penny to enter and then changed his mind and sought to leave without paying a further penny. The respondents prevented him from doing so. The Privy Council held that this was not a false imprisonment. How can this be so? Surely it was the case that the plaintiff was wholly restrained within the wharf? If so, it would seem to be the case that an action for false imprisonment should have succeeded. One explanation of the case is that the appellant was never completely restrained; he could still have used the ferry, as he had originally intended to do, and gained his freedom unconditionally on the other side. Thus, his contractual path was never closed to him and he was not, therefore, falsely imprisoned.

While this may be a convincing explanation of the case, it is not clear that this was the reason given by the Privy Council for their decision. An alternative view of the reasoning of the court was that there was no false imprisonment because an occupier of premises is entitled to impose reasonable conditions on the manner in which an entrant leaves his premises. On the facts, the Privy Council held that it was reasonable for the ferry company to insist that all persons leaving the wharf paid one penny. The plaintiff had contracted to leave the wharf via the ferry and the payment of one penny was not an unreasonable condition to impose for his leaving by a different route.

A similar case was that of *Herd* v. *Weardale Steel Coal and Coke Co Ltd* [1915] AC 67. A miner employed by the defendants, in breach of his contract, refused to do certain work in his pit. His employers refused to take him to the surface for some time after a cage was available to do so. He sued for false imprisonment. The House of Lords held that his action failed. Clearly, the restraint here was total; the only way out was via the cage to the surface. The court, relying on the decision in *Robinson* v. *Balmain New Ferry Co*, held that the miner had gone down the mine on certain terms and it was no false imprisonment to hold him to the conditions he accepted when he went down. Both cases are, therefore, authority for the proposition that the imposition of a reasonable condition may negate false imprisonment.

There may be a false imprisonment even in the absence of actual force or direct physical contact. Thus if a police officer informs a person that he is under arrest this, in the absence of lawful justification, will amount to a false imprisonment. It has even been held that requiring a person to come along to the police station and answer some questions may be sufficient. All that is required, therefore, is that there must be such constraint on the person's will that he believes that he is under restraint. The emphasis, as Fleming (1987) points out (p. 27) is on 'the impression created in the victim's mind.' Given this emphasis it is perhaps not surprising that differing views have been expressed on the question of whether a person can be falsely imprisoned where he does not know that he is under constraint. Despite an old decision suggesting that there cannot be liability in such circumstances, the more modern view is that there can be. In *Murray* v. *Ministry of Defence* [1988] 1 WLR 692 Lord Griffiths, with whom the other members of the House of Lords agreed, said that knowledge of the restraint was not an essential element of the tort. While in the absence of such knowledge the damages likely to be awarded will be nominal, 'the law attaches supreme importance to the liberty of the individual and if he suffers a wrongful interference with that liberty it should remain actionable even without proof of special damage'.

The essence of false imprisonment is, as we have seen, the restraint of a person without lawful justification. In most cases this restraint will be of a person who is lawfully at large. A difficult problem is posed by the question of whether a person who is lawfully imprisoned can ever complain of false imprisonment in relation to acts subsequent to his imprisonment. This matter was considered by the House of Lords in *Hague* v. *Deputy Governor of Parkhurst Prison* [1991] 3 All ER 733 (see Mullis, 1991 pp. 396–8). Allegations were made against the prison authorities by two prisoners. H alleged that in breach of the Prison Rules he had been transferred to another prison and there segregated from other inmates for 28 days. W alleged that he had been falsely imprisoned by being placed in a strip cell overnight. The House of Lords held that no action for false imprisonment could lie in these circumstances. The prison authorities had a complete defence by virtue of section 12(1) of the Prison Act 1952 which provides that, 'a prisoner . . . may be lawfully confined in any prison'. This section, their Lordships said, provided a complete defence for the restraint of a prisoner within the bounds of a prison by the governor or someone acting with the governor's authority. Thus, where the prisoner was locked up in a part of the prison with the governor's authority there was no room for an argument that the prison authorities were liable for false imprisonment based on any 'residual liberty' of the prisoner's. They further held that holding a prisoner in intolerable conditions could not give rise to liability for false imprisonment because this was to confuse the fact of confinement with the conditions of confinement. The tort of false imprisonment was confined to remedying the former. They did accept, however, that an action for negligence might lie if a prisoner suffered injury as a result of such confinement.

While no action lay on the facts of this case, the House of Lords did not wholly reject the possibility of an action being brought by a person who is lawfully imprisoned. They said that if another prisoner, or a prison officer who acted in bad faith, locked up within the confines of a prison a person who was lawfully imprisoned, this could amount to false imprisonment.

17.5   Intentional Infliction of Physical Harm other than Trespass to the Person: *Wilkinson* v. *Downton*

In *Wilkinson* v. *Downton* [1897] 2 QB 57 the defendant, by way of a practical joke, falsely represented to the plaintiff that her husband had met with a serious accident. The plaintiff, believing the story, suffered a violent shock to her system and subsequently became ill. She brought an action against the defendant claiming damages for her psychiatric injury. Wright J held that where a person wilfully does an act calculated to produce an effect on the plaintiff of the kind which was actually produced, then a cause of action would arise in the absence of any legal justification. On the facts it was clear that the defendant must be treated as having intended to induce the psychiatric illness in the plaintiff and, therefore, the plaintiff's claim succeeded.

There has only been one further case in England applying this principle. In *Janvier* v. *Sweeney* [1919] 2 KB 316 the defendants, who were private detectives, told the plaintiff that unless she produced certain letters then in the possession of her employer they would disclose to the authorities that her fiancé was a traitor. She suffered a nervous shock as a result of these statements. The Court of Appeal held, applying *Wilkinson* v. *Downton*, that her action for damages succeeded.

What is the extent of the principle in *Wilkinson* v. *Downton*? Clearly within the principle are those cases where the defendant makes a statement intending to cause nervous shock. However, it will be comparatively rare that such an intention can be established. An intention to frighten or alarm the plaintiff may also suffice to found liability. Provided the statement made was of a kind which would have caused a reasonable person to sustain nervous shock of the sort which occurred, the intention to produce that effect would be imputed; *Wilkinson* v. *Downton* itself is a case of this type. Provided that some physical harm was intended, liability will be established. The full extent of the harm need neither be intended nor foreseen.

Although the injury in *Wilkinson* v. *Downton* resulted from a statement there is no reason why the principle should not extend to acts. As Dias and Markesinis (1989, at p. 247) point out, 'a statement is, after all, a kind of act, so it is hardly a large step to understand the principle as covering acts generally'. Neither does there seem to be any reason to confine the principle to nervous shock. If the plaintiff in *Wilkinson* v. *Downton* had fallen over as a result of the shock and in so doing had cracked open her head she should equally have been able to recover.

The relationship of *Wilkinson* v. *Downton* to the tort of trespass is not wholly clear. At present it appears to be confined to cases of intentional but indirectly inflicted physical harm. Thus it should be seen as a residuary form of liability supplementing the nominate torts of trespass to the person. However, there seems to be no reason why *Wilkinson* v. *Downton* could not give rise to a general principle of liability for all intentionally inflicted physical harm. Whether it will do so is a more difficult question. To form a new tort of intentionally inflicting physical harm would involve dismantling the current structure of the trespass torts. This is something the courts are unlikely to be willing to do. For the moment, therefore, it seems that the principle is likely to remain as a separate, complementary principle of liability covering cases of intentionally, though indirectly, inflicted physical harm.

17.6 Damages

Unlike negligence, where proof of damage is an essential element in the cause of action, trespass to the person is actionable *per se* (without proof of any damage). In actions for false imprisonment and assault, damages may also be awarded for insult or injury to the plaintiff's feelings. Additionally, exemplary damages may be awarded where the trespass occurred either as a result of arbitrary conduct by a government official, or was a result of a deliberate or reckless breach of the law done with a view for gain The fact that exemplary damages can be awarded in respect of arbitrary conduct by a government official gives trespass an important role in the protection of the liberties of the citizen against infringement by the state, even where no damage is caused and hence no action in negligence will arise.

17.7 Defences to Trespass to the Person

Once the plaintiff has proved the direct interference that constitutes the trespass, it is for the defendant to justify his action by reference to one of the defences. There are a number of defences to trespass to the person of varying degrees of importance. Thus the exercise of disciplinary powers by parents over children can be a defence provided the force used is reasonable. So too can statutory authority and, in limited circumstances, contributory negligence (see 12.5) and illegality (see 12.6). The fact that criminal proceedings have already been taken against the defendant may also, in certain circumstances, relieve him of civil liability (Offences Against the Person Act 1861, ss. 42–45). Probably the most important defences in practice are the powers of arrest conferred on police officers, and the more limited powers conferred on private citizens by the Police and Criminal Evidence Act 1984. Where a police officer or a private citizen, carries out a lawful arrest he will commit neither a false imprisonment nor a battery. Reference should be made to texts on constitutional law or civil liberties for details of the powers of arrest. Three defences – consent, self-defence and necessity – will now be considered in more detail.

Consent

Where a person consents either expressly or impliedly to a trespass to his person, no action will lie. There is some debate over the question of whether consent is strictly speaking a defence at all, because a defence is something which it is for the defendant to prove. In *Freeman* v. *Home Office (No 2)* [1984] QB 524, McCowan J held that the burden of proving absence of consent was on the plaintiff, thereby implying that absence of consent is an essential element of trespass to the person. While this is probably the prevailing view in English law today (cf. the view in Australia where McCowan's view has been rejected), it is suggested that Winfield and Jolowicz (1989) are correct when they say (at p. 683) that 'as a practical matter, however, the defendant may need to lead evidence to lay a foundation from which the court will infer consent as a specific issue in his statement of claim'. In this sense, therefore, consent may be treated as a 'defence'.

Consent can be given expressly: for example, where a patient signs a consent form to an operation. Alternatively, consent may be implied. An example of implied consent can be found in the old American case of *O'Brien* v. *Cunard* (1891) 28 NE 266, where the court held that by standing in line and holding out her arm the plaintiff impliedly consented to being vaccinated. Similarly, participants in 'violent sports' impliedly consent to the risks ordinarily incidental to such sports. They do not, however, consent to excessive violence or to deliberate unfair play.

The relevance of consent in a civil action may differ from that in criminal proceedings. While certain consensual activities may be considered so contrary to public policy that they are treated as criminal, it would be wrong to allow one consenting participant to sue another (so long as the latter did nothing excessive). Thus in the infamous case of *R* v. *Brown* [1992] 2 All ER 552, the Court of Appeal held that the participants in homosexual sado-masochistic 'games' could not rely on the defence of consent to negate their criminal liability. Much stress was laid by the court on the public interest that people should not injure each other for no good reason. While this is clearly a relevant matter when considering a criminal prosecution, it is less clear that it is relevant in a civil action where the court is primarily concerned with the reciprocal rights and liabilities of the parties *inter se*. Thus, had one of the participants in the activities brought an action for battery it is suggested that his consent should amount to a complete defence.

For consent to be valid it must be genuine. Thus, consent obtained by duress would be no defence. So, for example, consent to sexual intercourse obtained by threats of violence would not be valid. By way of contrast, the

Court of Appeal held in *Freeman* v. *Home Office (No 2)* [1984] QB 524
that the consent given by a prisoner to medical treatment was genuine.
The institutional pressures imposed in those circumstances were held not
to negate the consent given.

Consent will not be valid unless the plaintiff understands the nature and
purpose of the touching. In *Chatterton* v. *Gerson* [1981] 1 All ER 257
Bristow J said that 'once [a person] is informed in broad terms of the
nature of the procedure which is intended and gives her consent, that
consent is real'. The difficulty is to determine what information is relevant
to the 'nature' and 'purpose' of the touching and what is merely collateral
to it. In circumstances where the consent was induced by deceit or given
under a misapprehension as to the nature and purpose of the touching the
courts have held that the consent was vitiated. In *R* v. *Williams* [1923] 1
KB 340, for example, it was held that there was no valid consent by a
woman to sexual intercourse where she was told that this was therapy for
her voice. There the deceit was as to the nature and purpose of the
touching.

More uncertainty surrounds the situation where the plaintiff is aware of
the nature and purpose of the touching but unaware of its harmful
consequences. This issue was considered in *R* v. *Clarence* (1888) 22 QB
23. The defendant had sexual intercourse with his wife with her consent.
Unknown to the wife, the defendant had gonorrhoea and she became
infected. The defendant was charged with 'assault occasioning actual
bodily harm' and 'unlawfully and maliciously inflicting grievous bodily
harm'. A majority of the court held that both offences required the proof
of an assault or battery: Hence it was necessary to prove that the
defendant's wife had not consented. The court held that the woman's
consent was valid even though she had no knowledge of her husband's
condition.

Despite, or perhaps because of, its antiquity this case has attracted
much academic criticism. Grubb and Pearl (1990) argue that the case
should be narrowly confined. *Clarence* was a decision relating to a
criminal prosecution for a serious offence and, given the prevailing social
and sexual mores of the time, it was unsurprising that the result was
reached. It should not, however, be treated as authority for the proposition that in a civil action for trespass to the person consent to a touching is
valid where the person touched knows the nature and purpose of the
touching but does not know its harmful consequences. The consequences
of accepting the *Clarence* approach would be to refuse an action to a
person who consents to being touched by a metal rod which (unknown to
him, but known to the holder of the rod) is charged with electricity. This is
surely wrong and recovery should be permitted (see Fleming, 1987).

Finally, something should be said about consent in medical cases as this
is probably the most important area of the defence's operation. As a
general rule, the principles explained above apply equally to medical cases.
Indeed, many of the leading authorities involve medical treatment. Thus,
provided the broad nature of the proposed operation is explained to a

patient, any consent given will excuse what would otherwise be a battery (see, e.g., *Chatterton* v. *Gerson*). However, particular difficulties arise in medical cases in three types of case: treatment of children, treatment of the mentally disordered or ill and treatment of the unconscious. In the case of children, section 8 of the Family Law Reform Act 1969 provides that a minor between the ages of 16 and 18 can give an effective consent to surgical, medical or dental treatment as if he were an adult. As regards a child who has not reached his sixteenth birthday, the House of Lords held in *Gillick* v. *D.H.S.S.* [1986] AC 112 that a child can give effective consent to medical treatment providing he has the ability to understand what is involved in the medical procedure proposed. In *Gillick* itself, Lord Scarman said that in relation to contraceptive advice and treatment this would involve not only understanding the reasons for the doctor touching the child and the purposes behind the touching, but also an understanding of the wider social and moral implications. In the case of a very young child, consent must be sought from a proxy (usually a parent) in order for the touching to be lawful.

As far as mentally disordered or ill persons are concerned the position is more difficult. Clearly, such persons may be unable to give a real consent if they are not able to understand any explanation given to them as to the nature and purpose of the touching. This is obviously the case with regard to unconscious patients. Both class of patients are, in law, incompetent to consent to medical treatment. In *F* v. *West Berkshire Health Authority* [1989] 2 All ER 545, the House of Lords held that treatment of such patients could not be justified by any extension of the notion of implied consent; it would be a pure fiction to suggest that such patients impliedly agreed to medical treatment in their best interest. However, medical treatment might be justified on the ground of necessity. This point is considered below.

Self-Defence

Where a person hits another in defending himself from an attack by that other person, he may be able to plead self-defence as a justification. The defence may succeed even where no physical touching has actually been committed by the aggressor. So, for example, if a person threatens another with a gun the defence would succeed if the threatened person sought by force to disarm the aggressor. A reasonable apprehension of threatened aggression is all that is required to justify the use of reasonable force in self-defence.

In addition to proving that he was justified in using force to defend himself, the defendant must also prove that the force used was reasonable. This is in essence a question of fact, and the answer given will depend on such factors as the degree of violence offered, its immediacy and whether any weapons were used. It was held not to be self-defence in *Cook* v. *Beal* 1 Lord Raym 177, for example, for the defendant to draw his sword and cut off the hand of a person who had merely struck the defendant. Having said that, the use of even lethal force may be justified if the initial attack is sufficiently violent. There is no *duty* on the defendant to retreat in the face of an assault. The fact that the person attacked did not retreat is merely a factor to be taken into account in determining whether the action taken by the defendant was reasonable.

In addition to the right to defend oneself if attacked, a trespass to the person may be justified if the defendant acts in defence of other persons or even to protect his property. It is clear that a person may defend any member of his family. As with self-defence, the force used must be reasonable. It is suggested that it is also legitimate to use force in protection of persons other than one's own family. Nobody should have to stand idly by and watch a person seriously assault another because he is afraid of a civil action being brought against him for trespass.

A similar principle applies in relation to protection of property. A person is entitled to use reasonable force to defend land or chattels in his possession. So, for example, an occupier of land may use reasonable force in ejecting a trespasser. As with the defence of another person the force used must be reasonable. In *Collins* v. *Renison* (1754) Say. 138, Ryder CJ held that overturning a ladder on which the plaintiff was standing in order to eject him from the defendant's property was not justifiable. As the judge put it: 'the overturning of the ladder could not answer the purpose of removing the plaintiff out of the garden; since it only left him upon the ground at the bottom of the ladder, instead of being upon it'. It may be that these cases should now be considered as examples of the principle of necessity (see below).

Necessity

In *F* v. *West Berkshire Health Authority* Lord Goff acknowledged that English law recognises a principle of necessity which 'may justify action which would otherwise be unlawful'. The cases on necessity, he said, could be conveniently divided into three different categories. First, there are cases of public necessity. A typical example of this category would be where a person pulls down another man's house in order to prevent the spread of a catastrophic fire. Secondly, there are cases of private necessity. Typically these occur where a person damages another's property or inflicts injury to another in order to save his own person or property. Finally, there are a series of cases concerned with action taken as a matter of necessity in order to assist another person without his consent. As an example of this category Lord Goff suggested the case of a man who forcibly seizes another to drag him from the path of an oncoming vehicle. As Fleming (1987) has pointed out, the defence of necessity involves 'more obviously than any [other] a hard choice between competing values and a sacrifice of one to the other'. Its basis lies in a mixture of altruism, public protection and the maintenance of 'acceptable' social values. As a result, determining when it applies will be no easy task.

Most of the cases on public necessity are cases which justify trespass to land or to chattels and are, therefore, not compelling authority on the question of whether public necessity justifies the infliction of a trespass to the person. In principle, however, there seems to be no reason why, given an appropriately strong case, it should not. For example, consider the case of a fire chief who, in attempting to prevent the spread of a fire to a hospital, orders that a burning house causing most danger to the hospital be pulled down. He knows that there are three people trapped in the house and that if he pulls down the house they will almost inevitably be killed. Would the inevitable killing of the three occupants in the house be justified by the saving of the patients? Can the taking of one or more lives ever be justified on the ground that it is neccesary to save others? It is suggested that, provided the fire chief's action was reasonable in all the circumstances, he should be able to rely on the defence of public necessity.

As with public necessity, cases of private necessity justifying the infliction of harm are very rare. Most of the cases on private necessity concern trespass to land or chattels carried out to protect the defendant's own land or chattels. In principle, private necessity may justify a trespass to the person. However, the circumstances in which the defence will succeed are likely to be more limited than for public necessity. Acts of self-protection are more likely to be motivated by selfish concerns, and therefore are not likely to be encouraged by the courts. For example, a person who pulls an innocent third party in front of him as a shield against an attack by another is extremely unlikely to be able to rely on the defence of necessity.

Finally, there are the cases where the defendant acts for the purpose of protecting the plaintiff's own health or property. One of the most famous cases of this type is *Leigh* v. *Gladstone* (1909) 26 TLR 139. A suffragette prisoner who was on hunger-strike was force-fed through the mouth and nose by prison officers. The court held that this was justified. It is unlikely, given the fact that suicide was then a crime but is no longer, that such a decision would be followed today. Today, forcible treatment of a competent adult patient is probably never justified by any principle of necessity (*Re S* [1992] 4 All ER 671).

The defence of necessity may, however, have an important role to play in the case of treatment of incompetent (including unconscious) patients. In *F* v. *West Berkshire Health Authority* the House of Lords upheld a declaration made by a judge allowing the sterilisation of a mentally incompetent woman. Such treatment, although not consented to, could be justified on the principle of necessity. Lord Goff said that for the defence to succeed there must have been (a) a necessity to act in circumstances where it was not practicable to communicate with the assisted person, and (b) the action taken must have been such as a reasonable person would in all the circumstances take, acting in the best interests of the assisted person.

In determining what is in the best interests of the assisted person, Lord Goff said that in non-medical cases the test was that of the reasonable man. In medical cases, however, the principles set out in *Bolam* v. *Friern Hospital Management Committee* [1957] 1 WLR 582 should be applied. Provided a doctor acts in accordance with a responsible and competent body of medical opinion, he will not be liable.

Summary

17.1 The modern trepass to the person torts – assault, battery and false imprisonment – are derived from the ancient writ of trespass which provided a remedy for directly inflicted intentional interference with the person.

17.2 A cause of action will only lie in trespass where a person *intentionally* applies force directly to another. Where force is applied negligently the action is in negligence (cf Diplock LJ in *Letang* v. *Cooper*).

17.3 Where a person intentionally applies force directly to another, that is a battery. Where a person intentionally makes a threat which causes the plaintiff reasonably to apprehend the immediate infliction of a battery on him, that is an assault. Directness is a requirement in both assault and battery. A touching will only amount to a battery where it falls outside the category of generally acceptable physical contacts. For there to be an assault some conduct is usually required to cause the plaintiff to apprehend the infliction of a battery; it is questionable whether mere words will suffice.

17.4 The tort of false imprisonment is committed when the defendant intentionally and without lawful justification restrains a person's liberty within an area delimited by the defendant. The restraint must be total, although it is not necessary for a person to be locked up in a prison. A person may impose reasonable conditions on the manner in which an entrant leaves his premises; it is not necessary that the imprisoned person knows that he is imprisoned. A change in the conditions of a lawful imprisonment cannot render the imprisonment unlawful.

17.5 Where a person intentionally, but indirectly, inflicts physical harm on another, that person may be liable on the basis of the principle in *Wilkinson* v. *Downton*.

17.6 The trespass torts are actionable without proof of damage.

17.7 A number of defences which apply generally in the law of tort apply equally to trespass to the person. Thus, illegality and statutory authority are both defences to trespass to the person. The use of reasonable force in defending oneself, one's property or another person may also justify a trespass. Probably the most important defences in practice are the arrest powers contained in the Police and Criminal Evidence Act 1984, consent, self-defence and necessity.

Exercises

17.1 If A negligently touches B's breasts, does this give rise to an action in trespass?

17.2 Is Lord Denning MR's judgment in *Letang* v. *Cooper* preferable to that of Diplock LJ in the same case?

17.3 A persuades B, who is 16 years old, to pose naked for him. A tells B that he intends to use the photographs to try to win a prestigious art prize. In taking the photographs A touches B's leg to show him how to pose. A subsequently publishes the photographs in a pornographic magazine. Would B have any action against A? (See also *Kaye* v. *Robertson* [1990] FSR 62.)

17.4   Was the infliction of harm in *D.P.P.* v. *K* direct?

17.5   A points a purple water pistol at B, and B, wholly unreasonably, is terrified. Is this an assault?

17.6   In *Robinson* **v.** *Balmain New Ferry Co Ltd* would the result reached by the court have been different if, instead of the vessel going on a short journey, it had been bound for America? What would the result have been if the defendant had demanded £5 from the plaintiff before he could exit? How long could the defendants in *Herd* **v.** *Weardale Coal and Coke Co Ltd* have left the plaintiff down the mine? Are these two cases reconcilable with *Sunbolf* v. *Alford* (1838) 3 M & W 247, which decided that you cannot imprison a person for breach of contract?

17.7   A goes to his doctor for a blood test for glandular fever. Without A's consent the doctor tests the blood for the HIV virus. Would the doctor be able to rely on the defence of consent?

17.8   Are there any circumstances in which a doctor should be able to treat a competent person against his express wishes? (See *Re S* [1992] 4 All ER 671.)

Part III

Interference with Land

18 Interference with Land: Introduction

18.1 Property, Tort and Crime

A number of torts can be seen as an adjunct to the law of real property. Speaking in broad terms, we can say that legal rules relating to interests in land may be grouped under three headings. First, there are rules which determine who has precisely what interest in land. Secondly, there are rules which serve to protect those various interests in land against interference. Thirdly, there are rules which govern the passing on of those interests to others, for instance by sale or by inheritance. Rules under the first and third headings are primarily the concern of books on land law; those under the second, however, are the preserve of the law of tort. The torts of trespass and nuisance, in particular, are the means by which those with interests in land prevent their enjoyment of those interests being eroded unlawfully. In performing this function, the torts of trespass and nuisance also add flesh to the skeleton furnished by land law's list of interests in land: where land law specifies who has what interest in land, tort law specifies what in practice those interests entitle one to do.

Trespass is concerned with 'direct' encroachments on land; nuisance with interference that is 'indirect'. If I step on your land without your permission or deliberately place something on it (e.g. my rubbish) that is a trespass, whereas if I pollute your land with noise, smells and fumes, or let things inadvertently escape from my land on to yours (as where my wall falls down through disrepair), that is a nuisance. 'Nuisance' is used here in a technical sense to denote the unreasonable interference with the use and enjoyment of another's land.

Sometimes this tort is called 'private nuisance' in order to distinguish it from 'public nuisance' which is a crime of ill-defined scope: the courts have the power to label any conduct that causes annoyance to a substantial portion of the community a 'public nuisance' (see Spencer, 1989). Public nuisances need not have any impact on the use and enjoyment of land. Examples have included making a telephone bomb hoax, selling food that was unfit for human consumption and holding an ill-organised pop festival. A public nuisance, though primarily a criminal offence, will also give rise to tortious liability where an individual suffers 'special damage' as a result of the conduct in question. In view of the nebulous nature of public nuisance, our discussion of it is confined to its most common manifestation: obstruction of the highway (see 19.6).

A third type of nuisance is 'statutory nuisance'. Statutory nuisances, like public nuisances, are criminal offences. Under the Environmental

Protection Act 1990, Part III a number of activities that are harmful to the environment are listed as statutory nuisances, and the courts are empowered to order the cessation of those activities. The creation of these offences is a crucial prong of environmental policy. Unlike public nuisance, there is no rule that a person who suffers special damage as the result of a statutory nuisance may bring an action for damages in tort. The facts which give rise to a criminal liability for statutory nuisance may, however, give rise to an independent tortious liability for public or private nuisance if they satisfy the requirements of those causes of action.

18.2   Trespass, Nuisance and Negligence

As elsewhere in the law, the expansion of the tort of negligence has had an impact on the more established torts, particularly the tort of nuisance. Many claims which involve the competing rights and duties of neighbouring landowners, and which historically would therefore have been viewed as the concern of the law of nuisance, are today brought under negligence. This tendency was most noticeable in relation to liability for the acts of third parties and natural hazards on one's land (see 19.4). In both these areas, liability in nuisance was slow to develop and negligence, which was thought for a time to treat the foreseeability of harm to the plaintiff as the sole criterion of liability (see 3.2), seemed to offer plaintiffs better prospects of success. It is now clear that foreseeability is not enough to establish liability in negligence in such cases. There is no advantage to be gained from framing one's action in negligence rather than nuisance (see *Goldman* v. *Hargrave* [1967]) 1 AC 645). Nevertheless, the liability of landowners for the acts of third parties and natural hazards on their land is now an established part of the tort of negligence (see 6.4) and has substantiated what Markesinis (1989) views as negligence's 'unstoppable tendency to subsume under its heading the role of older nominate torts'.

The effect of the rise of negligence is not only that negligence is in practice tending to take over the role of nuisance: it is also the case that doctrines of nuisance law have been infused with the 'fault principle' which negligence embodies. Areas of nuisance law in which liabilities had been imposed irrespective of fault (eg under the rule in *Rylands* v. *Fletcher*; see Chapter 20) – or, conversely, in which liability did not arise however reprehensible the conduct in question – came to be regarded as anomalous. Consequently, the courts took every opportunity to enlarge the category of cases in which liability turned upon the reasonableness of what was done (see 19.1) and to stress that liability should not be imposed without proof of fault (see 19.7). Some commentators have responded to these developments by arguing that, in reality, 'nuisance is a branch of the law of negligence' (Williams and Hepple, 1984, p. 124). The strength of this claim is considered below (see 19.7).

The tort of trespass to land shares with other types of action in trespass the characteristic that it is actionable without proof of damage. Negligence is different: liability will not arise unless the plaintiff suffers loss. For this reason, negligence might be said to be concerned primarily with compensation for loss. The role of trespass has, over the course of time, stretched far beyond the recovery of damages in respect of loss (e.g. in its guise as the action of ejectment: see Baker, 1990, pp. 341–3). Today, its chief practical significance is as a means of maintaining the privacy of one's home against unwanted intrusion and of settling boundary disputes with one's neighbours, purposes for which the tort of negligence is not suitable.

Summary

18.1 The torts of trespass to land and private nuisance provide protection against interference with the use and enjoyment of land. Trespass deals with 'direct' interferences, private nuisance with interferences that are indirect. Private nuisance should not be confused with public nuisance, a crime that may incidentally give rise to tortious liability if 'special damage' is suffered as a result. Public nuisances need not be connected with the use of land.

18.2 The tort of negligence has in practice subsumed areas of the law of nuisance; this has caused academic debate as to whether nuisance is merely a branch of the tort of negligence. Trespass, however, being actionable without proof of damage, differs from negligence in that it is less concerned with compensation for loss than with the vindication of rights over property.

19 Private Nuisance

19.1 The Nature of Private Nuisance

The tort of nuisance is 'primarily concerned with conflict over competing uses of land' (Fleming, 1992, p. 409). It is remedied by the award of damages, or by the granting of an injunction, or both (see Chapter 23). That much is clear. The task of mapping out the contours of the tort, however, has caused excessive consternation in the legal mind since time immemorial. Even today, no consensus has emerged as to how the subject should be expounded and as to exactly what rules apply in different situations. The difficulty the subject presents stems largely from the fact that no coherent thread of argument can unite the disparate rules that the courts have applied under the general rubric of 'nuisance'. This lack of principle means that there are no short cuts to understanding the tort of nuisance. The obscure nooks and crannies of the subject can only be illuminated by reference to a long and apparently arbitrary list of what one can and cannot do with one's land. Looking at this list, we may learn that courts have said you will be liable to your neighbour for any damage caused by roots or branches of your tree which encroach on to her land (*Davey* v. *Harrow Corporation* [1958] 1 QB 60), but that you may with impunity dig a ditch on your land even if it means that your neighbour's recently constructed house falls down (*Dalton* v. *Angus* (1881) 6 App Cas 740). Reading on, we may find out that you may inflict on your neighbour the noise of speedboats racing on your lake a few times a year, but woe betide you if you organise too many race meetings, for that would constitute an actionable nuisance (*Kennaway* v. *Thompson* [1981] QB 88). Any attempt to identify a single general principle from which these diverse rules can be deduced is doomed to failure.

A long list of specific examples similar to the above is beyond the scope of an introductory book (and indeed of many tort courses). All that we can attempt to do here is to give some flavour of the variety of situations covered by the tort of nuisance and of the sort of rules that are applied in them. A useful starting point is to make a theoretical division between three categories of cases (see Spencer, 1987): (a) some aspects of the use and enjoyment of land are protected from interference regardless of the reasonableness of the conduct of whoever is responsible for the interference; (b) some are afforded no protection from interference at all, under any circumstances; and (c) some are protected to the extent that the interference with them is unreasonable.

Interference Leads to Liability Regardless of Reasonableness

That nuisance incorporates instances of this first category – sometimes called cases of strict liability (i.e., liability irrespective of fault) – is undeniable (see *Davey* v. *Harrow Corporation*, above). Where you have what property lawyers call a 'natural right' to some amenity derived from your land, or where you have acquired a right to an amenity as an 'easement', your neighbour has no right to interfere with that amenity no matter how reasonable she may regard her conduct to be (see Green, 1989, Ch. 7).

Natural rights are regarded as part and parcel of every landowner's interest in her land; they impose restrictions on what an adjacent owner may do on her property. Natural rights include rights to the support of land in its natural state and certain water rights. Let us take rights in respect of water running on or under the land as an example for further discussion. Where water runs in a clearly-defined channel, you may take as much water from that stream as you need for your domestic purposes, but if you want to take water for other uses (e.g., spraying your crops) your conduct will cause an actionable nuisance if it affects the stream's flow as it runs through other properties (*Miner* v. *Gilmour* (1858) 12 Moo PC 131). Where by contrast the water 'percolates' under your land without flowing in a defined channel, then you have an absolute right to abstract it, no matter who else has an interest in receiving the water: it is simply a matter of first come, first served (*Chasemore* v. *Richards* (1859) 7 HLC 349).

Easements, like natural rights, are rights attached to one piece of land which impose restrictions on the proprietary right attached to another piece of land. They differ from natural rights in that they are not natural incidents of land ownership but have to be acquired by grant or prescription. Easements include certain rights to the uninterrupted passage of light or air through windows or other inlets in your property. They also include the right to have buildings on your land supported against subsidence by earth or buildings on your neighbour's land: thus, if your neighbour withdraws support which you have enjoyed for twenty years or more and your buildings collapse, that constitutes a nuisance no matter what reasons your neighbour had for acting as she did (*Dalton* v. *Angus* (1881) 6 App Cas 740).

When we move on from natural rights and easements, the extent of the category of rights afforded absolute protection becomes more debatable. One body of thought goes as far as to say that any act which causes physical damage to land constitutes a nuisance regardless of the reasonableness of those acts. This view receives some support from a dictum of Veale J in *Halsey* v. *Esso Petroleum Co Ltd* [1961] 1 WLR 683 that, in cases of physical damage, 'Negligence is not an ingredient of the cause of action' (see also Spencer, 1989). Most commentators, however, agree that, in cases of physical damage as in cases of mere personal discomfort, a court must look at the reasonableness of the interference before characterising it as a nuisance (see Winfield and Jolowicz, 1989, p. 388;

Salmond and Heuston, 1992, p. 61). The principal exceptions to this rule occur with respect to artificial structures adjacent to the highway under the rule in *Wringe* v. *Cohen* [1940] 1 KB 229, and land put to ultra-hazardous use under the rule in *Rylands* v. *Fletcher* (1865) LR 1 Ex 265, (1868) LR 3 HL 330 (see 19.6 and Chapter 20).

Interference Never Leads to Liability no matter how Unreasonable

The second group of rules brings together a number of cases in which the law grants no protection at all, no matter how unreasonable the interference. Again we should begin in the world of easements and natural rights. In the first place, you have no cause for complaint if your neighbour's enjoyment of her natural right or easement causes you harm. We saw above that every landowner has the natural right to abstract any water percolating under her land: if your neighbour does so, you have no legal redress if your buildings are caused to subside as a consequence (*Langbrook Properties Ltd* v. *Surrey CC* [1970] 1 WLR 161). Put another way, you have no right to water support for your buildings. Secondly, where an amenity connected with land is of a sort that can be protected as an easement, but it has not been so protected, interference with that amenity is entirely lawful. As we noted earlier, you may acquire an easement of support for your buildings with the result that your neighbour will be liable if her removal of that support caused your buildings to fall down; the other side of the coin is that, where you have acquired no easement of support (e.g., because you have enjoyed the support for less than 20 years), your neighbour is free to develop her land without heed to any subsidence her development might cause next door (*Dalton* v. *Angus*).

Other amenities enjoyed by landowners also belong in this group. It has long been the law that no action lies for blocking a pleasant view or prospect, the reason given in the sixteenth century by Wray CJ being that 'the law does not give an action for such things of delight' (*Bland* v. *Moseley* (1587), unreported but reproduced in Baker and Milsom, 1986, p. 597). This reasoning has led some to conclude that no remedy lies for interference with purely recreational facilities. In *Bridlington Relay Ltd* v. *Yorkshire Electricity Board* [1965] Ch. 436, one of the reasons given by Buckley J for rejecting a claim by a television broadcasting station whose signals were disrupted by pylons erected by the electricity board was that domestic television viewing was purely recreational and could not be regarded as so important a part of the ordinary enjoyment of land as to warrant legal protection. However, Buckley J denied the existence of any hard-and-fast rule that interference with purely recreational facilities can never be a nuisance and, as the law's view of what interests deserve protection changes with the times, it may well be that his view of the importance of television viewing in 1965 would be regarded as out of date today (cf. *Nor Video Services Ltd* v. *Ontario Hydro* (1978) 84 DLR (3d) 221).

Another type of case in which the courts have been slow to give landowners legal protection is that which involves interference caused by the forces of nature. For centuries, the courts denied that one landowner could complain if her neighbour failed to prevent her land in its natural condition, or wild animals on it, causing damage next door. Thus in *Giles* v. *Walker* (1890) 24 QBD 656 it was held that it was no nuisance if thistle seeds were blown from A's land to B's, where they took root and did damage. Lord Coleridge brusquely dismissed the claim with the words: 'I have never heard of such an action as this.' Here again, times have changed and, with the expansion of the tort of negligence, the tort of nuisance has become more willing to impose liability for natural nuisances that landowners might reasonably be expected to prevent, as in *Leakey* v. *National Trust* [1980] QB 485 where the Court of Appeal held the owner of hill-top land liable when rocks and other debris fell naturally on to property below (see 19.4). It is disputed whether the earlier caselaw justified the court in *Leakey* in adopting a general rule of liability for natural nuisances (see Wedderburn, 1978). Nevertheless it is undeniable that the tendency of the law – exemplified by *Leakey* – is to narrow the anomalous categories of interests that receive absolute protection or no protection at all and to expand the category of cases which are treated flexibly by the application of the standard of reasonableness.

Interference Leads to Liability only if Unreasonable

It is to this third category that we now turn our attention. This category is residual in the sense that all aspects of the use and enjoyment of land that have not been specified above fall within it. It covers a vast array of things which might affect that use and enjoyment, amongst them smells, noise, vibration, fumes and dust. Interference taking such forms is permitted so long as it satisfies the test of reasonableness. This test surfaces throughout the law of tort, in particular in the tort of negligence where the test is said to be whether the defendant exercised reasonable care. In the tort of nuisance, the question put appears in various forms: sometimes the court asks whether there was 'unreasonable interference' with the plaintiff's enjoyment of land; sometimes whether the defendant was engaged in a 'reasonable user' of her land. The way the question is framed makes no difference to the result which is determined by balancing the interests of each party and of society as a whole. In performing this balancing exercise, it is customary to isolate a number of factors as being of particular significance and we consider these in turn in our next section.

19.2   The Test of Reasonable User

Where reasonableness is relevant in determining liability in the tort of nuisance, the following factors are taken into account by the courts in deciding whether a given interference with the use and enjoyment of land is to be characterised as reasonable or unreasonable.

The Extent of the Interference

The extent of an interference in the use and enjoyment of land is the product of its gravity and its duration. Physical damage is a graver form of injury than mere personal discomfort, and so interference which causes the former is more likely to be regarded as unreasonable than that which causes the latter. In relation to the latter, the courts have made it plain that a certain amount of noise and smell must be tolerated as part of everyday life. Where the plaintiff complains of mere personal discomfort, the question to ask – according to the much-quoted formula of Knight Bruce VC in *Walter* v. *Selfe* (1851) 4 De G & Sm 315 – is: 'Ought this inconvenience to be considered in fact as more than fanciful, more than one of delicacy or fastidiousness, as an inconvenience materially interfering with the ordinary physical comfort of human existence, but according to plain and sober and simple notions among the English people?'

The duration of the interference also bears on the question of reasonableness. A continuing interference, if more than trivial, will often be regarded as unwarranted. However, this is not to say that an isolated incident cannot give rise to a cause of action, especially in cases of physical harm. All that the plaintiff must show is that the incident was attributable to a continuing state of affairs on the defendant's land (see *British Celanese Ltd* v. *AH Hunt Ltd* [1969] 1 WLR 959).

Locality

In *Sturges* v. *Bridgman* (1879) 11 Ch. D. 852, Thesiger LJ famously remarked: 'What would be a nuisance in Belgrave Square would not necessarily be so in Bermondsey.' The point he was making is that the reasonableness of any use to which land is put will depend on, amongst other things, the character of the neighbourhood the land lies in ('the locality'): factories billowing out smoke might be all right in an industrial estate but not in an idyllic rural village.

This 'locality principle' applies only to cases of personal discomfort, not to cases of property damage. This was decided by the House of Lords in *St. Helens Smelting Co.* v. *Tipping* (1865) 11 HLC 642. In that case, noxious vapours from the defendant's smelting works damaged trees and shrubs on the plaintiff's land. The defendant alleged that, as almost the whole neighbourhood was devoted to copper smelting or similar manufacturing activities, those activities could be continued with impunity. Lord Westbury LC dismissed this argument. In his view, it was necessary to distinguish two types of case, the first being where the nuisance produces what he refers to as 'material injury to property' or 'sensible injury to the value of the property', and the second being where it merely produces 'personal discomfort.' Locality was relevant only in relation to the latter: 'If a man lives in a street where there are numerous shops, and a shop is opened next door to him. . . he has no ground for complaint, because to him individually there might arise much discomfort from the trade carried on in that shop. ' In relation to the former, however, locality was of no significance. It followed that the injury to the plaintiff's trees and shrubs in the case before him gave rise to a cause of action in nuisance, irrespective of whether the pollution from the defendant's works was exceptional for the locality.

Lord Westbury's ruling has been criticised on a number of grounds. First of all, the precise meaning of what he says is obscure. He talks of 'sensible injury to the value of property' and distinguishes this from 'personal discomfort', yet if land becomes uncomfortable to live on then its value will surely be diminished. Perhaps it is best to assume that Lord Westbury merely intended to draw a line between cases of physical damage and those of more ephemeral loss. A more substantial criticism is made by Buckley (1981) pp. 8–9: in his view, the rigid distinction between material damage to property and mere personal discomfort might produce arbitrary results. He advocates a more flexible approach in which the locality is just one of several factors weighed up in considering the reasonableness of the plaintiff's user of land. He imagines a case where the plaintiff lives in an exposed mountainous region. In the region, rock fragments regularly fall from higher to lower land. The plaintiff's property is damaged by such falls coming from the defendant's land. Buckley argues that the defendant should be entitled to have the court take into account the locality in applying the overall test of reaonableness.

Hypersensitive Activities

In the words of Lord Robertson, 'A man cannot increase the liabilities of his neighbour by applying his own property to special uses, whether for business or pleasure' (*Eastern and South African Telegraph Co* v. *Cape Town Tramways* [1902] AC 381). It follows that one cannot complain about interference with abnormally sensitive activities where ordinary activities would not be affected. This rule was applied by Buckley J in *Bridlington Relay Ltd* v. *Yorkshire Electricity Board* [1965] Ch. 436 in deciding that interference with the signals received by a television broadcast relay station, caused by a nearby electricity power line, did not amount to a nuisance. The judge pointed to the abnormal nature of the plaintiff's business which, if it were to prosper, required an exceptional degree of immunity from interference. This was not a case of interference with ordinary domestic television reception. (As an alternative, he was prepared to rule that television reception was not so important a part of the ordinary enjoyment of land that it should be protected at all: see 19.1.)

The only exception to this rule is where the plaintiff complains of interference by something which is inherently noxious. In *Cooke* v. *Forbes* (1867) LR 5 Eq 166, the plaintiff was in the business of making coconut matting which was hung out to dry after it had been bleached. He alleged that emissions of hydrogen sulphide from the defendant's premises dulled the colours of the matting, requiring it to be dyed again at considerable expense. The court disregarded the fact that the matting required such unusually delicate handling that the fumes might impair its value and concluded that the defendant was liable in nuisance. The later case of *Robinson* v. *Kilvert* (1889) 41 Ch. D. 88, however, makes it clear that the crucial factor in that case was the noxious nature of the interference; in all other cases, the hypersensitivity of the plaintiff's activities might be a good defence. The plaintiff kept stocks of brown paper which he sought to sell at a profit; the defendant occupied the premises below in which he made paper boxes, for which he required heat and dry air. The heat passed into the plaintiff's premises and dried out his paper, causing it to lose weight; as the paper was sold by weight, the plaintiff suffered a loss of profit. The Court of Appeal viewed the plaintiff's business as exceptionally sensitive, for ordinary paper would not have dried out in the same way. Accordingly his action failed. *Cooke* was distinguished on the grounds that the hydrogen sulphide emitted from the defendant's premises was 'inherently noxious': this made the hypersensitivity of the plaintiff's activity irrelevant.

Motive

The reasonableness of one's user of land depends in part on the reasons one has for using the land in such a way. What is not a nuisance if done for a good reason may become one if done for a bad reason. This means that an activity carried out carelessly may give rise to liability when none would arise if due care had been employed (though it does not follow from the fact that due care was exercised that liability will not arise, for the activity may be one that should not have been carried out at all: see 19.7). The importance of the defendant's reasons for acting can be demonstrated by considering how the courts approach cases involving disturbance caused by demolition or building work. According to Vaughan Williams J in *Harrison* v. *Southwark and Vauxhall Water Co* [1891] 2 Ch. 409:

> '[A] man who pulls down his house for the purpose of building a new one no doubt causes considerable inconvenience to his next door neighbour during the process of demolition; but he is not responsible as for a nuisance if he uses all reasonable skill and care to avoid annoyance to his neighbour by the works of demolition. Nor is he liable to an action, even though the noise and dust and the consequent annoyance be such as would constitute a nuisance if the same had been created in sheer wantonnesss.'

If the defendant's wanton or thoughtlessly inconsiderate behaviour makes it hard to justify her disturbance of the plaintiff, her case is even weaker if she acts maliciously out of a desire to harm the plaintiff. This is made plain by *Christie* v. *Davey* [1893] 1 Ch. 316. The plaintiffs' was a musical family. Mrs Christie and her daughter were music teachers; her son was a cellist. Mr Christie seems not to have been a musician and, as the judge remarked dryly, 'perhaps fortunately for himself is very deaf'. The defendant, who occupied the adjoining house, was disturbed by the noise, particularly of singing which he claimed was hard to distinguish from the howling of a dog. He wrote to the Christies in protest (this entertaining correspondence is well worth reading in the law report), but his complaints were ignored. In retaliation, he decided to pursue his own brand of musical studies. Whenever he heard the sound of music coming from the Christies' house, he would begin to bang on the wall, beat on trays and blow a whistle. North J found that this behaviour constituted a nuisance on account of the fact that the defendant had acted maliciously, for the purpose of annoying the Christies. The judge contrasted the noise made by the latter: their music-making had been a legitimate use of their house.

Mayor of Bradford v. *Pickles* [1895] AC 587 is a case that has given rise to controversy in this area. The source of the problem is a dictum of Lord Halsbury LC that 'Motives and intentions. . . seem to me to be absolutely irrelevant.' This should not be taken as laying down a rule for the law of nuisance as a whole; indeed, Lord Halsbury expressly limited it to cases of the same type as that before him. The case arose out of the defendant's action in draining his land. This threatened to diminish the supply of water available for the domestic use of the inhabitants of Bradford, for a proportion of this supply was drawn from water that percolated under the defendant's land. The plaintiffs alleged that the defendant had acted maliciously, as his intention was to get the city to pay for the water. This motive was rightly held to be irrelevant, for this was a case in the second category identified above (see 19.1) in which the defendant has an absolute natural right to do as he did (i.e. to abstract water percolating under his land), no matter how unreasonable his behaviour appeared to others. The decision has no bearing on those cases in which the reasonableness of the defendant's user of land is the decisive factor (category (c)). This was acknowledged in *Hollywood Silver Fox Farm* v. *Emmett* [1936] 2 KB 468. In that case, the defendant threatened to fire his gun during the fox breeding season – saying 'I guarantee you will not raise a single cub' – if the farm continued to advertise its breeding activities which the defendant feared would put off potential purchasers of his land. When the farm refused to comply, the defendant carried out his threat with the result that some vixens ate their cubs and others did not mate at all. McNaughten J held that the defendant's malice made the disturbance actionable as a nuisance, rejecting the contention that *Mayor of Bradford* v. *Pickles* had any bearing on cases such as that before him. These cases are those falling in category (c) listed above: only in categories (a) and (b) is the defendant's motive of no significance.

19.3   Who Can Sue?

To bring an action in nuisance, you must have an interest in the land in the enjoyment of which you claim to have been disturbed. In *Malone* v.

Lasky [1907] 2 KB 141, the plaintiff was the wife of the tenant of a certain house; she herself had no interest in the property. While she was making use of the lavatory, the cistern was dislodged by vibrations from the defendant's electricity generator next door and fell on top of her. The Court of Appeal held she could not sue in nuisance in respect of her personal injuries as she lacked any interest in land.

In fact, spouses of an owner or tenant may now have a sufficient interest in land to allow them to sue in nuisance, for they are given a statutory right of occupation by virtue of the Matrimonial Homes Act 1967. The principle of *Malone* v. *Lasky*, however, remains good law, although it is viewed by many as unduly restrictive: it has not been followed in Canada where the Court of Appeal of New Brunswick in *Devon Lumber* v. *MacNeill* (1988) 45 DLR (4th) 300 recognised the right to sue of all those in actual occupation of the property in question. This approach is supported by Kodilinye (1989). He argues that there is no reason to distinguish the children of an owner or tenant from the owner or tenant herself: their occupation is just as substantial as that of the parent and the interference with their use and enjoyment of land just as great.

19.4   Who Can Be Liable?

Those whose activities cause unlawful interference with another's use or enjoyment of land will be liable in nuisance. For these purposes, the activities of an occupier of land include not only those carried out personally or by employees, but also those carried out by independent contractors, at least where the activities involve 'a special danger of nuisance' (*Matania* v. *National Provincial Bank* [1936] 2 All ER 633). This represents an exception to the normal rule of vicarious liability, which requires proof of a contract of employment before responsibility will arise (see Ch. 22). In *Matania*, the defendants employed independent contractors to make extensive alterations to their flat. The plaintiff's flat underneath was affected by dust and noise which amounted to an actionable nuisance. The defendants were held liable for actions of the contractors whose activities were found to involve a special danger of nuisance, it being inevitable that the noise and dust would interfere with the plaintiff unless precautions were taken.

The liability on those who 'create' a nuisance extends beyond those in occupation of land themselves, however, and covers those who create nuisances while on somebody else's land or even on the public highway. Although doubts have been expressed on the latter score (see *Esso Petroleum Ltd* v. *Southport Corporation* [1954] 2 QB 182, 204 (Devlin J), [1956] AC 218, 242 (Lord Radcliffe)) the bulk of the authorities assume that a nuisance need not emanate from private land. Thus it has been held that striking workers mounting a picket in the road outside a factory may be liable in private nuisance (*Thomas* v. *NUM (South Wales Area)* [1986] Ch. 20), as may the owners of an oil refinery in relation to the noise of lorries approaching and leaving the refinery on a road running by the plaintiff's house (*Halsey* v. *Esso Petroleum* [1961] 1 WLR 683).

An occupier of land may be liable for interference caused by trespassers and natural hazards on her land as well as for interference caused by her own activities (or those of her employees and independent contractors). In the idiosyncratic language of the tort of nuisance, she may face liability not merely for a nuisance she 'creates', but also for one that she 'adopts' or 'continues'. She adopts a nuisance if she makes any use of the thing that constitutes the nuisance; she continues it if she allows it to remain after she knew, or ought to have known, of its existence and when she could easily have put an end to it.

The leading case on liability in nuisance for the acts of a third party is *Sedleigh-Denfield* v. *O'Callaghan* [1940] AC 880. The defendants owned property on which they located a religious commune. The plaintiff owned the adjoining property. At the boundary between the two properties, there was a ditch which belonged to the defendant. Local authority workers laid a drainage pipe in the ditch, in so doing trespassing on the defendants' land which they had no permission to enter. The workers neglected to place a grid at the mouth of the pipe to keep it clear of refuse. All these activities were observed by the defendants' representative at the commune, Brother Dekker. Some three years later, after a heavy rainstorm, the pipe had become so obstructed with refuse that rainwater overflowed from the ditch and flooded the plaintiff's land. The House of Lords held the defendants liable for they had both continued and adopted the nuisance, either of which alone would have been sufficient to make them liable. Viscount Maugham explained the application of the principles to the facts of the case:

'After the lapse of nearly three years, they must be taken to have suffered the nuisance to continue, for they neglected to take the very simple step of placing a grid in the proper place, which would have removed the danger to their neighbour's land. They adopted the nuisance, for they continued during all that time to use the artificial contrivance of the conduit for the purpose of getting rid of water from their property without taking the proper means for rendering it safe.'

For some time after this case, it was questioned whether the same duty of positive action on the part of an occupier of land might arise in the context of natural hazards rather than the acts of trespassers. Such a duty was finally recognised to be part of English law in the case of *Leakey* v. *National Trust* [1980] QB 485. The natural hazard in that case was debris in the form of rocks, soil, tree roots and the like that fell from the steep banks of a hill owned by the National Trust, Burrow Mump in Somerset, on to the plaintiff's property below. The falls threatened to damage houses on that property. The Court of Appeal held that a nuisance had been established. Megaw LJ, who delivered the leading judgment, said that it would be a grievous blot on the law if such a duty were not recognised.

He countered fears that this might result in injustice where those affected by the hazard were much wealthier than those on whose land it arose by saying that the scope of the duty imposed on the latter was limited. In contrast to the objective standard of care generally imposed in the tort of negligence (see 9.2), the standard proposed by Megaw LJ was that of what the particular occupier could be expected to do. Where physical effort was required to avert an immediate danger, this would reflect the occupier's age and physical condition; where the expenditure of money was required, it would reflect her means. Megaw LJ even went so far as to suggest that the duty on the defendant might depend upon what it was reasonable to expect the plaintiff to do to protect herself, for instance by erecting a barrier on her own land or by paying for repairs on the defendant's. It is possible that the same rule limiting the scope of an occupier's duty of positive action will apply whether cases like *Leakey* are argued in nuisance or, as they might very well be, in negligence. This at least was the view of Lord Goff who, in *Smith* v. *Littlewoods* [1987] AC 241 doubted whether there could be any material difference between what was required of the occupier in nuisance and what was required in negligence.

The position of landlords merits separate attention as they may be held liable for nuisances arising on premises they have let out even though they neither occupied those premises nor created the nuisance. Such liability will arise where they let out the premises (a) with the knowledge that the tenant will create a nuisance, as in *Tetley* v. *Chitty* [1986] 1 All ER 663 in which a local authority let land for the specific purpose of go-karting which was inevitably going to disturb local residents; or (b) with the knowledge that a nuisance already existed at the date of the lease; or (c) retaining the right to enter and repair the premises if a nuisance arises. With regard to the last category of case, an additional claim is now possible under section 4 of the Defective Premises Act 1972, which requires landlords who have a right to repair to take reasonable care to ensure that those who might be affected by defects in the state of the premises, whether on or off the premises, are reasonably safe. This makes the liability at common law largely redundant except in so far as *Wringe* v. *Cohen* (see 19.6) imposes a stricter duty in respect of artificial structures on the highway.

19.5   Defences

Prescription

No liability arises if the defendant has acquired a prescriptive right to commit a nuisance after having done so without objection from the plaintiff for a period of 20 years. This only applies to interferences which can develop into easements. It is possible to acquire an easement to discharge water on to your neighbour's land, or to send smoke through openings in the wall dividing your house from your neighbour's, but it is doubtful that the right to disturb your neighbour by smell or noise can be acquired as an easement (see Clerk and Lindsell, 1989, para 24–80).

Statutory Authority

Where a statute empowers the defendant to carry out a certain activity, she cannot be held liable in tort if she interferes with adjoining land, so long as the interference was an unavoidable consequence of the exercise of the statutory power. Such interference is regarded as impliedly authorised even if it is not expressly permitted. In *London, Brighton and South Coast Railway* v. *Truman* (1886) 11 AC 45, a railway company was empowered to purchase station yards to accommodate cattle that were to be carried by rail. When it did so, occupiers of nearby houses complained of the noise of the cattle and drovers. The House of Lords held that a yard such as the defendants' had inevitably and of necessity to be located close to stations which in turn had to be located close to centres of population; in consequence, the yard would have been a nuisance wherever located and Parliament must have been taken to authorise that nuisance.

The policy behind the defence was described by Lord Roskill in *Allen* v. *Gulf Oil Refining* [1981] AC 1001 in the following terms:

'The underlying philosophy plainly is that the greater public interest arising from the construction and use of undertakings such as railways must take precedence over the private rights of owners and occupiers of neighbouring lands not to have their common law rights infringed by what would otherwise be an actionable nuisance. In short, the lesser private rights must yield to the greater public interest.'

That case provides an example of the lengths to which plaintiffs will go to urge a narrow interpretation of a statute on the courts. Gulf Oil had been authorised to build a refinery on land it had acquired compulsorily but the relevant statute said nothing about putting the refinery to use. Responding to an argument that no refinery could be operated on the land at all if the inevitable result was unreasonable disturbance of neighbouring landowners, Lord Diplock noted wryly: 'Parliament can hardly be supposed to have intended the refinery to be nothing more than a visual adornment to the landscape in an area of natural beauty. Clearly the intention of Parliament was that the refinery was to be operated as such.' Nevertheless, the House of Lords agreed that it was still open to the plaintiff landowners to prove that the interference caused by Gulf Oil's refinery was in excess of that which was the inevitable consequence of the operation of any refinery whatsoever on the land.

Plaintiff's Act

The defendant may be able to defend an action for nuisance by pointing out that the plaintiff was responsible for all or some of the injury she suffered. If the plaintiff, by word or deed, has shown her willingness to accept the interference, then a defence of voluntary assumption of responsibility would bar her claim; if she carelessly contributed to her own loss, then a defence of contributory negligence might reduce any damages payable to her. These defences will only avail a plaintiff if the defendant has done something unreasonable and the courts have been adamant that those who move to a previously inhospitable environment have done nothing unreasonable: it is no defence that the plaintiff 'came to the nuisance' (*Bliss* v. *Hall* (1838) 4 Bing NC 183). Those who move to inhospitable areas must, however, put up with whatever degree of personal discomfort, though not physical damage, that is appropriate in the locality (see 19.2).

19.6   Nuisances on or Adjacent to the Highway

The public interest in freedom of passage along the highway has resulted in the courts imposing liabilities of exceptional stringency on those who impede that passage. Obstruction of the highway amounts to the criminal offence of public nuisance, and it may give rise to tortious liability if an individual suffers 'special damage' as a result. This liability was first recognised, and the special damage requirement explained, by Fitzherbert J in *Sowthall* v. *Dagger* (1535), (see Baker, 1990, p. 493). The judge considered a case where the highway was obstructed by a ditch dug across it. In his view, no one could complain about mere delay caused by the obstruction but, if a man fell into the ditch, he should be allowed to sue the person who had dug it in respect of this special loss. This liability is anomalous because, in contrast to cases in which a moving vehicle causes a collision, where negligence must be proved, the defendant will be liable if she intentionally caused the obstruction whether or not she could reasonably have foreseen damage to the plaintiff (see Newark, 1949). It is also anomalous in that the plaintiff may be able to recover pure economic loss resulting from the obstruction, – e.g. where, as in *Rose* v. *Miles* (1815) 4 M&S 101, she has to pay for alternative transport – thus evading the limitations on such recovery in the tort of negligence.

Another area in which ordinary principles of liability have been cast aside relates to the collapse of artificial structures adjacent to the highway. In *Wringe* v. *Cohen* [1940] 1 KB 229, Atkinson J laid down the following rule: 'if, owing to a want of repair, premises upon a highway become dangerous, and, therefore, a nuisance, and a passer-by or adjoining owner suffers damage by their collapse, the occupier. . . is answerable, whether or not he knew, or ought to have known of the danger'. He went on to exclude liability in cases where the collapse was caused by the act of a trespasser or 'a secret and unobservable act of nature, such as a subsidence under or near the foundations of the premises.' The liability arises even where the plaintiff suffers injury not on the highway but on private property. This indeed was the case in *Wringe* in which the Court of

Appeal found the defendant liable when his wall collapsed and fell on to the roof of the plaintiff's shop next door. Once again, it seems unreasonable to have one rule when the nuisance is a threat to users of the highway and another when it is not.

19.7 The Relationship between Nuisance and Negligence

Much controversy attends the issue of whether nuisance is best regarded as a branch of the law of negligence or as a wholly separate tort. The former view finds particularly persuasive advocates in Williams and Hepple (1984) pp. 123–7. To see whether they are right, we shall consider a number of claims made by those who insist that negligence and nuisance are very different entities. As will be seen, the differences between the two are in many respects more apparent than real.

Nuisance Protects a Wider Range of Interests than Negligence

Admittedly, there are many interests not protected by a duty of care in negligence which are recognised in nuisance. Whereas negligence generally limits liability to cases of physical damage, nuisance can be employed to prevent interference with personal comfort by ensuring, for example, freedom from unreasonable noise and smells. Williams and Hepple, however, argue that this is simply a matter of terminology: 'Why should we not say that people are under a duty of care not to be noisy and not to allow a noxious escape of such a nature that the plaintiff cannot reasonably be expected to tolerate it?' In other words, nuisance might be encompassed within negligence if we were just prepared to recognise that particularly extensive duties of care are owed to owners and occupiers of land.

Liability in Nuisance is Strict whereas Liability in Negligence Depends on Proof of Fault

We should at the outset make it clear that there are indeed cases of strict liability (i.e. liability irrespective of fault) that fall under the general heading of the tort of nuisance. They fall within the first category of case identified at the outset of this chapter. In the vast majority of cases (those in category (c)), interference with the use and enjoyment of land will only be regarded as actionable if it is unreasonable, and the real controversy is whether this requirement of unreasonable user can be satisfied even where the defendant cannot be said to be at fault. Distinguished judges seem to rule out this possibility: in *Sedleigh-Denfield* v. *O'Callaghan* [1940] AC 880, Lord Wright insisted that the 'liability for a nuisance is not, at least in modern law, a strict or absolute liability' and, in *The Wagon Mound (No 2)* [1967] 1 AC 617, Lord Reid argued that 'fault of some kind is almost always necessary' for liability to arise. (It appears that he inserted the word 'almost' to take account of the exceptional instances of strict liability in category (a) as in *Wringe* v. *Cohen*.)

One persistent source of confusion in this regard is a remark made by Lindley LJ in *Rapier v London Tramways* [1893] 2 Ch. 588. Delivering judgment for the plaintiff in an action for nuisance in respect of the smell coming from the defendant's excessively large and overcrowded stables, he commented: 'At common law, if I am sued for a nuisance, and the nuisance is proved, it is no defence on my part to say, and to prove, that I have taken all reasonable care to prevent it.' As Williams and Hepple point out, however, this does not mean that liability was being imposed without fault, for, if all else failed, the only reasonable course left to the defendant would be to close his stables down. This was clearly in the mind of Lindley LJ for he says, 'If the defendants are right in saying that they cannot concentrate their stables to such an extent as is desirable without committing a nuisance to the neighbourhood, then they cannot concentrate their operations to such an extent.' Their failure to cease or cut back their operations itself amounted to fault.

In summary, then, we can say that an interference will only be regarded as unreasonable if the defendant was at fault either in the way an activity was carried out or in carrying on with the activity at all. For this reason, it is appropriate to rely upon the *Wagon Mound* test of remoteness of damage in nuisance as well as negligence (*The Wagon Mound (No 2)*; see Chapter 12).

'[T]he distinguishing aspect of nuisance, as compared with other heads of liability like negligence, is that it looks to the harmful result rather than to the kind of conduct causing it.' (Fleming, 1992, p. 401)

In negligence actions, we put the question: 'Did the defendant take due care?'; in nuisance actions, we ask: 'Was there unreasonable interference with the plaintiff's use and enjoyment of her land?' Despite this difference in emphasis, it would be wrong to conclude that negligence looks only at the defendant's conduct, and nuisance only at the plaintiff's injury. In fact, both torts look both at the nature of the damage suffered by the plaintiff and at the nature of the defendant's conduct. In negligence, the court compares the extent of the risk faced by the plaintiff with the ease with which the defendant might have eliminated that risk before deciding whether the latter took reasonable care. If the foreseeable risk to the plaintiff is greater than that to ordinary people (as in *Paris* v. *Stepney Borough Council*: see 9.3) then the defendant will be expected to alter her behaviour accordingly. Similarly, in nuisance, the court enquires not only into the extent of the interference with the plaintiff, but also into the motive with which the defendant acted: what might be reasonable if done with care might be a nuisance if done wantonly (see 19.2).

The Function of Negligence is to Allocate Losses after one-off Accidents whereas the Function of Nuisance is the Provision of Guidelines to Neighbours in a Continuing Relationship

Neighbouring owners and occupiers of land are in a continuing relationship that is very different from the relationship between those involved in the paradigmatic instances of negligence, accidents on the roads and the like. They need much clearer guidelines as to how they should conduct their affairs than the simple injunction to take reasonable care not to injure their neighbours. In response to this need, categories of the law of nuisance have grown up in which the limits of what one can do with one's land are spelt out in black and white terms; the vague but appealing standard of reasonableness is put on one side (see 19.1). On the one hand, as we have seen, you may stop up your neighbour's water supply by abstracting that water as it percolates under your land no matter how ill your motive (category (b)); on the other hand, you may not take water from a stream that passes through your land to supply your factory if the result is that your neighbour's supply is diminished, irrespective of the importance of your business and of the difficulty of obtaining another supply (category (a)). To this extent, the law of nuisance gives occupiers and owners of land very clear guidelines as to what they can and cannot do with their land.

Yet in the majority of cases, neighbours can get no clear guidance as to how they may use their land, for all is left to the court's view of what is reasonable in the circumstances. Admittedly, once the court has given its view, then the parties are bound to continue their affairs in accordance with this view, at least until the character of the neighbourhood changes sufficiently to justify a re-assessment. But this is no more than what happens in many cases in negligence, for the parties to a negligence action may well be in a continuing relationship, such as that between employer and employee: a decision that it was negligent not to provide safety goggles or the like to employees may serve to lay down a standard for the future for a whole industry.

Summary

19.1 The tort of nuisance consists of a number of very disparate rules, with no common rationale, which are treated together because they are all concerned with one particular field of activity: the use and enjoyment of land. An elementary classification might distinguish these rules according as to whether (a) they impose liability in respect of a particular interference with the use and enjoyment of land regardless of its reasonableness; (b) they oppose liability no matter how unreasonable the interference in question might be; or (c) they treat the reasonableness of the interference as the test of liability. Most cases fall under the last category as the reasonableness test allows greater flexibility in the balancing of competing land uses.

19.2   Where the reasonableness of an interference is relevant, this is assessed after consideration of (a) its extent; (b) the locality in which it takes place (except in cases of physical harm); (c) the sensitivity of the plaintiff to interference of that kind; and (d) the motive with which the defendant acted. This last factor prejudices the defendant who acted carelessly or maliciously.

19.3   Only those with an interest in the land affected by the defendant's activities can sue in the tort of nuisance.

19.4   Liability is imposed on those who create, adopt or continue a nuisance, whether by their own acts or the acts of their independent contractors. In certain circumstances, landlords may be liable in respect of nuisances created on land they have let out.

19.5   Various defences may be raised to an action in nuisance, notably prescription and statutory authority. Although the unreasonableness of the plaintiff's conduct may give rise to a defence of contributory negligence or *volenti*, it is no defence that the plaintiff 'came to the nuisance'.

19.6   The public interest in free passage along the highway has resulted in the imposition of liabilities of exceptional stringency on those who cause obstructions. Such liabilities arise in the tort of public nuisance rather than private nuisance, as there is no interference with the use or enjoyment of any private property. Liability in public nuisance depends on proof of special damage. A stringent liability is also imposed under the rule in *Wringe* v. *Cohen* in respect of the collapse of structures adjacent to the highway.

19.7   It is a disputed question whether nuisance is best regarded as a branch of the tort of negligence or as an entirely independent tort. Careful analysis of the alleged differences between the two suggest that these are often more apparent than real.

Exercises

19.1   To what extent is nuisance a tort of strict liability?

19.2   What is the test of 'reasonable user'? Is it relevant in all cases of nuisance? What factors determine whether a user of land is reasonable?

19.3   What is the significance of *St. Helen's Smelting* v. *Tipping*? Do you agree with the views of Lord Westbury LC in that case?

19.4   Can *Mayor of Bradford* v. *Pickles* be reconciled with *Christie* v. *Davey*?

19.5   Who may sue in the tort of nuisance? Is the law satisfactory on this issue?

19.6   In what circumstances will liability in the tort of nuisance be imposed on one who has not personally created the nuisance?

19.7   Will the mere fact that a defendant has statutory authority to carry out a particular activity absolve her of any liability in nuisance?

19.8   Is it a defence that the plaintiff 'came to the nuisance.' Should it be?

19.9   Should obstruction of the highway be any of the following: (a) a crime; (b) a tort; (c) the tort of private nuisance?

19.10 Is nuisance in reality nothing more than a branch of the tort of negligence?

(For a problem on nuisance and the rule in *Rylands* v. *Fletcher*, please see the end of Chapter 20.)

20 The Rule in *Rylands* v. *Fletcher*

20.1 Introduction

Rylands v. *Fletcher* (1866) LR 1 Exch 265, (1868) LR 3 HL 330 lays down a rule of strict liability for harm caused by exceptionally hazardous activities on land. Although historically it seems to have been an offshoot of the law of nuisance, it is sometimes said to differ from nuisance in that its concern is with escapes *from* land rather than interference *with* land. Accordingly, some authorities hold that there is no requirement – like that in the tort of nuisance – that the plaintiff should have a proprietary or possessory interest in land, though the point is far from uncontroversial (see 20.4). If this is so, the rule in *Rylands* v. *Fletcher* may be more appropriately classified amongst those torts which have as their primary purpose the protection of interests in the person and personal property than amongst those protecting interests in real property.

The case concerned the flooding of the plaintiff's mine with water from the defendants' recently-constructed reservoir. A coal seam had previously been worked on the site of the reservoir and, although the mine shaft had been filled up, water from the reservoir was able to escape down the shaft and from there to the plaintiff's mine. The existence of the disused shaft had not been discovered before the reservoir was filled with water and thus no precautions had been taken to guard against the risk which eventuated. The fault for this lay with the independent contractors the defendants had engaged to construct the reservoir; the defendants were not personally to blame. Furthermore, the general rule is that, while one may be vicariously liable for the acts of an employee, one is not responsible for the acts of an independent contractor (see Chapter 22). This difficulty, though, was avoided in the case by treating the defendants as personally liable irrespective of fault.

In the Court of Exchequer Chamber, Blackburn J set out the rule to be applied in such cases, together with the defences to it (his formulation was subsequently approved by the House of Lords in the same case):

'[T]he person who, for his own purposes, brings on his land, and collects and keeps there anything likely to do mischief if it escapes, must keep it in at his peril, and, if he does not do so, he is prima facie responsible for all the damage which is the natural consequence of its escape. He can excuse himself by showing that the escape was owing to the plaintiff's default, or, perhaps, that the escape was the consequence of vis major, or the act of God.'

This formulation makes it clear that there are two essential ingredients of *Rylands* v. *Fletcher* liability: first, the bringing of a dangerous thing on to one's land (treated under the heading 'non-natural user of land'); secondly, the escape of that thing.

20.2   Non-Natural Use of Land

The requirement that the defendant must bring something on to his land was inadvertently transformed in the House of Lords by Lord Cairns. He paraphrased Blackburn J's words, saying that the rule applied only to a 'non-natural use' of land, not to a case in which a substance had accumulated naturally on the land. As Newark (1961) points out, the word 'natural' is ambiguous and, although Lord Cairns meant to exclude from the scope of the rule only those things which were present on the land in its natural state, his words were misinterpreted so as also to exclude man-made objects and accumulations, so long as they could be described as 'ordinary' ('ordinary' sometimes being a synonym for 'natural'). What will be regarded as ordinary and natural will depend on the exact circumstances of the case. Changes in perceptions brought about by the passage of time must be taken into account: keeping a motor car in one's garage might be unremarkable in the late twentieth century, but at the beginning of the century it might have been thought unusually dangerous (see *Musgrove* v. *Pandelis* [1919] 2 KB 43). So too must more transient shifts in community standards: in *Read* v. *Lyons* [1947] AC 156 it was held that it was 'natural' to use land for the manufacture of explosives at time of war.

The leading statement of the non-natural user requirement is that of Lord Moulton in *Rickards* v. *Lothian* [1913] AC 263: 'It must be some special use bringing with it increased danger to others and must not merely be the ordinary use of the land or such a use as is proper for the general benefit of the community.' Lord Moulton's statement of principle effectively robs the rule in *Rylands* v. *Fletcher* of its primary justification, for strict liability is premised upon the belief that the rights of individuals should not be sacrificed in the furtherance of the public interest (see 13.2). It is precisely where land is put to 'such a use as is proper for the general benefit of the community' that strict liability should arise. Furthermore, Lord Moulton's view that hazardous activities cannot give rise to liability under *Rylands* v. *Fletcher* if beneficial to the community leaves the (supposedly) strict liability derived from that case hard to distinguish from liability in negligence: exposing others to danger without generating a countervailing benefit should, as a matter of logic, amount to negligence.

20.3   Escape

The requirement that the thing brought on to the land must have escaped from the land is also illustrated by *Read* v. *Lyons*: in that case, the plaintiff was injured in her employment as an inspector of munitions in the defendant's arms factory when an artillery shell exploded on the production line. The House of Lords held that the rule in *Rylands* v. *Fletcher* had no application to her case as she had been injured on the defendant's land; the shell had not escaped and injured her on neighbouring land.

20.4 Parties

The primary liability under the rule in *Rylands* v. *Fletcher* is upon the owner or controller of the thing that escapes. The escape need not be from that person's own land but can be from land she is merely licensed to use or indeed from the highway: in *Rigby* v. *Chief Constable of Northamptonshire* [1985] 1 WLR 1242, Taylor J said that he could 'see no difference in principle between allowing a man-eating tiger to escape from your land on to that of another and allowing it to escape from the back of your wagon parked on the highway'. The owner or occupier of land on to which the thing is brought may also be held liable (*Rainham Chemical Works* v. *Belvedere Fish Guano Co* [1921] 2 AC 465), though she may have a defence where the actions are those of a stranger (see 20.5).

It is clear that the owner or occupier of the land affected can sue in relation to the damage to her property. Two significant areas of doubt, however, arise when we consider the question of to whom the liability is owed. First, it is not clear whether it is possible to claim in respect of personal injuries as opposed to property damage. In *Read* v. *Lyons*, Lord Macmillan said that 'an allegation of negligence is in general essential to the relevancy of an action of reparation for personal injuries' and would not countenance *Rylands* v. *Fletcher* as an exception to that general rule. Yet the point cannot be regarded as decided, for none of the other judges in *Read* was prepared to express a view on the issue and the Court of Appeal had previously awarded damages for personal injury under the rule, as in *Hale* v. *Jennings Bros* [1938] 1 All ER 579 where the plaintiff, the tenant of a shooting gallery at a fairground, was injured when a chair, with its occupant, became dislocated from the defendant's rotating 'chair-o-plane' ride. Secondly, different opinions have been expressed as to whether the plaintiff must have a proprietary interest in the land invaded. Again, the courts have awarded damages to those who had no interest in the land on which they were injured; for example, the plaintiff in *Schiffman* v. *Order of St John* [1936] 1 All ER 557 who was injured in Hyde Park when the defendants' flag-pole fell on him. A more recent decision, however, may give some support to the opposing view that the plaintiff must have an interest in the land invaded: where the business of cattle auctioneers was disrupted after local livestock was infected by foot and mouth disease which had escaped from the defendant's laboratories, Widgery J resisted the auctioneers' claim for compensation under the rule in *Rylands* v. *Fletcher* (*Weller & Co* v. *Foot and Mouth Disease Research Institute* [1966] 1 QB 569). The true basis of the judge's decision on this point is, however, not clear for he dealt with the issue very briskly and his words are equally consistent with what is perhaps a better rationale for the decision, namely that plaintiffs should not be able to evade the limits of liability for pure economic loss in the tort of negligence by suing under the rule in *Rylands* v. *Fletcher* instead. In any case, the point remains controversial, though it has been said that it is not open to the Court of Appeal to limit the rule to cases of interference with a proprietary interest (*Perry* v. *Kendricks Transport Ltd* [1956] 1 WLR 85 at 92, per Parker LJ).

20.5   Defences

Blackburn J indicated three defences to liability under *Rylands* v. *Fletcher* in the passage extracted above (20.1). First in his list was default of the plaintiff. In extreme cases, no liability at all will arise as where it was the plaintiff's mining operations beneath the defendant's canal, performed with full knowledge of the likely consequences, that caused water to escape and damage his mine (*Dunn* v. *Birmingham Canal Co* (1872) LR 7 QB 244). More mundane instances of fault can be dealt with through the apportionment provisions of the Law Reform (Contributory Negligence) Act 1945 (see 12.5). The second defence indicated by Blackburn J was *vis major*, which in this context refers to cases in which the escape was caused by the independent acts of a third party. The act of a third party will be considered 'independent' unless it would not have occurred without the negligence of the defendant. Hence, in *Perry* v. *Kendricks Transport Ltd*, the Court of Appeal declined to hold the defendants liable when a motor coach in their car park was set on fire by young boys: the motor coach was not left in such a condition that it was reasonable to expect that children might meddle with it and cause the fire. Last, the defence of Act of God will arise where the escape was caused by some wholly unforeseeable natural event (e.g. an earthquake or hurricane). The question of whether exceptionally heavy rains or violent winds give rise to this defence is a matter of degree (compare *Nichols* v. *Marsland* (1876) 2 Ex D 1 with *Greenock Corporation* v. *Caledonian Railway* [1917] AC 556).

In addition to the defences listed by Blackburn J, the defendant may be able to rely upon the defences of necessity (see 17.7), consent to the non-natural user of land (see 20.2) and statutory authority (see 19.5).

20.6   Fire

Notwithstanding the narrow approach to *Rylands* v. *Fletcher* liability evident above, the courts have shown some flexibility when it comes to cases in which things brought on to land catch fire and the fire escapes to neighbouring land. Although Blackburn J's words, taken literally, would seem to require the thing that escapes to be the same as the thing brought on to the land, in *Mason* v. *Levy Auto Parts of England* [1967] 2 QB 530,

McKenna J accepted that the same rule of strict liability applies where the non-natural thing catches fire and the fire escapes from the land.

Section 86 of the Fires Prevention (Metropolis) Act 1774, confers a tortious immunity in respect of fires beginning accidentally on the defendant's land. This does not apply, however, when liability can be established on *Rylands* v. *Fletcher* principles or indeed in negligence (*Musgrove* v. *Pandelis* [1919] 2 KB 43). Even where a fire begins without any negligence or non-natural user, the defendant may lose her immunity under the Act if she negligently allows the fire to spread. Thus, in *Musgrove*, the defendant was held liable after the engine of his motor car caught fire on being started up in his garage; the crucial factor in the case was that the spread of the fire to the plaintiff's premises above the garage would not have occurred without his servant's negligence (an alternative ground for the decision was that keeping the car was a non-natural user of land which itself deprived the owner of any immunity: see 20.2). The converse is true when a fire is lit intentionally but in a controlled environment and subsequently spreads from the defendant's land without any fault on her part. In such circumstances, the statutory immunity may be raised. Hence, in *Musgrove*, Warrington LJ considered that if a lump of coal should jump unexpectedly from a fire lit in a domestic hearth the resulting conflagration should be regarded as having begun accidentally and the statutory immunity would apply.

A similar rule to that under *Rylands* v. *Fletcher* governs the liability of those engaged in dangerous operations involving the creation of fire. The leading case is *Honeywell and Stein Ltd* v. *Larkin Bros (London's Commerical Photographers) Ltd* [1934] 1 KB 191, in which contractors engaged to work in a cinema themselves employed photographers to record their handiwork on film. The primitive flashlights used by the photographers set fire to the cinema. The contractors were held liable for the fire damage, even though they were not personally at fault, because they had instigated the dangerous operation. This liability differs from that under *Rylands* v. *Fletcher* in three main respects. First, it applies even in the absence of a non-natural user of land. Secondly, there is no requirement of any *escape* from the land on which the dangerous operations are carried out. Last, it seems that the liability is not properly regarded as strict but a hybrid form of liability for which negligence must be shown, even if it is the negligence of an independent contractor (see Chapter 22).

Summary

20.1   *Rylands* v. *Fletcher* lays down a rule, originally formulated by Blackburn J in the Court of Exchequer Chamber, of strict liability for harm caused by the escape of dangerous things accumulated on land.

20.2 The requirement that the defendant must bring something on to his land was inadvertently transformed in the House of Lords by Lord Cairns who, despite fully endorsing everything said by Blackburn J, said that the rule only applied where the accumulation of dangerous things represented a 'non-natural user of land'. This requirement has been applied restrictively so as to exclude liability in many cases in which the accumulated things were artificial but not unusual.

20.3 The plaintiff must be injured by an escape from the defendant's premises: no liability under the rule can arise when she is injured *on* those premises.

20.4 Both the owner or controller of the dangerous thing and (if they are not one and the same) the owner or occupier of the land from which it escapes may be held liable under the rule.

20.5 Defences which may be raised against the imposition of liability under the rule include default of the plaintiff, the independent act of a third party and act of God.

20.6 The escape of fire may give rise to a liability analogous to that under *Rylands* v. *Fletcher*. The tortious immunity conferred by the Fires Prevention (Metropolis) Act 1774 does not apply to cases which fall within the rule, or indeed to cases where a fire was started negligently. Even when fire does not escape from premises, something approaching strict liability may be imposed under the rule in *Honeywell and Stein* v. *Larkin Bros*.

Exercises

20.1 What are the ingredients of liability under the rule in *Rylands* v. *Fletcher?*

20.2 Is the imposition of liability without fault justifiable? To what extent have the courts paid heed to the objectives of strict liability in developing the rule in *Rylands* v. *Fletcher?*

20.3 Can liability for fire damage ever arise in the absence of negligence? If so, when?

20.4 D and E are neighbours in Meadow Lane. Four weeks ago, F started to sell roasted chestnuts from a mobile stall in the lane outside D and E's houses. Many passers-by have been inconvenienced by the fact that F's stall gets in their way; D and E have more particular grievances. D alleges that she can no longer host her regular wine appreciation evenings as the smell from the stall overwhelms the bouquet of the wines. E, who is trying to sell her property, has been told that the fact that 'a dirty old tramp' has set up a stall in the vicinity, 'spoiling the view' and 'making a terrible smell', means that she will have to reduce the price considerably. When E asks F to move on, the latter replies: 'There've been stalls like mine in the area for hundreds of years. You should value your heritage. Besides, I'm only here a couple of hours a night.' Angered by E's attitude, F starts to burn an even more pungent fuel than before. Yesterday sparks from F's stall set fire to D's hedge. D's gardener, G, who comes to work for D one afternoon a week, tried to put out the fire with the garden hose. However, her efforts to direct the jet of water at the fire were ineffectual as she is elderly and suffers greatly from arthritis. As a result, a fire spread to D's rubbish tip and thence to E's property where it burnt down an outhouse. Despite this damage, F vows to continue selling chestnuts from the same place in the future. Advise the parties as to their rights and liabilities in tort.

Part IV

Interference with Reputation

21 Defamation

21.1 Interference with Personality Generally

How much protection should English law give to 'interests in personality'? Should a person, for example, have a remedy where another person makes untrue, or even true, statements about him which affect his sense of dignity or honour? Should a person be able to bring an action where another person appropriates his name or picture for commercial use without his permission? Should a person be able to prevent another planting listening devices in his house or taking photographs of him by surreptitious means? These are vexed questions which have troubled lawyers, both practising and academic, for at least 100 years. In this chapter we will look principally at the law of defamation and the way in which it protects a particular interest in personality, namely, a person's reputation. As we shall see, the law of defamation is primarily concerned with providing a remedy to a person who has been the victim of an untrue statement which lowers him in the estimation of others. The law of defamation, however, leaves other interests in personality unprotected. It provides no protection, for example, where true but unflattering or even extremely damaging statements are made by one person about another. It does not protect a person from physical intrusions into his private life, such as the opening of confidential letters or the taking of unauthorised photographs. It also provides no protection where one person uses another person's name or image for his own benefit.

Although the protection given to interests in personality by the law of defamation is limited, there are other legal principles which may be used in order to protect interests in personality. First, the law of negligence gives some protection to an individual's reputation in cases where that individual is inaccurately criticised by the defendant. Thus, it was held in *Lawton* v. *B.O.C. Transhield Ltd* [1987] ICR 7 that misrepresentations about the plaintiff made in a reference to a potential employer could give rise to liability if negligence was established. Secondly, in a number of cases, disclosure of true facts about another has been prevented through an action for breach of confidence. For example, in *Argyll* v. *Argyll* [1967] Ch. 302 a man was prevented from disclosing information given to him by his ex-wife during their marriage which concerned her private affairs. However, the equitable remedies available through an action for breach of confidence are available only where the information (a) had the necessary quality of confidence about it; (b) was conveyed in circumstances importing an obligation of confidence, and; (c) was used in an un-authorised way to the disadvantage of the person who had communicated it. Thirdly, certain statutes may also prevent the disclosure of true facts. For example, section 49 of the Children and Young Persons Act 1933 prohibits the revelation in any report of juvenile proceedings of the name, address, school or any other particulars identifying any juvenile involved unless the court grants leave.

As we have already said, the tort of defamation is usually limited to protection of a person's reputation from untrue imputations which lower him in the estimation of others. However, in *Tolley* v. *Fry* [1931] AC 333) the court used the law of defamation to provide what looks, in essence, like a remedy for the unauthorised appropriation of another's personality. A caricature of a well-known amateur golfer with a bar of Fry's chocolate in his back-pocket was held to be defamatory of the golfer. In reality, the plaintiff appears to have been given an action, under the guise of defamation, restraining the unauthorised use of his picture for commercial purposes. Apart from this case, the courts have not shown themselves willing to allow an action for the unauthorised use of another's picture or name though, as Fleming (1987, p. 576) points out, 'the decision has potentially far reaching implications and could be stretched to serve as a basis for restraining the unauthorised use of anyone's name or picture for commercial use under the guise of protecting reputation'.

Protection may also be given against physical intrusions into a person's private life. For example, the owner of land may be able to rely on the torts of trespass to land and nuisance in order to protect his privacy. Additionally, many statutes provide protection against physical interference. For example, section 14 of the Post Office Act 1969 makes it an offence to open the letters of another without authorisation.

It can be seen, therefore, that English law does protect interests in personality other than the right not to have untruths spoken to another about oneself. However, the protection offered is at best haphazard and gaping holes still exist. Are there really free speech implications which prevent there being an action for appropriation of personality for commercial use? The haphazard nature and the inadequacies of the remedies offered have led some people to call for the introduction of a tort of infringement of privacy. Various definitions of privacy have been offered, ranging from 'the right to be let alone' to the identification of various personality interests, such as intrusion by spying, the unauthorised use of another's personality and the publication of personal information. At present, despite increasing intrusion by the press into the private lives of politicians, members of the royal family and members of the public generally, it seems unlikely that such a tort will be introduced. Indeed, the latest government report on privacy (Calcutt, 1990) expressly recommended against the introduction of such a tort. However, while these inconsistencies and inadequacies remain it is unlikely that the issue will go away. How far the law should protect interests in personality is likely to remain an area of great controversy.

The remainder of this chapter will look at the protection afforded to a person's reputation by the law of defamation.

21.2   The Law of Defamation

The law has, from the earliest times, recognised the making of false statements about another as a wrongful act. The high value accorded to a person's reputation has led to virtually every legal system in the world affording it protection. In English law, this function is performed by the law of defamation. Whilst a reputation is deservedly afforded substantial protection by the law, the need to protect reputations must be balanced against the competing demands of free speech. No system of law does or should offer absolute protection for reputation. This is particularly the case where the maker of the statement is discussing a matter of public interest. One of the concerns, therefore, of the law of defamation is to achieve a satisfactory balance between these two interests. The difficulty of achieving this balance has led to the development of an area of law of considerable complexity.

In order for a statement to be actionable in the tort of defamation a defamatory statement must be published about the plaintiff to a third person. In the case of slander actual injury must also be proved. Each of these elements of the tort will now be considered in turn.

21.3   The Statement must be Defamatory

A defamatory statement is one which adversely affects a person's reputation. Vulgar abuse or insulting name calling will not generally be defamatory because such behaviour is usually only insulting to a person's pride and does not affect his reputation. Traditionally, the test as to whether or not a statement was defamatory was whether the words complained of brought the plaintiff into 'hatred, ridicule or contempt'. However, the difficulty of bringing some statements which appeared adversely to affect a person's reputation within the traditional definition led Lord Atkin in *Sim* v. *Stretch* [1936] 2 All ER 1237 to put forward a broader test. He said:

'[T]he conventional phrase exposing the plaintiff to "hatred, ridicule or contempt" is probably too narrow. . . . I do not intend to ask your Lordships to lay down a formal definition, but after collating the opinions of many authorities I propose in the present case the test: would the words tend to lower the plaintiff in the estimation of right thinking members of society generally?'

This test now commands almost universal usage.

Whether or not a statement is capable of being defamatory is a question of law for the judge. Whether or not it is in fact defamatory is one of fact for the jury. In considering the standard to be applied when determining whether or not the words used are defamatory, the courts have not been wholly consistent. However, the formulation most used is that of the 'right thinking man' or 'the good and worthy subject of the [Queen]'. The question asked is, therefore, whether the 'right thinking man' would construe the words in a way defamatory of the plaintiff. It may, of course, be a controversial question what the 'right thinking man' would think. For example, would the 'right thinking man' consider that an allegation that a woman had been raped, or that she was not a virgin when she married, lowered her in the estimation of society? Similarly, would a 'right thinking man' consider that an allegation of insanity or alcoholism lowered a person's reputation? It may be that the courts in considering what the 'right thinking man' thinks, are inclined to look to what he *should* think rather than what he does in fact think. A good illustration of this tendency is seen in the case of *Byrne* v. *Deane* [1937] 1 KB 818 .

In that case automatic gambling machines, which were kept illegally on the premises of a golf club, were removed by the police after someone had informed them of the machines' presence. A verse appeared soon after this on the notice board of the club. The last two lines of the verse read, '[b]ut he who gave the game away, may he byrnn in hell and rue the day'. The issue for the Court of Appeal was whether the trial judge had been correct to leave to the jury the question whether the words were defamatory of the plaintiff, Mr Byrne, in the sense that they meant he was guilty of underhand disloyalty to his fellow members. The court held that the words were not capable of a defamatory meaning as no 'good and worthy subject of the King' could consider such an allegation against a person to be defamatory. Thus the case should not have been left to the jury.

As Greene LJ admitted in his judgment, many people in the country would not consider any moral reprobation attached to the playing of gambling machines. Thus, for them at least, the allegation made against the plaintiff – whom they might regard as officious – could be defamatory. Why should not the question of whether the words are defamatory be judged according to what they think? The answer given by the court to this is that it is always possible to discover a small group in society who would not find the words complained of defamatory. For example, among certain groups to describe someone as a *'professional* thief' would be a compliment. The ordinary meaning of words cannot be left to such anti-social groups, but must instead be considered by a more respectable body of opinion. However, it must not be assumed that a body of opinion is anti-social merely because it is opposed by the majority. For example, to accuse someone of being a homosexual would be defamatory in the estimation of many, despite the fact that the homosexual lifestyle is regarded by some as perfectly proper. Care must be taken to respect minority rights.

In deciding whether or not the words used are in fact defamatory the jury are asked to consider the meaning of the words in their 'natural and ordinary' sense. In many cases, of course, the words used only have one meaning and that meaning is clearly defamatory. However, a word may be capable in its ordinary usage of having more than one meaning. For example, in a recent case a woman was described as an 'international boot'. Three 'dictionary' meanings were considered; first, that a boot was a type of footwear (unlikely!); secondly, that boot meant a physically unattractive person; finally, and the meaning that was accepted by the jury, that boot meant a promiscuous person. Where more than one natural and ordinary meaning is possible and pleaded it is left to the jury to decide which meaning the words have.

In some cases the plaintiff may allege that the meaning that ought to be attributed to the words is not an ordinary or natural meaning but is instead a meaning which can only be ascertained by drawing an inference or implication from the words themselves or perhaps only from the use of evidence separate from the statement itself which makes the true meaning of the words clear. In the former case, known as a false or popular innuendo, the plaintiff seeks to argue that the words themselves convey an impression of, or mean something different from, their ordinary and natural meaning. In the latter, known as a true or legal innuendo, the plaintiff seeks to argue that certain facts which were already known to the addressee gave the words a defamatory meaning.

An example of a false innuendo can be seen in *Lewis* v. *Daily Telegraph* [1963] 2 All ER 151. Two newspapers published a story in which it was reported that officers of the London Fraud Squad were 'inquiring into the affairs of the R Co and its subsidiary companies'. Three possible meanings were considered by the House of Lords: first, that there was an investigation in progress; secondly, that the plaintiffs were suspected of fraud; and finally, that the plaintiffs were guilty of fraud. Lord Reid held that in determining the meaning to be given to the words the question to be asked was what meaning would be conveyed to the ordinary person. Such a person 'does not live in an ivory tower and he is not inhibited by a knowledge of the rules of construction. So he can and does read between the lines in the light of his general knowledge and experience of world affairs'. Their Lordships held that only the first two meanings were possible. It was impossible in this case, they said, for the statement that an enquiry was taking place to convey the impression that the subject of the enquiry was *guilty* of fraud. Acceptance of the second meaning, that the plaintiffs were suspected of fraud, involves a false innuendo. No extrinsic evidence is required for this meaning to be attributed; it is simply an implication that can be drawn or an impression that may be gained from a reading of the words themselves.

Where the meaning that the plaintiff is seeking to establish can only be ascertained by the use of extrinsic evidence this is known as a true innuendo. A true innuendo arises solely from facts or circumstances which are not apparent from the words themselves but which give the words a meaning they would not ordinarily have. A good illustration of a true innuendo can be seen in the case of *Cassidy* v. *Daily Mirror Newspapers Ltd* [1929] 2 KB 331. In that case the defendants published a photograph taken of Kettering Cassidy, also known as Michael Corrigan, and another woman. Below the photograph were the words: 'Mr M. Corrigan, the race horse owner, and Miss X, whose engagement has been announced.' Mr Cassidy had told the photographer of this announcement. The action was brought by Mrs Cassidy, who was in fact the lawful wife of Cassidy; although they lived apart, Cassidy occasionally visited her. She argued that the words and picture were capable of meaning that 'Corrigan' was a single man, and that therefore she was living in immoral co-habitation with him. The Court of Appeal held that the publication was capable of bearing this defamatory meaning. On their own, the words and picture were not defamatory. However, in the light of the extrinsic evidence that Cassidy was in fact married, a defamatory meaning was possible. It did not matter that the defendant newspaper did not know of the extrinsic facts, provided that the paper had been read by those who did and who understood the statement to apply to the plaintiff.

21.4   The Statement must be Published to a Third Person

The law of defamation is concerned, as we have seen, with the protection of a person's reputation in the eyes of other people. As a person's reputation is, in simple terms, the opinion or view that others hold of him, it follows that unless the statement is published to a third person there can be no damage to the person's reputation. If nobody but the maker of the statement and the person about whom the statement was made know of the contents of that statement, how can the statement have affected the person's reputation in the eye's of his fellow man? Thus English law requires that the defamatory statement must be published to a person other than the person whose reputation is impugned.

Publication is the communication of a defamatory statement to a person other than the plaintiff. An unexpressed defamatory thought or even the writing of such a thought on paper will not be actionable unless and until it is actually communicated to another. The publication must also be made to a person capable of understanding the defamatory meaning. Where, for example, the statement is not defamatory on its face but is only defamatory when considered in the light of extrinsic evidence (a case of true innuendo), the hearer must know of the extrinsic facts which make the statement defamatory. More obviously, if a defamatory statement contained in a letter is written in a foreign language, the recipient must be able to understand that language.

It is not necessary for the plaintiff to prove that the publication was intentionally made. As long as he can show that the defendant ought reasonably to have foreseen that the statement would come to a third party's attention, the requirement of publication will be satisfied. Thus in *Theaker* v. *Richardson* [1962] 1 All ER 229 the defendant wrote a defamatory letter to the plaintiff who was a married woman. The letter, which was addressed to the plaintiff, was contained in a manilla envelope similar to the kind used for distributing election addresses. The plaintiff's husband opened the envelope thinking it was an election address. At the trial the jury found there had been a publication of a defamatory statement and awarded damages to the plaintiff. On appeal to the Court of Appeal, Pearson LJ said that the question that should be asked was, '[Was] his (i.e. the recipient's) conduct so unusual, out of the ordinary and not reasonably to be anticipated, or was it something which could quite easily and naturally happen in the ordinary course of events?' This was pre-eminently a jury question, and as the jury had decided that the opening of the letter by the husband was something that could quite easily happen in the ordinary course of events the Court of Appeal would not interfere with its decision. By way of contrast, the Court of Appeal held in the case of *Huth* v. *Huth* [1914–15] All E Rep 242 that where a defamatory letter about the wife and children was sent by a husband to his wife, the fact that it had been opened and read by the butler did not constitute publication. As Lord Reading CJ said, 'it is no part of a butler's duty to open letters that come to the house of his master or mistress addressed to the master or mistress'.

Every repetition of a defamatory statement is a new publication and creates a fresh cause of action in the person defamed. The person repeating the statement will be treated in the same way as if he had originated it. 'Tale bearers are as bad as tale makers' is a well-established maxim. It is no defence that the speaker did not originate the scandal, but heard it from another, even though it was current rumour and he believed it to be true.

Although every repetition creates a new cause of action, common sense dictates that liability must cease somewhere. Whilst there may be arguments of policy for holding the author of a statement and his publisher liable even in the absence of fault, there is perhaps less reason for imposing liability upon mere 'mechanical' publishers of a defamatory statement, (e.g., booksellers, libraries or distributors). Where 'mechanical' publishers are concerned they generally have no control over the content of the statement and in many cases have no reason to suspect that the publication contains any defamatory matter. To expect them to read every line of a publication is to expect too much. Whilst 'mechanical' publishers are presumptively liable for publication, the case of *Vizetelly* v. *Mudie's Select Library Ltd* [1900] 2 QB 170 provides them with a defence of innocent dissemination if they can prove (a) that they were innocent of any knowledge of the libel; (b) that there was nothing in the work or in the circumstances in which it came to, or was disseminated by, them which ought to have led them to suppose it contained a libel; and (c) that when the work was disseminated by them it was not by any negligence on their part that they did not know it contained a libel. Although the defence does give 'mechanical' publishers a substantial degree of protection, the protection is not absolute. A distributor might not, for example, be able to rely on the defence where he distributes a publication which has a reputation for publishing defamatory material. This may discourage distributors from selling certain journals (W.H. Smith & Son Ltd, for example, declined for a long time to distribute 'Private Eye').

A related question was considered by the Court of Appeal in *Slipper* v. *British Broadcasting Corporation* [1991] 1 All ER 165: is the original maker of the statement liable for subsequent re-publications of his statement by others? The Court of Appeal held that the law relating to re-publication in defamation cases is simply an example of the rule of causation encapsulated in the Latin phrase *novus actus interveniens* familiar throughout the law of tort (see Chapter 10.4). Thus, in any case involving the repetition of a libel, the following question should be asked: was it a foreseeable or natural and probable consequence of the libel that the third party to whom it was published would repeat it?

21.5   Reference to the Plaintiff

The third essential requirement to found an action for defamation is that the statement refer to the plaintiff. Where the plaintiff is expressly mentioned by name there will usually be no difficulty. However, it is not essential that the plaintiff be expressly referred to. In *Morgan* v. *Odhams Press Ltd* [1971] 2 All ER 1156 the fact that the plaintiff was not expressly referred to was not held to be fatal to his claim. The defendants published an article which stated that a girl had been kidnapped by a dog-doping gang. The girl had in fact been staying voluntarily with the plaintiff around this time. At the trial the plaintiff produced several witnesses who said that they thought that the article referred to him. The House of Lords held that in determining whether the article referred to the plaintiff, the test to be adopted was to ask whether a 'hypothetical sensible reader who knew of the special facts' could reasonably come to the conclusion that the article referred to the plaintiff. Such a reader is not expected to read a newspaper article with the care that a lawyer would read an important legal document; it is accepted that he may read it quickly in order to get a general impression. What is important is the inferences that such a reader would draw from the article. On the facts of the case, despite the fact that a close reading of the article would have made it clear that it could not refer to the plaintiff, their Lordships upheld the jury's decision.

The fact that the defendant in making the statement did not intend to refer to the plaintiff has been held by the courts to be irrelevant. In *Hulton* v. *Jones* [1910] AC 20 Artemus Jones, a barrister, brought an action against the defendants in respect of a newspaper article which he claimed referred to him. The article referred to 'Artemus Jones', a church warden in Peckham, and cast imputations on his moral behaviour at a motor festival in Dieppe. The defendants argued they had never intended the article to refer to the 'real' Artemus Jones but instead had intended to create a fictitious character. The House of Lords held that the defendants' intentions were irrelevant. Lord Loreburn said, '[a] person charged with libel cannot defend himself by shewing that he intended in his own breast not to defame, or that he intended not to defame the plaintiff, if in fact he did both'. The test to be applied was to ask whether a reasonable person would consider in all the circumstances that the article referred to the plaintiff.

In *Newstead* v. *London Express Newspaper Ltd* [1940] 1 KB 377 the Court of Appeal applied the principle of *Hulton* v. *Jones* to the situation where the defendant had intended to refer to a person about whom the statements were true, but the plaintiff said that the statement also referred to him and was defamatory. Provided a reader of the article would reasonably think that the statement referred to the plaintiff it is no defence for the defendant to prove that the words were intended to refer to another person of whom they were true.

Where words are spoken of a group of people, proof that the article refers to a particular member of the group is likely to be difficult. If a person were heard to say 'all lawyers are thieves', such a statement would be unlikely to give rise to a cause of action on the part of any individual lawyer. The fact that proof of reference in such a case is difficult does not mean that no 'group defamations' will be actionable at the suit of a member of that group. In *Knuppfer* v. *London Express Newspapers* [1944] AC 116 the House of Lords was asked to consider whether the trial judge had been correct to hold that an unflattering article concerning the activities of a pro-German group referred to the plaintiff. The membership of the British branch of the organisation, of which the plaintiff was head, numbered about 24. The House of Lords held that the article could not be understood as referring to him. As Lord Atkin pointed out, there was no special rule to be applied where group defamation was concerned; '[t]he only relevant rule is that in order to be actionable the defamatory words must be published of and concerning the plaintiff'. He accepted that this was likely to be difficult in most group defamations. However, in two situations apparent 'group defamations' may be capable of referring to individual members of that group: first, where the words are spoken of a group which is so small or so ascertainable that the words spoken of the group are necessarily said of each individual member; and secondly, where although the words purport to refer to a group they can in fact be read as applying to a particular individual (for instance, where his photograph appears next to the defamatory words).

21.6 Damage: The Distinction between Libel and Slander

English law draws a distinction between libels and slanders, libels generally being written, slanders, spoken. In the case of libel, actual injury need not be proved: in cases of slander, by contrast, the courts require proof of injury before the defamatory statement can give rise to an action. Although the basis of this distinction is historical there have been a number of modern attempts to justify its continued existence. It has been said that, as libels are generally written, they are likely to remain in effect for longer and to be read by more people, and that more significance is likely to be attached to them. It has also been argued that libel conveys the impression of a deliberate calculated attack on reputation, in the sense that more time for reflection is required for a written statement than a slander, which is often the result of a moment's outburst of anger. Whilst there is some truth in all this, a slander may have just as serious an effect on a person's reputation as a libel. For example, a well placed remark at a board meeting of a large company concerning the chairman's competence could be just as deleterious for him as an article in a major newspaper. It is surely such factors as the status of the person making the statement, the statement's seriousness and the circumstances in which it is made that are important rather than the means by which the remark is conveyed.

What is the basis of the distinction? Originally, it lay in the difference between written and oral statements. However, as methods of communication developed and changed this distinction was no longer wholly satisfactory. How, for example, should radio defamation be treated? Or a defamatory statement made on a video recording or on television? While Parliament has legislated on some of these issues, the basic test for distinguishing libels and slanders must still be sought in the cases.

It is doubtful if today there can be said to be one single test as to what is a libel or a slander. Some cases, such as *Monson* v. *Tussauds Ltd* [1894] 1 QB 671, have looked to the permanence or transience of the 'statement', libels being those 'statements' found in a permanent form, whereas slanders take a transient form. In *Monson*, a wax model of the plaintiff was placed in an exhibition entitled 'the chamber of horrors'. This was held to be a libel. As Lopes LJ said: '[l]ibels are generally in writing or printing, but this is not necessary; the defamatory matter may be conveyed in some other permanent form. For instance, a statue, a caricature, an effigy, a chalk-marks on a wall, signs or pictures may constitute a libel.' On the other hand, the underlying basis for the distinction in other cases seems to be that libels are communications conveyed to the sense of sight, whereas, slanders are conveyed to the ear. The best view is that permanence and perception by sight are both factors which indicate a libel rather than a slander. Neither should, however, be treated as conclusive.

Libel is actionable *per se*, whereas slander generally requires proof of actual damage. What amounts to actual damage? Mere loss of reputation has been held to be insufficient. The courts have instead insisted that there must be proof of some 'material' or 'pecuniary' loss. Thus, if it could be proved that the plaintiff had lost his job or lost trade as a result of the slander this would be actionable.

Whilst slander generally requires actual damage to be proved, there are four exceptional situations where slander is actionable *per se*. These are: imputations of criminal conduct punishable with imprisonment; imputations that the plaintiff is suffering from a contagious or infectious disease; imputations of unchastity against a woman; and imputations calculated to disparage the plaintiff in any office, profession, calling, trade or business.

21.7 Defences

In addition to certain general defences dealt with elsewhere in the book, such as voluntary assumption of responsibility and consent, the law of defamation has its own special defences. These defences must now be considered.

21.8 Justification

Where a plaintiff succeeds in showing that the words complained of are defamatory of him and have been published to a third party, the law presumes in his favour that such words are untrue. However, to such a claim the defendant can plead justification. The essence of the defence of justification is that the words complained of are 'true in substance and in fact'. The policy behind allowing justification as a complete defence was well put by Littledale J. in *M'Pherson* v. *Daniels* (1829) B & C 263 at p. 272, '[t]he law will not permit a man to recover damages in respect of an injury to a character which he either does not or ought not to possess'. Unlike other defences, such as fair comment or qualified privilege, the motive of the defendant in making the original statement is irrelevant. Thus, even where the defendant makes the statement with the express intention of damaging the plaintiff's reputation, if the words are true the defendant will escape liability.

In order to establish the defence the defendant must prove that the defamatory matter complained of is true. However, it is not necessary that every 't' should be crossed and every 'i' dotted. As Lord Shaw said in *Sutherland* v. *Stopes* [1925] AC 47 at p. 79:

'[t]he plea [of justification] must not be considered in a meticulous sense. It is that the words employed were true in substance and in fact . . . all that was required to affirm the plea was that the jury should be satisfied that the sting of the libel or, if there were more than one, the stings of the libel should be made out.'

Thus, if I accused A of having stolen my car on 20 March from outside my house, proof that A had stolen my car would justify the sting of the accusation. The fact that A stole the car on 21 March from outside my office would not prevent reliance on the defence. Such minor inaccuracies in no way add to the seriousness of the charge against A.

In order for the plea of justification to be successful it must cover the meaning attributed by the jury to the words complained of. You will recall that the plaintiff may, and must if he wishes to rely on them, give particulars of defamatory meanings which arise by way of innuendo. In a similar fashion, a defendant who pleads justification must state the meaning which he seeks to justify. If the defendant fails to justify the meaning which the jury finds the words to have then the defence will fail: the fact that the defendant can prove some other meaning is irrelevant. Thus, in *Lewis* v. *Daily Telegraph* the fact that the defendant could justify the literal meaning of the words – that the company was under investigation by the police – would not have justified the innuendo meanings (that the company was suspected or guilty of misconduct).

A defamatory statement may contain more than one charge. At common law where more than one charge was alleged, a plea of justification would only have been successful where the defendant justified the sting of all the charges. If A says of some person that 'he has murdered his father, stolen from his mother and does not go to church on Sundays', and A can prove the first two allegations but not the last, A will remain liable in damages in respect of the last charge. The common law has now been altered by section 5 of the Defamation Act 1952. This provides:

> 'In an action for libel or slander in respect of words containing two or more distinct charges against the plaintiff, a defence of justification shall not fail by reason only that the truth of every charge is not proved if the words not proved to be true do not materially injure the plaintiff's reputation having regard to the truth of the remaining charges.'

Under this rule, in the example given above, failure to prove that the plaintiff does not go to church on Sundays would not be fatal to a defence of justification if it was felt by the jury that an allegation of failure to go to church on Sundays did not add to the gravity of the other charges.

The provisions of section 5 are, however, only applicable in an action where the plaintiff relies upon a defamatory statement which contains two or more distinct charges. It would appear to be open to a plaintiff to complain simply of one allegation out of number made against him. Hence the defendant would not be allowed to justify other defamatory allegations contained in the publication in the hope of persuading the jury that the defamatory statement was substantially true or to influence the jury to award lower damages. However, although the plaintiff may isolate one particular allegation in the expectation of being able to prevent the defendant justifying other allegations, the defendant will only be prevented from justifying other allegations where they are 'separate and distinct'. Where the allegations have a common sting, the defendant will be allowed to adduce evidence of the truth of the other allegations in order to justify the common sting. In *Polly Peck (Holdings) PLC* v. *Trelford* [1986] 1 QB 1000, O'Connor LJ held that whether allegations are 'separate and distinct' or have a common sting is a question of fact and degree in each case. In *Khashoggi* v. *I.P.C. Magazines Ltd* [1986] 1 WLR 1412, a magazine article contained what purported to be an account of the plaintiff's life with her husband, an international arms dealer, before and after the dissolution of their marriage. The article contained a series of allegations regarding the plaintiff's sexual behaviour. The plaintiff objected to one of the allegations in the article suggesting that she had committed adultery with a named friend of her husband. The Court of Appeal held that, although the defendants could not prove the allegation of adultery with that particular person, the article was capable of meaning that the plaintiff was guilty of promiscuity generally. Evidence of other 'affairs', therefore, was relevant in considering whether the common sting of the article could be justified.

21.9 Fair Comment

The defence of fair comment on a matter of public interest is, like justification, a complete defence to an action for defamation. The defence is an essential aspect of the greater right of freedom of speech and a safeguard allowing protest at the undemocratic exercise of power. These considerations are of such social importance that in the area covered by the defence they are taken to outweigh the competing claim of protecting a person's reputation. In order for the defence to succeed it must be shown: (a) that the words used are comment and not fact; (b) that the comment is on a matter of public interest; (c) that the comment is based on true facts; and (d) that the comment is 'fair'. Once the defendant has proved these points he will be entitled to rely on the defence unless the plaintiff can show that the defendant was actuated by malice.

Comments or Statements of Fact

In order to be able to rely on the defence the defendant must indicate with reasonable clarity that the statement is one of opinion as opposed to one of fact. Where there is any doubt as to whether the words are fact or comment the trial judge is required to decide whether the words are capable of being comment, the question whether they are in fact comment being left to the jury. How, then, are facts to be distinguished from comment? The distinction is often elusive but an approach which has some merit is that suggested by Sutherland (1992). There he says:

> 'generally, the issue . . . can be determined by examining the statement in isolation. If the statement is at least theoretically susceptible of proof by objective criteria, then it is a statement of fact. If, on the other hand, it represents the statement of a moral or aesthetic judgment, then it constitutes opinion or comment.'

Thus a statement that 'A is a convicted burglar and is, therefore, unfit for public office' is a statement of opinion that A is unfit for public office based on a statement of fact that A is a convicted burglar. More problematic is a statement that A has been guilty of 'disgraceful conduct'. This has been assumed by more than one judge to be a statement of fact, yet it is difficult to see that such a statement is susceptible of proof by objective criteria. Is it not in reality a statement of moral judgment and therefore comment?

Matter of Public Interest

The comment must be on a matter of public interest. A matter is of public interest 'whenever . . . [it] is such as to affect people at large, so that they may be legitimately interested in, or concerned at, what is going on; or what may happen to them or others' (per Lord Denning MR in *London Artists Ltd* v. *Littler* [1969] 2 QB 375 at p. 391). So, for example, discussion of national or local politics or the administration of justice would clearly fall within this definition, as would discussion of a published book or play.

Whilst comment on both the substance of public debate and the conduct and behaviour of those engaged in such debate is essential in any democracy, care must be taken not to stray from comment on a person's conduct in their public capacity to comment on their private life. The private character of a person is of interest only in so far as it affects their capabilities or qualifications for public office. The mere fact of being in the public eye does not legitimise comment on every aspect of a person's character.

Based upon True Facts

A defendant must prove that his comment was based upon true facts. At common law failure to prove the truth of any material basic facts, as distinct from the comments on, or inferences drawn from, those facts, prevented the defendant relying on the defence. However, this strict position has been mitigated by section 6 of the Defamation Act 1952. This provides:

> 'in an action for libel or slander in respect of words consisting partly of allegations of fact and partly of expression of opinion, a defence of fair comment shall not fail by reason only that the truth of every allegation of fact is not proved if the expression of the opinion is fair comment having regard to such of the facts alleged or referred to in the words complained of as are proved.'

Thus where it is said of A that he is unfit for public office because he is a 'liar, a cheat and he has never held office before', failure to prove that the plaintiff has never held office before would not prevent the defendant relying on the defence. The comment is still fair comment having regard to such of the facts as have been proved. However, if the defendant had failed instead to prove that the plaintiff was a cheat, section 6 would probably not provide a complete defence.

The facts on which the comment is based need not be fully set out in the publication complained of. In *Kemsley* v. *Foot* [1952] AC 345 the defendant wrote an article accusing the Beaverbrook Press of the 'foulest piece of journalism perpetrated in this country for a long time'. The defendant's article was headed 'Lower than Kemsley'. The plaintiff, a rival newspaper proprietor, alleged that the statement implied that his companies knowingly published false statements and that 'his name was a byword in this respect'. The defendant pleaded fair comment. The House of Lords held that a plea of fair comment may succeed provided there is a 'sufficient substratum of fact stated or indicated in the words which are the subject matter of the action.' On the facts there was a sufficient substratum of fact – namely, that the plaintiff was in control of the newspapers and that his conduct in this regard was in question – to justify leaving the defence to a jury.

The Comment must be 'Fair'

The question of the appropriate test to be applied in determining whether or not a comment was 'fair' had, until the decision of the House of Lords in *Telnikoff* v. *Matusevitch* [1991] 4 All ER 817, become so shrouded in confusion that the two leading practitioners' works on defamation suggested different answers. In *Telnikoff*, the plaintiff had argued that, in addition to satisfying an objective test (could any man, however prejudiced or obstinate, honestly hold the view expressed by the defendant?), the defendant must prove that he honestly held the views expressed. The House of Lords rejected this argument. They held, approving the judgment of Lloyd LJ in the Court of Appeal ([1990] 3 WLR 725), that the test is a purely objective one: 'could any fair-minded man honestly express that opinion on the proved facts' (per Lloyd LJ at p. 740). Objectivity does not here require an investigation into whether a reasonable man would hold that opinion; the test instead appears to be whether *any* reasonable man could hold the opinion. Provided the opinion is within the sphere of reasonableness, the comment will be fair even if others would not have held that opinion.

Once the defendant has established that the subject matter is a matter of public interest, that the facts on which the comment is based are true and that the comment is such as an honest-minded man might make, the burden is then on the plaintiff to show that the defendant was actuated by malice. As the question of malice arises in almost identical terms in relation to the defence of qualified privilege, the issue of what amounts to malice will be considered later.

21.10 Absolute Privilege

In certain situations deemed to be of sufficient social or political importance the law allows a person to speak or write about others without restraint. Where an occasion is deemed to be of sufficient importance, statements made on that occasion will be absolutely privileged. This is a complete bar to an action for defamation, no matter how false the words may be or how malicious the defendant is. Since the effect of the defence is so drastic, preventing as it does a person from vindicating his reputation, the number of absolutely privileged occasions is small. The defence is not, however, designed to protect abusers of such occasions. Instead the immunity is granted to protect the makers of statements on certain occasions from being forced to defend themselves against unjustified accusations that they were actuated by malice. The following are occasions of absolute privilege:

Parliamentary Proceedings

Article 9 of the Bill of Rights 1688 provides that 'the freedom of speech and debates on proceedings in Parliament ought not to be impeached or questioned in any court or place out of Parliament'. This has been held to have the effect that any statement made by members of the Houses of Parliament in the course of parliamentary proceedings are absolutely privileged. Whilst the full extent of the privilege has not been fully worked out, it would appear that statements made in committees of either House, whether made by MPs or those called to give evidence, are within the privilege as are documents laid before Parliament. On the other hand, statements made by a politician outside the environs of the Houses of Parliament will not be protected by absolute privilege.

In addition to the protection afforded to the maker of the statement, section 1 of the Parliamentary Papers Act 1840 provides that the court is compelled to stay any action brought against the publisher of any reports or papers published by order of, or under the authority of, either House of Parliament. As yet there is no similar provision with respect to the televising of Parliament, although the broadcasting authority would almost certainly be protected by qualified privilege.

Judicial Proceedings

An absolute privilege attaches to all statements, whether oral or written, made in the course of judicial proceedings. All concerned in judicial proceedings, whether as one of the parties to the action, counsel, judge, members of the jury or witness, are immune from an action for defamation. The privilege is not confined to proceedings before a court properly so called. It extends to 'tribunals' which, although not courts of justice, nevertheless act in a manner similar to courts. Also covered by absolute privilege are communications between solicitors and their clients, at least where such communications are made in contemplation of litigation.

High Executive Communications

Where a statement is made by one high-ranking member of the executive to another such a statement will be protected by absolute privilege. In

Chatterton v. *Secretary of State for India in Council* [1895] 2 QB 189, the Court of Appeal held that a statement made by the Secretary of State for India to an Under-Secretary of State was protected by absolute privilege. The court attached great importance to the need for independence in such officers and the interest of the public in allowing them to get on with their work unhindered by libel actions.

The scope of this head of privilege remains uncertain. Whilst communications between ministers of state or between ministers and high-ranking civil servants are clearly within the scope, doubt exists as to how high-ranking the official must be and what executive bodies might be covered. Should the privilege extend, for example, to high-ranking officers in the police force or army? The best approach to this problem is that suggested in Winfield and Jolowicz on Tort (1989, p. 336). Absolute privilege should be confined to those cases where complete freedom of communication is so important that it is right to deprive the citizen of his remedy for any defamatory statements. Care should be taken not to extend the privilege beyond this point.

Statements of Public Officials Protected by Statute

A number of statutes expressly provide that publications made by certain officials, such as the Ombudsman and the Director General of Fair Trading, are absolutely privileged. The underlying rationale of these statutes appears to be that the nature of the work of these individuals makes it likely that they will be subject to actions for defamation. To allow a defamation action against them would make their work intolerable and leave them looking over their shoulder fearful of such an action. To avoid this, and to facilitate the proper working of these individuals, an absolute privilege is needed.

21.11 Qualified Privilege

In addition to those occasions of sufficient social importance to justify the application of absolute privilege, there are others which, while not of sufficient importance to attract absolute privilege, are nevertheless of sufficient importance to attract qualified privilege. As with absolute privilege, the reason for allowing statements made on such occasions to be privileged is 'the common convenience and welfare of society'. However, unlike absolute privilege, the protection given is not absolute. Where the plaintiff can show that the maker of the statement was actuated by malice the defence will be defeated.

Unlike absolute privilege it is impossible fully to categorise all the occasions on which qualified privilege arises. As the legal concepts used to determine the existence of the defence of qualified privilege have regard to such matters as the 'interests' and 'duties' of society, the matters considered worthy of protection are likely to change over time. What was considered to be of public interest at the end of the last century may not be of public interest today, and vice versa. The following classifications of qualified privilege should, therefore, not be taken as exhaustive.

Statements made in Performance of a Legal, Moral or Social Duty

Statements made in the discharge of a legal, moral or social duty to a person who has a reciprocal interest in receiving them are protected by qualified privilege. The determination of whether a duty to communicate exists is a question solely for the judge. The state of mind of the maker of the statement is not relevant to this question. Honest belief in the existence of a duty cannot create a duty to communicate. Whether a legal duty to communicate exists is not usually a difficult question. Certain contracts or statutes may, for example, impose an obligation to make a statement or disclosure. Section 18 of the Marine Insurance Act 1906 makes material non-disclosure in marine insurance contracts a ground for the insurer to avoid the contract. Disclosures made in order to comply with this section would in all likelihood be protected by qualified privilege.

Problems have arisen in determining whether a social or moral duty to communicate exists. In *Stuart* v. *Bell* [1891] 2 QB 341, at 350 Lindley LJ suggested the following test:

'the question of moral or social duty being for the judge, each judge must decide it as best he can for himself. I take moral or social duty to mean a duty recognized by English people of ordinary intelligence and moral principle, but at the same time not a duty enforceable by legal proceedings, whether civil or criminal.'

The circumstances in which courts have held a moral or social duty to exist are extremely diverse. Where the statement is made in answer to an enquiry, the courts appear to be more willing to hold that a duty to communicate exists. However, it does not follow that where there is no request there is no duty. For example, unsolicited warnings by one member of a family to another regarding the 'moral dangers' of a suitor have been held to attract qualified privilege. The case of *Watts* v. *Longsdon* [1930] 1 KB 130 illustrates, however, that not all well-intentioned interventions will be protected. There, the unsolicited repetition by an acquaintance to the plaintiff's wife of unsubstantiated information concerning the plaintiff's sexual conduct was held not to be protected. Other common examples of circumstances attracting qualified privilege include the writing of a reference for an ex-employee at the request of someone proposing to employ him, and a banker's reference on the credit standing of one of its customers.

The existence of a duty to communicate is not enough of itself to attract the defence. In addition the statement must be made to a person who has a legitimate interest to receive it. Without this reciprocity there can be no privilege. A person may have a legitimate interest to receive the contents of a statement by virtue of some legal or social relationship: for example, an employer has an interest in receiving a complaint concerning the fitness of an employee to do his job, and a solicitor has an interest in receiving his client's instructions. The interest may also arise by virtue of the public position of the receiver. A police officer has a legitimate interest to receive information regarding the alleged commission of an offence. Similarly, it has been held that an MP is legitimately interested in the way a constituent was treated by a local solicitor. Where, however, the statement is published in a newspaper or on television to the general public, the courts have been less willing to uphold the existence of the privilege. Something out of the ordinary will be required to satisfy the courts that the public at large, and not just a section of the public, has sufficient interest to receive the information. An example might be where the information relates to a public emergency such as a scare (later unsubstantiated) over the safety of a particular food product (see *Blackshaw* v. *Lord* [1984] QB 1, per Stephenson LJ).

Statements made in Futherance or Protection of an Interest

Private Interest   Where a person makes a statement in protection of his own personal interests to a person who has a reciprocal interest to receive it, the statement will attract the defence of qualified privilege. As Lord Oaksey said in *Turner* v. *Metro-Goldwyn-Mayer Pictures Ltd* [1950] 1 All ER 449 at p. 470:

> 'there is . . . an analogy between the criminal law of self defence and a man's right to defend himself against written or verbal attacks. In both cases he is entitled . . . to defend himself effectively, and he only loses the protection of the law if he goes beyond defence and proceeds to offence.'

Therefore, statements are protected if made in reply to an attack on a person's reputation or proprietary interests, or in protection of one's employer's interests. For example, if A is accused of theft by a police officer, A's reply that B was the thief would attract qualified privilege. By accusing B, there is no evidence that A has gone beyond what is reasonably necessary to defend his reputation.

In order to attract privilege, the communication must be made to a person with a corresponding interest or duty to receive it. This point has already been discussed with regard to statements made in performance of a duty.

Public Interest   A defamatory statement has no claim to privilege merely because it concerns a matter of public interest. As Stephenson LJ said in *Blackshaw* v. *Lord* at p. 26, 'no privilege attaches yet to a statement on a matter of public interest believed by the publisher to be true in relation to which he has exercised reasonable care'. In order to attract the privilege, the nature of the matter published, its source, the position or status of the publisher and the position or status of the recipient must be considered in order to determine whether the publisher has a duty or interest to publish the matter to the intended recipient. Publication to the general public will only rarely be protected. In *Blackshaw* v. *Lord*, the Court of Appeal held that the publication by a national newspaper of unsubstantiated allegations that the plaintiff was involved in the loss of several million pounds of public money was not protected by qualified privilege. Whilst publication of details of wastage of tax-payers' money may attract qualified privilege, the public had no interest in the half-baked rumours and guesses published by the defendant. The circumstances where a publication of such suspicions or speculations would be justified would be very rare; Stephenson LJ gave as examples where 'there is danger to the public from a suspected terrorist or the distribution of contaminated food or drugs.'

Common Interest   A communication on a matter in which the defendant and the recipient share a common legitimate interest is privileged. For the privilege to exist, both parties must be interested in some matter which concerns them both. Where the recipient's interest is mere idle curiosity or meddling in the affairs of others, the defence will not be established. The common interest may be financial. All employees were said in *Bryanston Finance Ltd* v. *De Vries* [1975] 1 QB 703 to have an interest in the survival and prosperity of the business in which they are employed, therefore communications made to them for the purpose of informing them about the affairs of the business would be privileged. Other examples include: statements made to a trade or professional association by one member about another, or by a member of the public about the conduct of a member of the association; and statements by an employer to his employees as to why he had dismissed one of their workmates.

Statements made in Certain Classes of Report

Fair and Accurate Reports of Parliamentary Proceedings   Fair and accurate reports of parliamentary proceedings are protected by qualified privilege. Thus, reports in newspapers, on the radio or on television are privileged whether the whole statement or merely extracts from such a statement are published. A report is fair and accurate where it gives a substantially fair account of what took place. The fact that the report is not verbatim will not preclude reliance on the defence (Parliamentary Papers Act 1840, s.3 as amended).

Fair and Accurate Report of Judicial Proceedings   A fair and accurate report of judicial proceedings, whether or not published contemporaneously, is protected by qualified privilege.

Statements Privileged by Virtue of Section 7 of the Defamation Act 1952 Section 7 of the Defamation Act 1952 (as amended by s.166(3) of the Broadcasting Act 1990) affords a qualified privilege to a publication in a newspaper or in a public broadcast of any report or matter mentioned in the schedule to the Act. The privileged reports and matters are divided into two categories: first, those comprising statements privileged without explanation or contradiction (Pt I); and, secondly, those statements privileged subject to explanation or contradiction (Pt II). Section 7(2) provides that the defence is lost as regard statements in Pt II:

'if it is proved that the defendant has been requested to publish in the newspaper in which the original publication was made a reasonable letter or statement by way of explanation or contradiction, and has refused or neglected to do so, or has done so in a manner not adequate or not reasonable having regard to all the circumstances.'

To attract the privilege the publication must be in a 'newspaper' (as defined in section 7(5) of the Act) and must not be of 'any matter the publication of which is prohibited by law, or of any other matter which is not of public concern and the publication of which is not for the public benefit' (section 7(3)). The matters and reports protected are listed in the schedule to the Act and include such matters as fair and accurate reports of proceedings of international organisations and Commonwealth legislatures and their courts, fair and accurate reports of the findings and decision of certain domestic associations, and fair and accurate reports of proceedings of any public or local authority meeting. For a full list, reference should be made to the schedule.

Malice

Where a defendant is proved to have been actuated by 'malice' the defences of fair comment and qualified privilege will be defeated. In broad terms a defendant will be found to have been so actuated where he desires to injure the person defamed and this is the predominant motive for the defamatory publication. The motive with which a person publishes defamatory material can, of course, only be inferred from what he did or said. Evidence of malice may be found in the words themselves or from extrinsic facts. For example, use of intemperate language in conveying information to a person who has an interest in hearing the information may be evidence of malice. Furthermore, the fact that the defendant knew the statement was untrue at the time he made it itself constitutes malice (*Horrocks* v. *Lowe* [1975] AC 135). The burden of proving that the defendant was actuated by malice is on the plaintiff. It is for the judge to determine whether there is enough evidence of malice to be left to the jury, and for the jury to decide whether the defendant was in fact malicious.

Where more than one person has been involved in the publication of the defamatory material, difficult questions have arisen in relation to malice. Where several defendants are sued as authors in respect of the same publication, does the proof of malice against one prevent the others from relying on the defences of fair comment or qualified privilege? In *Egger* v. *Viscount Chelmsford* [1965] 1 QB 248 the plaintiff sued all eight members and the secretary of a committee of the Kennel Club in respect of a letter written by the secretary on the instructions of the committee. The trial judge held that the letter was written on an occasion of qualified privilege, and the jury found that five of the members were actuated by malice but that the other three and the secretary were not. The Court of Appeal held that the non-malicious members were not tainted by the malice of the malicious members. As Lord Denning MR put it, 'each defendant is answerable severally, as well as jointly, for the joint publication: and each is entitled to his several defence whether he be sued jointly or separately from the others'. Whilst *Egger* v. *Viscount Chelmsford* was concerned with the defence of qualified privilege, there seems to be no reason why the principle in the case should not apply to the defence of fair comment as well (but cf. Davies LJ).

21.12 Unintentional Defamation

It has been seen that liability for a defamatory statement does not depend on the intention of the maker of the statement. As we saw, the fact that a writer or publisher intended an article to refer to a different person from the plaintiff, or did not intend to refer to a living person at all is irrelevant at common law to their liability. This may produce hardship for writers and publishers. Section 4 of the Defamation Act 1952 was passed to remedy this situation. The section can be summarised as follows.

1. The defence only applies to words 'published innocently'. By section 4(5) words are treated as having been published innocently where the publisher took all reasonable care in relation to the publication and either (a) did not intend to publish the words of the plaintiff and did not know circumstances by which it might be understood to refer to him (e.g., *Hulton* v. *Jones*) or (b) the words were not defamatory on their face and the publisher did not know of circumstances by virtue of which they might be understood to be defamatory of the plaintiff (e.g. *Cassidy* v. *Daily Mirror Newspapers Ltd*). Where the words are defamatory on their face, even where this is not known to the defendant and despite his taking all reasonable care, the provisions of the section will not be satisfied.

2. Where the publisher claims the words have been published innocently he must make an offer of amends (section 1) as defined in section 4(3).

3. If the offer of amends is accepted and performed, no proceedings for defamation can be taken or continued against the person making the offer (section 4(1)(a)).

4. If the offer of amends is not accepted then it is a defence for the defendant to prove that: the words complained of were published innocently; the offer was made as soon as practicable after the defendant received notice that the words were or might be defamatory of the plaintiff; and the offer has not been withdrawn (section 4(1)(b)). In addition, by virtue of section 4(6), if the defendant is not the author of the published words, he must show that the words were written by the author without malice.

21.13 Damages

Unusually for civil cases, defamation actions are generally still tried by a judge and a jury. The assessment of the amount of damages is, in such a case, a matter for the jury. The primacy of the jury in this matter is well established and the courts have generally shown themselves unwilling to disturb a jury award. Only where the amount awarded is so unreasonable that it must have been arrived at capriciously, unconscionably or irrationally will an appeal court interfere with a jury's decision. Until recently, in the event of the appeal court deciding that the award was unreasonably high or low, it could only order a re-trial. However, under the Rules of the Supreme Court, Order 59, rule 11(4), the Court of Appeal now has a discretion to substitute such sum in damages as appears to it to be proper (the first case in which an appeal court reduced an award of damages using this provision was an action brought by Teresa Gorman MP against an Essex businessman; the Court of Appeal reduced the jury's award of £150 000 to £50 000).

Damages in a defamation action are primarily intended to be compensatory. The jury is required to assess the sum required to vindicate the plaintiff's reputation and to compensate him for the injury to his feelings. In addition to compensatory damages, exemplary damages are also available in appropriate cases. In *Cassell & Co* v. *Broome* [1972] AC 1027, the House of Lords held that exemplary damages are available where the defendant's conduct had been calculated by him to make a profit for himself which would exceed what he would have to pay the plaintiff in compensation (see 23.2). In addition to compensatory and exemplary damages, some cases have appeared to suggest that there are two further heads of damages: namely, aggravated and vindicatory damages. It was made clear, however, in *Sutcliffe* v. *Pressdram* [1990] 1 All ER 269 that separate awards are not to be made under these heads. Whilst the defendant's behaviour (by, e.g., a violent cross-examination of the plaintiff, or persisting in a plea of justification which he is unable to establish) may aggravate the original injury suffered by the plaintiff and thus may make it appropriate for the jury to increase the compensatory damages to some degree, there is no separate head of 'aggravated damages'. Similarly, a jury can be told of the need to vindicate the plaintiff's character: the need for the plaintiff to be 'able to point to a sum awarded by a jury sufficient to convince a bystander of the base-lessness of the charge'. This is also not a separate head of damages. It is merely a matter the jury can take into account in assessing the compensatory award.

Summary

21.1 'Interests in personality' are protected by a number of legal mechanisms in English law. The primary tort in this area is the tort of defamation, which protects a person's reputation. However, additional protection is provided by the torts of negligence, breach of confidence, malicious falsehood, trespass, nuisance and passing off. Additionally, a number of statutes protect interests in personality. English law, however, knows no tort of infringement of privacy.

21.2 The tort of defamation is committed whenever a person publishes defamatory material about another to a third person.

21.3 A defamatory statement is one which 'lowers the plaintiff in the estimation of right thinking members of society generally'. In applying this test the courts tend to look to what right thinking members of society *should* think, rather than what they actually think. Words are often capable of more than one meaning. The plaintiff can seek to show that the words convey an impression or mean something different from their ordinary meaning ('false' innuendo). Alternatively, the plaintiff can argue that the meaning of the words can only be understood by having regard to extrinsic evidence ('true' innuendo).

21.4 The statement must be published to a third person. However, the statement need not have been intentionally published. Provided the defendant ought reasonably to have foreseen that the statement would come to the attention of a third person, that is sufficient. Every repetition of a defamatory statement gives rise to a fresh cause of action. However, the original maker of the statement only remains liable for the repetition where it was foreseeable.

21.5 The defamatory statement must refer to the plaintiff. There is no need for the plaintiff to be expressly referred to. Provided a 'hypothetical sensible reader with knowledge of the special facts' would have thought that the statement referred to the plaintiff, that is sufficient. A defamatory statement made about a group is not actionable unless the group is so small that the words can be treated as referring to all the group, or where the words should be treated as having been intended to refer to the plaintiff.

21.6 English law draws a distinction between libel and slander. Libel is actionable without proof of damage. Slander, unless falling within one of the exceptional categories, requires proof of damage. There is no single test for distinguishing between libel and slander. However, generally a statement made in a permanent form and conveyed to the sense of sight will be treated as a libel, while a statement made in transitory form and conveyed to the ear will be treated as a slander.

21.7 In addition to certain general defences, such as voluntary assumption of risk and consent, the law of defamation has its own special defences.

21.8 Where a plaintiff succeeds in showing that the words complained of are defamatory, their falsehood is presumed. Justification or truth is, however, a defence. The essence of a plea of justification is that the 'words are true in substance and in fact'. Where there are two or more distinct charges against the plaintiff, the defence will not fail merely because one or more cannot be proved, provided the untrue words do not materially injure the plaintiff's reputation.

21.9 The defence of fair comment is, like justification, a complete defence. In order for the defence to succeed it must be shown: (a) that the words used are comment and not fact; (b) that the comment is on a matter of public interest; (c) that the comment is based on true facts; and (d) that the comment is fair. The plaintiff can rebut the defence by showing that the defendant was actuated by malice.

21.10 Some situations are deemed to be of such social or political importance that the law allows a person to speak or write about another without restraint. These are situations of absolute privilege and they include statements made by MPs in Parliament, statements made in judicial proceedings, high executive communications and statements made by certain officials.

21.11 Some occasions, although not of sufficient importance to attract absolute privilege, are nevertheless considered to be of sufficient importance to attract qualified privilege. Statements covered by qualified privilege are protected unless the plaintiff can show that the maker of the statement was actuated by malice. In broad terms a defendant will be found to have been actuated by malice where his motive is to injure the person defamed or where he does not believe in the truth of what he says. Statements attracting qualified privilege include: statements made in performance of a legal, moral or social duty; statements made in furtherance or protection of an interest (whether that interest is a private interest, public interest or a common interest); and statements made in certain classes of report.

21.12 Where a statement is published 'innocently' a publisher may be excused from liability where he makes an offer of amends and the provisions of section 4 of the Defamation Act 1952 are satisfied.

21.13 Generally defamation actions are tried by a judge and jury. Where they are, the assessment of damages is a matter for the jury. Appeal courts are unwilling to interfere with jury awards. Damages in a defamation action are primarily intended to be compensatory. However, exemplary damages may be awarded.

Exercises

21.1 Was Calcutt (1990) right to oppose the introduction of a statutory tort of infringement of privacy? Who would benefit from the enactment of such a tort?

21.2 Is it defamatory to accuse someone of being HIV positive? (see *Bloodworth* v. *Gray* (1844) 7 Man & G 334). Does the 'right thinking person' provide a satisfactory concept to determine what is defamatory?

21.3 Were the House of Lords correct in *Lewis* v. *Daily Telegraph* to say that the words complained of could not convey the impression that the plaintiff was guilty of the allegations?

21.4 What is the difference between a true and a false innuendo?

21.5 Would an action lie against the maker of a television programme in respect of remarks made in a review in a newspaper which repeated the defamatory allegations made in the programme? (see *Slipper* v. *B.B.C.*)

21.6 Should *Hulton* v. *Jones* and *Newstead* v. *London Express Newspapers Ltd* be followed today?

21.7 How satisfactory is the test for distinguishing between libel and slander? Should the courts continue to draw this distinction? Does the existence of the 'exceptional' cases, where slander is made actionable *per se*, make it unnecessary to continue to draw the distinction?

21.8 A writes that B has a number of convictions for theft and robbery. Additionally, he accuses B of having been convicted of rape. B brings a libel action in respect of the allegation that he has been convicted of robbery. This is untrue, though the other allegations are true. Would A be able to rely on the defence of justification? Would your answer be different if B sued in respect of the rape allegation where this was untrue, although the other allegations were true?

21.9 A writes of B, an MP, that he is a drunkard who beats his dog and that he is therefore unfit to represent his constituents. A beats his dog but is not a drunkard. Does B have any remedy?

21.10 MPs are so irresponsible that their historical right to say what they like in Parliament should be abandoned. Do you agree?

21.11 Juries have shown themselves to be so irresponsible when it comes to the award of damages that they should no longer perform this task. Do you agree? Is the new provision in Order 59 of the Rules of the Supreme Court sufficient protection for a defendant?

21.12 Anarchy plc is the owner of 'Your Investments', a weekly magazine devoted to stock market comment and City gossip. Brian, a journalist on the magazine, was preparing an article about the take-over of Holy Securities Ltd by Satanic Securities plc, a company in which the principal shareholder was Robert, a well-known entrepreneur. The article, transcribed on to Brian's word-processor, alleged that Robert had obtained control of Holy for Satanic by 'strong-arm' tactics and by threatening to expose the extra-marital affair of Holy's principal shareholder, David, to David's wife, Edna. Felicity, an executive employed by Anarchy plc to manage the magazine's affairs, saw the final draft of the article on the word-processor screen when she went into Brian's office while he was out to lunch. Felicity was about to resign her job as she was unhappy with the way the senior management of Anarchy interfered in the running of the magazine. She was also a friend of Edna and decided to disclose the contents of the story to her and also to David's fellow shareholder, Gaynor. On receiving the information from Felicity, Edna became irate and telephoned a gossip magazine called 'City Slicker', informing the editor, Ian, that one of David's affairs was with a well-known rock singer whose name was 'synonymous with Satan'. These words appeared in a report in last week's 'City Slicker'. In using the words Edna had intended to refer to a rock singer named Cyn with who she thought David was having an affair. In fact David was having an affair with a rock singer called Devilla.

The edition of 'Your Investments' containing the article was published last week. The allegations contained about Robert are untrue.

Advise the parties as to their rights and liabilities in tort.

General Principles of
Tortious Liability

22 Vicarious Liability and Joint Torts

22.1 Introduction

As we have seen, the modern law of torts is still generally based on some notion of fault or blameworthiness. Liability will not, subject to certain well-known exceptions, be imposed on a person unless he has intentionally or negligently caused some loss or damage to the plaintiff. Thus, liability is usually based on personal fault. However, a person may incur liability as a result not only of his own acts but also as a result of the acts of another. Vicarious liability is an example of just such a situation. Where certain criteria are satisfied the law holds the defendant vicariously liable for the misconduct of another. This is the case even though the defendant is not himself in any way at fault. In this chapter we will examine the criteria required to establish a vicarious liability and look at the justifications for a rule of law which appears to run counter to two basic principles of English law: namely, that a person should not be liable in the absence of fault, and that a person should only be liable where his act or omission caused the injury.

Vicarious liability may be defined as the liability imposed on one person (D) for the tortious act or omission of another (X) which causes loss to a third person (P). For one person to be vicariously liable for another's tort, certain requirements must be met. First, P must be injured or suffer loss as a result of a tortious act committed by X. This was for some time a source of judicial and academic debate in that some had argued that unless D himself owed P a duty of care, D could not be liable. X's acts were to be attributed to D, but D was not liable for them unless *he* owed P a duty of care. This view was known as the master's tort theory. It is clear today that the view expressed in the master's tort theory is not correct. All that is required is that X commits a tortious act which injures P. Secondly, some relationship must exist between the tortfeasor X and the defendant D. The relationship which most characteristically satisfies this requirement is that of master and servant or, as it would be more frequently called today, that of employer and employee. Thirdly, there must be some connection between the tortious act and the relationship. This requirement is satisfied where the servant acts in the 'course of his employment'.

Where the requirements of vicarious liability are met, the employer will be liable for the acts of his employee regardless of his own culpability and regardless of whether he owes the injured person any duty recognised by law. The liability of the employee in such a case is not extinguished but, for reasons of policy, the courts have considered it desirable to give the injured person an action against the employer. The employer is still entitled to proceed against his employee to recover any damages he has to pay. However, because the employee is unlikely to be able to satisfy any substantial claim and because of the danger to good labour relations, an employer is unlikely to bring such a claim.

22.2   Justifications for Vicarious Liability

Despite vicarious liability being one of the longer established principles in English law, its existence is still considered by English lawyers to be somewhat exceptional and to require some special justification. The reason for this is, as we have seen, that the doctrine seems to run counter to two well-established principles of the law of tort. Various arguments of policy have been put forward from time to time to justify the doctrine's existence. Today the most accepted justification is that as the master derives an economic benefit from his servant's work, so he ought to bear any losses or liability incurred in the course of the enterprise. It is felt to be fairer to impose liability on the master, who in most cases is likely to have substantially greater means than his servant, because these losses are a normal incident of his business and therefore he should bear responsibility for them. He is also better able to spread the cost of the accident. As the employer knows that he has to bear the cost of any accidents, he will usually take out insurance to cover such losses and increase the price of his products to take account of the cost of the insurance. By this mechanism, rather than one person having to bear the whole of the loss, the loss is distributed amongst those who derive a benefit from either the sale or use of the product.

22.3   Master and Servant Relationship

As a general rule, in order for a person to be vicariously liable for the tort of another the relationship between them must be governed by a contract *of* service. Where the person is employed under a contract *for* services the employer will not generally be vicariously liable for his torts. In the latter case the 'employee' is more properly known as an independent contractor and, in the absence of a personal non-delegable duty on the employer, the latter will incur no liability in respect of the torts of the independent contractor.

The courts have not found it easy to articulate a single test to answer the question whether a person is a servant or – which amounts to the same thing – whether a person is employed under a contract of service. The changing nature of employment, the increasing technicality of many jobs and professions and the complexity of corporate structures makes it considerably more difficult today, compared with a hundred years ago, to say of a person that they are definitely employed by a particular employer. For example, if a lawyer is seconded from his law firm to a government department, does he remain employed by his law firm? Similarly, is a consultant, who normally only does private work, a servant of the local health authority if he does an operation for the authority under the NHS? It might be thought that the answer to the question of whether a person is a servant or an independent contractor will depend upon how the parties themselves have classified the relationship. However, whilst any classification made by the parties will be taken into account by the courts, it can never be conclusive.

The conventional test used by the courts for distinguishing a servant from an independent contractor is the 'control' test. The test was well expressed by Bramwell B in *Yewens* v. *Noakes* (1880) 6 QBD 530, at pp. 532–3 where he said, '[a] servant is a person subject to the command of his master as to the manner in which he shall do his work'. An employee is, therefore, a servant if his employer can not only tell him what to do but also how to do it. Such a test is, however, only satisfactory in an agricultural or primitive industrial society where the employer has at least as much technical knowledge as the employee and is able to instruct him in how to do the work. In a modern, complex industrial society it is doubtful whether the test is capable of any sensible meaning except in its application to the simplest of jobs. People are employed today in many cases precisely because they have the technical knowledge and skill that their employer does not have. If a hospital authority told a doctor how to resuscitate a patient or a warehouse owner told a fork-lift truck driver how to drive his truck they are likely to be told, in no uncertain terms, to mind their own business.

Whilst the courts continue to use the 'control' test in its traditional formulation where that is appropriate, they have not hesitated to hold an employer liable even where the work on which the servant is employed is highly technical and the method of its performance is something of which the employer is ignorant. In order to do so what they have done is to re-interpret the 'control' test so that what they now look for is 'not so much the power to direct *how* the work shall be done but instead the power to control the servant in relation to the incidental features of his employment – what has been termed the 'when' and the 'where' of the work' (Atiyah, 1967, at p. 47). Thus the courts, in seeking to answer the question of who is in 'control', have taken into account a wide variety of factors, such as who has the power of appointment and dismissal, who pays the wages, where the 'employee' works, who provides the 'tools of the trade', who pays national insurance contributions or deducts tax and whether the contract itself makes any provision as to the parties' relationship.

The case of *Ready Mixed Concrete (South-East) Lt*d v. *Minister of Pensions and National Insurance* [1968] 1 All ER 433 illustrates some of the factors the courts are likely to take into account in considering whether a contract of service exists. The case raised the question of whether an owner-driver was employed under a contract of service for the purposes of section 1(2) of the National Insurance Act 1965. Although not concerned with the question of vicarious liability, it highlights the problem of identifying a contract of service in a modern 'atypical' employment context. A company organised a scheme for the delivery of ready-mixed concrete to its customers through so-called 'owner-drivers'. The contract with each driver provided, amongst other things, that each driver was to buy the vehicle on hire-purchase from a finance company owned by the company; the driver was not to use the vehicle for any haulage business other than that of the company; the driver was not to make any alterations, change or sell the vehicle without the consent of the company; the driver was to make the vehicle available to the company at all times of the day and night and was generally to comply with all rules, regulations and reasonable orders given by the company. Mackenna J held, despite these provisions which were suggestive of a high degree of control by the company, that this was not a contract of service. Whilst there were a number of provisions suggestive of such a contract, the fact that the driver owned the vehicle, was free to maintain the vehicle as he chose, to hire another driver in the event of holiday or sickness and to buy fuel where he chose were more in line with this contract being a contract of carriage. As Mackenna J put it, 'the ownership of the assets, the chance of profit and the risk of loss in the business of carriage are [the driver's] and not the company's'.

22.4   The Course of Employment

The existence of the relationship of master and servant is not, however, a sufficient ground of liability in itself. The tort committed by the servant may have absolutely no connection with his employment and in such a case the master will not be vicariously liable for his servant. For example, if a servant chose to murder her husband at home, the mere fact that she happens to be a servant is manifestly no ground for imposing liability upon the master. In addition, therefore, to the requirement of a contract of service the servant must commit the tort in the 'course of his employment'.

Clearly, if the tort committed by the servant has been expressly authorised or ratified by the master, the master will be liable for the tort (though this will not be on the basis of vicarious liability but instead a distinct principle that applies even outside the employment relationship). Such cases are probably rare and it is clear that the course of employment is not limited to such circumstances. However, articulating a clear test to determine whether a tort was committed in the course of employment is not an easy task. As Fleming points out (1987, p. 350):

> 'the course of employment is an expansive concept which provides ample scope for policy decisions and, despite the vast volume of case law, has failed to acquire a high degree of precision. No statistical measurement is possible, and precedents are helpful only when they present a suggestive uniformity on parallel facts.'

The standard starting point adopted by the courts is the test set out by Salmond and Heuston (1992, p. 457). The learned authors there state that in addition to torts authorised or ratified by the master, torts committed by the servant are within the course of employment provided they are 'so connected with acts which [the master] has authorised that they may rightly be regarded as modes – although improper modes – of doing them'. The test makes clear that the master is liable not only for those acts he has authorised but also for those acts which, although he has not directly authorised them, are nevertheless to be treated as wrongful and unauthorised modes of performing an authorised task. Where the servant embarks on an unauthorised, independent jaunt of his own the limit is exceeded. Until that moment in time he acts in the course of his employment. It is all a question of degree. If, for example, a company employs a person as a bus conductor he may still be acting in the course of his employment if he merely drives the bus out of the way of another bus while in the bus terminal. However, he will almost certainly be acting outside the course of his employment if he takes the bus out on to the streets and engages in a race with another bus-driver. In order to consider the application of the test, a number of problem areas will be considered.

Frolic, Detour and Incidental Duties

In *Joel* v. *Morison* (1834) 6 C & p. 501, at p. 503 Parke stated that a servant acts outside the course of his employment 'when embarking on a frolic of his own'. This clearly encompasses egregious behaviour entirely for the servant's own benefit. For example, if an employer instructs his employee to drive from London to Glasgow to deliver a parcel and the employee deviates via Land's End to pick up a friend, it can be said that he has deviated from his route so extensively that he has gone on an entirely new journey and is acting outside the course of his employment. On the other hand, if he stops off between London and Glasgow in order to buy himself lunch and negligently runs someone over in the restaurant car park, he is likely to be treated as acting in the course of his employment. In this case the diversion from the most direct route would be likely to be treated as incidental to his employment. In *Century Insurance Co Ltd* v. *Northern Ireland Road Transport Board* [1942] AC 509, a petrol tanker driver lit a cigarette while delivering petrol and threw away the match, causing an explosion which damaged the plaintiff's property. The House of Lords held that he was still acting within the course of his employment. Even though the act of lighting the cigarette was done purely for his own benefit and convenience and not for his employer's benefit, the act could not be treated as a wholly independent act but was instead an improper mode of doing that which he was employed to do.

Some difficulty has been experienced by the courts in dealing with cases of negligence committed by employees while on their way to work or while travelling between different workplaces on the instructions of their employer. In the recent case of *Smith* v. *Stages* [1989] 1 All ER 833, the House of Lords, whilst recognising that it was impossible to provide for every eventuality, set out a number of presumptions. First, an employee travelling to or from work is in ordinary circumstances not acting within the course of his employment. Of course, it may be said that in order to carry out a day's work he must travel to and from work and thus the travel should be seen as an incidental part of his work. The House of Lords was, however, of the view that, while a person was employed to work at his place of work, he was not in ordinary circumstances employed to travel from his home to his workplace. Their Lordships recognised that, where a person is obliged to travel to work by means provided by his employer, he may be held to be acting within the course of his employment. Secondly, where an employee is instructed or required by his job (for example, if he were a travelling salesman) to travel from one workplace to another or from his home to a succession of workplaces and he is paid for this travelling, he will usually be acting within the course of his employment. Finally, payment of wages while travelling or allowing the employee a discretion as to the mode and time of travel are factors to be taken into account, but are not conclusive of the question whether a person is acting within the course of his employment.

Prohibited Conduct

If a master expressly prohibits a servant from doing a particular act, and the servant in breach of that instruction does that very act and injures another, it might be thought that he would be acting outside the course of his employment. This is, however, not necessarily the case. Some prohibitions do, and some prohibitions do not, take the servant outside the course of his employment. Whether or not a prohibition takes the servant outside the course of his employment depends on whether it limits the sphere of employment or whether it only seeks to deal with conduct within the sphere of employment. It is often a very difficult question which side of the line a prohibition falls, and fine judgments may be called for. In some cases the breach of a prohibition makes the servant's conduct so unconnected with his employment that he will be treated as acting outside the course of his employment. For example, if a company expressly forbade the drivers of its buses from racing other buses, an employee who causes an accident while racing a rival firm's buses would in all likelihood be treated as acting outside the course of his employment. On the other hand, if a company prohibits its employees from using their own cars for work unless they are properly insured, an employee driving his own, uninsured, car who causes an accident will not be acting outside the course of his employment as the prohibition merely affects the way in which he is to do his job. It does not restrict him in what he is employed to do.

As a general rule prohibitions which affect the manner, time or place of performance are not held to affect the sphere of performance and, therefore, breach of the prohibition will not take the employee outside the course of his employment. In *Rose* v. *Plenty* [1976] 1 All ER 97, Mr Plenty was a milk roundsman employed by the defendants. His duties included driving a float on his round and collecting money. He was expressly prohibited by the terms of his employment from employing children in the performance of those duties. In breach of this prohibition, he invited the infant plaintiff to help him and the plaintiff was injured when Plenty drove the float negligently. The Court of Appeal, by a majority, held that Plenty was acting within the course of his employment. The judges held that the prohibition affected only the sphere of employment in that it went only to the manner in which the work was to be performed.

Intentional Misconduct

As with express prohibition, it might be thought that if by intentional misconduct a servant injures another person that would take him outside the course of his employment. If a university lecturer were to strike and injure a student who was annoying him, in all likelihood the university would not be vicariously liable for the lecturer's tort. Striking a student can only with great difficulty be viewed as an improper mode of performing an authorised duty. Having said that, there are cases where even intentional misconduct by the servant may be within the course of his employment. Such cases are usually situations where the servant was prompted by a desire to further the interests of his employers and was acting with what turned out to be unfortunate enthusiasm. In *Poland* v. *John Parr & Sons* [1926] All ER Rep 177 Mr Hall, an employee of the defendants, reasonably believed that the 12-year old plaintiff was stealing sugar from his employer's wagon. Hall struck the child causing him to fall under one of the wheels of the wagon, and the child was seriously injured. The Court of Appeal held that Hall was acting in the course of his employment. He had acted in defence of his employer's interests and such defence was reasonably incidental to the duties he was employed to perform.

Where, however, the act of the servant goes beyond unfortunate enthusiasm or an error of judgment the courts have generally been careful to avoid imposing too heavy a burden on the employer. In *Poland* v. *John Parr & Sons*, for example, Atkin LJ said that the answer given by the court may well have been different had Hall shot the plaintiff. Similarly, in another case a dance hall 'bouncer', having lawfully ejected a customer from the hall, later wholly gratuitously struck him and injured him. The court held he was acting outside the course of his employment.

22.5 Liability for Independent Contractors

As a general rule employers are not liable for the acts of independent contractors whom they employ to do a particular task, or series of tasks.

The reason given for this qualification of vicarious liability is that the employer lacks detailed control over the independent contractor who is, in any event, better able to distribute the losses caused by his work than his employer. In many cases this is of course true. If someone hires a taxi to drive him from London to Heathrow he has little control over the way in which the driver drives, and it is surely more appropriate to expect the taxi driver to insure against any losses caused by his negligence rather than the passenger. However, as McKendrick points out (1990b), it may no longer be realistic to treat all 'independent contractors' in the same way. Some are without doubt large, well-organised organisations who are capable of including provision for insurance within their pricing policy. However, over the last few years there has been a vast increase in the number of home-workers and the 'self-employed'. Neither category may be 'servants' as that word has been defined by the courts and yet, unlike their employers, they may be unable to bear or shift any loss that may be caused by their negligence. This change in work patterns may suggest a need to re-evaluate the courts' traditional opposition to liability for independent contractors and indicate a need either for a wider view of who is a 'servant' or for a relaxation of the rules against recovery against an employer of an independent contractor.

Although the courts have traditionally refused to allow a plaintiff to recover damages against the employer of an independent contractor, there are a number of exceptional categories where recovery has been allowed. In recent years the courts have shown themselves willing to expand upon these exceptions, though unfortunately they have not articulated the basis on which they have done so. The mechanism by which liability is imposed on an employer is that of the non-delegable duty. By saying that an employer owes such a duty, the courts mean that he cannot acquit himself of liability by exercising reasonable care in entrusting an independent contractor with the work. As Glanville Williams (1956) has pointed out there is unfortunately no coherent theory which explains when a duty will be classified as non-delegable. Nevertheless, there are now a substantial number of duties which are classified as non-delegable, and in the remaining part of this chapter we will seek to identify some of these.

Unsurprisingly, many of the duties that have been classified as non-delegable are strict duties. For example, there are a number of strict statutory duties which cannot be discharged by the employment of an independent contractor (see, e.g., many of the provisions of the Factories Act 1961). So, also, the duty imposed upon land owners to prevent the escape of dangerous things imposed by *Rylands* v. *Fletcher* is a non-delegable duty, as are the strict duties to maintain premises abutting a highway and to provide lateral support for adjacent land (*Tarry* v. *Ashton* (1876) 1 QBD 314). An analogous case to *Rylands* v. *Fletcher* is the non-delegable duty owed by all those who engage independent contractors to do 'extra-hazardous' acts. In the leading case of *Honeywell and Stein Ltd* v. *Larkin Bros Ltd* [1934] 1 KB 191, a cinema company engaged contractors to do some acoustic work in their theatre. The contractors employed photographers to take photographs of their work inside the theatre. At the time, the taking of flashlight photographs involved the ignition in a metal tray of magnesium powder which, on being ignited, flared up and caused intense heat. As a result of the negligence of the camera operator the magnesium ignited too close to the curtains and they caught fire, causing damage. The Court of Appeal held that the contractors were liable for the harm done. Where, as here, an act 'in its very nature involved a special danger to others', it was not possible to discharge that duty by hiring a competent independent contractor.

In addition to the strict duties which the courts have classified as non-delegable, they have in a number of cases classified situations where the duty on the employer is merely one to ensure that reasonable care is taken as giving rise to non-delegable duties. Examples of such duties include the obligation of employers to provide a safe system of work (*Wilson and Clyde Coal Co* v. *English* [1938] AC 57); of hospitals to care for their patients (*Cassidy* v. *Ministry of Health* [1951] 2 KB 343, per Denning LJ) and of school authorities to care for their pupils (*Carmarthenshire County Council* v. *Lewis* [1955] AC 549).

Finally, it must be pointed out that an employer is not liable for any 'casual' or 'collateral' acts of negligence of the independent contractor. The distinction between 'collateral' acts of negligence and those for which the employer is responsible is by no means clear. What appears to be meant is that the employer is only liable when the independent contractor commits the tort while engaged in doing that which he was actually employed to do. Thus, in *Honeyweill & Stein Ltd* v. *Larkin Bros* the employer would probably not have been liable for the independent contractor had he managed to set fire to the curtains while throwing fire-crackers.

22.6   Joint and Several Liability: The Distinction between Joint, Several Concurrent and Separate Tortfeasors

Where damage is caused to the plaintiff by two or more tortfeasors he may be uncertain as to who to sue. Must he sue all of them or can he sue one only? Can he recover the full amount of his loss from one of the tortfeasors or must he bring separate actions against each tortfeasor to recover from each their proportionate share of his loss? If the plaintiff is required to sue all those involved in causing him damage he may be faced with problems if, for example, one of the tortfeasors cannot be found, is uninsured or insolvent. On the other hand, if a plaintiff is allowed to recover all his loss from one tortfeasor, fairness would seem to dictate that that tortfeasor should have some right to contribution from the other tortfeasors. In the remainder of this chapter we will examine some of the problems which arise where more than one tortfeasor causes damage to the plaintiff, and also consider the rights of tortfeasors to claim contribution from each other.

There are three possible types of case where a person may suffer damage as the result of a tortious act committed by two or more tortfeasors. First, the same damage may be caused to the plaintiff by two or more tortfeasors acting in pursuance of a common design. This may happen in at least three classes of case: namely, agency, vicarious liability and common action. Thus, for example, where two people were looking for an escape of gas and one lit a match thereby causing an explosion, it was held that they were engaged on a joint enterprise and were jointly liable for the damage caused (*Brooke* v. *Bool* [1928] 2 KB 578). Similarly, where a master is vicariously liable for the tort of his servant, both are jointly liable for the damage caused by the servant's tort. Where two or more people *jointly* participate in the commission of the tort the plaintiff may sue any of them separately for the full amount of the loss. Alternatively, he may sue all of them jointly in the same action. The liability of *joint* tortfeasors is, therefore, joint and several.

Secondly, two or more tortfeasors may cause the same damage to the plaintiff in circumstances where they are acting independently and, therefore, do not fall within the first category. In such a case the tortfeasors are known as 'several concurrent' tortfeasors. Where, for example, two cars driven by A and B respectively crash into the plaintiff's car causing him 'whiplash' injuries, A and B are several concurrent tortfeasors. As with joint tortfeasors, each several concurrent tortfeasor is answerable in full for the whole damage caused to the plaintiff.

At common law there were two principal distinctions between joint tortfeasors, and several concurrent tortfeasors. First, judgment against one joint tortfeasor, even if it remained unsatisfied, barred any subsequent action. Secondly, the release of one joint tortfeasor operated as a release of all. Neither of these rules applied to several concurrent tortfeasors. The first rule has now been abolished and the second much diminished in importance such that there is now little substantive distinction between joint and several concurrent tortfeasors.

Finally, where two or more persons not acting in pursuance of a common design cause different damage to the same plaintiff, they are treated as separate and independent tortfeasors. For example, as a result of A's negligent driving the plaintiff's wrist is broken and requires hospital treatment. At the hospital Dr B bandages the plaintiff's wrist but does it so negligently that the plaintiff permanently loses all feeling in his arm. A will not be responsible for Dr B's negligence. A and Dr B are separate and independent tortfeasors who have caused different damage to the same plaintiff. The cases of *Performance Cars* v. *Abraham* [1962] 1 QB 33 and *Baker* v. *Willoughby* [1970] AC 467 (see 10.2) are also good example of separate and independent tortfeasors. No special rules are required where two or more tortfeasors cause different damage to the plaintiff.

22.7 Contribution between Tortfeasors

General Right to Claim Contribution

As a general rule the common law allowed no contribution to be claimed between joint or several concurrent tortfeasors, even where one tortfeasor had satisfied the plaintiff's claim in full. This rule has, however, largely been reversed by statute. The rules relating to contribution are now found in the Civil Liability (Contribution) Act 1978. Section 1(1) of the Act provides that:

'subject to the following provisions of this section, any person liable in respect of any damage suffered by another person may recover contribution from any other person liable in respect of the same damage (whether jointly with him or otherwise).'

The Act is not limited in its application to tort. It also applies where the legal basis of liability is 'breach of contract, breach of trust or otherwise'.

Who May Claim Contribution?

In order to be able to claim contribution the person seeking contribution must either have been found by a court to have been liable or be able to show that liability could be established against him at trial (section 1(6)). Where, therefore, no action could be brought against him because a limitation period has expired, his claim for contribution will fail. However, if one of the tortfeasors has paid the plaintiff he is still entitled to contribution even if he has ceased to be liable to the original plaintiff, provided 'he was liable immediately before he made or was ordered or agreed to make the payment in respect of which contribution is sought' (section 1(2)). If one of the tortfeasors settles his claim with the plaintiff, without admitting liability, he will only be able to claim contribution if he could prove that he was legally answerable (section 1(4)).

From Whom may Contribution be Claimed?

Section 1(1) provides that contribution is recoverable from anyone who is liable for the same damage. A person may still be liable to make contribution even where he has ceased to be liable to the plaintiff (s.1(3)). For example, a person may have ceased to be liable to the plaintiff because the plaintiff waived his claim against that person or because the claim was settled. More commonly, the period of limitation within which the plaintiff must sue the defendant may have expired. Provided, however, the person seeking contribution brings the action against his co-defendant within two years from the date of judgment or settlement an action for contribution may still lie.

242 General Principles of Tortious Liability

Assessment of Contribution

Section 2(1) of the Act provides that 'in any proceedings for contribution under section 1 above the amount of contribution recoverable from any person shall be such as may be found by the court to be just and equitable having regard to the extent of that person's responsibility for the damage in question'. The assessment of the amount of contribution payable is made by having regard only to the parties before the court: the negligence or contributory negligence of a party not before the court cannot be taken into account. In determining the 'responsibility for the damage' the courts have looked at both the blameworthiness of the tortfeasor and the extent to which that person's act directly caused the loss. Thus, the question of responsibility is assessed on the basis of fault plus causation, and not simply moral blameworthiness.

Where the amount of damages payable by one of the tortfeasors to the plaintiff has been limited by agreement or by virtue of the operation of the Law Reform (Contributory Negligence) Act 1945, then the maximum amount recoverable in contribution is that limited or reduced amount (section 2(3)).

Summary

22.1 Vicarious liability may be defined as the liability imposed on a master (D) for the tortious act of his servant (X) which causes loss to a third party (P). For one person to be vicariously liable for the tort of another three conditions must be satisfied: first, the relationship of master and servant must exist: secondly, the servant must commit a tort: thirdly, the tort must be committed within the course of the servant's employment.
22.2 The most commonly accepted justification for the principle of vicarious liability is that, as the master derives a benefit from his servant's work, so he ought to bear any losses or liability incurred in the course of the employment. Other justifications have, however, been put forward.
22.3 In order for the master to be liable for the torts of his servant a contract *of* service, as opposed to a contract *for* services, must exist. Traditionally, the 'control' test was used to establish this relationship. However, the more modern approach is to look at all the terms of the contract and the surrounding circumstances in order to see whether a relationship *of* service exists.
22.4 The tort must be committed by the servant *in the course of his employment.* Torts are committed by the servant within the course of his employment where they are so connected with acts which the master has authorised that they may be rightly regarded as modes, albeit improper modes, of doing that which the servant was employed to do. The fact that the servant intentionally committed a tort, was doing something he had been prohibited from doing or committed a tort while on a frolic of his own are relevant factors in considering whether a servant was acting within the course of his employment. They are not, however, conclusive against the imposition of vicarious liability.
22.5 As a general rule an employer will not be liable for the acts of his independent contractors. However, in recent years the courts have held that an employer will be

liable where he owes the plaintiff a non-delegable duty. The circumstances in which non-delegable duties have been found to exist are many and various.

22.6 Where two or more tortfeasors cause the same damage to a plaintiff, the plaintiff may sue any or all of them to recover his loss. In such a case the tortfeasors will either be joint tortfeasors (where they act in pursuance of a common design to cause the same damage) or several concurrent tortfeasors (where they act separately to cause the same damage). Where two or more tortfeasors act separately to cause different damage they are separate and independent tortfeasors and must be sued separately.

22.7 Joint and several concurrent tortfeasors may recover contribution from the other tortfeasors. The rules on contribution are contained in the Civil Liability (Contribution) Act 1978.

Exercises

22.1 In what circumstances will a master be liable for his servants?

22.2 Is the principle of vicarious liability justifiable?

22.3 If a master is liable for the torts of his servant, why should he not be liable for the torts of his independent contractors?

22.4 A Ltd own a number of nightclubs. B Co hire out 'bouncers' for night-club work. A Ltd hire Kevin, who is on B Co's books, for six months. B Co pay their 'bouncers' a nominal £25 per week when they are not employed by another company. Under the terms of the agreement between A Ltd and B Co, A Ltd agree to pay B Co £50 per week for Kevin's services. It is also agreed that A Ltd can dismiss Kevin for 'misconduct' and that A Ltd will pay Kevin £200 per week in cash (to avoid any tax problems). Kevin's contract with A Ltd describes him as self-employed.

A Ltd tell Kevin that under no circumstances must he drink on duty or strike a customer unless he is attacked first.

One night Kevin gets drunk in the club with a 'friend' of his, C. C, who is very drunk, starts to cause trouble. The manager of the club tells Kevin to eject C. Kevin tries to persuade C to leave. C starts to leave but on his way out he turns around and calls Kevin a coward. Kevin chases after C and catches him. Kevin stabs C with a knife he carries for 'protection'. C is seriously injured.

Advise the parties as to their rights and liabilities in tort.

22.5 What is meant by the control test? Is it a satisfactory determinant of the question whether a master–servant relationship exists?

22.6 Should an employer ever be liable where an employee does something which the employer has expressly forbidden him to do?

22.7 Why should an employer not be liable in respect of torts committed by an employee on the way to work?

22.8 Is there any coherent principle underlying the cases where the courts have held that an employer owes a non-delegable duty?

23 Remedies

In this chapter we will consider the remedies available to the victim of a tort. We will concentrate in particular on the formal rules governing the recovery of damages for personal injuries and death. In addition, we will examine the rules governing the recovery of damages for loss of or damage to property and the circumstances in which an injunction may be granted in a tortious action.

23.1 The Indemnity Principle

In contrast to the law of contract, where the purpose of an award of damages is to put the injured party in the position he would have been in had the contract been performed, the purpose of an award of damages in tort is to put the person who has suffered the loss in the position he would have been in if no tort had occurred. As Lord Scarman said in *Lim Poh Choo* v. *Camden and Islington Area Health Authority* [1980] AC 174, at 187, 'the principle of the law is that compensation should as nearly as possible put the party who has suffered in the same position as he would have been in if he had not sustained the wrong'. Thus, the overriding principle of the law of damages is that the person who has suffered the loss should be fully *compensated* for the loss he has suffered. Damages are, therefore, generally awarded to compensate the plaintiff and not to punish the defendant.

23.2 Contemptuous, Nominal, Aggravated and Exemplary Damages

There are three situations, however, in which an award of damages may not be made with a compensatory intent; these are (a) contemptuous damages, (b) nominal damages, and (c) exemplary damages. Additionally, a court may award aggravated damages which, despite appearances, are compensatory in intent.

Contemptuous Damages

Although the plaintiff may succeed in his action, the court may indicate that it has formed a low opinion of the merits of the plaintiff's claim or of the plaintiff's conduct by awarding a derisory amount. Such damages are contemptuous and the amount awarded is usually the smallest coin 'in the realm'. An award of contemptuous damages may imperil the plaintiff's chances of recovering his costs. The reason for this is that while costs usually 'follow the event' (i.e. are borne by the losing party), the award of costs is at the judge's discretion. Thus, although the award of contemptuous damages does not necessarily lead to the conclusion that costs will not be awarded to the successful plaintiff, the fact that the court awarded contemptuous damages only is a material factor for the court to take into account in exercising its discretion. Contemptuous damages are most commonly awarded in the context of libel actions.

Nominal Damages

Nominal damages are awarded where a person's legal rights have been infringed but he has suffered no actual loss. Where, for example, a person succeeds in an action for assault (which is actionable without proof of damage) but fails to prove that he has in fact suffered any injury or loss, the damages awarded will be nominal. The function of nominal damages is, therefore, to mark the fact that the plaintiff's rights have been vindicated albeit that he has suffered no damage. The award of nominal damages does not involve any finding that the plaintiff was guilty of any misconduct nor does it reflect on the merits of the plaintiff's case. However, as is the case with contemptuous damages, the fact that the court made an award of nominal damages is a material factor for the judge to consider in exercising his discretion in awarding costs.

Exemplary Damages

The express aim of an award of exemplary damages is to punish the defendant and to deter him from such behaviour in the future. In *Rookes* v. *Barnard* [1964] AC 1129 Lord Devlin, with whom the other members of the House of Lords concurred, restated the law on exemplary damages. As a general proposition, Lord Devlin was of the opinion that exemplary damages were objectionable because they confuse the civil and criminal functions of the law. Thus, the circumstances in which exemplary damages could be awarded should be limited. Apart from the cases where exemplary damages are allowed by statute there are only two classes of case where exemplary damages can be awarded.

The first class is where there is oppressive, arbitrary or unconstitutional action by servants of the government. Exemplary damages, therefore, can play a significant role in the protection of an individual's liberties against interference by the state. It is clear since *Cassell & Co Ltd* v. *Broome* [1972] AC 1027, that this class should not be narrowly interpreted. Thus, it includes not only servants of the government in the strict sense of the word, but also police officers, local authority officers and other 'government' officials. However, the House of Lords in *Cassell* v. *Broome* reiterated what Lord Devlin had said in *Rookes* v. *Barnard*: this class of case did not encompass the misuse of powers by non-governmental bodies. Thus, oppressive behaviour by a large company or trade union would not give rise to an award of exemplary damages.

The second category covers cases where the defendant's conduct has been calculated by him to make a profit for himself which may well exceed the compensation payable to the plaintiff. Once again it is clear that a broad interpretation should be given to these words. The aim of the category is, to use the words of Lord Hailsham in *Cassell* v. *Broome*, 'to teach the wrongdoer that tort does not pay'. Thus, it is not essential that the defendant should be seeking to profit in *monetary* terms; it is enough that the defendant was, for example, seeking to gain some property at the plaintiff's expense. It is not uncommon for exemplary damages to be awarded in defamation cases. In *Cassell* v. *Broome,* where the defendant published a book containing grave imputations on the plaintiff's conduct, an award of £25 000 exemplary damages was upheld by a majority of the House of Lords. The book was only published after the publishers had been warned as to the defamatory material it contained. Further, there was, according to their Lordships, enough evidence for the jury to have reached the decision they did that the defendant had made a cynical calculation that the damages they might have to pay would not exceed the profit they would make. This is not to say, however, that all defamatory material published in a newspaper and published with a view to selling the newspaper should be redressed by an award of exemplary damages. Something more, in the nature of greater calculation and deliberation as to the financial benefits likely to be derived, is required.

There are arguments both in favour and against exemplary damages. The opponents argue that the award of exemplary damages confuses the function of civil and criminal law and imports the possibility that a person may be 'punished' without receiving the protections he would get in a criminal trial. On the other hand, it is argued that there is no clear dividing line between the functions of criminal law and civil law (see 1.1). Tort still has an important deterrent role to play in, for example, trespass to the person and defamation, and the possibility of limited awards of exemplary damages confirms that role. Further, the award of exemplary damages in the second category prevents the unjust enrichment of the defendant. It seems unlikely, for the moment at least, that the House of Lords will depart from their decisions in the two cases cited above.

Aggravated Damages

Aggravated damages are typically awarded where the defendant has compounded the original tort in some way (for an example of a case where aggravated damages were awarded, see *Sutcliffe* v. *Pressdram,* 21.13). At first glance, it may appear that when aggravated damages are awarded the court is punishing the defendant. This is not in fact the case.

What the court is asked to assess is the extent to which the defendant's behaviour has aggravated the original injury. How much extra mental distress and injury to his feelings has the plaintiff suffered as a result of the defendant's conduct? Aggravated damages are, therefore, truly compensatory in nature.

23.3 Damages Recoverable Once Only

The damages which the plaintiff is entitled to recover from the defendant can be recovered once only. This rule has two aspects to it. First, the plaintiff cannot bring a second action on the same facts simply because the initial loss turned out to be more serious than was thought when judgment was given in the first action. This rule was laid down in *Fetter* v. *Beal* (1701) 1 Ld Raym 339. The plaintiff recovered damages from the defendant in respect of a trespass to the person. After the judgment had been given 'part of [the plaintiff's] skull came out of his head'. The plaintiff sought to bring a second action in respect of the deterioration in his condition. The court held that the recovery in the first action for trespass barred the second action in respect of the subsequent loss.

The second aspect of the rule is that damages are awarded on a once and for all basis in a lump sum. This requires that the court make an assessment not only of what the plaintiff has lost between the accident and the trial, but also of what he will lose in the future as a result of the accident. Future contingencies must therefore be translated into a present value. In the case of property damage this rarely gives rise to much difficulty in that future losses can usually be estimated with some accuracy. However, where personal injury has been suffered the difficulty of predicting whether the plaintiff will recover, and if so when and to what extent, has caused problems for the courts. There has, as a result, been a great deal of debate as to whether the system of once and for all payments should be retained or whether some form of periodic payments should replace it.

Proponents of the existing system argue that it leads to finality in litigation, the defendant (usually an insurance company) can close its files and the plaintiff can concentrate on getting better free of any 'compensation neurosis'. Further, the plaintiff is given a free hand in how to spend the money. Opponents argue, however, that these advantages, to the extent that they are advantages, are outweighed by the disadvantages of the existing system. First, as Lord Scarman acknowledged in the *Lim Poh Choo* case, assessment of future losses is replete with problems: '[K]nowledge of the future being denied to mankind, so much of the award as is attributed to future loss and suffering . . . will almost surely be wrong. There is only one certainty: the future will prove the award to be either too high or too low.' Secondly, there is a danger that if the plaintiff fritters away his award society will have to maintain him when the award runs out. Periodic payments would to a large extent solve these problems.

Although the general rule remains that the award must be made in a lump sum, there exist a number of exceptions. Two of these arise from legislation while the third, and potentially the most important, depends on the parties reaching an agreed settlement. The first is the award of provisional damages. Where there is a chance that at some time in the future an injured person will 'develop some serious disease or suffer some serious deterioration in his physical or mental condition' (section 32A of the Supreme Court Act 1981), the court can award damages assessed in the first place on the basis that the disease or deterioration will not occur and can, should such disease or deterioration occur, award further damages at a later date. Secondly, an award of interim damages may be made prior to the trial of the action provided the defendant has admitted liability, or a court is satisfied that at a trial the plaintiff would recover substantial damages and the defendant is either insured, a local authority or a person of substantial means. Assuming these criteria are satisfied, an interim award may be made to cover pressing financial needs, and the plaintiff will not be precluded from recovering further damages at the trial.

Finally, and perhaps of the greatest potential importance, there is the possibility of the parties, where the defendant has liability insurance, agreeing to a structured settlement. The concept of such a settlement was until recently virtually unknown in the UK because it offered few advantages over the traditional lump sum payment. However, as a result of an agreement between the Association of British Insurers (ABI) and the Inland Revenue that certain forms of structured settlements should no longer attract liability to income tax, increasing use has been made of the concept. A structured settlement was first given court approval in 1990 in *Kelly* v. *Dawes* (1990) *The Times* 27 September.

A structured settlement will usually consist of two parts: a lump sum to cover the past losses and existing needs of the plaintiff at the date of the settlement, and a pension payable annually to cover the claimant's future needs. In practice, the parties agree how much the claim would have been worth according to the usual principles of damages. Part of that sum will then be allocated to meet any existing needs, leaving the balance to be structured. As to the balance, the insurer assumes a direct liability to the claimant in place of the defendant insured's liability to the claimant. The insurer then purchases an annuity, which he holds for the benefit of the claimant, which provides for the payment of fixed sums to the beneficiary over a specified period (often the claimant's life). The sums payable to the claimant take the form of a pension, and can be structured such that they are index-linked or are larger in some years than others.

The structured settlement has substantial advantages to both the insurer and the claimant. The insurer pays out less money than before because the income can be paid into the plaintiff's hands free of tax. At the same time, because the holder of the annuity is not taxed on the income element of the annuity, he can draw a higher income from the damages obtained. These gains are made at the expense of the tax-payer.

Structured settlements do, however, have their limitations. First, they can only be arranged via a settlement out of court. A judge has no power to order the structuring of any settlement. Secondly, as periodic payments for pre-trial losses are inappropriate, a structured settlement will only be used where there are losses which will continue after the trial. In addition such schemes can only be justifiably used where the damages awarded are substantial. For the smaller, and quantitatively more usual, claims the lump sum system is likely to continue in use. Having said that, it seems likely that increasing recourse will be had to structured settlements in the future.

23.4 Special and General Damages

When a court makes an award of damages the amount awarded will be divided between special and general damages. The distinction between the two is a matter of pleading. General damages are awarded in respect of loss which is *presumed* to flow from the wrong and which therefore does not have to be specially pleaded. Special damages are those damages beyond general damages which arise from the particular facts of the plaintiff's case. If the plaintiff wishes to claim special damages he must specifically plead them. Examples of general damages would include loss of amenities, pain and suffering and loss of future earnings. Expenses already incurred in travelling to and from hospital, the cost of an operation which the plaintiff has had done privately and pre-trial loss of earnings would, however, be classified as special damage. The distinction is important not only for pleading purposes but also for the calculation of interest. It is, however, of little importance so far as the substantive law of damages is concerned.

23.5 Damages for Personal Injuries

Before examining the formal rules on the recovery of damages for personal injury, something must be said by way of general introduction. It might be thought that for most people who have been injured as a result of an accident, their most important consideration is how much can they get for their injury. Readers of newspapers cannot have failed to notice that awards of damages in excess of £1 million are becoming more common. Is this, therefore, the sort of award that a person who has been injured in an accident can expect? The answer to this is 'No'. First, studies have shown that only a small proportion of accident victims succeed in recovering any damages at all. Most people simply give no thought to attempting to recover any damages: they are concerned solely with physically recovering from their injuries. A survey done in 1976 by the Oxford Centre for Socio-Legal Studies (the 'Oxford Survey') showed that only one in seven accident victims reached the stage of consulting a lawyer and, of these, one out of seven failed to get any damages (Harris, 1984). Thus in most accidents the victim will recover nothing at all.

Second, the majority of claims are settled out of court as a result of negotiations between the parties' representatives. In the 'Oxford Survey', for example, only 2 per cent of those who received some award of damages received these after a contested trial. In many ways this is a good thing. Parties to litigation should be encouraged to settle their differences quickly and as cheaply as possible. Staying out of court means that the lawyer's costs will be lower and the plaintiff's claim should be dealt with more expeditiously. Further, if all personal injury actions were actually litigated the courts would be totally overwhelmed with work, and the already unacceptably long time it takes to complete a personal injury action would be lengthened.

It must be borne in mind, however, that there are serious disadvantages to the settlement process. As Harris (1988) points out, the parties to a typical personal injury action are unlikely to have the same bargaining strength. The advantage almost invariably lies with the defendant, which is usually an insurance company. For the plaintiff this is a one-off action which he cannot afford to lose. He is often without a job as a result of the accident and has no other source of income. He may have little or no recollection of the accident and will almost inevitably want to get the whole thing over as quickly as possible. Further, he may well have gone to his local solicitor, who may not have had much experience of personal injury litigation. For the defendants, however, this is one of many actions in which they are involved. Insurance companies have no personal interest in the outcome of the action and are inevitably represented by personal injury specialists. Further, the longer an insurance company can avoid paying out the better as it is able to invest the plaintiff's damages in the meantime. The pressures on a plaintiff to settle and to settle for less than a court may award are, therefore, very real. Looking only at sums awarded in contested trials distorts the picture, and ignores the fact that the vast majority of cases are settled out of court for considerably less than the awards made in court.

Finally, even where cases do reach a court and are contested it is only in the most serious cases of disabling injury or death, and sometimes not even then, that a plaintiff is awarded a sum in excess of £1 million. Most actions for personal injury or death are for much smaller amounts as a quick glance at Kemp and Kemp 'The Quantum of Damages', will show.

With this background in mind, we now turn to examine the way in which the courts assess damages for personal injury or death.

23.6   The Assessment of an Award of Damages

As we have seen, the purpose of an award of damages in tort is to put the injured person into the position he would have been in had no tort occurred. In order to see how this principle is given effect in practice let us consider the following hypothetical accident:

> Arnold and his daughter Jane are injured in a car accident for which Simon admits full responsibility. At the trial on the amount of damages recoverable the following facts are established.
>
> Arnold is a 35-year old brick layer working for a major building company. Prior to the accident he was earning £18 000 per annum gross. Out of his gross income he paid £4500 in income tax and £1500 per annum in national insurance contributions. Although the building industry is currently in a recession, Arnold is a very good brick layer and it is highly probable that he would have continued to be employed to the normal retirement age. Prior to the accident Arnold was a keen footballer, playing each weekend for a local side.
>
> In the accident Arnold suffered a broken back, which resulted in paralysis from the waist down, and fractured ribs. He also suffered an injury to his lungs when he inhaled poisonous fumes given off as a result of the fire caused by the accident. The injury to his lungs is so serious that his life expectancy has been reduced to 10 years. He was in hospital for 12 weeks after the accident, during which time he had three operations to try to remedy the paralysis. This time in hospital was spent in a private hospital as Arnold's employer pays for him to be a member of a private health care scheme.
>
> Despite the operations Arnold will not be able to work as a brick layer again. He is also unable to find any alternative work and will, in all likelihood, never work again. Arnold also requires round the clock nursing supervision. During the day this is provided by his wife, Gina, who is 29. Gina finds it impossible to provide the round the clock care that Arnold requires and so a nurse is hired at a cost of £10 000 per annum to provide the necessary night cover.
>
> Arnold's friends are very upset about his accident and decide to launch an appeal for him. They manage to raise £15 000. In addition to this sum Arnold receives a state mobility allowance of £15 per week and a £50 per week pension from his employer.
>
> Jane is a 7-year old school girl who was, by all accounts, doing well at school. As a result of the accident she was rendered permanently unconscious, a state from which she will never recover. Her life expectancy is, however, unchanged. She now requires round the clock care which is provided in an NHS hospital.

23.7 Non-Pecuniary Loss

As we have already seen, non-pecuniary losses are those losses which are not readily quantifiable in monetary terms. Despite this, English law does seek to put a value on such losses. The problem arises, however, of how such losses are to be valued. What is the loss of a leg or arm worth? How much money would compensate for the loss of the ability to play football or to dance? Undoubtedly any award made for such losses is likely to be perceived as arbitrary, yet this is the task facing the court. Whilst accepting that any award is likely to seem too much to some people and yet inadequate to others, the courts do at least seek to treat like cases alike. The trial judge will have previous awards cited to him and, taking these into account, will award a sum that is fair and reasonable in all the circumstances. An appeal court will not interfere with this assessment unless the judge has misdirected himself as to the law, misapprehended the facts or has for some other reason made an award that is wholly erroneous.

Pain and Suffering

Under this head the court will award damages to reflect the pain and suffering felt as a consequence of the accident. In our example Arnold would be able to recover a sum to compensate him for the pain he suffers which is attributable to his injuries (in other words the pain of his fractured ribs and damaged lungs). He would also be entitled to recover for any pain or suffering attributable to medical treatment he receives. Prior to the Administration of Justice Act 1982 Arnold would have had a separate claim for the shortening of his life expectancy and would have received a token sum in respect of this. This has now been abolished by section 1(1)(a) of the Act. However, the court may still award him a sum (under the head of pain and suffering) for the mental distress he suffers in knowing that his life expectancy has been shortened.

Jane, however, will not be able to recover any damages for pain and suffering. The courts have held, and this has now been confirmed by the House of Lords in *Lim Poh Choo*, that no damages will be awarded where the plaintiff suffers no pain because she is unconscious or otherwise incapable of experiencing pain.

Loss of Amenities

Damages under this head are awarded for the deprivation of some form of enjoyment or the loss of some ability. Arnold was a keen footballer and would, as a result, be able to recover damages to compensate him for the loss of this form of enjoyment. By way of example, awards have been made under this head to compensate a pianist for the loss of his ability to play the piano and a woman for the loss of sexual desire.

A more difficult problem, however, arises as to whether or not Jane, who is unconscious and therefore presumably unable to appreciate her loss of amenity or to pursue alternative amenities, can recover a sum for that loss. It might be thought, and indeed this view was put forward in dissenting speeches in the House of Lords in *H. West & Son* v. *Shephard* [1964] AC 326, that loss of amenity, like pain and suffering, is something that goes to reduce the 'pleasures or happiness' of life. On this view, where a plaintiff is unaware of her loss, she should not be entitled to recover.

However, the majority of their Lordships in that case and also the unanimous House of Lords in *Lim Poh Choo*, held that damages for loss of amenities were awarded for the fact of their deprivation. Such loss, they said, did not depend upon the perception of the plaintiff; the plaintiff has suffered an objective loss of amenity and should be compensated regardless of her state of consciousness.

The approach of the House of Lords has been criticised. The Pearson Commission recommended that damages for loss of amenities should not be awarded to an unconscious plaintiff, taking the view that damages for non-pecuniary loss were in essence given to relieve suffering which they viewed as 'by nature an experience subjective to the victim'. This is of course counter to the traditional judicial approach which treats loss of amenity as analogous to loss of property. Whilst there seems to be much merit in the Pearson Commission's approach it would, as Lord Pearce pointed out in *West* v. *Shephard*, 'be lamentable if the trial of a personal injury claim put a premium on protestations of misery and if a long face was the only safe passport to a large award'.

The Injury Itself

The injury itself is also a proper subject of a claim in a personal injury action. This claim is in addition to any amount that may be awarded for pain and suffering and loss of amenities. Once again, a conventional figure tends to be awarded.

23.8 Pecuniary Loss

Although damages for non-pecuniary losses in a serious accident may be substantial, damages for pecuniary loss will usually make up the greater part of the plaintiff's claim. As we have already seen, the usual practice is that damages are awarded on a once and for all basis in a lump sum. In assessing the plaintiff's pecuniary loss the court must, therefore, award a sum to take account of both the plaintiff's actual pre-trial loss and also any future pecuniary losses he will suffer.

Where a seriously injured person is in employment, the majority of any damages awarded for pecuniary loss are likely to be for loss of earnings. However, this is not the only head of damages awarded under pecuniary loss. Damages, as we shall see, can also be awarded for other expenses reasonably incurred, both before and after the trial.

Loss of Earnings

Damages for loss of earnings can conveniently be divided into two categories, pre-trial and post-trial. The assessment of pre-trial loss of earnings is relatively straightforward. The court will simply seek to ascertain the sum of money which the plaintiff would have been paid had he not been injured. If we assume, using our hypothetical accident, that Arnold's case comes to trial exactly three years after the accident and that his wages would not have altered during that period of time, his pre-trial loss of earnings would be calculated in the following way. First, his net annual loss would be established. This would be arrived at by deducting from his gross annual income the amount he would pay in tax (*British Transport Commission* v. *Gourley* [1956] AC 185) and national insurance contributions (*Cooper* v. *Firth Brown Ltd* [1963] 2 WLR 418). In earning his annual income Arnold would have to pay tax and national insurance and thus, to avoid overcompensating him, these must both be deducted from his gross income. After tax and national insurance Arnold would have earned £12 000 per annum. This is then multiplied by the number of years between the accident and the trial, and yields a sum of £36 000 for his pre-trial loss of earnings.

The calculation of post-trial or future loss of earnings is more complicated. As damages are payable at the time of the trial in a lump sum, it is necessary for a court to convert the plaintiff's future loss of earnings into a lump sum which reflects that future loss. This is an exercise fraught with difficulty. To take some examples, how long would the plaintiff have lived if he had not had the accident? Would he have remained in the same job? Would he have been promoted or would he have been sacked? What will the rates of wage and price inflation be? Will the tax or national insurance rates change? Some or all of these problems are likely to arise in all claims for future loss of earnings. In the light of these problems it might be thought that the courts would enlist the help of experts such as actuaries or economists to assist them. The courts have not, however, been keen to do so. Indeed, in one case Oliver LJ said: 'the predictions of an actuary can be only a little more likely to be accurate (and will almost certainly be less entertaining) than those of an astrologer'.

How, therefore, do the courts assess future loss of earnings? The general approach taken is the 'multiplier method'. The starting point is to work out the multiplicand. This is, in essence, the net annual loss of income that the plaintiff suffers as a result of the accident (in other words, the plaintiff's gross income less tax and national insurance). This sum is then multiplied by a 'multiplier' to reflect the fact that the plaintiff's annual loss will continue for some years.

How do the courts decide upon the appropriate multiplier? To return to our example, at the time of his accident Arnold is 35 years old. If it is assumed that he would have worked until the usual retirement age, he would have another 30 years of potential earnings. Should the courts, therefore, simply set the multiplier at 30? The courts have answered this question in the negative. In determining the multiplier, the courts make certain deductions to avoid overcompensating the plaintiff. First, a deduction of between 5 per cent and 10 per cent is made to allow for 'the general vicissitudes of life'. The plaintiff might, independently of the defendant's tort, have contracted some fatal illness or lost his job This must be taken into account. Secondly, and more importantly, some reduction in the multiplier must be made to take account of the fact that the plaintiff is getting his money early. The payment of £1000 today is worth considerably more than a promise to pay £1000 in a year's time. In the former case, the money can be invested and will be worth, at an interest rate of, say, 10 per cent, about £1100 in a year's time. In our example, paying Arnold 30 times £12000 would considerably overcompensate him. Invested prudently, the lump sum would probably be sufficient to enable Arnold to maintain himself wholly out of his investment income and he would be left at the end of 30 years with the entire capital sum intact. Therefore the court choses a multiplier to ensure that the plaintiff receives a sum of money which, when invested, will produce annually out of capital and investment income a sum equivalent to the total earnings that the plaintiff has lost. The effect of this is that the multiplier awarded in Arnold's case will be considerably less than 30, and will in fact be likely to be around 16. In practice, the highest multiplier applied by the courts is 18. Once the plaintiff reaches his mid-thirties the multiplier awarded will fall, and obviously the older the injured plaintiff is the lower the multiplier will be.

Somewhat surprisingly, at least at first sight, young children are not awarded the highest multipliers. If we return to our hypothetical example and consider the case of Jane, she too would be entitled to claim for loss of earnings. A number of problems, however, arise. First, how to assess the multiplicand? As she has never worked it is obviously impossible to assess the multiplicand in the ordinary way. As a result the courts have tended to award infants the national average earnings as the multiplicand (see, as an example, *Croke* v. *Wiseman* [1982] 1 WLR 71). One exception to this approach is where the infant is a child prodigy (the so called 'Shirley Temple' case. In such a case the court will make an assessment of the lost earnings on the basis of what has actually been lost and what the child was likely to earn in the future.

As to the multiplier awarded, these have generally been comparatively low. The reasons for this are twofold. First, the uncertainties in such cases are greater than in cases of working adults. The child might never have reached the age of majority. The child might never have worked or might only have been able to get very low-paid work. The imponderables are many and justify the award of a lower multiplier. Secondly, where a child is very young there will be several years before he would have been able to work. As a result a lump sum awarded to a young child can be invested for a considerable period before the loss is deemed to accrue. Less capital will, therefore, be needed to compensate fully the child for the loss of future earnings.

The most obvious problem with the multiplier method is that it seems to ignore the effects of inflation. The last 20 or 30 years have demonstrated that both wage and price inflation are facts of life in a modern economic society. Price inflation has the effect of eroding the value of money so that £1000 today will be worth more (in the sense that you can buy more with it) than £1000 in a year's time. Obviously, the greater the likely duration of the plaintiff's loss, the greater the effect inflation will have on the real value of the award. Do the courts take inflation into account when assessing the multiplier? The answer to this question, rather confusingly, is yes and no. The House of Lords, in a number of cases, have made clear that no adjustment to the multiplier is to be made to take account of future inflation. Inflation is to be ignored and money treated as retaining the value it had at the time of the trial. One reason that is often given for this is the real difficulty of anticipating what the rate of inflation will be. As Lord Scarman said in *Lim Poh Choo*, 'it is pure speculation whether inflation will continue at present, or higher rates, or even disappear. The only sure comment one can make upon any inflation prediction is that it is as likely to be falsified as borne out by the event.' However, the real reason why no adjustment is necessary to the multiplier to take account of inflation is that existing multipliers already take account of future inflation. The multipliers applied by the courts assume that the plaintiff invests the lump sum he gets and receives a real rate of return on that investment (i.e., the rate of return after taking out the effect of inflation) of between 4 per cent and 5 per cent. For example, it is assumed by the courts that when inflation is running at 10 per cent per annum the plaintiff, through the use of a prudent investment policy, can find a safe investment returning 14–15 per cent per annum.

Is the assumption of a 4–5 per cent real rate of return realistic? Whilst it is true that it is possible to achieve through prudent and safe investments a real rate of return on investment of between 4 and 5 per cent this may involve a level of investment sophistication that is simply not possessed by the average person. For example during the early 1980s investing in safe 'blue chip' shares would have yielded a return of at least 4–5 per cent. However, anybody who invested in shares during 1987 (the year in which shares fell over 20 per cent in one day) would have found it extremely difficult to make any return. Similarly, for much of the early 1980s government bonds offered a rate of return of at least 4–5 per cent. However, during the late 1970s the real return on such investments was negative. Is it realistic to expect the average plaintiff to show the necessary level of sophistication to cope with the difficulties inherent in obtaining a 4–5 per cent real rate of return? Kemp and Kemp (1985) argue that the better, and more realistic, approach would be to assume that a plaintiff invests his damages in government index-linked bonds (popularly known as 'granny bonds'). These are obviously a very safe, trouble-free investment and guarantee the investor a real rate of return of approximately 2½ per cent. He points out that the 'the use of a discount rate of 4–5 per cent effects a reduction far greater than the real advantage gained by the present receipt of a capital sum and so offends against the governing principle of law that full compensation should be given'. If it is assumed that the injured person will only receive a real rate of return of 2½ per cent then multipliers should be increased by 25–30 per cent. This increase would reflect a more realistic appraisal of investment opportunities open to the plaintiff and would ensure that he is fully compensated, so far as possible, for his pecuniary loss.

The 4–5 per cent chosen as the real rate of return achievable by the plaintiff on his investment is the rate achievable *after* tax. Do the courts take some account of the fact that if the lump sum awarded is large enough the plaintiff will become liable to pay tax at a higher rate? Despite initially taking the view that some increase in the multiplier should be made where the plaintiff will be liable to pay tax at a higher rate, the House of Lords have decided in the recent case of *Hodgson* v. *Trapp* [1989] AC 807 that no addition, except in exceptional circumstances, should be made to the multiplier in respect of a liability to pay higher rate tax. Two main reasons were given in the speech of Lord Oliver. First, since 'future taxation . . . is as much as an imponderable as future inflation', the courts should not guess as to the likely direction of tax rates. Secondly, as with inflation, taxation is already taken into account in the existing multiplier. Any addition to the multiplier would simply overcompensate the plaintiff.

The 'Lost Years'

In our hypothetical example, Arnold suffered such a serious injury to his lungs that his life expectancy was reduced to 10 years. As we have seen, damages are no longer available for loss of expectation of life as a separate head, though a plaintiff may recover a sum under pain and suffering for the knowledge that he is going to die early. However, the problem we are concerned with here is whether Arnold can claim for the earnings he will lose in the 'lost years' (in other words those years in which, but for the accident, he would have expected to be alive and working), or whether he can only claim in respect of the years for which he is expected to be alive.

In *Pickett* v. *British Rail Engineering Ltd* [1980] AC 136 the House of Lords rejected the view that '[N]othing is of value except to a man who is there to spend or save it. The plaintiff will not be there when these earnings hypothetically accrue: so they have no value to him.' Their Lordships held that where an injury reduces the plaintiff's normal life expectancy, the pre-accident life expectancy is still the relevant one for assessing the appropriate multiplier. Their Lordships justified this in the following way. They took the view that an injured person in such a case has lost something of present value to him: that is, the opportunity to spend the money he will earn or to make provision for his dependants, if he has any. Earnings that a plaintiff would have made in the lost years are, therefore, recoverable.

Two further points need to be made. First, a deduction is made from the wages that would have been lost in the 'lost years' to account for the plaintiff's living expenses. The plaintiff would only have what was left after he had paid his living expenses to spend on his dependants and others. As he will have no living expenses in the lost years, his only loss is the balance. Secondly, the courts have generally refused to allow a child to recover for the 'lost years' (see, e.g., *Connolly* v. *Camden and Islington*

Area Health Authority [1981] 3 All ER 250). The reason for this is that, in the case of children, whose future earning capacity is in any case uncertain, the many uncertainties increase. Not only do the factors already mentioned in relation to a lost earnings claim by a child apply, but there is also the problem of assessing what the child's living expenses would have been in the lost years. As a result of these uncertainties the courts have generally refused to allow a claim for the lost years by an infant plaintiff. The possibility of a lost years claim in a child prodigy case or a case where the infant plaintiff is the heir to a large estate has been left open.

Future Prospects

In our example, Arnold was likely to have remained a brick layer for the rest of his working life. Would the damages he would receive be any different if, for example, he had just completed a part-time degree in law and wanted to become a solicitor? As a solicitor he would probably earn more than a brick layer. The courts take account of prospective pay increases like this by increasing the multiplicand for the plaintiff. Conversely, if the plaintiff was likely to have lost his job or was in work which was inherently dangerous, the multiplicand or the multiplier may be reduced.

As well as making this adjustment in the multiplicand to take account of the plaintiff's future prospects, the courts have also awarded damages for 'loss of earning capacity'. Under this head of damages the court compensates the plaintiff for the possibility that if he loses his existing job he may, as a result of the injury, find it more difficult to get another job. Assessment of damages under this head is somewhat speculative. However, the courts have required that there is a 'real' or 'substantial' risk that the plaintiff will suffer this disadvantage before the end of his working life. Once the court has decided that there is a real risk, the chance of the risk eventuating must be valued.

Medical, Hospital and Other Nursing Expenses

The plaintiff is entitled to recover for all medical, hospital and other rehabilitation expenses that he has reasonably incurred as a result of the accident. To return to our example, Arnold would be able to recover the cost of the operations and the cost of his hospital stay. The fact that Arnold could have taken advantage of the facilities available on the National Health Service (NHS) is, by virtue of section 2(4) of the Law Reform (Personal Injuries) Act 1948, disregarded. The Pearson Commission proposed the repeal of this section and its replacement with a section which would allow recovery for private medical expenses only where it was reasonable on medical grounds that the plaintiff should incur them, but this proposal has not been implemented. If Arnold had, instead, decided to be treated by the NHS and had therefore not incurred any medical or hospital expenses, he would not be able to make a claim in respect of medical expenses.

Before we consider the question of recovery for nursing care, reference must be made to a potential problem of duplication between loss of earnings and cost of care. In our example, Jane is after her accident being nursed 24 hours a day in an NHS hospital. As we have seen, she is entitled to be compensated for the loss of earnings she would had made when old enough to work. If she is allowed to claim her full loss of earnings she will be overcompensated because, as she will still be fully maintained by the state, she will not have to apply any of her earnings to living expenses as she would otherwise have to do. To guard against this danger, section 5 of the Administration of Justice Act 1982 provides that a deduction must be made from the loss of future earnings claim to take account of the living expenses saved.

Finally, in relation to medical expenses the question of home nursing must be considered. Arnold is being nursed partly by his wife and partly by a professional nurse. Where the hire of a professional nurse is reasonable there will be no problem with the cost being recovered. Arnold can also recover a sum in respect of his wife's nursing care, his need for the care being regarded as a compensable loss (*Donnelly* v. *Joyce* [1974] QB 454).

Other Expenses

Any other expenses that the plaintiff can show he has reasonably had to incur as a result of the accident are recoverable. So, for example, if Arnold had to travel to and from hospital for a number of appointments, his travel expenses will be recoverable. Similarly, if his house had to be adapted to provide easier access for him in his injured state, the cost of the conversion would be recoverable. If the plaintiff's expenses are unreasonable they will either be disallowed in full or reduced to a level the court considers reasonable.

23.9 Interest

In our example, Arnold had to wait three years for his case to come to court. His right to damages for the injuries he suffered accrued at the moment he was injured and he has, therefore, been deprived of the damages to which he was entitled for three years. In order to compensate him for the loss of the right to use the money during those three years the court will, and indeed must, make an award of interest. The courts have in a series of cases laid down guidelines for the awarding of interest. First, no interest is awarded on damages for the future pecuniary or non-pecuniary loss. This is logical in that the purpose of an award of interest is to compensate a plaintiff for having been deprived of the use of money he would otherwise have had. At the time of the trial the future loss has not yet been suffered, and hence the plaintiff has not been deprived of the use of the money due to him.

Secondly, the amount of interest varies according to whether the loss is pecuniary or non-pecuniary. The former attracts a rate approximately equivalent to half the normal short-term commercial rates for the period, but for the latter a conventional figure of only 2 per cent is employed. The reason for this comparatively low figure is that the damages for non-pecuniary loss are calculated at the date of trial and therefore already reflect any changes in the value of money up to the date of trial. The additional 2 per cent simply represents what the plaintiff could have gained over and above inflation by investing his damages.

23.10   Collateral Benefits

In our hypothetical example Arnold received a number of 'benefits' as a direct result of his accident. The benevolence of his friends, his prudence in paying his pension premiums and the 'benevolence' of the state in providing him with a mobility allowance all contributed to an improvement in his position after the accident. One might have thought that where the plaintiff's position has been, or will be, improved as a result of the tort these benefits would be taken into account; if they are ignored the plaintiff would be left in a better position than if no tort had been committed. However, the position with regard to collateral benefits is one of some complexity, and whilst some collateral benefits are deducted, many are not. Our concern here is to indicate in outline the rules on deductibility.

The main source of compensation for accident victims is the social security system. There has for a long time been considerable controversy over whether social security payments should be deducted. The current position is to be found in section 22 and schedule 4 of the Social Security Act 1989, as amended. This provides that where an accident occurred on or after 1 January 1990, the full value of all specified benefits received or to be received, within five years of the injury or the date of compensation (whichever is the earlier), is to be deducted from the plaintiff's damages before they are paid to him. The amount deducted is then paid directly to the Secretary of State by the tortfeasor who issues the plaintiff with a certificate of deduction. Thus in Arnold's case, the Secretary of State could 'claw-back' from Simon payments made in respect of the mobility allowance for a period of three years after the accident (i.e. until the date of the trial). Thereafter, the allowance would not be deducted.

Although section 22 has the effect of ending 'double compensation', at least for five years, the area of collateral benefits remains of considerable complexity. For example, the recoupment provisions of section 22 do not apply to 'exempt payments'. Included amongst 'exempt payments' are 'small payments', a term applied to payments not exceeding £2500. In respect of small payments, the complicated rules of section 2(1) of the Law Reform (Personal Injuries) Act 1948, which previously governed all cases regardless of size, are applied. Under these rules the compensator is entitled to offset half of any specified benefits received or to be received, for five years from the date the cause of action accrued. The Secretary of State has no right to 'claw-back' any of the sums so deducted.

Where the benefit received is not specified in section 22, the common law continues to apply. The decisions in this area are often not easy to reconcile. However, it is possible to identify a number of factors that appear to have influenced the courts in reaching their decisions. Where the benefit received is the result of the generosity of others, the courts have refused to allow deduction. Thus charitable or *ex gratia* payments are not deducted. The reason behind this appears to be a understandable reluctance to discourage charitable giving. The £15 000 paid to Arnold as a result of the appeal would not, therefore, be deductible.

Where a plaintiff has paid for, or in some sense earned, his 'benefit' the courts have generally refused to deduct the 'benefit'. Thus, where a person benefits from a contract of insurance he has taken out or sets up his own pension scheme, this has been held to be non-deductible. By way of contrast, where the benefit is financed by taxation or by the defendant himself, the courts have tended to insist on deductiblity. Thus long-term sickness benefits payable under an insurance scheme run by the defendant employers have been held to be deductible, as have sick pay and wages.

23.11 Damages for Death

The death of a person can have two effects in the law of torts. First, it may affect existing tortious actions in which the plaintiff is involved. Secondly, it may give rise to a cause of action in favour of the deceased's dependants. The first part of this section deals with the effect of death on existing causes of action. In the second part, the question of an action for dependency will be considered.

23.12 The Effect of Death on Existing Causes of Action: The Law Reform (Miscellaneous Provisions) Act 1934

At common law any cause of action in which the deceased person was involved, whether as plaintiff or defendant, died with that person. This rule was abolished by the Law Reform (Miscellaneous Provisions) Act 1934. This provides, in section 1(1), that 'all causes of action subsisting against or vested in [the deceased] shall survive against, or, as the case may be, for the benefit of, his estate'. Thus if in our hypothetical example Arnold had been killed instantaneously in the accident caused by Simon, Arnold's cause of action would survive for the benefit of his estate. Similarly, if Simon had also been killed in the accident, Arnold's estate would still have an action against Simon's estate.

However, the Act sets out a number of limitations on the right of the plaintiff to sue or claim damages. First, by virtue of section 1(2)(a)(ii), no claim can be made in respect of loss of income for the period after the person's death. In the case of instantaneous death, therefore, as there will be no non-pecuniary loss, all the estate will be able to recover are the funeral expenses (section 1(2)(c)). If, however, the victim died some time after the accident but before the trial of any action against the tortfeasor, his estate will be able to recover damages for the earnings lost up to the date of death and also a sum of money in respect of any non-pecuniary losses suffered in that period. Secondly, section 1(2)(c) provides that the damages recovered for the benefit of the estate are to be calculated without reference to any loss or gain to the estate consequent on the death of the deceased. Thus if, to use our example, Arnold had taken out an insurance policy which accrued to the benefit of his estate on his death, this would not be taken into account in calculating the damages payable under the Act. Finally, any action for defamation dies with the deceased.

23.13   Claims by the Deceased's Dependants: The Fatal Accidents Act 1976

The original Fatal Accidents Act was passed in 1846, a time when, as a result of the Industrial Revolution, the number of industrial accidents was on the increase and an increasing number of close dependants were being left uncompensated for the loss of the family breadwinner. The purpose of the original Act was to remedy the perceived unfairness of the rule in *Baker* v. *Bolton* (1808) 1 Camp. 493. This rule denied the existence of any claim on the part of dependants of a deceased person. In its original form the Act gave actions to the widow and children only: however, subsequent Acts have widened the class of those entitled to bring an action for the loss of dependency.

The Act of 1976, which was a consolidating statute, gives 'dependants' an action for the loss of their dependency provided certain criteria are met. The first requirement is that the death must have been 'caused by such wrongful act, neglect or default which is such as would (if death had not ensued) have entitled the person injured to maintain an action and recover damages in respect thereof' (section 1(1)). Thus, if the deceased would not have had an action neither will his dependants. For example, if A went for a joyride in B's light aircraft knowing that B was extremely drunk and the aircraft crashed killing A, A's action would be likely to fail on the grounds that he had voluntarily assumed the risk (see 12.3). In such a case A's dependants would also be barred.

The second requirement is that the person claiming must be within the class of dependants set out in the Act. Since the first Fatal Accidents Act of 1846, the class of persons categorised as dependants has been widened considerably. Section 1(3) of the Act provides that not only are immediate natural family members to be regarded as dependants, but so too are natural ascendants and descendants; any persons treated as ascendants or descendants of the deceased; adopted and illegitimate children, brothers, sisters and uncles and aunts; and any person who has been living as husband or wife of the deceased in the same household for at least two years prior to the death. Whilst this may seem a broad classification there are a number of glaring omissions, the most obvious of which is homosexual partners. The current system, under which Parliament adds to the existing list of dependants as and when it wakes up to changes in society's view of the 'acceptable' family, is unsatisfactory. Surely the better approach is to allow anyone who can show they were factually dependant on the deceased (other than as business associates) to bring an action.

To claim under the Act not only must the plaintiff show that he is within the class of dependants, but also that he was in fact *financially* dependant on the deceased. No damages are awarded to dependants under this head for their own mental distress or for the loss of society of the deceased. A fairly broad approach has, however, been taken to what is a financial dependency. If we were to assume in our example that Arnold had been killed as a result of the accident, both Gina, his wife, and Jane, his daughter, could recover for the loss of any financial support they suffered as a result of Arnold's death. As well as this, Gina would also be entitled to claim for loss of her husband's services, such as the cost of hiring a gardener or general handy-man, if he did such jobs (similarly, Arnold would be able to claim for the loss of his wife's services if she had been killed). Jane would also be entitled to recover for the loss of Arnold's services as her father.

As well as a dependant being able to claim for the loss of an *actual* dependency, claims for loss of a *potential future* dependency are allowed. Thus, in *Taff Vale Railway* v. *Jenkins* [1913] AC 1, the House of Lords allowed parents to recover for the loss of support which their daughter, who was at the time of her death training to be a dressmaker, would have provided when she finished her training. Despite the *Taff Vale Railway* case it seems unlikely, if Jane had been killed in our example, that Arnold and Gina would have any claim in respect of any potential future support they might have received. The House of Lords stressed the requirement of a reasonable expectation of pecuniary benefits. In the case of very young children the possibility of future pecuniary benefit is too speculative to be recoverable.

In order to be able to recover for the loss of a dependency, not only must the loss be a financial one, but the pecuniary advantage that has been lost must also stem from a familial relationship. In *Burgess* v. *Florence Nightingale Hospital for Gentlewomen* [1955] 1 QB 349, the deceased and her husband were professional dancing partners. The husband sought to recover for the loss of his wife's services as a dancing partner. The court held that no damages were available to compensate the husband for this loss as the lost benefit arose out of their business partnership rather than the family relationship.

In addition to the claim for loss of dependency, two further claims may be made under the Act. First, damages for bereavement may be claimed by a spouse, in respect of his partner's death, or by a child, while still a minor, in respect of a parent's death (section 1A). A sum of £7500 is awarded under this head. Secondly, a claim may be made in respect of funeral expenses.

23.14   Assessment of Damages for Loss of Dependency

Once the plaintiff has established that he falls within the category of dependants, and that he has suffered a loss of dependency which arose solely from the familial relationship, the court will consider what is the appropriate measure of damages. The purpose of an award of damages in a fatal accidents claim is, in the words of Lord Diplock in *Mallet* v. *McMonagle* [1970] AC 166:

> 'to provide the widow and other dependants of the deceased with a capital sum, which, with prudent management will be sufficient to supply them with material benefits of the same standards and duration as would have been provided for them out of the earnings of the deceased had he not been killed by the tortious act of the defendant.'

As in a personal injuries claim, damages are assessed by using the multiplier method.

In assessing the multiplicand, the starting point for the calculation is the deceased's net earnings (the deceased's earnings after tax and national insurance have been deducted). From this must be deducted the amount the deceased would have spent exclusively on himself. The deceased's share of the joint expenses, such as rent or mortgage payments, the cost of running a car and other general household bills are not, however, deducted. The sum left after deducting the plaintiff's personal expenditure from his net earnings is, in essence, what is left for the dependants. In practice, unless there is compelling evidence to the contrary, the courts simply deduct a conventional percentage from the net earnings to represent the plaintiff's personal expenditure. Where the family consists of husband and wife, a deduction of 33 per cent is made to represent the plaintiff's personal expenditure. Where there are children the deduction for personal expenditure is reduced to 25 per cent.

Once the multiplicand has been calculated, the court proceeds to assess the appropriate multiplier. The multiplier will be set at a figure which, when multiplied by the multiplicand, provides the dependants with a sum of money that will compensate them for the loss of the material benefits that the deceased was likely to provide for them over the estimated period of the dependency. However, unlike a personal injuries action where the multiplier is assessed as at the date of the trial, the multiplier is assessed as at the date of death. The reason for this is explained in Lord Fraser's speech in the case of *Cookson* v. *Knowles* [1978] 2 All ER 604 at 614–5. There he said:

'in a personal injury case, if the injured person has survived until the date of trial, that is a known fact and the multiplier appropriate to the length of his future working life has to be ascertained as at the date of trial. But in a fatal accident case the multiplier must be selected once and for all as at the date of death, because everything that might have happened to the deceased after that date remains uncertain.'

In assessing what multiplier should be awarded in the case of a fatal accident there are, as Purchas LJ pointed out in *Corbett* v. *Barking Havering and Brentwood Health Authority* [1991] 1 All ER 498 at 508–9, at least five essential elements that must be considered: first, the likelihood of the provider of the support continuing to exist; secondly, the likelihood of the dependants being alive to benefit from that support; thirdly, the possibility of the providing capacity of the provider being affected by the changes and chances of life either in a positive or in a negative manner; fourthly, the possibility of the needs of the dependant being altered by the changes and chances of life, again in a positive or negative way; finally, the discount necessary to take account of (a) the immediate receipt of compensatory damages in advance of the date when the loss would actually have been incurred, and (b) the requirement that the capital should be exhausted at the end of the period of the dependency.

To illustrate the application of this we must return to our original hypothetical case. If we assume that Arnold has been killed immediately as a result of Simon's tortious act and, for the present, that his wife, Gina, is his only dependant, then in assessing the multiplier account must be taken of Arnold's and Gina's life expectancy. In ordinary circumstances a wife will be presumed to outlive her husband and thus the starting point for the calculation will be Arnold's life expectancy. This figure is then adjusted to take account of the vicissitudes of life, for example that Arnold or Gina may have died at a particularly young age due to illness or an accident, or that Arnold may have lost his job or retired early. This figure is then adjusted to take account of the fact that Gina will receive the sum awarded before she suffers the actual loss and that the capital must be exhausted at the end of the period of dependency. As in a personal injuries action the multiplier awarded is unlikely to be close to the actuarial figures of the deceased's life expectancy. In our example Arnold's actuarial life expectancy would be about 37 years; however, the multiplier awarded would be no more than 16.

Once the multiplier has been assessed, the sum awarded is divided into special damages and general damages. Special damages are awarded for the pre-trial loss and attract interest at the same rate as pre-trial damages for pecuniary loss in a personal injuries action. General damages are awarded for the loss thereafter and do not attract interest.

So far we have dealt with the general approach taken by the courts in assessing the sums awardable in a fatal accidents case. Some comments must now be made as to particular difficulties that arise in fatal accident claims. First, by virtue of section 3(3) of the 1976 Act, the benefits accruing to a wife as a result of the prospects or fact of re-marriage are not to be taken into account when considering a wife's claim in respect of her husband's death.

Secondly, claims by children of the deceased, although assessed using the same general approach as above, raise a number of different issues. In most cases the child's dependency will be presumed to end after he has completed his secondary education. Where a child is likely to proceed to tertiary education or, alternatively, to leave school at 16, the multiplier will be adjusted accordingly.

More problematic is the assessment of the multiplicand in respect of a child's claim. If we return to and adapt our original example and assume that Gina had been killed in the accident and Jane had been uninjured, how would the court assess the multiplicand? Clearly Jane has been deprived of the services (physical, educational and moral) of her mother. These services have a value. How do the courts value such a loss? If Gina was not employed but was instead looking after Jane full-time, the approach taken is usually to value the loss as the cost of a full-time nanny. Further, the Court of Appeal held in *Corbett* that the award of an additional sum to be added to the cost of hiring a nanny, to take account of the fact that a parent does not work set hours and is in constant attendance may be justified. However, where the mother is in full-time employment and could only care for the children on a 'part-time' basis, a discount may be made to the multiplicand.

23.15   Apportionment between Dependants

Section 2(3) of the Fatal Accidents Act 1976 provides that 'not more than one action shall lie for and in respect of the same subject matter of complaint'. Thus an action under the Act must be brought by the executor or administrator of the deceased's estate in the name of the dependants. As to the apportionment of any award, sections 3(1) and (2) of the Act provide that such damages may be awarded as are proportioned to the injury resulting from the death to the dependants respectively, and shall be divided among the dependants in such shares as may be directed. In practice the compensation paid to the spouse of the deceased will be the larger amount; the children, if any, will receive smaller shares. This may be justified on the basis that the spouse will maintain the children so long as they are dependants. Sums paid to a younger child will usually be greater than those paid to an older child on the basis that the expected dependency was longer.

23.16 Deductions

By section 4(1) of the Act 'the benefits which have accrued or will or may accrue to any person from [the deceased's] estate or otherwise as a result of his death shall be disregarded'. Unlike the case of a living plaintiff, the general position in respect of a claim by dependants is, therefore, that no deductions will be made in respect of 'collateral benefits' accruing either to the estate or to dependants directly. Thus not only will no deduction be made where there would be no deduction in the case of a living plaintiff, but there will also be no deduction even in the case of benefits which are deductible in the case of a living plaintiff. In the light of this difference in approach, it must be asked why it should be that dependants are more favourably treated than live plaintiffs? If the answer is that no reason exists, then which is the correct approach as a matter of policy: general deductibility of benefits or non-deductibility?

In *Stanley* v. *Saddique* [1991] 1 All ER 529 the Court of Appeal held that section 4 applied to all forms of material benefit and was not just confined to direct pecuniary benefits. In *Stanley* v. *Saddique* the infant plaintiff's mother was killed. The court held that the benefits, in terms of a more stable family situation accruing to the infant plaintiff as a result of his father's remarriage, were, by virtue of section 4, to be disregarded. Thus, it would appear to be the case that if the plaintiff's wife is killed and he remarries a much richer woman, this should not be taken into account in assessing his loss of dependency. (cf. *Hayden* v. *Hayden* [1992] 4 All ER 681)

23.17 Property Damage

The basic principle for the assessment of damages is that the plaintiff should be put in the same position as if the tort had not occurred, and this principle applies to the recovery of damages for loss of, or damage to, property as well as to the recovery of damages for personal injury. In this section we examine the rules governing the assessment of damages where property is lost or damaged.

23.18 Assessment of Damages in Property Damage Cases

Where, as a result of the defendant's tort, the plaintiff's property has been lost or damaged, the plaintiff is entitled to compensation for the loss of its value to him. The usual measure where there is *total* loss or destruction is the market value of the lost property assessed at the time and place of the loss. So, for example, if due to the defendant's negligence the plaintiff's car was damaged beyond repair, the plaintiff would be entitled to recover in damages an amount which would enable him to replace his lost car valued as at the time the loss occurred.

Where the plaintiff obtains a brand new replacement for his damaged property, must he give credit for his 'betterment'? No clear answer can be given. In *Harbutt's Plasticine Ltd* v. *Wayne Tank and Pump Co* [1970] 1 QB 447, it was held that no credit should be given as to insist on this would be to insist that the plaintiff improve his property. However, where the plaintiff's property is very old and would have needed replacement in the near future, it is likely that the courts would insist that credit be given and the damages reduced accordingly.

Where the plaintiff's property is merely *damaged* and can be repaired, the normal measure of damages is the amount by which the property has been diminished in value. In many cases this will be ascertained by reference to the cost of repair. However, if the cost of repair greatly exceeds the diminution in value, the victim of the tort may only be able to recover an amount to represent the amount by which his property has declined in value as a result of the tort. For example, suppose A negligently carries out work on his land which causes subsidence on B's property. The cost of putting the subsidence right is £30 000, whereas the diminution in the value of the plaintiff's property is only £3000. It is likely that a court would hold that the plaintiff could not recover the cost of repair but was confined instead to the diminution in value.

In the case of both loss of and damage to property, consequential damage may be recoverable. In *Liesbosch Dredger (Owners)* of Dredger Liesbosch v. *Edison* [1933] AC 449, the plaintiff's dredger was engaged in working on a contract for a third party. The contract provided for heavy financial penalties in the case of delay. Due to the defendant's negligence the plaintiff's dredger was sunk and lost. The Court of Appeal held that the plaintiffs could recover (a) the market price of a dredger comparable to the one they had lost; (b) the cost of adapting the new dredger and transporting and insuring her from her old moorings to the plaintiff's place of work; and (c) compensation for disturbance and loss suffered in carrying out the contract from the date of the loss until the new dredger could reasonably have been available at the plaintiff's place of work.

23.19   Injunctions

Instead of, or sometimes in addition to, the award of damages, a court may grant the plaintiff an injunction. An injunction is an order of the court restraining the commission of some wrongful act or ordering the defendant to take some positive steps to rectify a wrongful act. Originally an injunction could only be issued by the Court of Chancery; however, today any division of the High Court may do so. As an injunction is an equitable remedy it is never available 'as of right'. Instead the issue of an injunction lies within the discretion of the court. In this section we will look briefly at four different types of injunction: prohibitory, mandatory, interlocutory and quia timet injunctions.

A prohibitory injunction is, as its name suggests, an order of the court which restrains or prohibits the defendant from committing or continuing a wrong. Injunctions are commonly sought to prevent or stop a nuisance, or in cases of continuing or repeated trespasses. However, there seems to be no reason why an injunction should not be issued to prevent the commission or continuation of other torts. Where liability has been established and where there is a likelihood of recurrence or continuation, the plaintiff will nearly always be granted this type of injunction unless damages are an adequate remedy. Lord Cairn's Act of 1858 (now s.50 of the Supreme Court Act 1981) enables a court to award damages in addition to or substitution of an injunction. However, the courts have stressed that the defendant should not be allowed to buy off the plaintiff. In *Shelfer* v. *City of London Electric Lighting Company* [1895] 1 Ch. 287 Smith LJ held that the jurisdiction under the Act should only be exercised if it would be oppressive to the defendant to issue an injunction, if the injury to the plaintiff's rights is small, if the damage is capable of being estimated in money and if money payment would be an adequate compensation.

A mandatory injunction differs from a prohibitory injunction in that, instead of preventing or restraining the defendant from doing a wrongful act, it orders the defendant to take positive steps to rectify that which he has already done. In *Redland Bricks Ltd* v. *Morris* [1969] 2 All ER 576, the House of Lords held that a mandatory injunction would only issue where three criteria are satisfied. These are: (a) damages are not a sufficient or adequate remedy; (b) the defendant has acted wantonly or unreasonably in relation to his neighbour; (c) the terms of the injunction can be stated clearly such that the defendant can know what it is he has to do.

An interlocutory injunction is a provisional and temporary injunction which is designed to restrain the commission or continuance of an activity pending the final settlement of the plaintiff's claim. In *American Cyanamid Co* v. *Ethicon Ltd* [1975] AC 396, the House of Lords held that for an interlocutory injunction to issue there must be a serious question to be tried. If there is, then the court must decide whether, on the balance of convenience, to issue an injunction. In considering whether the balance of convenience lies in favour of or against, interlocutory relief the court should take into account whether damages would be an adequate remedy for the plaintiff, whether the plaintiff's undertaking in damages gives the defendant adequate protection if the plaintiff loses at trial and whether the preservation of the status quo is important enough to demand an injunction. Where, after considering these factors, the court is of the opinion that the balance of convenience is 'even', the court may consider the relative merits of the two parties' cases.

Usually an injunction will only issue where a tort has already been committed. However, where, to use the language of Lord Upjohn in *Redland Bricks Ltd* v. *Morris*, 'the plaintiff shows a very strong probability on the facts that grave damage will accrue to him in the future', a *quia timet* injunction may issue. *Quia timet* actions are, therefore, ordered to prevent threatened torts. Lord Upjohn, however, made clear that a *quia timet* injunction would only issue where the threatened or intended damage was imminent, and where damages would be an inadequate remedy.

Summary

23.1 The purpose of an award of damages in tort is to put the injured person in the position he would have been in had no tort occurred. The overriding principle of the law is to compensate the plaintiff fully for his loss.

23.2 In certain circumstances the purpose of an award of damages may not be to compensate the victim. Awards of contemptuous, nominal or exemplary damages are made for purposes other than to compensate the plaintiff. Aggravated damages are, however, intended to be compensatory.

23.3 Damages are recoverable once only. This rule has two aspects. First, the plaintiff cannot bring a second action on the same facts simply because his injury turned out to be worse than he had originally thought. Secondly, damages are payable in a lump sum once and for all. There exist three exceptions to this: an award of interim damages; an award of provisional damages; and structured settlements.

23.4 Where a court makes an award of damages the amount will be divided between special and general damages.

23.5 Newspapers often report the conclusion of litigation involving a very large award of damages. Excessive concentration on these reports obscures the fact that most people who are injured as a result of a tort do not think of pursuing any legal action and, of those who do, the vast majority of their claims are settled out of court for comparatively small sums of money. The formal rules of damages must be set against that background.

23.6 Damages may be awarded for both pecuniary and non-pecuniary losses.

23.7 Non-pecuniary losses are those which are not readily quantifiable in money terms. Pain and suffering, loss of amenities and the injury itself are examples of non-pecuniary loss. An award of damages for loss of amenities is made for the fact of their deprivation, while an award of damages for pain and suffering is made only when the plaintiff actually experiences the pain and suffering. Although it is obviously difficult to put a figure on these non-pecuniary losses, the courts assess damages by having regard to previous cases.

23.8 Pecuniary loss is the financial loss the plaintiff suffers consequent upon his injury. The main item of pecuniary loss is likely to be loss of earnings, but also included are medical and other expenses. Damages for loss of earnings are divided into pre-trial and post-trial loss. For post-trial losses the court seeks to award a sum of money which, when invested, will produce annually out of capital and investment income a sum equivalent to the total earnings that the plaintiff has lost. This is assessed by the multiplier method.

23.9 Interest is payable on all pre-trial losses. The rate of interest payable depends upon the type of loss suffered. No interest is payable on post-trial losses.

23.10 Charitable payments and payments under an insurance policy are not to be taken into account in assessing the damages payable to the plaintiff. Virtually all other benefits which accrue to the plaintiff as a result of the tort must be taken into account in some way. The deduction of social security benefits is governed largely by statute.

23.11 The death of a person can have two effects in the law of torts. It may affect existing causes of action in which the plaintiff is involved, and it may give rise to a cause of action in favour of the deceased's dependants.

23.12 Section 1(1) of the Law Reform (Miscellaneous Provisions) Act 1934 provides that any cause of action subsisting against or vested in the deceased survives for the benefit of, or against, the deceased's estate. No damages are payable under the Act in respect of loss of income for the period after the deceased's death.

23.13 The Fatal Accidents Act 1976 gives a cause of action to 'dependants' (defined in section 1(3)) in respect of their loss of dependency. In order to recover, a dependant must show that he was financially dependent on the deceased and that that dependency arose from a familial relationship. A more limited class of persons can recover damages for bereavement (section 1A). Funeral expenses are recoverable under the Act.

23.14 The purpose of an award under the Fatal Accidents Act 1976 is to provide the dependant with a capital sum which will be sufficient to supply him with material benefits of the same standard and duration as would have been provided for him out of the earnings of the deceased had he not been killed. The method of assessment is again the multiplier method, appropriately modified.

23.15 An action under the Fatal Accidents Act 1976 is usually commenced, on behalf of the dependants, by the deceased's executor or administrator. Each dependant recovers such damages as are proportioned to the loss suffered as a result of the death.

23.16 By virtue of section 4 of the Act, any benefit accruing to a person as a result of the deceased's death is not to be taken into account when assessing damages. The courts have held that section 4 is not confined to direct pecuniary benefit but instead applies to all forms of material benefit.

23.17 The basic principle that the victim of a tort should be put in the same position as if the tort had not occurred applies equally to property damage as it does to personal injury.

23.18 Where property has been totally lost, the usual measure of damage is the market value of the lost property assessed at the time and place of the loss (ie the replacement value). Where the plaintiff's property is only damaged, the usual measure of damage is the amount by which the property has diminished in value. In both total loss and damage cases, damages may be recovered for any consequential loss.

23.19 Instead of, or sometimes in addition to, the award of damages a court may grant an injunction. An injunction is an order of the court restraining the commission of some wrongful act or ordering the defendant to take some positive steps to rectify a wrong. The injunction is an equitable remedy and is never available as of right. Four types of injunction are considered in the text. These are: prohibitory, mandatory, interlocutory and quia timet.

Exercises

23.1 What is the purpose of an award of damages in tort? How does it differ from the purpose of an award of damages in contract?

23.2 When are exemplary damages available in a tortious action? Should the victim of a tort be able to recover exemplary damages?

23.3 What is a structured settlement? Why has it been described as 'the greatest advance in personal injury law of recent times' (Lewis, 1988)?

23.4 Why should an unconscious plaintiff be able to recover damages for loss of amenities? Should the courts continue to award damages for non-pecuniary loss?

23.5 How do the courts assess loss of future earnings? Why is the multiplier rarely equal to the number of years of work the plaintiff would have been likely to do? Why do the courts not use actuarial evidence?

23.6 Should a plaintiff be able to recover damages for the 'lost years'?

23.7 Why are the multipliers awarded in cases of personal injury to young children comparatively low? Why can a child not recover for the 'lost years'?

23.8 A's partner gives up her job as a partner in a City solicitor's office to nurse him. She was earning £100 000 per annum. Can A recover this amount in respect of cost of nursing?

23.9 Why should the cost of private medical care be recoverable?

23.10 Why are benefits generally taken into account when considering an action for personal injuries when they are not taken into account when assessing damages in respect of death? Is there an underlying rationale for the different treatment of different benefits in a personal injuries action?

23.11 Why are no damages recoverable under the Law Reform (Miscellaneous Provisions) Act 1934 in respect of loss of income in the period after the deceased's death?

23.12 Is the current list of 'dependants' in the Fatal Accidents Act 1976 satisfactory? How do the courts assess damages under the Act of 1976? Should the fact of re-marriage be taken into account when assessing damages for loss of a dependency?

23.13 What are: prohibitory injunctions, mandatory injunctions, quia timet injunctions and interlocutory injunctions? When will damages be awarded in lieu of an injunction?

23.14 A car crash leaves a number of people dead or injured. Liability for the accident is not disputed. Advise the following parties on the damages they may recover.

(i)   Alpesh, aged four, is left unconscious in a coma from which it is feared that he will never recover. His life expectancy is 47 years. He is sustained in a private hospital. All the costs of the private care are covered by a health insurance policy.

(ii) Bettina, a 32-year old bus driver and keen fun-runner, loses a leg in the accident. Before the accident she was earning £10 000 per annum. Afterwards, she is unemployed for two years while she recovers and then is able to take a clerical job earning £8000 per annum. For the first 18 months of her recovery Bettina's lover, Cynthia, is given unpaid leave from her job at a bank where she was earning £50 000 per annum, to nurse Bettina back to health. A year after the accident, the Department of Social Security agree to pay Bettina £20 per week in severe disablement allowance. Her case on quantum is heard four years after the accident.

(iii) Deborah is killed immediately in the accident. She is survived by Edward, her boyfriend of the last several years, and their two young children. As a result of an argument Deborah and Edward had lived apart for the four months preceeding the accident; however, hopes of a reconciliation were high. Deborah was 36 at the time of the accident and earned £50 000 per annum as a partner in a major solicitor's firm. Edward, also a solicitor, had left work to bring up the children, but expects to return to work after a couple of years. Just before the trial on quantum, Edward marries Fiona, who has just inherited £2 million. Fiona wants to stay at home and look after the children full time.

How would your advice have been different if Deborah and Edward had been married?

Bibliography

Alexander (1972) 'The Law of Tort and Non-Physical Loss: Insurance Aspects', 12 *JSPTL* 119.

Allen *et al.* (1979) *Accident Compensation after Pearson* (Sweet & Maxwell).

Atiyah (1967) *Vicarious Liability in the Law of Torts* (Sweet & Maxwell).

Atiyah (1972) *Res Ipsa Loquitur* in England and Australia', 35 *MLR* 337.

Atiyah (1987) *Accidents, Compensation and the Law*, 4th edn, ed, P. Cane (Weidenfeld & Nicolson).

Atiyah (1989) *An Introduction to the Law of Contract* 4th edn (Oxford University Press).

Baker, (1990) *An Introduction to English Legal History*, 3rd edn (Butterworths).

Baker and Milsom (1986) *Sources of English Legal History* (Butterworths).

Bell (1983) *Policy Arguments in Judicial Decisions* (Oxford University Press).

Beyleveld and Brownsword (1991) 'Privity, Transivity and Rationality', 54 *MLR* 48.

Birks (1985) *An Introduction to the Law of Restitution* (Oxford University Press).

Bishop (1980) 'Negligent Misrepresentation through Economists' Eyes', 96 *LQR* 360.

Bishop (1982) 'Economic Loss in Tort', 2 *OJLS* 1.

Bowman and Bailey (1986) 'The Policy Operational Dichotomy – A Cuckoo in the Nest', 45 *CLJ* 430.

Buckley (1981) *The Law of Nuisance* (Butterworths).

Calabresi (1970) *The Costs of Accidents* (New Haven, CT).

Calcutt (1990) *Report on Privacy and Related Matters* (HMSO), Cmnd 1102.

Cane (1989) 'Economic Loss in Tort: Is the Pendulum out of Control', 52 *MLR* 200.

Cane (1991) *Tort Law and Economic Interests* (Oxford University Press).

Clerk and Lindsell (1989) *Torts*, 16th edn, ed. R.W.M. Dias (Sweet & Maxwell).

Cornish and Clark (1989) *Law and Society in England 1750–1950* (Sweet & Maxwell).

Craig (1989) *Administrative Law* (Sweet & Maxwell).

Dias (1967) 'Trouble on Oiled Waters: Problems of *The Wagon Mound (No 2)*' [1967] *CLJ* 62.

Dias and Markesinis (1989) *Tort Law*, 2nd edn (Oxford University Press).

Dworkin (1986) *Law's Empire* (Fontana).

Flemming (1987) *The Law of Torts*, 6th edn (The Law Book Co.).

Fleming (1988) *The American Tort Process* (Oxford University Press).

Fleming (1989a) 'Probabilistic Causation in Tort Law', 68 Can. Bar Rev. 661.

Fleming (1989b) 'Property Damage-Economic Loss: A Comparative View', 105 *LQR* 508.

Fleming (1990) 'Requiem for *Anns*', 106 *LQR* 525.

Fleming (1992) *The Law of Torts*, 7th edn (The Law Book Co.).

Furmston (ed.) (1986) *The Law of Tort: Policies and Trends in Liability for Damage to Property and Economic Loss* (Duckworth).

Gearty (1989) 'The Place of Private Nuisance in the Modern Law of Torts', 48 *CLJ* 214.

Gilmore (1974) *The Death of Contract* (Ohio State University Press).

Green (1989) *Land Law* (Macmillan).

Grubb and Mullis (1991) 'An Unfair Law for Dangerous Products: The Fall of *Anns*' [1991], *Conv.*, 225.

Grubb and Pearl (1990) *Blood Testing, Aids and DNA Profiling: Law and Policy* (Jordan).

Harlow (1987) *Understanding Tort Law* (Fontana).

Harris (1988) *Remedies in Contract and Tort* (Weidenfeld & Nicolson).

Harris, Maclean, Genn, Lloyd Bostock, Fenn, Corfield and Brittan (1984) *Compensation and Support for Illness and Injury* (Oxford University Press).

Harris and Veljanovski (1986) 'Liability for Economic Loss in Tort', in Furmston (1986), 45.

Hart & Honoré (1985) *Causation in the Law*, 2nd edn (Oxford University Press).

Hepple and Matthews (1991) *Tort: Cases and Materials*, 4th edn (Butterworths).

Hitcham (1986) 'Some Insurance Aspects', in Furmston (1986), 191.

Holmes (1881) *The Common Law* (London).

Honoré (1983) 'Causation and Remoteness of Damage', *Int. Enc. Comp. L.*, XI, Torts, Ch. 7.

Jaffey (1985) 'Volenti Non Fit Injuria', 44 *CLJ* 87–110.

Jackson and Powell (1992) *Professional Negligence*, 3rd edn (Sweet & Maxwell).

Jolowicz (1987) 'Product Liability-Directive and Bill', 46 *CLJ* 16.

Kemp (1984) 3 *CJQ* 120.

Kemp and Kemp (1985) *The Quantum of Damages*, 4th edn.

Kodilinye (1986) 'Public Nuisance and Particular Damage in Modern Law', 6 *LS* 182.

Kodilinye (1989) 'Standing to Sue in Private Nuisance', 9 *LS* 284.

Law Commission (1969) 'The Interpretation of Statutes', *Law Com.*, 21.

Lewis (1988) 'Pensions Replace Lump Sum Damages: Are Structured Settlements in Most Important Reform of Tort in Modern Times', 15 *JLS* 392.

Likierman (Chairman) (1989) *Professional Liability Review* (HMSO).

McKendrick (1990a) *Contract Law* (Macmillan).

McKendrick (1990b) 'Vicarious Liability and Independent Contractors – A Re-examination', 53 *MLR* 770.

Maitland (1936) *The Forms of Action at Common Law* (Cambridge University Press).

Markesinis (1987) 'An Expanding Tort Law – The Price of a Rigid Contract Law', 103 *LQR* 354.

Markesinis (1989) 'Negligence, Nuisance and Affirmative Duties of Action', 105 *LQR* 104.

Markesinis and Deakin (1992) 'The Random Element of their Lordships' Infallible Judgement: An Economic and Comparative Analysis of the Tort of Negligence from *Anns* to *Murphy*', 55 *MLR* 619.

Mullis (1991) 'Review of Tort Cases', *All England Rev.*, 396–8.

Newark (1949) 'The Boundaries of Nuisance', 65 *LQR* 480.

Newark (1961) 'Non-Natural User and *Rylands* v. *Fletcher*', 24 *MLR* 557.

Newdick (1985) 'Strict Liability for Defective Drugs in the Pharmaceutical Industry', 101 *LQR* 405.

Newdick (1988) 'The Development Risk Defence of the Consumer Protection Act 1987', 47 *CLJ* 455.

North (1972) 'Breach of Confidence: Is there a New Tort?', 12 *JSPTL* 149.

O'Dair (1991) '*Murphy* v. *Brentwood District Council*: A House with Firm Foundations?', 54 *MLR* 561.

Pearson, Lord (Chairman) (1978) *Royal Commission on Civil Liability and Compensation for Personal Injury* (HMSO), Cmnd 7054.

Priest (1987) 'The Current Insurance Crisis and Modern Tort Law', 96 *Yale LJ* 1521–90.

Salmond and Heuston (1992) *The Law of Torts*, 20th edn by R.F.V. Heuston and R.A Buckley (Sweet & Maxwell).

Schlechtriem (1989) 'Presentation of a Product and Products Liability under the EC Directive', 9 *Tel Aviv Studies in Law* 33.

Smith and Burns (1983) '*Donoghue* v. *Stevenson* – the Not So Golden Anniversary', 46 *MLR* 147.

Spencer (1987) 'Flooding, Fault and Private Nuisance', 46 *CLJ* 205.

Spencer (1989) 'Public Nuisance – A Critical Examination', 48 *CLJ* 55.

Stanton (1986) *Breach of Statutory Duty* (Sweet & Maxwell).

Stapleton (1986a) *Disease and the Compensation Debate* (Oxford University Press).

Stapleton (1986b) 'Products Liability Reform – Real or Illusory?', 6 *OJLS* 392.

Stapleton (1988a) 'The Gist of Negligence: Part I (Minimum Actionable Damage)', 104 *LQR* 213.

Stapleton (1988b) 'The Gist of Negligence: Part II (The Relationship between Damage and Causation)', 104 *LQR* 389.

Stapleton (1991) 'Duty of Care and Economic Loss: A Wider Agenda', 107 *LQR* 249.

Stevens (1964) '*Hedley Byrne* v. *Heller*: Judicial Creativity and Doctrinal Possibility', 27 *MLR* 121.

Sutherland (1992) 'Fair Comment by the House of Lords?', 55 *MLR* 278.

Tunc (1983) 'Introduction', *Inc. Enc. Comp. L.*, XI, Torts, Ch. 1.

Wedderburn (1978) 'Natural Nuisances Again', 41 *MLR* 589.

Weinrib (1975) 'A Step Forward in Factual Causation', 38 *MLR* 518.

Weir (1989) 'Government Liability' [1989] *PL* 40.

Weir (1990) 'Statutory Auditor not Liable to Purchaser of Shares', 49 *CLJ* 212.

Weir (1991) 'Fixing the Foundations', 50 *CLJ* 24.

Weir (1992) *A Casebook on Tort*, 7th edn (Sweet & Maxwell).

Whittaker (1989) 'European Product Liability and Intellectual Products', 105 *LQR* 125.

Williams (1960) 'Penal Legislation in the Law of Tort', 23 *MLR* 232.

Williams and Hepple (1984) *Foundations of the Law of Tort*, 2nd edn (Butterworths).

Winfield and Jolowicz (1989) *Tort*, 13th edn, ed. by W.V.H. Rogers (Sweet & Maxwell).

Wright (1985) 'Causation in Tort Law', 73 *Cal. L. Rev.* 1737.

Index